Against Returning to Egypt

Against Returning to Egypt

Exposing and Resisting Credalism
in the
Southern Baptist Convention

by
Jeff B. Pool

MERCER UNIVERSITY PRESS

ISBN 0-86554-553-7 perfectbound   MUP/P162

Against Returning to Egypt
Exposing and Resisting Credalism in the Southern Baptist Convention
Copyright ©1998 by Mercer University Press
Cover photograph ©1998 by Thomas V. Brisco
Mercer University Press, Macon, Georgia 31210-3960 USA

The paper used in this publication meets the minimum requirements
of American National Standard for Information Sciences—
Permanence of Paper for Printed Library Materials, ANSI Z39.48-1984.

Library of Congress Cataloging-in-Publication Data

Pool, Jeff B., 1951–   .
Against returning to Egypt : exposing and resisting credalism
in the Southern Baptist Convention / by Jeff B. Pool.
xxvi+340pp. 6x9" (15x23cm.).
Includes bibliographical references and index.
ISBN 0-86554-553-7 (perfectbind : alk. paper).
1. Southern Baptist Convention—Creeds.
2. Baptists—United States—Creeds.
3. Southern Baptist Convention—Doctrines—History—20th century.
4. Baptists—United States—Doctrines—History—20th century.
I. Title.
BX6462.7.P66   1997
286'.132—dc21   97-27099
                                CIP

Contents

To the memory
of my Baptist maternal grandparents

Lela Pearl Hughes
(1907–1969)
Church Secretary, Sunday School Teacher, Charter Member,
Fairview Baptist Church, Seminole, Texas

and

Karl Leslie Hughes
(1897–1988)
Deacon, Sunday School Teacher, Charter Member,
Fairview Baptist Church, Seminole, Texas

Preface to a Vocation

In this book, I have examined a volatile historical issue for Baptist Christians: credalism in the Southern Baptist Convention (SBC).[1] I have addressed this issue with special attention to its peculiar forms in the SBC's contemporary context. Toward that end, I have written from the standpoint of my particularity as a systematic theologian in a seminary of the SBC, Southwestern Baptist Theological Seminary (SWBTS), a theological school located in Texas, on the western periphery of the Old South. I have also engaged the larger problem of credalism among Baptists through my analysis and criticism of one recent, yet very significant, doctrinal document of the SBC: "The Report of the Presidential Theological Study Committee" (*RPTSC*).[2] In the most specific sense, then, with this book I offer a critical commentary on that document.

When the SBC adopted the *RPTSC* in the summer of 1994, I began to write a short assessment of the document's problematic features. In spite of the disturbing characteristics of the *RPTSC*, at that time I soon discontinued my response to the *RPTSC* for two reasons. First, the then-recent termination of Russell Dilday's employment as president of SWBTS in March 1994 had already required the commitment of much of my energy to struggles in my most immediate Baptist environment. As

---

[1]Instead of the more common term, "creedalism," I have used the alternative spelling of this word, "credalism." According to *Merriam Webster's Collegiate Dictionary* (10th ed., 1993), under "creed" (273a), the adjective may be spelled as "creedal" or "credal." Although I have not altered quotations that employ the term "creedalism," I have obviously followed the second spelling in my conversion of this word into a noun. Thus, in my own references to this phenomenon, I will consistently use the term "credalism."

[2]"The Report of the Presidential Theological Study Committee," in *Annual of the Southern Baptist Convention* (1994): 112-18 (hereafter cited as *RPTSC*). I have included the complete text of the *RPTSC* in appendix 2. Timothy George has also included the *RPTSC* in *Baptist Confessions, Covenants, and Catechisms*, vol. 11, Library of Baptist Classics, ed. Timothy George and Denise George (Nashville: Broadman & Holman, 1996) 147-58. With no explanation other than that the *RPTSC* has affirmed these documents and without even listing the following documents in the book's table of contents, George attaches to the *RPTSC* both the "Chicago Statement on Biblical Inerrancy" and the "Chicago Statement on Biblical Hermeneutics," as if the SBC had adopted the latter two non-Baptist documents as part of that report (*Baptist Confessions, Covenants, and Catechisms*, 13-14, 159-69).

a consequence, rather than writing about the document and its adoption
by the SBC, I began to express my concern about the *RPTSC* both to
some of my colleagues and in illustrations during the courses that I
taught. Second, at that time, I decided not to exert excessive theological
energy on such a weak and manipulative doctrinal statement. Nonetheless, discussions with students during a class in February 1995 led me to
change my mind. As the students in that class discussed a specific
doctrinal issue with me, I pointed to the *RPTSC* as an example of a deficient doctrinal formulation related to the issue under discussion. One
student informed me that, in his discussions about employment with the
Home Mission Board (HMB), he had received a packet of material from
the HMB containing the *RPTSC*. In its letter to this student, the HMB
indicated the necessity for the student to affirm the contents of the
RPTSC in order to be a viable candidate for the HMB. Learning that the
HMB had begun to employ the *RPTSC* as a doctrinal criterion motivated
me to renew my critical study of this document.[3]

In that context, I sensed an invitation from God's Spirit to engage in
this work, to accept this calling or this specific task as one expression of
my vocation with God. Thus, I offer this book on the following convictional basis. In his presidential address to the SBC in 1992, Morris
Chapman issued the following call to the SBC's seminaries:

> Give us theological leadership for the renewal of this denomination. Provide
> us with traning [*sic*] for preachers, teachers, missionaries, and fellow
> servants. Model for us the united disciplines of faith and learning. Be true
> to the convictions which birthed you and called you into being.[4]

---

[3]An awareness of the SBC's larger historical situation, similar to the alarmed prophetic insight of Charles W. Deweese, has motivated my work. "Baptists of the world, take
note! Since 1979, the top leaders of the Southern Baptist Convention—fundamentalists
obsessed with power and control under the guise of biblical inerrancy—have trashed the
historic Baptist vision of freedom, instituted stifling patterns of creedalism and authoritar-
ianism, exalted pastoral authority to irresponsible levels, distorted the character of God
and the Bible, twisted Baptist history to make it support personal and political objectives,
seized the capital assets of the largest evangelical denomination in America, turned its
news organization into a propaganda machine, employed strategies and methods that treat
with disdain individuals and churches which pay the bills, driven out of leadership persons who objected to their schemes, and forced into exile Southern Baptists uncomfort-
able with their destructive tendencies" (Deweese, *Defining Baptist Convictions: Guidelines for the Twenty-First Century*, ed. Deweese [Franklin TN: Providence House
Publishers, 1996] 21).

[4]Morris H. Chapman, "It's Time to Move," in *Annual of the SBC* (1992): 101.

In spite of the very different theological posture, styles of ecclesial leadership, and denominational renewal envisioned by Chapman, quite simply, with these studies, I have endeavored to fulfill such a commission. As an employee of an institution in the SBC and, more specifically, by virtue of my role as a teacher of systematic theology in a seminary of the SBC, I possess not only the right, but also the responsibility or commission, to address any issues that concern or affect those who have built these institutions, those who continue to maintain these institutions, those educated and served by these institutions, and those who serve with me in this seminary and other related institutions. Yet, more than as a fulfillment of my denominational responsibility as a *Baptist* Christian theologian, I offer this book as a step in my faithfulness to the creative and liberating God of love, accompanied by the Holy Spirit of love, as fidelity to my Christian community, as loyalty to my role as a Baptist in the SBC, even as a Baptist who has supported and does support the SBC, and, therefore, especially as one among the many to whom the SBC also must account. As an illustration of this, I have inscribed my entire study of the *RPTSC*, in an attitude of reverence, between verses from two Baptist hymns, one at the beginning of the prologue and one at the end of the epilogue.

My attention to the problem of credalism among Baptists through such personal and social particularities, however, may elicit a variety of responses. From a first perspective, for some readers, especially those readers who agree with me about the weaknesses of the document through which I have focused my inquiry, I have written too much about so little. Other readers also will agree with my opposition to this document and will concur with my evaluations of it, yet may think, for those very reasons, that I have written far too little about so much.

Yet, other readers who disagree with my assessments of the document itself, those who consider the document under scrutiny to be an honest or a straightforward effort (however adequate or inadequate), may judge my own studies as too harsh or too critical. From the opposite perspective, some of the readers who agree with my critical approach may think that I have approached a manipulative and deceptive document with not nearly enough critical intensity.

Still other readers, whether they agree or disagree with everything in this book, may label such an effort as futile or wasted in the SBC's presently triumphalistic, fundamentalist environment. Some readers, whether they consider my assessments to be correct or incorrect, whether or not they believe these studies to be necessary for the SBC's health, will describe my analyses as ineffective in the face of widespread apathy among Baptists.

Thus, while I acknowledge with readers the negative tone signaled by the title of this book, on the one hand, I do not apologize for that posture. No genuine Baptist can afford to ignore either the continuance or the intensification of the severe problems that the fundamentalist subjugation of the SBC originally initiated. By pretending that all is well when dis-ease and bondage abound, by refusing public discussion of private abuse, oppression, and victimization within this Baptist family, Baptists in the SBC perpetuate and legitimize, not only a family with problems, but a dysfunctional family at that. Rather, I offer this study precisely because such dis-ease and bondage persist and increase within the SBC even today. Nonetheless, on the other hand I admit one regret about this book's negative tone: I regret both that abuse as well as bondage (as well as the denial of those evils) do exist in the SBC today and that such a situation requires such a book as this.

Lamentably, in the SBC's present environment, the SBC's fundamentalist leaders characteristically, mistakenly, and unwisely distinguish Christian truth from Christian freedom. Those who make and apply this distinction virtually restrict the concept of *Christian truth* to the category of communicable, correct, accurate, and precise divine information, cognitive constructs, propositions, facts, or data. Accordingly, this perspective tends almost exclusively to equate truth with objectivity, communal or social norms, uniformity, or absolute epistemological and theological parameters, boundaries, or controls. Those who employ this distinction also restrict the concept of *Christian freedom*, by contrast, to the category of personal, ambiguous, and diverse human experience. Hence, this perspective also tends almost exclusively to equate freedom with subjectivity, risk, diversity or plurality, individual preferences, or epistemological and theological openness or relativity.[5] This often amounts to a contrast

---

[5]Observe the operation of this distinction in writings by key members of the SBC's Presidential Theological Study Committee. R. Albert Mohler, Jr. refers to Baptists in the SBC who emphasize Christian freedom as the "liberty party" or the "experience party," while he refers to Baptists who emphasize Christian truth as the "truth party" or "doctrine party": R. Albert Mohler, Jr., "A Call for Baptist Evangelicals and Evangelical Baptists: Communities of Faith and A Common Quest for Identity," in *Southern Baptists and American Evangelicals: The Conversation Continues*, ed. David S. Dockery (Nashville: Broadman & Holman, 1993) 227-32; cf. idem, "Has Theology a Future in the Southern

between responsibility or integrity (in a word, truth) and freedom, as if the two categories mutually exclude one another.

Invariably, those who utilize this particular distinction between truth and freedom tend to emphasize the priority and superiority of truth to freedom, at least as they have interpreted these realities. Additionally, those who operate with this distinction often seem to assume that all Baptists accept it as an accurate or valid basis from which to develop their perspectives, or that all Baptists in the SBC either do share or ought to share this distinction as a presupposition. Hence, with this distinction fully operational and unquestioned, those who operate on the basis of this distinction both can advance a specific version of Christian orthodoxy as truth and can legitimize the legislation (and its enforcement) of that particular orthodoxy.

In this book, however, I have refused the previous contrast or dichotomy between *truth* and *freedom*. That contrived distinction both

---

Baptist Convention? Toward a Renewed Theological Framework," in *Beyond the Impasse? Scripture, Interpretation, and Theology in Baptist Life*, ed. Robison B. James and David S. Dockery (Nashville: Broadman & Holman, 1992) 91-117; idem, "A Response," in *Beyond the Impasse*, 244-54; idem, "The Conflict of Visions," *Christian Index* 168 (22 June 1989): 2.

Timothy George distinguishes two similar categories from one another in the tension between "individual responsibility" (freedom) and "theological integrity" (truth or orthodoxy): Timothy George, "The Priesthood of All Believers and the Quest for Theological Integrity," *Criswell Theological Review* 3 (Spring 1989): 287-91; idem, "The Priesthood of All Believers," in *The People of God: Essays on the Believer's Church*, ed. Paul Basden and David S. Dockery (Nashville: Broadman, 1991) 88-91; cf. idem, "Conflict and Identity in the SBC: The Quest for a New Consensus," in *Beyond the Impasse*, 195-214; idem, "The Renewal of Baptist Theology," in *Baptist Theologians*, ed. Timothy George and David S. Dockery (Nashville: Broadman, 1990) 13-25. See Andrew L. Pratt's insightful assessment and critique of this trend in light of the SBC's history: Andrew L. Pratt, "A New Question in Baptist History: Seeking Theological Renewal in the 1990s," *Perspectives in Religious Studies* 20 (Fall 1993): 255-70.

Furthermore, according to Walter Shurden, moderate Baptists have also accepted this dichotomy, yet contending for the opposite perspective and thus emphasizing freedom and diversity: Walter B. Shurden, "Major Issues in the SBC Controversy," in *Amidst Babel, Speak the Truth: Reflections on the Southern Baptist Convention Struggle*, ed. Robert U. Ferguson, Jr. (Macon GA: Smyth & Helwys Publishing, 1993) 4.

Nonetheless, see a far more adequate understanding of this distinction in two resolutions adopted by the SBC in its annual meeting of 1963, for which meeting the SBC selected the theme "To Make Men Free" ("Resolution No. 2—Human Freedom" and "Resolution No. 3—Christian Responsibility," in *Annual of the SBC* [1963]: 65). Two addresses to the convention concerned these issues: Wayne Dehoney, "To Make Men Free," in *Annual of the SBC* (1963): 79; Henry L. Lyon, "Freedom through Responsibility," in *Annual of the SBC* (1963): 81.

distorts this dual divine gift and misrepresents Baptist Christian experience of it. Introducing a dichotomy between these two realities often precedes the favoring of one reality over the other, however vehemently one may argue for a balance between the two. Thus, insofar as a person effectively conceptualizes one reality as superior to the other, that person has misconstrued both realities. The dichotomy (or the alleged distinction) is false, because the concepts of truth and freedom at the basis of this dichotomy are, at best, deficient, if not entirely misconstrued.

As a foundation for these studies, I presuppose the identity of Christian truth with Christian freedom rather than a dichotomy between them. In Christian experience, freedom and truth do not compete with one another. The very name of the one who described himself as *the truth* (John 14:6), "Jesus," announces the good news from God in summary: "Yahweh *liberates!*" By applying to himself a text from the prophecies of Isaiah, Jesus even qualified the heart of his own vocation from God as the liberation of humans from their bondage (Luke 4:16-21; Isaiah 61:1-2; cf. Isaiah 58:6). Jesus even identified the trust of his disciples in him as their experience of the truth that liberates them (John 8:31-36). If the meaning of the name "Jesus" is accurate or true (even in terms of a *correspondence* between this claim and that to which it refers), and if the Messiah's name truly summarizes the point of his ministry, message, and person, then truth is freedom or liberation and freedom is truth. Truth as well as freedom is thoroughly relational.[6]

Thus, humans know the truth when they experience liberation from their bondages through the Christ, Jesus of Nazareth. To have the truth is to live this freedom fully; to be free is to hold the very heart of the truth disclosed by God. This claim, however, does not alleviate the insecurities that produced the false dichotomy between Christian truth and Christian freedom. Rather, my claim intensifies the problem and, hence, deepens the need for radical trust in God through Jesus of Nazareth. Insofar as ambiguity, risk, subjectivity, and even relativity genuinely characterize human freedom through Jesus of Nazareth, then these qualities also characterize Christian truth in its identity with Christian freedom. In creation and history, neither truth nor freedom escape the characteristics and limitations of finitude.

---

[6]Similarly, see Charles H. Talbert, "The Bible's Truth Is Relational," in *The Unfettered Word: Southern Baptists Confront the Authority-Inerrancy Question*, ed. Robison B. James (Waco TX: Word Books, 1987) 39-46.

Those who would deny any aspect of Christian freedom in order to exalt any quality of Christian truth or vice versa, therefore, distort not only Christian freedom but also Christian truth. In this book, I argue that the *RPTSC* instantiates precisely this dual distortion: part one primarily addresses this document's abuse of freedom, while part two primarily addresses the document's abuse of truth. Consequently, on the one hand, part one unmasks or exposes and resists the manipulative methods through which the SBC's fundamentalist leaders have exercised their own freedoms, in order to control the Christian freedom of all Baptists in the SBC. On the other hand, part two exposes and resists the distorted doctrines to which the SBC's fundamentalist leaders seek to secure allegiance from all Baptists in the SBC. By the same token, part one exposes and resists the deception and falsehood in the *RPTSC*'s manipulative methods, while part two exposes and resists the restrictions on Christian freedom in the *RPTSC*'s distorted doctrines.

I have written primarily about one phenomenon, as I have previously characterized it: *the truth of freedom in Christ*. Russell H. Dilday has recently described freedom as an "identifying trait of Baptists," the basic trait really threatened "from within, from pseudo-Baptists, rogues inside the family who either never knew or have forgotten what our true identity is." These pseudo-Baptists seek to impose their own perspectives on all Baptists, to coerce conformity to a very narrow perspective. Dilday called for the elimination of credalism in every form, as one way to meet this threat to Baptist identity. With regard to the present situation for Baptists and the SBC, Dilday quite rightly perceived a need for "Baptist freedom fighters."[7]

I fully concur with Dilday's assessment. Within the SBC today, masquerading as Baptists or hiding under the veneer of the name "Baptist," roam those who either ignorantly (never having known or having forgotten) or knowingly (and, therefore, malevolently) have begun systematically to eradicate the traits of genuine Baptist identity. As a consequence, genuine Baptists, those who have neither forgotten nor abandoned the SBC's historic perspectives, have become targets for attack in this campaign of eradication. During the sixteenth century, the dominant yet challenged ecclesiastical and governmental authorities ordered special detachments of police to search for or to hunt Anabaptists—forces desig-

---

[7]"Dilday Says 'Authentic' Baptists Face Extinction," *Western Recorder* 169 (4 July 1995): 2.

nated in German as *Täuferjäger*, literally, "baptist-hunter." Currently, many such *hunters* of Baptists control the SBC. Such authorities and hunters employ various credal documents as devices to aid them in their eradication of Baptists who hold different theological and political perspectives. The credal impulse within the SBC, at the very least, expresses, on the one hand, a heterophobia or an almost frantic fear of *the other* and, on the other hand, a homophilia or an equally desperate desire or love for *the same*.

I similarly attest with Dilday to the need for "Baptist freedom fighters." To some extent, with this book I take my own place among those who struggle to liberate Baptists in the SBC from their present disease and bondage, in this case, specifically from the constraints of credalism. In the following studies, then, I strive to expose and to resist credalism among Baptists with the historic resources of the SBC itself.

Notwithstanding the very different responses that this book may occasion, I hope, in light of the previous thoughts, that this book will function as a sign to others along the journey of freedom to which this book attests. I have endeavored both to expose credal aberrations in the SBC and to resist those anomalies with the SBC's more adequate historic resources. In this respect, I have tried to discern the muted voices and traditions within the SBC's confessional heritage, as resources in the struggle against contemporary forms of credalism in the SBC. By no means have I idealized the history of the SBC prior to the advent of the present conflict (conveniently dated 1979). Neither have I elevated any individual Baptist in the SBC—however significant that individual's contribution to the SBC—to the status of hero. Certainly, as one of my friends reminded me, "the ideals of priesthood of all believers and equality in the democratic process have never been fully realized because of our patriarchal theology and polity." I imitate, however, the attitude expressed by John Leland about his own "description of the Baptist principles": "if I have inadvertently misrepresented the general opinion, and only written my own, I should be glad to be corrected."[8] Nonetheless, although every book deserves criticism while only a few deserve praise, readers of this book will err most if they preoccupy themselves with

---

[8]John Leland, "Preface" to "The Virginia Chronicle," in *The Writings of John Leland*, ed. L. F. Greene, Religion in America Series, ed. Edwin S. Gaustad (New York: G. W. Wood, 1845; repr., New York: Arno Press and the N.Y. Times, 1969) 91 (page references are to the reprint edition).

either criticism or praise of this text, not to deny or claim that perhaps this book deserves either one or both. This book only, and even inadequately, points to something far greater than itself. The book will succeed and readers will profit only insofar as both the book and its reading do not become ends in themselves and readers finally turn from the sign to that about which the book testifies. Only such a result can ultimately validate the claims of the following pages.

Fort Worth, Texas
31 October 1996

Jeff B. Pool

Acknowledgments
of a Convocation

I have affectionately dedicated this book to the memories of my Baptist maternal grandparents: Lela Pearl Hughes and Karl Leslie Hughes. Their lives as Baptist Christians indelibly imprinted themselves into my own trust in and fidelity to God through Jesus of Nazareth. As charter members of Fairview Baptist Church near Seminole, Texas, they demonstrated the essential importance of genuine Christian community. Through these memories of my maternal grandparents, I also remember that Baptist Christian community with unending appreciation and love, for there I began to identify my awareness of and participation in life's ultimate mystery through Baptist Christian social experience and language. My connections with that community, however brief, planted the seeds of historic Baptist principles deep within me, seeds that later germinated in my life and eventually yielded the fruit of my commitment to them: principles such as the competency of every person before God, religious freedom, the priesthood of every Christian, the autonomy of each local church.

Although I have dedicated this book to the memories of the grandparents who by example and word gave to me a Baptist Christian vision of life, I have written this book in the interstices between the dissolution of the historic Southern Baptist Convention and the reemergence of numerous new yet still small Baptist Christian communities. Thus, I especially acknowledge all Baptists who also find themselves in these gaps—those exiles and pilgrims *en route* from the ruined spectacle of the former community to the restored vision of a future community. These cotravellers have often inspired and encouraged me both throughout my own larger journey and especially in the writing of this book.

Additionally and more specifically, I want to identify the many friends, both longtime and newly discovered on this journey, who have critically, kindly, and lovingly helped to shape the thoughts of the following pages into a book. I have received wonderful counsel, suggestions, corrections, and even caution from these friends. Much of their wisdom I have incorporated into this work. I have chosen in several respects, however, to diverge from the wise guidance offered in their generous commentaries on my work. For that in this book which remains inadequate or deficient in any way, on the one hand, I fully accept the responsibility. On the other hand, for much of the value possessed by this book, these friends deserve credit. I gratefully acknowledge their contributions to this work: Darrel Baergen, Jann Aldredge-Clanton, Dave Dinkins, William R. Estep, Harold Freeman, Steve Harmon, Boo Heflin, William L. Hendricks, Kip Ingram, Robert P. Jones, Ron Kafer, Bill J. Leonard, Andrew McIntosh, Molly Truman Marshall, Kyle Pasewark, Bruce Prescott, Jan Richardson, Velma Stevens, Bill Tillman, Nancy Thurmond, E. Frank Tupper, and Carl Wrotenbery.

I greatly appreciate the commitment of Mercer University Press to publish work on the life and theology of Baptists—especially during this crucial period of the SBC's history. I thank my publisher for adding this book to its list of titles. I especially thank Marc Jolley, assistant publisher of Mercer University Press, for his encouragement and support since my first contact with him about this project. Another person deserves very special acknowledgment and my deepest gratitude: Edmon L. Rowell, Jr., senior editor of Mercer University Press. Edd's expert attention to the smallest details and the wisdom of his editorial experience have significantly enhanced the quality of this work. I have thoroughly enjoyed working with him on this book.

I also thank the departments of theology and church history at SWBTS for their encouragement at the inception of this project. I owe much as well to the staff of Roberts Library at Southwestern Baptist Theological Seminary, especially to Alan Lefever, archivist, and Naomi Harmon for their help in obtaining copies of several important documents for my research. Among the many friends who have supported me in various ways either during the entire process of producing this book or at some stage along the way, I also remember the members of the Artist's Way Cluster at Connections Book Store in Fort Worth, Texas: for sharing with me their insights into the creative processes, I thank them. I also thank the members of the Baptist Spirituality Gathering in Texas for their companionship and prayers.

To continue, I owe a special debt of gratitude to Martin Marty, one of my former teachers at the University of Chicago Divinity School, for his comments on this work. Additionally, I thank the following friends and mentors for commenting on this book, as well as for offering spiritual, practical, and pastoral guidance to me during this project: Ralph

H. Elliott, formerly my pastor at North Shore Baptist Church in Chicago; H. Stephen Shoemaker, presently my pastor at Broadway Baptist Church in Fort Worth, Texas; and Gayland Pool, friend and relative, Rector at Christ the King Episcopal Church in Fort Worth.

For contributing material support to complete this project, I admiringly thank several very special Christians who perceived the importance of this project. These friends became significant participants in delivering this book to both the larger Christian community and to Baptist Christian communities: Gerald and Diane Haddock, Ron Kafer, and Gayland Pool and the administrators of the Unwin Fund of Christ the King Episcopal Church in Fort Worth, Texas.

Finally, I mention several members of my family, loved ones who have patiently discussed this topic with me from its conception as an idea to its birth as a book, the ones who have allowed me to vent my frustrations about this project, the ones who have encouraged me to pursue this inquiry as far as necessary, the ones who have lived and will live with the effects of this book. Although God has supplied me with both the determination to complete this work and the courage to face the consequences of its publication, without my family's faith, love, and hope, the threatening dimensions of this task often would have overshadowed my own joy in accepting the invitation to accompany the Spirit on this journey. With all my love, I thank them: my mother, Billie Faye Hughes Pool; my sister, Karen Diane Pool Dansby; my brother, David Bryan Pool; my son, Jonathan; my daughter, Kristen; and my wife, Laurinda Lynne.

Divine Spirit of freedom, I thank You for the invitation to accompany You on this journey into the open spaces of life in Christ. You invited me to accept a difficult and dual task: both to conservation through criticism and to criticism through conservation of the SBC's diverse heritage. As a grain of sand carried high in the ecstatic current of Your love's courageous coursings, I yield myself to Your gift of freedom. Even as You led and accompanied the ancient Hebrews into and through the wilderness, You have also led and accompanied me from the desert along the sea in North Africa, through the dusty yet fertile plains of West Texas, and even through this present task. I offer this book to You as the result of my acceptance of Your invitation. I thank You for the gifts to commence and complete this work: courage, knowledge, insight, wisdom, endurance, joy, peace, and love. Without these resources, as you supplied them through my friends and family, I could not have fulfilled this task. Most of all, without *Your presence*, I could not have accomplished this work: You who have brought good news to me in my poverty, have healed my blindness, have released me from captivity, have liberated me from oppression. For this freedom, You have liberated me. In my grateful love to You, I refuse to submit again to enslavement. May all my Baptist sisters and brothers love You with their complete freedom. May each grain of sand refract Your love for creation into adoration of You, O' Creator of liberty. Let the winds across the plains love you with their wild freedom and may this book love You as it announces the liberation in Your name, Jesus.

Abbreviations

Documents

AP (1858)

"Abstract of Principles." In *Annual of the Southern Baptist Convention.* Ninety-Seventh Session. St. Louis, Missouri. June 2-5, 1954. From "Recommendation No. 3, Charter of the Southern Baptist Theological Seminary." In "Proceedings," Wednesday morning, 2 June, item 15. Edited by the Executive Committee, Southern Baptist Convention (EC/SBC), pages 38-39. Nashville: Southern Baptist Convention (SBC), 1954.

BFM (1925)

"Report of Committee on Baptist Faith and Message." In *Annual of the Southern Baptist Convention.* Seventieth Session. Memphis, Tennessee. May 13-17, 1925. In "Proceedings," second day, afternoon session, 14 May, item 53. Edited by the secretaries, SBC, pages 70-76. Nashville: Marshall and Bruce Company, 1925.

BFM (1963)

"Committee on Baptist Faith and Message." In *Annual of the Southern Baptist Convention.* One Hundred Sixth Session. Kansas City, Missouri. May 7-10, 1963. In "Proceedings," Thursday morning, 9 May, items 112-24. Edited by the EC/SBC, pages 63, 269-81. Nashville: SBC, 1963.

BI (1963)

Baptist Ideals. Nashville: Sunday School Board of the SBC (BSSB), 1963.

CNC

"Covenant for a New Century, The Spirit and Structure of the Southern Baptist Convention: The Report of the Program and Structure Study Committee." In *Annual of the Southern Baptist Convention.* One Hundred Thirty-Eighth Session. Atlanta, Georgia. June 20-22, 1995. From "Sixty-Eighth Annual Report of the Executive Committee." In "Proceedings," Tuesday morning, 20 June, item 30. Edited by the EC/SBC, pages 45-46, 151-76. Nashville: SBC, 1995.

CSBH

"The Chicago Statement on Biblical Hermeneutics." *Journal of the Evangelical Theological Society* 25 (December 1982): 397-401.

CSBI

"The Chicago Statement on Biblical Inerrancy." *Journal of the Evangelical Theological Society* 21 (December 1978): 289-96.

DHR (1978)

"Declaration of Human Rights." In *Annual of the Southern Baptist Convention*. One Hundred Twenty-First Session. Atlanta, Georgia. June 13-15, 1978. In "Proceedings," Wednesday morning, 14 June, item 129. Edited by the EC/SBC, pages 57-58. Nashville: SBC, 1978.

DS

Enchiridion Symbolorum: Definitionum et Declarationum de Rebus Fidei et Morum. Thirty-third edition. Edited by Henricus Denzinger and Adolfus Schönmetzer. Freiburg im Breisgau: Verlag Herder, 1965.

DWC (1923)

"Defining the Work of the Convention." In *Annual of the Southern Baptist Convention*. Sixty-Eighth Session. Kansas City, Missouri. May 16-20, 1923. From "Report of Executive Committee." In "Proceedings," Friday evening session, 18 May, item 86. Edited by the secretaries, SBC, page 74. Nashville: Marshall and Bruce Company, 1923.

ECT (1994)

"Evangelicals and Catholics Together: The Christian Mission in the Third Millennium." *First Things* 43 (May 1994): 15-22.

FASB (1920)

Fraternal Address of Southern Baptists. Southern Baptist Convention, 1920.

NHC (1833)

"The New Hampshire Confession, 1833." In *Baptist Confessions of Faith*. Revised edition. Edited by William L. Lumpkin, 361-67. Valley Forge PA: Judson Press, 1959.

PCSBC (1845)

"Preamble and Constitution of the Southern Baptist Convention." In *Proceedings of the Southern Baptist Convention*. Augusta, Georgia. May 8-12, 1845, pages 3-5. Richmond: H. K. Ellyson Printer, 1845.

PCU (1914)

"Pronouncement on Christian Union and Denominational Efficiency." In *Annual of the Southern Baptist Convention*. Fifty-Ninth Session. Nashville, Tennessee. May 13-18, 1914. From "Report of Commission on Efficiency to the Southern Baptist Convention." In "Proceedings," fourth day, morning session, 16 May, item 97. Edited by the secretaries, SBC, pages 73-78. Nashville: Marshall and Bruce Company, 1914.

PRL (1939)

"A Pronouncement upon Religious Liberty." In *Annual of the Southern Baptist Convention*. Eighty-Fourth Session. Oklahoma City, Oklahoma. May 17-21, 1939. In "Proceedings," Saturday morning session, 20 May, item 82. Edited by the EC/SBC, pages 114-16. Nashville: SBC, 1939.

RIR (1938)

"Report on Interdenominational Relations." In *Annual of the Southern Baptist Convention*. Eighty-Third Session. Richmond, Virginia. May 12-15, 1938. In "Proceedings," Thursday, afternoon session, 12 May, item 15. Edited by the SBC, pages 24-25. Nashville: SBC, 1938.

RPC (1987)

"Special Reports: Southern Baptist Convention Peace Committee." In *Annual of the Southern Baptist Convention*. One Hundred Thirtieth Session. St. Louis, Missouri. June 16-18, 1987. In "Proceedings," Tuesday evening, 16 June, item 153. Edited by EC/SBC, pages 56-57, 232-42. Nashville: SBC, 1987.

RPTSC

"Report of the Presidential Theological Study Committee." In *Annual of the Southern Baptist Convention*. One Hundred Thirty-Seventh Session. Orlando, Florida. June 14-16, 1994. Edited by the EC/SBC, pages 112-18. Nashville: SBC, 1994.

RWCC (1940)

"Reply to World Council of Churches." In *Annual of the Southern Baptist Convention*. Eighty-Fifth Session. Baltimore, Maryland. June 12-16, 1940. In "Proceedings," Friday afternoon session, 14 June, item 66. Edited by the EC/SBC, page 99. Nashville: SBC, 1940.

SB (1920)

"A Statement of Belief." In *Annual of the Southern Baptist Convention*. Sixty-Fifth Session. Washington, D.C. May 12-17, 1920. From "Appendix A: Seventy-Fifth Annual Report of the Foreign Mission Board." Edited by the secretaries, SBC, pages 197-99. Nashville: Marshall and Bruce Company, 1920.

SBCBUS (1845)

"The Southern Baptist Convention, to the Brethren in the United States; to the congregations connected with the respective Churches; and to all candid men." In *Proceedings of the Southern Baptist Convention*. Augusta, Georgia. May 8-12, 1845, pages 17-20. Richmond: H. K. Ellyson Printer, 1845.

SP (1945)

"Statement of Principles." In *Annual of the Southern Baptist Convention*. 1945. Edited by the EC/SBC, pages 59-60. Nashville: SBC, 1945.

SP (1946)

"Statement of Principles." In *Annual of the Southern Baptist Convention*. Eighty-Ninth Session. Miami, Florida. May 15-19, 1946. In "Proceedings," Thursday morning session, 16 May, item 27. Edited by the EC/SBC, pages 38-39. Nashville: SBC, 1946.

SR (1923)
    "Science and Religion." In *Annual of the Southern Baptist Convention.*
    Sixty-Eighth Session. Kansas City, Missouri. May 16-20, 1923. In "Proceed-
    ings," Wednesday morning session, 16 May, item 11. Edited by the secre-
    taries, SBC, pages 19-20. Nashville: Marshall and Bruce Company, 1923.

Institutions, Organizations, and Committees

BP	Baptist Press
BSSB	Baptist Sunday School Board (Sunday School Board, SBC)
CLC	Christian Life Commission
EC/SBC	Executive Committee, SBC
FMB	Foreign Mission Board
HMB	Home Mission Board
MBTS	Midwestern Baptist Theological Seminary
NOBTS	New Orleans Baptist Theological Seminary
PTSC	Presidential Theological Study Committee
RPTSC	Report of the PTSC
SBC	Southern Baptist Convention
SBTS	Southern Baptist Theological Seminary
SEBTS	Southeastern Baptist Theological Seminary
SWBTS	Southwestern Baptist Theological Seminary
WCC	World Council of Churches
WMU	Woman's Missionary Union

One of the strangest lessons that our unstable life-passage teaches us is that the unwanted is often creative rather than destructive. . . . This is a common mystery of life, an aspect, if you will, of common grace: out of apparent evil new creativity can arise if the meanings and possibilities latent within the new situation are grasped with courage and with faith.

—Langdon Gilkey, *Shantung Compound: The Story of Men and Women under Pressure* (New York: Harper & Row, 1966) 242.

Crying in the Wilderness against Returning to Egypt*

My faith has found a resting place,
Not in device nor creed;
I trust the Everliving One,
*His wounds for me shall plead.***

In 1992, the president of the Southern Baptist Convention (SBC), H. Edwin Young, appointed a committee to examine the doctrines held by and taught among—as Young's committee described it—"that people of God called Southern Baptists."[1] This committee announced its report, the "Report of the Presidential Theological Study Committee" (*RPTSC*), in May 1993 and circulated the report among the messengers to the

---

*I have adapted, with permission from the publisher, portions of this prologue from my previously published article: " 'Sacred Mandates of Conscience': A Criteriology of Credalism for Theological Method among Baptists," *Perspectives in Religious Studies* 23 (Winter 1996): 353-86.

**"My Faith Has Found a Resting Place," lyrics by Lidie H. Edmunds, in *Baptist Hymnal* (Nashville: Convention Press, 1975) no. 380, verse 1.

[1]*RPTSC*, 112 (intro., ¶1). The editor of *SBC Life* also included this report as an insert in that publication (*SBC Life* [June/July 1994]: n.p.). I will cite all subsequent quotations from and references to this document, first, in terms of the page numbers on which they may be found in *Annual of the SBC* (1994) and, second, in terms of their places within the document's parts, articles, and paragraph numbers (e.g., *RPTSC* 113 [1.1] or 114 [2.1.1]). I have counted all paragraphs within this document, starting again with one in each part and article, following the committee's publication of those divisions. The *RPTSC* leaves its first paragraph outside its two major parts. For purposes of citation, I will refer to that paragraph as the "introduction," although the committee itself has left that paragraph untitled. The committee that formulated this report included the following persons: Timothy F. George (cochairperson); Roy L. Honeycutt (cochairperson); William E. Bell; J. Walter Carpenter, Jr.; Mark T. Coppenger; Stephen D. C. Corts; Carl F. H. Henry; Herschel H. Hobbs; Richard D. Land; R. Albert Mohler, Jr.; and William B. Tolar. As a careful study of the *RPTSC* indicates, however, Timothy George clearly controlled this committee, with aid, of course, principally from Land, Mohler, and Coppenger. One will search in vain for traces of Honeycutt's voice as the other cochairperson of this committee. The SBC's fundamentalist leadership openly acknowledges this fact. Paige Patterson describes the PTSC as "Timothy George's committee" (Paige Patterson, "Conversations with Evangelicals," *Texas Baptist* 2 [July 1995]: 7).

annual meeting of the SBC in June of that same year. At its next annual meeting in June 1994, the SBC adopted "Resolution No. 3—On the Presidential Theological Study Committee." During the annual meeting, messengers to the SBC, using some of the report's own language, resolved to "*commend*" this report "to the institutions and agencies of the Southern Baptist Convention as a *guide* to enable them to bear a faithful gospel witness to a culture in disarray, to be salt and light in a society that has lost its moral compass, and *to serve as a resource* for a new denominational consensus rooted in theological substance and doctrinal fidelity."[2] The messengers to the SBC in 1994 both commended this document to the SBC's agencies and institutions as a "guide" or "resource" and encouraged the dissemination of this document among Baptists in the SBC by the Sunday School Board.

On 14 December 1994, during a meeting of its board of directors, the SBC's Home Mission Board (HMB) instituted use of the *RPTSC* as a tool in its appointive and employment processes: "It is recommended that a copy of the *Report of the Presidential Theological Study Committee* be included with materials sent to missionary personnel candidates and potential Home Mission Board staff as an interpretive guide for a clearer understanding of Article 1 of *The Baptist Faith and Message* statement."[3]

---

[2]"Resolution No. 3—On the Presidential Theological Study Committee," in *Annual of the SBC* (1994): 102; emphasis mine. In a very different spirit, a little more than seventy years ago (during its 70th session, in the 80th year of its existence), in May 1925, the SBC adopted both a new confession of faith, the "Baptist Faith and Message," and a new method of support for the common missionary work of the SBC's participating churches, the Cooperative Program: "First Annual Report of Future Program Commission to Southern Baptist Convention" and "Report of Committee on Baptist Faith and Message" (hereafter cited as *BFM [1925]*), in *Annual of the SBC* (1925): 25-37, 70-76. In 1963, the SBC revised this statement: "Committee on Baptist Faith and Message," in *Annual of the SBC* (1963): 63, 269-81 (hereafter cited as *BFM [1963]*).

[3]"Minutes," HMB board of directors meeting (14 December 1994) 6-7. See the HMB's related application of stricter doctrinal standards (specifically, issues related to biblical inerrancy) to candidates for appointments to the chaplaincy ("HMB Tightens Scrutiny of Chaplain Candidates," *Western Recorder* 169 [29 August 1995]: 2). Not by coincidence, the HMB has instituted this policy under the leadership of Larry Lewis, the HMB's president. During the SBC's annual meeting in 1979, although Larry Lewis introduced a resolution concerning "doctrinal integrity" as related to the SBC's seminaries ("Resolution No. 17"), the chair of the Convention ruled the resolution out of order, because a previous motion had addressed the same issue. Wayne Dehoney had introduced the previous motion: "that this Convention reaffirm the 1963 Baptist Faith and Message Statement on the Scriptures which was overwhelmingly adopted to 'serve as information to the churches, and which may serve as guidelines to the various agencies of the

By November 1995, even Midwestern Baptist Theological Seminary (MBTS), under the leadership of its then newly elected president Mark Coppenger, had begun to use the *RPTSC* similarly. The seminary published a "Faculty Questionnaire" for persons seeking faculty positions at MBTS. In its questionnaire, on the surface, MBTS probes its prospective

---

Southern Baptist Convention.' . . . " The motion concluded by quoting the *BFM*'s article on the Christian scriptures. Even though the SBC did not adopt Lewis's resolution, Lewis, as well as Herschel Hobbs, spoke in favor of Dehoney's motion. According to James C. Hefley, however, whose source was a taped interview with Lewis, Lewis supported Dehoney's motion only because (after a call to Dehoney from Adrian Rogers and a brief conference between them for clarification) Dehoney had interpreted his own motion as an affirmation of inerrancy in scripture's *original autographs* (Hefley, *The Truth in Crisis: The Controversy in the Southern Baptist Convention* [Dallas: Criterion Publications, 1986] 69-71; idem, *The Conservative Resurgence in the Southern Baptist Convention* [Hannibal MO: Hannibal Books, 1991] 39-40). The SBC adopted Dehoney's motion, but did not publish in the *Annual* the inerrancy-interpretation of that motion. Furthermore, Welton Gaddy (a member of the Committee on Resolutions in 1979) moved that the SBC adopt "Resolution No. 16—On Gratitude for our Seminaries." This resolution spoke against "recent accusations" that "have brought into question the *doctrinal integrity* of some seminary staff and faculty members in relation to the 'Baptist Faith and Message' statement adopted by the Southern Baptist Convention in 1963. . . . " Larry Lewis, who had questioned the "doctrinal integrity" of some seminary faculty and staff members in his "Resolution No. 17," both "raised a parliamentary question" about "Resolution No. 16" and "moved to table the motion to adopt the resolution." Nevertheless, in 1979, the SBC adopted "Resolution No. 16" (*Annual of the SBC* [1979]: 31, 32, 45, 55-56; emphasis mine).

The president of the SBC in 1980, Adrian Rogers, however, appointed Larry Lewis to the Committee on Resolutions for the SBC's meeting in that year. Given Lewis's participation on the Committee on Resolutions during the SBC's meeting in 1980, apparently, the presentation and adoption of "Resolution No. 16—On Doctrinal Integrity," represented the substance of Lewis's "Resolution No. 17" from 1979 and, consequently, both a reversal of "Resolution No. 16" from the SBC of 1979 and the vindication of Lewis's still passionate conviction (*Annual of the SBC* [1980]: 25, 50-51; emphasis mine). In a related matter, during the annual meeting of the SBC at its Tuesday afternoon session, 9 June 1981, Hobbs introduced the following motion: that "we reaffirm our historic Baptist position that the Holy Bible, which has truth without any mixture of error for its matter, is our adequate rule of faith and practice, and that we reaffirm our belief in 'The Baptist Faith and Message' adopted in 1963, including all seventeen articles, plus the preamble which protects the conscience of the individual and guards us from a creedal faith." In the Wednesday morning session, 10 June 1981, when the Convention considered scheduled motions, Hobbs discussed his motion. Larry Lewis sought clarification of the motion's intent, expressing specific concern about the motion's "effect on Resolution No. 16 (Doctrinal Integrity) adopted by the 1980 Convention" (*Annual of the SBC* [1981]: 35, 45). In 1987, the HMB's trustees elected Larry Lewis as president of the HMB. More than likely, the HMB's recent adoption of the *RPTSC*, as an "interpretive guide" to the *BFM*'s article on the Christian scriptures, represents another partial release of Lewis's longstanding frustrations or a further alleviation of his deep concerns.

faculty members about a variety of doctrinal and moral positions or issues. While concerns about a prospective teacher's political alignments in the SBC clearly motivate the questions in this document, more importantly at this stage, MBTS employs the *RPTSC* and other confessional documents as credal criteria on the basis of which to interrogate prospective teachers about their doctrinal and moral perspectives. MBTS openly communicates its intention to pursue only candidates in agreement with the documents, including the *RPTSC*, to which this questionnaire refers.[4]

In light of both the *RPTSC*'s content and the ways some of the SBC's agencies have already begun to use this document, despite the Presidential Theological Study Committee's claims about the document to the contrary, more than any other document produced during the preceding seven decades, but especially during the two most recent decades, of the SBC's history, *this document and its adoption by the SBC programmatically and officially establish the most severe threat among recent threats to distinctive Baptist Christian experience and community: credal Baptist Christianity or Baptist credalism.*[5] Three other hypotheses

---

[4]"Having read the Report of the President's Theological Study Committee and the two Chicago statements, do you agree with them?" ("Midwestern Baptist Theological Seminary: Faculty Questionnaire," insert in *SBC Life* 4 [November 1995]: p. 2 of the insert, question 3).

[5]Obviously, many faithful Baptists in the SBC have warned the SBC about the impending danger of credalism. I only endeavor to imitate their courage and to stand openly with those prophets. Thus, with my claims about this greatest credal threat, I do not pretend to disclose anything hitherto completely unknown or unsaid (e.g., see Cephas C. Bateman, "Baptists versus Creeds," *Baptist Standard* 26 [16 April 1914]: 7, 11). Very early in the SBC's most recent controversies, Grady C. Cothen boldly and carefully identified the credal tendencies of the fundamentalist aggression in the SBC and the dangers of those tendencies for the SBC (Cothen, "The Real Issue of Our Times," *Facts and Trends* 25 [February 1981]: 2; idem, "The Bottom Line of a Creed," *Facts and Trends* 25 [April 1981]: 2; idem, "A Difference between Believing and a Creed," *Facts and Trends* 25 [May 1981]: 2; idem, "Now, I'm Scared," *Facts and Trends* 25 [June 1981]: 2; cf. Linda Lawson, "Cothen Underscores Ideals," *Facts and Trends* 27 [February 1983]: 5; "Cothen Recommends 'Ideals,' " *Facts and Trends* 27 [June 1983]: 11-13). Even in retirement, Cothen continues to alert Baptists to the danger of "creeping credalism" in the SBC (Cothen, *What Happened to the Southern Baptist Convention? A Memoir of the Controversy* [Macon GA: Smyth & Helwys, 1993] 157-63; cf. idem, *The New SBC: Fundamentalism's Impact on the Southern Baptist Convention* [Macon GA: Smyth & Helwys, 1995] 65-85, 143-78). Similarly, also more than a decade ago, Slayden Yarbrough discussed the dangers of the SBC's drift into credalism for its historical commitments and self-definition, for its understanding of the production and use of theology, and for its concept of missions as cooperative not coerced endeavors (Yarbrough, "Is Creedalism a Threat to Southern Baptists?" *Baptist History and Heritage* 18 [April

accompany and expand this initial or guiding hypothesis: (1) the Presidential Theological Study Committee has camouflaged the *RPTSC*'s credalism with the SBC's historic anticredal language and heritage; (2) the *RPTSC*'s credalism originates from and promotes a Calvinistic heritage; and (3) the restructuring of the SBC has secured the political power with which to enforce conformity to this credal document among Baptists in the SBC. With the following series of studies, I endeavor to confirm this fourfold hypothesis.

In the initial hypothesis, the phrases "credal Baptist Christianity" and "Baptist credalism," however, contradict themselves: the terms "Baptist" or "Baptist Christianity" and the terms "credalism" or "credal," as the SBC has understood them, do not consistently cohere as components of the same thoughts. This actually constitutes the problem addressed by this book. In order to confirm this book's guiding hypothesis, consequently, first the meaning of the term "credalism" requires clarification. Clarification of that term will disclose the self-contradictory character of the threat identified by this book's guiding hypothesis.

I. The Phenomenon of Credalism

Several components, when operating conjointly, produce the phenomenon of credalism. While I will not necessarily consider credalism as a problem in itself, Baptists in the SBC and the SBC itself have historically considered this phenomenon to be a threat to the very substance of the Baptist experience and understanding of life in God through Jesus Christ. This description of credalism, then, addresses only its dangerous characteristics with reference to the SBC's historic self-understanding, and neither credalism's positive roles in nor its threats to Christian communi-

---

1983]: 21-33). Russell Dilday, former president of SWBTS, also warned about the dangers of credalism, in a brief discussion of the historic Baptist principle of the individual human's competency in religion (Dilday, "Individuals Must Respond to God Personally," *Facts and Trends* 25 [March 1981]: 5). Even more recently, Fisher Humphreys has correctly observed a very different phenomenon in the new SBC. "The new majority tradition will no longer include a resistance to prescriptive creeds. The new leaders of the Convention do not share the conviction of earlier Baptists that creeds are pernicious" (Humphreys, *The Way We Were: How Southern Baptist Theology Has Changed and What It Means to Us All* [New York: McCracken Press, 1994] 170). Humphreys, Dilday, Yarbrough, Cothen, and Bateman represent only a small portion of an even larger group of faithful Baptists who have boldly warned against the threat of credalism in the SBC.

ties with ecclesial polities in which creeds hold official or authorized roles and functions.[6]

---

[6]As the primary points of reference for identifying the SBC's official and historic self-understanding, I have examined confessional statements authorized or adopted by the SBC during its annual sessions. See one very different approach to identifying shifts in the SBC's theological perspectives, wherein, according to the editor of that volume, "in order to track the changes in the doctrines considered in this book, the authors have focused their attention on the major writing theologians who have published as and for Southern Baptists" (Paul A. Basden, "Introduction" in *Has Our Theology Changed? Southern Baptist Thought since 1845*, ed. Basden [Nashville: Broadman & Holman, 1994] 5).

Strictly considered, the decisions made and the actions taken by the SBC during its annual sessions define the Convention's perspective. This claim invites some qualification. First, references to the SBC's historic perspective do not automatically denote some *universal* Baptist perspective, as if history discloses one theological perspective shared by all Baptist groups. While a variety of confessional documents have influenced the development of the SBC's perspectives, the SBC itself has used those documents only as resources with which to develop its own unique theological perspectives. For this reason, insofar as I refer to other Baptist confessional statements, either antecedent or subsequent to the existence of the SBC, I will consistently subordinate them (in order of theological importance) to the statements and documents authorized, produced, and adopted by the SBC through its annual sessions. Second, individual Baptists, churches, associations of churches, and state conventions participating in the SBC, as well as various institutions and agencies of the SBC itself, have also produced and employed a variety of confessional statements. Nonetheless, although I will often refer to such documents, I have also subordinated them to the confessional statements authorized, produced, or adopted through the SBC's annual sessions, as a way of isolating an official perspective. Third, although the SBC's decisions during its annual sessions represent the Convention's definitive positions on various issues or topics, those decisions literally define the SBC's official perspective for only one year. From year to year, the SBC has shifted its perspectives on a variety of topics and issues. Nonetheless, by examining the 150-year history of the SBC's official pronouncements and decisions, as recorded in the Convention's annuals, one discovers a surprising theological continuity in the SBC's history, at least prior to the introduction of severe aberrations since the late 1970s. With the previous qualifications, I aim to remain sensitive to the variety of confessional documents (such as, articles of faith from associations of churches and local churches, church covenants, confessions produced by institutions of the SBC, or even theological literature published by leaders in the SBC) in use among Baptists who participate in the SBC (see Bill J. Leonard, "Types of Confessional Documents among Baptists," *Review and Expositor* 76 [Winter 1979]: 29-42; James Leo Garrett, Jr., "Sources of Authority in Baptist Thought," *Baptist History and Heritage* 13 [July 1978]: 41-49; Charles W. Deweese, *Baptist Church Covenants* [Nashville: Broadman, 1990]). Nonetheless, in order to simplify my argument, I have distilled the SBC's official perspective from the documents authorized and adopted through its annual sessions, and have abstracted the SBC's perspective from its broader and more diverse historical and contemporary contexts.

A. Distinction between Creeds and Confessions of Faith

For a variety of reasons that will also figure prominently in this description of credalism, Baptists often vehemently distinguish their own confessions of faith from creeds.[7] Despite my own agreement in principle with the intent and intuition behind this distinction, with some reservation, I concur with Bill Leonard's assessment of the use of such documents: "The line between a confession and a creed is thin indeed. . . . Since 1979 it has become a particularly academic distinction." I do not *fully* concur, however, with Leonard's elaboration of his own assessment, to the effect that Baptists in the SBC "were naive in their effort to distinguish between confessionalism and credalism."[8] Hermeneutical, ideological, practical, social, or moral abuses of such a distinction neither necessarily invalidate the distinction itself nor essentially qualify it as a naive effort. Furthermore, one cannot even properly speak about the danger of *credalism* for Baptists without this distinction, however care-

---

[7]See the following examples in which this distinction operates: James E. Carter, "Southern Baptists' First Confession of Faith," *Baptist History and Heritage* 5 (January 1970): 24; idem, "Guest Editorial: The Bible and 20th-Century Southern Baptist Confessions of Faith," *Baptist History and Heritage* 19 (July 1984): 2-3; W. R. Estep, "Baptists and Authority: The Bible, Confessions, and Conscience in the Development of Baptist Identity," *Review and Expositor* 84 (Fall 1987): 600-601; idem, "Biblical Authority in Baptist Confessions of Faith, 1610–1963," in *The Unfettered Word: Southern Baptists Confront the Authority-Inerrancy Question*, ed. Robison B. James (Waco TX: Word Books, 1987) 157; Claude L. Howe, Jr., "From Houston to Dallas: Recent Controversy in the Southern Baptist Convention," *Theological Educator* 41 (Spring 1990): 84-85; Humphreys, *The Way We Were*, 50-54; William L. Lumpkin, ed., *Baptist Confessions of Faith*, rev. ed. (Valley Forge PA: Judson Press, 1969) 16-17; W. J. McGlothlin, ed., *Baptist Confessions of Faith* (Philadelphia: American Baptist Publication Society, 1911) xi-xii; G. Keith Parker, *Baptists in Europe: History and Confessions of Faith* (Nashville: Broadman, 1982) 20; Edward B. Pollard, "What Shall We Think of Creeds?" *Review and Expositor* 12 (January 1915): 40-54; idem, "A Brief Study in Baptist Confessions of Faith," *The Chronicle* 7 (April 1944): 74-85; Walter B. Shurden, "Major Issues in the SBC Controversy," in *Amidst Babel, Speak the Truth: Reflections on the Southern Baptist Convention Struggle*, ed. Robert U. Ferguson, Jr. (Macon GA: Smyth & Helwys, 1993) 7-8; H. W. Tribble, "Individual Competency and Use of Creeds," *The Chronicle* 7 (April 1944): 94-95; Yarbrough, "Is Creedalism a Threat to Southern Baptists?" 21-33.

[8]Bill J. Leonard, "Southern Baptist Confessions: Dogmatic Ambiguity," in *Southern Baptists and American Evangelicals: The Conversation Continues*, ed. David S. Dockery (Nashville: Broadman & Holman, 1993) 173; similarly, Bill J. Leonard, *God's Last and Only Hope: The Fragmentation of the Southern Baptist Convention* (Grand Rapids: Eerdmans, 1990) 77-81.

fully one must qualify the application of this distinction to actual personal
and social Christian experience. If creeds and confessions do not differ
in principle according to the SBC's historic perspectives, then, insofar as
credalism constitutes a danger for the SBC, one must also identify *confessionalism* of any kind as a threat to the SBC's Baptist substance.

The previous conclusion represents, perhaps, the most healthy and the
least ambiguous perspective for Baptists in the SBC. Refusing all forms
of confessionalism obviously eliminates the need for a distinction between creeds and confessions of faith. Certainly, solid precedents among
early American Baptists support the rejection of confessionalism of any
kind. For example, when John Leland expressed his own misgivings
about confessions of faith, he advocated this perspective.

> Confessions of faith often check any further pursuit after truth, confine the
> mind into a particular way of reasoning, and give rise to frequent separa-
> tions. To plead for their utility, because they have been common, is as good
> sense, as to plead for a state establishment of religion, for the same reason;
> and both are as bad reasoning, as to plead for sin, because it is everywhere.[9]

Nonetheless, given the history of confessionalism in the SBC, many Baptists in the SBC would consider a wholesale rejection of confessions to
be unwise. Realistically, given the SBC's history, a complete avoidance
of confessionalism no longer remains a viable alternative, however great
the threat remains from every kind of confessionalism. In light of the
SBC's confessional history, then, what criteria enable Baptists in the SBC
to distinguish between credalism and confessionalism?

Two related and preliminary questions require answers, however,
before I can adequately respond to the previous question. First, what are
creeds? Second, what are confessions of faith as understood historically
by the SBC? On the basis of answers to these questions, I will describe
the criteria with which to identify the more threatening phenomenon of
credalism, as eschewed historically by the SBC.

1. *Creeds.* I begin, then, with a brief answer to the first preliminary
question: What characteristics do Christian creeds exhibit historically? Although the following description does not include every characteristic of
creeds, I have identified several of the essential characteristics, those
especially pertinent as one portion of the background for identifying the
criteriology of credalism with which the SBC has operated historically.

---

[9]Leland, "Virginia Chronicle," 114n.*

Whether formulated and written by individuals, anonymous or identified, or by councils of bishops or ministers, first, a Christian credal document *originates from a community and functions as the official voice of and for that community.* Most often, *a group of elite individuals in a social hierarchy* articulates this official voice.

Second, as formulations by human communities, *specific historical circumstances, issues, problems, and dilemmas contextualize all credal statements.* For example, often in Christian history, creeds have arisen from conflict. Furthermore, creeds always contain linguistic elements, historical references, ideas, or presuppositions that indicate the times and places from which they originate.

Third, those who produce a creed, nonetheless, conceive and promote it as *a universal statement,* as the faith of all Christians everywhere and for all times, as doctrinal orthodoxy or normative doctrine for all Christians (a *consensus fidelium* or *universus ecclesiae sensus*). The authors of creeds prescribe the content of the faith to which all participants in the community must assent in order to remain part of the community.

Fourth, credal communities consider such documents to be *more concise, fixed, and precise or exact formulations of the true faith's objective elements (sensus fidelium)* or the ancient Rule of Faith (the *regula fidei*). With creeds, a community aims to eliminate the dangers of subjectivity and multiple perspectives.

Fifth, a creed, then, functions as *the hermeneutical rule or presupposition* by which the community *must interpret* its tradition and the Christian scriptures, as well as measure or test the subjective faith (*sensus fidei*) of all participants in the community. As a hermeneutical criterion, a creed disallows the possibility of interpreting scripture differently, either cognitively or practically, from the interpretations that comprise the creed itself. Additionally, when an individual's faith or interpretation of scripture does not pass the test or differs from the rule, then that believer has violated the conditions of participation (*communio*) within the community, until the believer officially and publicly changes her or his opinion.

Sixth, on the previous foundations, consequently, creeds *operate authoritatively,* and even infallibly, to fulfill several ecclesial functions: as the precise content of the congregation's response during worship, as the unquestionable guide for the content of the minister's or priest's proclamation, as the content of the baptizand's confession of faith, as the content taught by the community's educational ministries, and so forth. By utilizing the same precise and objective doctrinal formulations across the entire spectrum of ecclesial ministry, a community shapes the experiential potential of its participants, thus perpetuating the doctrinal traditions themselves.

Seventh, credal statements, thus, often *function polemically* to identify and to eradicate heterodoxy (understood in such communities as heresy) within the Christian community. Creeds often contain anathemas or curses on those persons in the community who hold contrary beliefs or opinions. Historically, Christian communities have enforced such official and linguistic anathematization in various ways, such as with the torture and execution used by numerous Christian inquisitions, or even with the excommunication, exclusion, or termination of employment used in more modern and contemporary contexts.

Eighth and finally, creeds also *function apologetically and prophetically* in relation to historical circumstances and occasions affecting the community. Christian communities often use creeds as statements against destructive social, political, or cultural forces, or perspectives considered as such, or as standards with which to rally Christians during times when they suffer persecution.[10]

2. *Confessions of Faith.* I continue by answering more extensively the second preliminary question: what are confessions of faith as understood historically by the SBC? The SBC has registered its own concept of confessional statements or confessions of faith, delineating several of the most essential characteristics exhibited by confessional statements, both in the "Baptist Faith and Message" from 1925 (*BFM [1925]*) and in its revision, the "Baptist Faith and Message" of 1963 (*BFM [1963]*).[11]

---

[10]See the following works for discussions of these characteristics: Philip Schaff, *The Creeds of Christendom*, vol. 1, *The History of Creeds*, 6th ed., ed. Philip Schaff and David S. Schaff (New York: Harper & Row, 1931; repr., Grand Rapids: Baker Book House, 1990) 3-8; John H. Leith, *Creeds of the Churches: A Reader in Christian Doctrine from the Bible to the Present*, 3d ed., ed. John H. Leith (Atlanta: John Knox Press, 1973) 1-11; J. N. D. Kelly, *Early Christian Creeds*, 3rd ed. (Singapore: Longman Group Ltd., 1972); *Dictionary of Fundamental Theology*, ed. René Latourelle and Rino Fisichella (New York: Crossroad Pub. Co., 1994) s.v. "Creed" by Jared Wicks, "Deposit of Faith" by Jared Wicks, "Dogma" by Guy F. Mansini, "Magisterium" by Francis A. Sullivan, "Orthodoxy" by William Henn, "Orthopraxis" by William Henn, "Rule of Faith" by Jared Wicks, and *"Sensus Fidei"* by Salvador Pié-Ninot.

[11]I have principally derived the following characteristics of confessional statements from the introductory statements or preambles to these two most influential of the SBC's confessional documents (*BFM [1925]*, 71; *BFM [1963]*, 269-70). In this section of the prologue, without repeated citations, I will frequently refer to these few pages in the two confessions.

Although both the *BFM (1925)* and the *BFM (1963)* explicitly identify and enumerate five of these characteristics, I have exercised the same freedom operative in the *BFM (1963)* in its revision of the *BFM (1925)*. Building "upon the structure" of those two confessional statements, substituting "words for clarity," adding "sentences for emphasis," "combining" and distinguishing points "with minor changes in wording,"[12] I have more systematically described these characteristics, in order to distill from them the second portion of a background for a criteriology of credalism. As a result of that study, I have identified fourteen characteristics of confessional statements. The following characteristics roughly describe the SBC's historic understanding of the nature and function of confessional statements.

Express Christian consensus. First, a confession of faith expresses the *"consensus"* of a group of Baptists, however large or small, on certain doctrinal concerns. The word "consensus" literally means "to feel with or together." In this sense, consensus has its basis in personal experience and convictions, personal convictions shared with other persons. For Baptists, however, such consensus always follows the individual Christian's experience, not the reverse. Nonetheless, finally, either one person writes the confession, while a committee changes and approves it for recommendation to the entire community, or various individuals write specific portions of the confession and the whole document proceeds through the same or a similar process. In this way, the group produces a confessional statement, but only the individuals consenting together authorize it as the group's confession of faith. No elite hierarchy produces doctrinal statements to which the entire community must adhere.

Demonstrate common Christian privilege. Second, accordingly, *all Christians share the privilege* of producing and publishing confessions of faith. Any group of Baptists or any individual Baptist, in any period of history, whatever the racial, sexual, social, religious, economic, or political status of that Baptist individual or group, has *"the inherent right"* to formulate and to publish confessions of faith for itself. Again, individual Christian freedom to confess one's faith establishes the condition for any group's or individual's right publicly to confess its faith.

Emerge from living Christian faith. As a third characteristic, a *"living faith,"* or trust in and trustworthiness toward the living God, through the

---

[12]*BFM (1963)*, 269-70.

resurrected Jesus Christ, and empowered by the indwelling Holy Spirit, elicits confessions of faith. Confessions of faith result or emerge from, and do not produce, the human experience of salvation through and life in Christ. With confessions of faith, Baptists do not intend "to add anything to the simple conditions of salvation" as disclosed through the scriptures: specifically, "repentance towards God and faith in Jesus Christ as Saviour and Lord."

Interpret living Christian faith. Fourth, with confessions of faith, Baptist Christians interpret their living faith, their experience with both God and one another. Christian confessional statements encapsulate Christian *understanding* of Christian experience, in the form of carefully crafted and organized thoughts, *"concerning those articles of the Christian faith which are most surely held"* by the Baptists who produce the confessions of faith. By emphasizing this characteristic of confessional statements, Baptists acknowledge with the broader Christian tradition the desire of the believer more fully to comprehend the life in Christ: *fides quaerens intellectum,* faith seeking understanding.

Employ biblical language. Fifth, also characteristic of confessional statements, Baptist Christians employ biblical language to aid in the interpretation of life in Christ. Because the Christian scriptures constitute the primary and written attestations to and interpretations of God's involvement with creation and humanity, statements *"drawn from"* the Christian scriptures function as the foundational resources for the interpretation of Christian experience or life through and in Christ. Confessions always remain subordinate in value to the Christian scriptures themselves, never taking the place of scripture.

Possess religious not scientific status. As a sixth characteristic of confessional statements, because such documents concern the content of faith, as *"statements of religious convictions,"* confessions of faith possess *a religious not a scientific status.* A confessional statement makes claims about ultimate reality, claims not necessarily verifiable or demonstrable by empirical, scientific, or logical methods, whether those are the methods of the physical, biological, and social sciences, or even the methods of the philosophical disciplines. For this reason, Baptist Christians *should not use confessions of faith to inhibit or "to hamper freedom of thought or investigation in other realms of life."*

Serve as educational instruments. Seventh, with a confession of faith, Baptist Christians characteristically *teach the broad contours of the cognitive content,* "those articles of the Christian faith," shared or held by participants in the community or group. Confessional statements function to educate bidirectionally: first, to and among the members of the group themselves; and, second, "to the world" or to those who do not yet or who choose never to participate in the community. In the first case, a confession of faith functions as a tool with which and as a medium through which the members of the community can articulate to one another various aspects of their Christian experience—thus, educating one another about various aspects of their shared life in Christ. In this respect, a confessional statement supplies a common linguistic framework with a vast and broad range of possible combinations for dialogical interaction regarding Christian doctrine. Furthermore, no single member of the community can or may legitimately monopolize or control the linguistic medium; among members of the group, mutuality guides the educational dynamic. In the second case, a confessional statement serves to inform everyone outside the group about the community's cognitive, axiological, and practical commitments. In this second respect, confessions of faith function apologetically, dialogically, hence evangelistically, and even ecumenically.

Guide biblical interpretation. Eighth, confessions of faith characteristically function "*only as guides in interpretation*" of the Christian scriptures. Confessions supply broad, yet concise and dense, renderings of Christian doctrines and practices, in order to aid the interpreter of biblical texts to discover therein attestations to the essential elements that describe the shared Christian experience. Historically for the SBC, confessional statements have never disallowed the discovery of more or less than that described or claimed by confessions themselves. In other words, Baptists in the SBC do not require either the Christian scriptures or interpretations of biblical texts to conform to the interpretations contained within confessions of faith. Rather, the SBC has consistently claimed that all confessional statements must either conform to the testimony of the Christian scriptures or receive revision in light of those scriptures in the event that confessional statements fail to conform. Nevertheless, confessional statements can and do function as guides into the vast, diverse, and beautiful terrain of the Christian scriptures.

Reflect historical conditioning. As a ninth characteristic, because a human and a particular group of humans, or "*some Baptist body, large or small*," formulates and publishes a confession of faith, obviously such documents always *reflect historical conditioning*. A confessional statement always contains contemporary formulations or reinterpretations of ancient Christian doctrines and practices, in which those who have written the document have addressed problems, issues, crises, dilemmas, or concerns for a specific group of Christians within its own unique or peculiar historical circumstances. Confessional documents always reflect such particularity linguistically, conceptually, practically, axiologically, epistemologically, and ontologically.

Register only Christian opinions. Tenth, a Baptist group's confessional statement registers that particular group's "consensus of *opinion*" concerning "those articles of the Christian faith" believed by the group. Confessions of faith, according to the SBC's historic stance, do not contain, either in form or content, absolute knowledge; from the SBC's historic perspective, pretensions to absolute certainty with regard to doctrinal formulations never produce or accompany confessional statements. Because confessional statements represent *interpretations* of Christian experience in light of *interpretations* of scripture, and vice versa, such documents always remain within the category of opinions about the various doctrines considered. However more probable may be the truth of certain interpretations than others within confessional documents, such statements remain subject to the logic of probability and hence open to doubt and further inquiry. Confessions of faith record only the opinions of a group about various Christian doctrines, not *unalloyed* truth itself. Only God can possess and express such absolute certainty about the knowledge of anything.

Represent Christian beliefs incompletely. As an eleventh characteristic, according to the SBC's historic stance, Baptists in the SBC "*do not regard*" confessions of faith "as *complete* statements" of their faith. Confessional statements do not possess "any quality of finality." If such documents adequately or sufficiently represented Christian life through and in Christ, the Christian scriptures themselves would become irrelevant and unnecessary. Obviously, short summaries of Christian doctrine cannot adequately represent either the fullness of Christian experience or the whole wealth of the Christian scriptures. Furthermore, humans in their finitude, even as faithful Christians led by the Holy Spirit, have limitations of knowledge, understanding, ability, and so forth, that can affect and often have affected both the form and content of confessional statements.

Do not infallibly interpret Christian faith. From the SBC's historic perspective, confessions of faith also exhibit a twelfth characteristic: they *never* possess "*any quality . . . of infallibility*." Not only can confessions of faith err as a consequence of finitude's limitations, as the previous characteristic indicates, but human sin itself can also contribute to distortions of the form and content of confessional statements. Christians can represent and often have represented their own biases, prejudices, and selfish intentions as the truth of Christian faith, as pure Christian doctrine. Hence, not only can confessional statements be theologically mistaken or uninformed, but they can be morally wrong as well.

Remain open to revision. Consequently, as a thirteenth characteristic, confessional statements *remain open to revision.* The SBC has considered it a moral imperative for Baptists to maintain a critical posture toward confessional statements or to scrutinize diligently such documents: "as in the past so in the future, Baptists *should hold themselves free to revise* their statements of faith as may seem to them wise and expedient at any time." A bipolar attitude constitutes this critical posture. The first attitude of this critical posture requires Baptists to remain *hermeneutically suspicious* of confessional statements in two respects: (1) by examining such documents carefully for evidence of *serious errors in formulations of or omissions from* central Christian doctrines; and (2) by searching for any evidence or presence of *sinful distortions* in such doctrinal summaries. This critical posture's second attitude also requires Baptists to analyze their confessions of faith carefully (with both wisdom and expedience), in order to revise them *when historical circumstances change,* to meet the needs of new generations of Baptist Christians. Hence, when Baptists revise their confessions of faith, they remain "in historic succession of intent and purpose," as they endeavor to state for their "time and theological climate those articles of the Christian faith" that they "most surely" hold among themselves: "A living faith must experience a growing understanding of truth and must be continually interpreted and related to the needs of each new generation."

Exercise no inherent, ultimate, or mandatory authority. The previous characteristics of confessional statements imply a fourteenth and fundamental characteristic: confessions of faith *neither possess nor exercise any inherent, ultimate, or mandatory authority over either the individual Christian's conscience or Christian communities.* As a key to the interpretation of scripture, a confession of faith offers guidance to Christians and Christian communities into the meaning of biblical texts, but cannot function to command, coerce, or discipline either the Christian's conscience or the Christian community as a whole for refusal of such guidance. Finally, only the individual Christian's conscience and attestation can confer any functional authority to confessions of faith. The ultimate authority or supreme norm, *norma suprema* or *norma non normata*, for Christians and their communities is none other than the God disclosed in Jesus of Nazareth and attested presently by the Holy Spirit. As stated by the SBC, "the *sole authority for faith and practice among Baptists is Jesus Christ* whose will is revealed in the Holy Scriptures." Second to God alone, for the SBC, the scriptures even remain above confessions of faith. Confessions of faith can only point to or guide into the testimony of the Christian scriptures, and to God indirectly through the scriptures. Consequently, confessions of faith *cannot legitimately function* either as "parameters for cooperation" or as tools for ecclesiastical, much less denominational, discipline.[13]

B. Criteriology of Credalism

The dissonance between creeds and confessions of faith (at least, as historically understood by the SBC), as I have previously characterized those two genres, enables the formulation of several criteria with which to detect the presence or approach of credalism among Baptists in the SBC and in the SBC itself.[14] Although creeds and confessions of faith share several characteristics, they differ from one another significantly enough that, especially when the SBC's confessional statements begin to function as creeds, the phenomenon of credalism itself has appeared. Although a deep interdependence exists among the following criteria, credalism itself can appear in varying degrees. Sometimes evidence will indicate only the *approach* of credalism or even *weak forms* of credalism.

---

[13]See the qualification of this historic conviction by the Southern Baptist Convention Peace Committee, in the introduction to its first recommendation. "Although the Baptist Faith and Message Statement of 1963 is a statement of basic belief, it is not a creed. Baptists are non-credal, in that they do not impose a man-made interpretation of Scripture on others. Baptists, however, declare their commitment to commonly held interpretations which then become *parameters for cooperation*" (emphasis mine). Nonetheless, even there, the Peace Committee recommended the *BFM (1963)* as the guideline with the "parameters for cooperation" ("Special Reports: Southern Baptist Convention Peace Committee," in *Annual of the SBC* [1987]: 240; hereafter cited as *RPC 1987*).

[14]Although Edward Pollard does not distinguish explicitly between creeds and confessions of faith, he discerns characteristics in the historical functions and uses of creeds that resemble some of the criteria in this criteriology of credalism: "a twentieth-century creed should be individual, rather than *collective*; voluntary, rather than *compulsory*; educative, rather than *authoritative*; emotive, rather than *intellectual*; experimental, rather than *speculative*; practical, rather than *metaphysical*; fluid and not *fixed*" (Pollard, "What Shall We Think of Creeds?" 53-54; emphasis mine).

Therefore, all of the following criteria will not necessarily, or may not yet, apply to every specific object of analysis. Nonetheless, the applicability of one or more of these criteria to various doctrinal statements indicates the presence or approach of credalism to some degree, however slight that might be.

1. First, credalism erupts when *a group of elite individuals relegates to itself the privilege and authority to articulate the doctrinal commitments for an entire community.* In this respect, credalism depends on a highly efficient and extremely hierarchical social system or community, an organization in which one person makes, or several people make, decisions for the entire community: autocratic, oligarchic, or aristocratic systems of polity in practice, even if denied in principle. In effect, such posturing defines the community as the leadership itself. Such an ecclesiology represents the instantiation in Baptist communities of a perspective similar to that held by Ignatius of Antioch: "Wherever the bishop shall appear, there let the people be; even as wherever Jesus Christ may be, there is the catholic church."[15]

2. Second, when *the group* (as realized by the presence of its leadership) begins *to devalue the convictions of the individual Christian's conscience in relation to communal interests, concerns, decisions, and doctrinal formulations, and to subordinate the individual Christian's priesthood to the community itself,* whether cognitively or practically or aesthetically, credalism has appeared again. If the voice of the community—the first-person-plural pronoun or the "we"—absorbs or silences the voice of the individual—the first-person-singular pronoun or the "I"— then credalism has appeared.

3. Third, credalism, at the very least, *equates the faith which is believed ("fides quae creduntur") with the faith by which it is believed ("fides qua creduntur"),* if it, more seriously still, does not elevate the former above the latter.[16] In such a shift, only assent to the cognitive content, as formulated by the creed itself, produces or guarantees the appearance of faith in the second sense: faith as trust in the living God. Although the cognitive content remains soteriologically important, for Baptists, mere mental assent to the particularity of that content produces no soteriological effect in itself. Often, very little cognitive understanding accompanies a person's initial salvific experiences: comprehension of the

---

[15]Ignatius *Epistle to the Smyrnaeans* 8.
[16]See Augustine's formulation of this classic distinction: *De Trinitate* 13.2.5.

cognitive content very often only follows the experience of salvation, and then only occurs gradually: faith seeks understanding. When a creed becomes the object of faith, it has ceased to express or to elicit living faith.

4. As a fourth indication, credalism appears *when Christians, either theoretically or practically, place a confessional statement or a group of confessional statements on either an equal level with or a superior level to the Christian scriptures themselves.* This characteristic appears when interpretations of Christian faith in a confessional statement supersede in importance biblical attestations themselves. As John Leland commented about all forms of confessionalism, "after all, if a confession of faith, upon the whole, may be advantageous, the greatest care should be taken not to *sacradize*, or make a petty Bible of it."[17]

5. Fifth, the *use of doctrinal or moral statements to prescribe for participants in a given group the contents of their beliefs or practices,* rather than to describe the beliefs or practices presently affirmed or operative among the group's participants, indicates the presence of credalism.[18] By endowing doctrinal or moral statements with this prescriptive

---

[17]Leland, "Virginia Chronicle," 114n.* Fundamentalist leaders in the SBC mistakenly and almost exclusively identify credalism with this criterion alone. For example, according to Timothy George, "Baptists have never been *creedalistic* in the sense of placing manmade doctrinal constructs above Holy Scripture" (George, "The Priesthood of All Believers and the Quest for Theological Integrity," *Criswell Theological Review* 3 [Spring 1989]: 287; idem, "The Priesthood of All Believers," in *The People of God: Essays on the Believer's Church*, ed. Paul Basden and David S. Dockery [Nashville: Broadman, 1991] 88). Again, "the creeds and confessions of the church are not infallible artifacts of revelation" (George, "Dogma beyond Anathema: Historical Theology in the Service of the Church," *Review and Expositor* 84 [Fall 1987]: 700). Thomas J. Nettles similarly construes credalism. "Baptists have rejected creedalism, and rightly so, since that word implies the elevation of a human document to the detriment of biblical authority" (Nettles, "Missions and Creeds: Part I," *Founders Journal* 17 [Summer 1994]: 21). "All concerned parties in the current crisis must be careful not to place any other entity, whether existential or written, above Scripture. Neither catechism, creed, or confession—nor reason, conscience, or current experience should be allowed to eclipse a clear and plain Scripture affirmation at any time. . . . If the wording of the Baptist Faith and Message permits agreement with the confession and a concurrent disagreement with the Scripture, then, just like the Athanasian correction of the Eusebian Creed, unequivocal clarification is needed. To do less exalts the confession above the Scripture and gives it independent and idolatrous authority" (Nettles, "Creedalism, Confessionalism, and the Baptist Faith and Message," in *Unfettered Word*, 144, 154).

[18]Fisher Humphreys designates this as the key distinction between creeds and confessions of faith. "The fundamental difference is that confessions are descriptive and creeds are prescriptive. . . . Creeds are authoritative statements of what one must believe in order to belong to a particular church. Baptists do not have creeds. They insist that the only

character, credalists aim to guarantee every individual's conformity to the group's official definition of its identity, by leaving no doubt about the community's expectations for every individual. The faith as *fides quae*, the cognitive content, becomes the law to be obeyed with one's will and mind.

6. Sixth, as a result, credalism operates also when *doctrinal statements restrain, inhibit, or prohibit either certain methods for the study of the Christian scriptures or certain interpretations of the Christian scriptures.* If a participant in the community obeys the credal rule, then the participant cannot, and must not, find in the scriptures anything that differs from or contradicts the creed itself. Furthermore, the participant in the community must not use methods or approaches that would or might make such discrepancies possible. Thus, when doctrinal statements inhibit or prohibit genuine exploration of the scriptures by Christians, when credal formulations stifle or restrain Christian reflection on and thought about those ancient testimonies of faith, then credalism has appeared.

7. Seventh, on the basis of the posture exhibited through the previous characteristics, when *a creed or confession of faith expresses an absolute certainty about the whole document itself or even about portions of the document*, such a document discloses another characteristic of credalism. When credal statements contain claims, attitudes, or pretensions to unqualified or absolute certainty about the formulations that comprise those statements, the formulators of such documents have virtually endowed those credal statements with a divine status: in a spectrum of possibilities ranging from divinely inspired to God's own voice. This characteristic claims for credal statements more certainty than that expressed in scientific reports. Such pretensions signal the presence of credalism.

8. Eighth, credalism arises also when *credal statements deny, minimize, or even fail to acknowledge their own historical conditioning.* Various tendencies or claims, either explicit or implicit, disclose this dehistoricizing posture in a creed or confession of faith: claims to completeness, finality, or linguistic precision in expression; or claims, whether subtle or blatant, to infallibility in the communication of either the form or content of doctrinal truth. Of course, this characteristic accompanies the previous pretension to absolute certainty.

---

written authority for Christian life and faith is the Bible" (Humphreys, *The Way We Were*, 50, 52).

9. As a ninth characteristic of credalism, creeds or confessions with the previous characteristics, consequently, also *inhibit, if they do not eliminate altogether, any possibilities for genuine revision of credal or confessional statements*, either corrective or elaborative. Given the previous characteristics, the tradition's or the creed's conservators, or the successors of the creed's writer or writers, have no external perspective from which to examine such authoritative credal statements. Unless the creed contains its own self-critical principle or characteristics, such as the credal or confessional statement's admission of its own fallibility or incompleteness, then the creed remains the rule for all evaluation of doctrine and no criterion external to itself, with the exception of God's own self, qualifies to evaluate the document itself.

10. Tenth, when *creeds or confessions of faith serve as immutable standards for indoctrination*, credalism has appeared. Several of the previous characteristics of credalism generate the possibility of this characteristic, especially such a document's nonrevisability or infallibility. Even though the word "indoctrinate" means only "to teach," specifically referring to various ideas or beliefs, and while not inherently negative, this word has a long history of negative usage; it has often referred to the use of various processes or methods for producing the right, proper, or acceptable knowledge or convictions in learners, with the goal of preventing or eliminating all other possibilities from their considerations or thoughts. Hence, I distinguish indoctrination from genuine education. Rather than encouraging learners to think carefully and analytically, as in genuine education, those who use creeds or confessional statements to indoctrinate discourage any thinking that might lead to genuine questions about the form or content of credal statements themselves. In this sense, indoctrination represents the principal aim of credalism.

11. Eleventh, when *the authority of creeds or confessions of faith operates coercively*, credalism looms most threateningly. Credalism cannot sustain its previous characteristics, unless behind the creed or confession of faith various kinds or types of real power exist with which to enforce the document's purportedly absolute, immutable, legal, and divine claims on participants in the community. In many cases, creeds invoke anathemas or curses upon those who hold doctrines that differ from the creed itself. When political, social, economic, or cultural mechanisms exist through which to coerce participants in the community to conform to the creed publicly, then credalism operates most openly and efficiently. Hence, the community practically makes those anathemas real, in varying

degrees and with various methods, in the lives of those in the community who might dissent or have dissented from the creed. *The community corrects deviation from the creed by coercion.*[19] As I noted previously, in Christian history, communities have coerced dissenters with torture, excommunication, and even execution. More recently, communities have coerced conformity with various threats to the livelihood of dissenting participants.

In its final characteristic, credalism realizes the most negative sense of the original meaning of the word "religion," the sense which pervades the previous characteristics of credalism as well. The English word "religion" originates from the Latin word *religare*. The word *religare* means "to tie or fasten behind" or "to bind back." Thus, this characteristic of credalism emphasizes the real, raw power to bind, to restrict, or to restrain individuals, the power to make individuals conform to the dictates of the community—perhaps, figuratively, to tie the hands of their freedom in Christ behind their backs. With the previous criteria or indicators of credalism, I have examined the *RPTSC*, only to discover their applicability to that document. The criteriology of credalism, thus, serves the method that I have used in this study.

II. The Biblical Analogue

I have referred to the *RPTSC* and its official adoption by the SBC as the official inauguration of credalism in the SBC. Thus, returning to the concern of my guiding hypothesis, in light of the previous criteriology, the self-contradictory character of the phrase "Baptist credalism" becomes

---

[19]Slayden Yarbrough astutely describes the use of coercion to secure conformity to confessional statements as the most necessary criterion with which to identify the phenomenon of credalism, even though he also notes other criteria. For example, borrowing elements from Philip Schaff's definition of the word "creed," Yarbrough primarily defines credalism through the criterion of coercion. "With emphasis on the phrases 'with authority' and 'necessary for salvation,' credalism . . . will be understood as the use of authoritative statements of faith as official bases of organization and as tests of orthodoxy. Such statements are considered to be binding upon adherents" (Yarbrough, "Is Creedalism a Threat to Southern Baptists?" 23). By contrast, fundamentalist leaders who favor the employment of creeds, both as measures of orthodoxy and as devices to discipline divergent (morally or doctrinally) members of Christian communities, refuse to identify such uses as coercive (see George, "Priesthood of All Believers and the Quest for Theological Integrity," 287-91; idem, "Priesthood of All Believers," in *People of God*, ed. Basden and Dockery, 88-91; cf., idem, "Dogma beyond Anathema," 700-701, 703-706; Nettles, "Missions and Creeds: Part I," 23-26; idem, "Creedalism, Confessionalism, and the Baptist Faith and Message," 148-51).

evident. The phrase "Baptist credalism" contradicts itself, because, according to the SBC's historic stance, credalism neutralizes or aggressively negates the *Baptist* substance of the SBC's historic self-understanding. In this respect, the SBC's recent turn to embrace credalism (however preliminary, ambiguous, and camouflaged) in its production and adoption of the *RPTSC* signals, once again, a surrender of freedoms that Baptists historically struggled so fiercely to attain and so courageously to retain, the original attainment of which defined the very substance of Baptist experience and communities. With its adoption of the *RPTSC* in 1994, the SBC indicated most decisively its willingness to abandon the risk in its present and historic freedom, for the security of a former bondage: with this document, the SBC completes the reversal of its direction.[20]

An account of both the SBC's previous history and its contemporary reversal of direction closely resembles key episodes in the biblical narratives of Israel's deliverance from Egypt and subsequent wandering through the wilderness.[21] From this biblical analogue, I have drawn the

---

[20]This reversal of direction with regard to credalism, of course, forms only one component (more and more a central component) in the SBC's more comprehensive directional reversal. As my own study proceeds, this reversal's social and political dimensions will also emerge. Nancy Ammerman documented this change of direction, in the midst of several moments in its greatest flux, from a sociological perspective (Ammerman, *Baptist Battles: Social Change and Religious Conflict in the Southern Baptist Convention* [New Brunswick NJ: Rutgers University Press, 1990]). This reversal originates from deep insecurity and extreme fear of the risks in freedom. During the second meeting of the Baptist World Alliance, J. Moffat Logan also identified this source of the credal tendencies among Baptists. "The desire for an authoritative creed is surely a departure from the standpoint of our Baptist sires. It is an endeavor to escape from spiritual risks by artificial aids and so is scarcely honoring to one another nor to Him who is supposed to be our chosen Guide. Let us insist on spirituality and loyalty and having these be well content to pay the price of liberty" (Logan, "Vital Experience of God, No Authoritative Creed," in *The Baptist World Alliance: Second Congress, Philadelphia, 19-25 June 1911, Record of Proceedings*, by the Philadelphia Committee [Philadelphia: Harper & Brothers, 1911] 120).

[21]See especially the following texts: Exod 1:8-22; 2:23-25; 3:1-12; 6:1-9; 12:29-42; 13:1-22; 14:5-31; 15:22-26; 16:1-36; 17:1-7; 19:1-25; 20:1-26; 24:1-18; 32:1-24; Num 11:4-35; 14:1-45; 20:1-13; 21:4-9. With this reference to Egypt, I do not imply anything negative (either geographically, racially, religiously, politically, or socially) about that contemporary nation or its people. I use this phrase only as a reference to a powerful biblical symbol of oppression and bondage in the history of God's interaction with creation. In 1914, in his presidential address to the SBC, George W. McDaniel applied this narrative cycle to the SBC as Baptists faced the world's needs and crises during that critical period: McDaniel, "Southern Baptists at Kadesh-Barnea" (part I), *Baptist Standard* 26 (28 May 1914): 6-7; idem, "Southern Baptists at Kadesh-Barnea" (part II), *Baptist Standard* 26 (4 June 1914): 11-12.

metaphorical title of this book: *Against Returning to Egypt*. Before I discuss both the title in connection with *the method* used in these studies and *the path of inquiry* or the structure of this book, I recount several major moments in this analogue.

A. Israel's Journey

According to biblical narratives, when the Hebrews dwelled in Egypt, the Pharaoh enslaved them, impressed them for work on public projects, afflicted them with hard labor in construction and agriculture. In the midst of their suffering from this bondage, the people cried to Yahweh for help, for relief from their suffering, for deliverance from their slavery. Yahweh empathized with the Hebrew people and, calling Moses to work with God in this task, delivered them from their bondage or misery.

Yet, as Pharaoh's army pursued the Hebrews in their journey of freedom, and as the liberated people approached the sea, the Hebrews stopped trusting Yahweh. In their fear, they imagined for themselves only two possibilities: either death inflicted by Pharaoh's army in the wilderness or life dominated by Pharaoh's taskmasters in Egypt. They indicated their preference for the second possibility. Through Moses, Yahweh supplied another possibility: liberation of the people from the entire Egyptian threat, from both death and domination. Escaping such bondage, however, also entailed abandonment of certain sustenance, or forsaking guaranteed provisions for satisfying hunger and thirst, however abundant or meager such provisions might have been. Entering the wilderness of freedom, and leaving the civilization of slavery, required that the Hebrews trust Yahweh to secure daily provisions for them and eliminated the possibility for their reliance on Pharaoh.

Despite the demonstrations of Yahweh's dependability or fidelity, even after Yahweh's deliverance of the people from Pharaoh through the sea, and even after receiving from Yahweh fresh water for their thirst at Marah, when the people became hungry in the Wilderness of Sin, they grumbled against Yahweh. Again, they recalled, and longed for, the guaranteed cuisine in Egyptian bondage. The people preferred to die with full stomachs in Egyptian bondage, even if death occurred as their punishment from Yahweh for not leaving Egypt; the people even accused Moses of leading them into the wilderness to kill them with hunger. For the Hebrew people, Yahweh's liberating guidance through the wilderness implied ultimate threats in freedom's risk, while Pharaoh's dominating governance in Egyptian civilization supplied penultimate guarantees with slavery's security. To satisfy their hunger, however, Yahweh provided quail and manna. Israel repeated this pattern also at Rephidim, when the people thirsted and could not obtain water. Again, the people grumbled against Moses and accused him of bringing them from Egypt to kill them with thirst. Still, Yahweh not only gave the people water, but led them into the Wilderness of Sinai where Yahweh disclosed the terms of the covenant with them.

While Moses remained on the mountain with Yahweh, however, the people remembered Egypt and distrusted Moses. In their great fear of the challenges in the wilderness, the people constructed a golden calf as their image of Yahweh, a god they could see. The people declared that this god had delivered them from Egyptian bondage. Yet, even after the destructive results of the people's fearful distrust and infidelity, Yahweh renewed a relationship with them.

In spite of every divine kindness and mercy, when Yahweh finally led the people from Sinai, at Kibroth-hatta-avah, they complained even about the manna with which Yahweh had satisfied their hunger. They remembered the richer foods in Egypt and longed for meat instead of manna. The people lamented their departure from Egypt and remembered their servitude there as if it had been prosperity. Once more, Yahweh gave to the people exactly that which they desired, meat in the form of quail, allowing them to satiate their gluttony until they became ill and many died. Fulfilling the desire that arose from their ingratitude to Yahweh, however, produced the destructive consequences of their fearful longings.

Later during the journey to their new home, the people camped in the Wilderness of Paran, while Yahweh sent a reconnaisance team into Canaan in preparation for Israel to enter the promised land. After hearing reports from the majority of scouts, however, fear of the Canaanite opposition gripped the people. Characteristically, they grumbled against Moses, and declared either death in Egypt or death in the wilderness as preferable to war with the Canaanites. Furthermore, the people even initiated the selection of a leader to return to Egypt. Yet again, although the people could not return to Egypt, Yahweh allowed them to fulfill at least one of their desires: the people of that generation did not enter the promised land; rather, they wandered in the wilderness until that entire generation had died there.

During their lengthy sojourn in the wilderness, the people continued to repeat the previous pattern. At one point, they camped at Kadesh in the Wilderness of Zin; there, too, thirsting and remembering the fruits and water of Egypt, they contended with Moses, rather than trusting Yahweh their faithful provider. This pattern reappeared also in Israel's long journey around Edom. In their impatience, once more, they accused Yahweh and Moses of bringing them into the wilderness to die. In addition, the people loathed the manna with which God had sustained them, longing for the food and water in Egypt. An invasion of poisonous serpents accompanied the people's ingratitude and accusations.

B. The SBC's Journey

Although the SBC's lineage extends to the Baptists in the early seventeenth century who originated from the reformations of the sixteenth century, the SBC has developed several significant differences from those earliest Protestant traditions. With one distinctive emphasis, however, the SBC historically has distinguished itself from most other Christian churches and organizations: its often-repeated aversion to credalism, an aversion that actually gave birth to the SBC.[22]

Just as the Hebrew people desired and endeavored to return to the security of Egyptian bondage when faced with obstacles and adversity in the wilderness, by adopting the *RPTSC*, the SBC has also begun to seek protection against the threats and ambiguities of contemporary life in something other than the SBC's distinctive Baptist convictions and commitments. In its fear of the numerous contemporary obstacles and

---

[22]I do not deny the significance of slavery's role in the SBC's origin and formation. Nonetheless, the issue of slavery did not cause the division among Baptists in the United States; rather, it occasioned that bifurcation. When the Triennial Convention's Board refused to appoint slaveholders as missionaries, thus both supplementing (and moving beyond) the Convention's written qualifications for missionary service and ignoring the Convention's previous refusal to take either proslavery or antislavery positions, Baptists in the South rightly perceived those actions as violations of the Convention's polity and, further, correctly understood the enforcement of that perspective as the operation of credalism (William B. Johnson et al., "The Southern Baptist Convention, To the Brethren in the United States; to the congregations connected with the respective Churches; and to all candid men," in *Proceedings of the Southern Baptist Convention* [1845]: 17-20; hereafter cited as *SBCBUS [1845]*). Consequently, while the Triennial Convention's Board rightly opposed slavery, it wrongly addressed the problem of missionaries as slaveholders. By the same token, nonetheless, while the Baptists of the South rightly resisted both the appearance of a noncongregational polity in the Convention and the imposition of a credal article, they wrongly continued to support slavery. James M. Morton, Jr. identifies several illuminating factors about the authorship of this founding address (e.g., James M. Morton, Jr., "Leadership of W. B. Johnson in the Formation of the Southern Baptist Convention," *Baptist History and Heritage* 5 [January 1970]: 11-12).

adversities for Christian life, the SBC has surrendered its freedom in Christ and its guidance by the living Holy Spirit for the security of fixed formulas and rules. By embracing credalism, the SBC has decided to leave the wilderness where God's Spirit guides the people in freedom. The SBC has chosen the security of credalism over the risk of the Spirit's guidance, human documents over God's own self. According to prophecies by Jeremiah and Hosea, although the wilderness represented the place of Israel's infidelity to Yahweh, Yahweh also associated Israel's wanderings in the wilderness with times of joyful and faithful love between God and Israel.[23] The times of greatest risk and most severe threats offer the opportunities for the most intimate love and the most significant communion between God and humans. Only in the wilderness of Christ's freedom, with all of its ambiguity and risk, can the SBC remain faithful and, by remaining faithful, remain genuinely Baptist. With the *RPTSC*, the SBC has fulfilled its desire for credal security and has abandoned spiritual freedom. Much of the SBC's leadership has responded with desperate anxiety to the uncertainty and ambiguity of Christian freedom in the chaos of contemporary life. In satiating its anxious desire, however, the SBC loses its very substance. By producing a creed to define itself, the SBC dissolves itself. The SBC cannot truly return to that which contradicts itself without losing itself. Thus, rather than genuinely realizing this desire to return to a credalism, the SBC's present generation may die in the wilderness of its freedom without tasting the milk and honey of the true promised land.

III. Dialectical Method and Path of Inquiry

From my perspective as a Baptist systematic theologian teaching in a seminary of the SBC, initially the Presidential Theological Study Committee's formulation invited thorough critical review and, in light of the *RPTSC*'s conclusions and declarations, finally has elicited vehement response. I will confirm my broader hypothesis about this document's role in the promotion of credalism within the SBC through careful studies of this document's content.[24] A second hypothesis accompanies the broader

---

[23]Jer 2:1-3; Hosea 2:3, 14-15; 9:10; 13:15.

[24]Although I am familiar with the credentials of all participants on this committee, and, despite both the inflammatory public comments by some of these committee members (e.g., Mark Coppenger, "Conserve is a Transitive Verb," *SBC Life* [May 1994]: 8-9; idem, "Who Then?" *SBC Life* [June/July 1994]: 16-17) and the ways in which the

hypothesis that motivates these studies: *the RPTSC has camouflaged its credalism*. I initiate these studies, consequently, with a twofold purpose: (1) to *expose* the *RPTSC*'s camouflaged credalism and, therefore, (2) to *resist* the *RPTSC*'s reductive approach in that strategy to Baptist Christian experience in the SBC. Thus, an *analeptic intention* accompanies my critique of both the production and the SBC's adoption of the *RPTSC*. With this study, I aim to confirm my broader hypothesis and, thereby, hope to *restore* an awareness of credalism's danger for Baptists, *to counteract* the drowsiness among Baptists induced by fundamentalist or extreme right-wing sedatives. I will realize this intention with the following method. The specific path of inquiry on which this method guides my studies will supply this book's structure.

A. Method

As noted previously, I aim to accomplish two goals. On the one hand, I will *expose* the incipient credalism that accompanies the SBC's adoption of the *RPTSC*. In the title, operating with the previous biblical analogue, I have correlated the phenomenon of credalism with the narrative of Israel's recurring desire and effort to return to Egypt. On the other hand, with these studies, I vehemently *resist* the presence and operation of credalism within the SBC, specifically as it has taken shape in the SBC through the *RPTSC*. Hence, in the title, still working with the biblical analogue, I have paralleled the term "resisting" in the more conceptual subtitle with the preposition "against" in the metaphorical or main title. In order to fulfill this dual aim, I have adopted a dialectical method, a method unapologetically operating as a disciplined expression of an essential dimension in my own fidelity to God.

---

militant right wing of the SBC has manipulated well-intentioned Baptists (those hoping for an end to hostilities among Baptists, for a continued and renewed cooperative coexistence in the SBC of Baptists from diverse perspectives), two members of this committee served as participants clearly representing alternative perspectives and minority voices on this committee: Roy L. Honeycutt, and Herschel H. Hobbs. Together, these two leaders both represent (from their different perspectives) Baptist diversity and express admirable Baptist efforts to coexist with love and tolerance within that diversity. By no means do I intend to implicate these leaders in this recent credal maneuver. Because of the solid reputations among Baptists held by these two leaders, the leadership of the SBC that has motivated this credal effort has used both their (Honeycutt's and Hobbs's) participation on this committee and their names on the *RPTSC* itself as devices with which to increase both the respectability of the document and, thereby, the possibilities for its adoption by the SBC. Obviously, this tactic contributed to the SBC's actual adoption of the *RPTSC*.

1. *Aporetics of Faith*
With Gratitude to Thomas the Apostle
(John 11:1-16; 20:24-29)

I describe the first pole in this dialectical method as an aporetics of faith. The term, "aporetics," originates from the Greek verb ἀπορέω and means "to be at a loss, be in doubt, be puzzled." Philosophically, it refers to initiating an inquiry or a line of questioning, to exposing theoretical or practical difficulties in various proposals or courses of action. Thus, as the object of such inquiry or exposure, the word ἀπορία contains a range of related meanings: the "difficulty of passing" through constricted places; the personal states of "loss, embarrassment, perplexity"; personal "distress, discomfort in illness"; and, less metaphorically, a "question for discussion, difficulty, puzzle." From the verb, then, the Greek adjective ἀπορητικός means "inclined to doubt" or dubitative.[25]

Using the genitive case with which to formulate the first pole of this method, I refer to aporetics as a discipline belonging to Christian faith itself: *faith's aporetics*. Resembling the impulse understood by the Johannine Christian community as "testing the spirits," faith inquires about or questions the proposals made to it, in light of its living criterion, the divine Creator historically and redemptively disclosed most decisively in Jesus Christ and presently active through the Holy Spirit.[26] Through such labors, faith exposes the theoretical and practical difficulties or distortions that accompany the proposals made to faith, whatever the sources from which those proposals originate, whether from Christian or from non-Christian communities or individuals.

In the first pole of this dialectical method, then, I have systematically and rigorously applied faith's inquisitive or dubitative inclination to the proposals made to it by the *RPTSC*, with the goal of exposing the aporias

---

[25]Henry George Liddell and Robert Scott, eds., *A Greek-English Lexicon*, 9th ed. rev. by Henry Stuart Jones and Roderick McKenzie (Oxford: Oxford University Press, 1940; repr., 1968) s.v. "ἀπορέω" and "ἀπορία." Also see George Ricker Berry, *The Classic Greek Dictionary*, Classic Series (Chicago: Follett Publishing Co., 1943) 92.

[26]"Beloved, do not believe every spirit, but *test the spirits to see whether they are from God*; for many false prophets have gone out into the world. By this you know the Spirit of God: every spirit that confesses that Jesus Christ has come in the flesh is from God, and every spirit that does not confess Jesus is not from God. And this is the spirit of the antichrist, of which you have heard that it is coming; and now it is already in the world" (1 John 4:1-3 NRSV; emphasis mine).

contained within or produced by that document. Thus, this pole of the dialectical method resembles quite closely one pole in Paul Ricoeur's dialectical hermeneutics: his hermeneutical suspicion, reduction, or iconoclasm. Ricoeur includes various critical procedures in his hermeneutical theory with which to expose the systemic distortions and illusions within and promoted by texts.[27]

Without an aporetic impulse, faith remains thoroughly naive. An aporetics of faith, therefore, operates with a prophetic or critical impulse. Yahweh often commissioned prophets to identify and to expose the sins of God's people.

> Oh, rebellious children, says the Lord,
>   who carry out a plan, but not mine;
> who make an alliance, but against my will,
>   adding sin to sin;
> who set out to go down to Egypt
>   without asking for my counsel,
> to take refuge in the protection of Pharaoh,
>   and to seek shelter in the shadow of Egypt;
> Therefore the protection of Pharaoh shall become your shame,
>   and the shelter in the shadow of Egypt your humiliation.
> For though his officials are at Zoan
>   and his envoys reach Hanes,
> everyone comes to shame
>   through a people that cannot profit them,
> that brings neither help nor profit,
>   but shame and disgrace (Isaiah 30:1-5 NRSV).[28]

In this respect, an aporetics of faith always operates as the Christian community's self-criticism in light of divine illumination. For example, the apostle Paul alerted the Thessalonian Christians to this principle. "Do not quench the Spirit. Do not despise the words of prophets, but test

---

[27]See the following examples in Ricoeur's work: Paul Ricoeur, *Freud and Philosophy: An Essay on Interpretation*, trans. Denis Savage (New Haven CT: Yale University Press, 1970) 32-36; idem, *The Conflict of Interpretations: Essays in Hermeneutics*, ed. Don Ihde, Northwestern University Studies in Phenomenology and Existential Philosophy (Evanston: Northwestern University Press, 1974) 330-31; idem, *Lectures on Ideology and Utopia*, ed. George H. Taylor (New York: Columbia University Press, 1986) 307.

[28]James M. Dunn has properly described this prophetic impulse as the "capacity for outrage," "the perpetual indignation that marks all prophets," "holy rage," an impulse which "calls for courage, not tepidity" (James M. Dunn, "Called to Be Perpetually Indignant Prophets," *Theological Educator* 41 [Spring 1990]: 127, 128, 133).

everything; hold fast to what is good; abstain from every form of evil" (1 Thess 5:19-22 NRSV). Throughout their varied history, Baptists have acknowledged and exercised this dimension of their faithfulness to God. Although various commitments to the operation of this prophetic principle have consistently appeared in the SBC's confessional documents, the SBC has articulated this prophetic principle most explicitly and completely in a confessional statement that it produced in connection with its preparation for and observance of the Third Baptist Jubilee in 1964.[29] According to that document, *Baptist Ideals* (*BI [1963]*), the healthiness and fruitfulness of both local churches and the SBC itself depend upon acceptance by those entities of "the responsibility of constructive self-criticism." Furthermore, only damage to churches and to the SBC will result both from denials of "the right to differ" and pretensions to the finality or perfection of "methods and policies." After affirming the need for "frequent re-evaluation" of "methods" as well as of "historic principles and practices as they relate to contemporary life," the *BI*

---

[29]This event commemorated the formation in 1814 of the Triennial Convention, the first national organization of Baptists in the United States. To fulfill its own role in this commemorative event, the SBC authorized and appointed its own Jubilee Advance Committee, functioning during the entire Baptist Jubilee Advance program (1959–1964), to coordinate the SBC's calendar and activities with those of other participating Baptist organizations. For example, see "Special Committees: Jubilee Advance Committee," in *Annual of the SBC* (1963): 263-66 (also see "Proceedings," Thursday night, 9 May, item 195). The Committee on Baptist Ideals (chaired by Ralph A. Herring), a subcommittee of the SBC's Jubilee Advance Committee, interpreted its own assignment as an effort "to restate in relevant terms only those historic principles of Southern Baptists which with certain emphases serve to make clear their unique position and mission" (*Baptist Ideals* [Nashville: BSSB, 1963] 3 [intro., 4]; hereafter I will cite this document as *BI [1963]*; I will also refer to this document first with page numbers, followed by the part and section numbers in parentheses). In its last report to the SBC, this committee offered the following suggestion: "A copy of the pamphlet 'Baptist Ideals' produced by a committee of 17 dedicated scholars, with Ralph A. Herring as chairman, ought to be placed in the hands of every Southern Baptist" ("Special Committees: Jubilee Advance Committee," in *Annual of the SBC* [1964]: 261). In light of the HMB's recent adopton of the *RPTSC* as a doctrinal criterion for missionary candidates, the HMB's equally recent employment of the very different *BI (1963)* introduces severe dissonance into the HMB's official doctrinal commitments. Recently, the HMB has published a book in the Korean language, in which it includes a Korean translation of *Baptist Ideals*: see Dan Moon, *The Growth and Future of the Korean Southern Baptist Churches in America* (Atlanta: HMB, 1994) 42-68. Baptists disaffected by the SBC's fundamentalist leadership rightly continue to emphasize the *BI*'s significance for the SBC (e.g., see "Appendix VII 'Baptist Ideals,' " in *The Baptist Identity: Four Fragile Freedoms*, by Walter B. Shurden [Macon GA: Smyth & Helwys, 1993] 103-15).

(1963) defends the appropriateness of this principle's operation: "for one to criticize does not necessarily mean that he is disloyal; his criticism may stem from a deep commitment to the welfare of the denomination."[30]

Without hesitation, then, I describe the aporetic impulse in this methodical polarity as faith's holy, inspired, or sacred distrust. In the studies of the *RPTSC* that follow, consequently, although a severe line of inquiry emerges, this aporetic impulse always originates from faith itself.

2. *Tharsetics of Doubt*

With Gratitude to Peter the Apostle
(John 13:36-38; 21:1-23)

Correspondingly, then, the dynamism of this dialectical method relies on a second pole, a *tharsetics* of doubt. The word "tharsetics" originates from the Greek verb θαρσέω, which means "to be of good courage," to "have confidence in," to "be confident or assured." The noun θάρσος or θράσος can signify either the "courage, boldness, confidence" to perform a particular action or "that which gives courage" or the "grounds of confidence." Thus, the Greek adjective θαρσητικός means "courageous" or "confident."[31]

Again, I have formulated the second moment in this dialectical polarity with the possessive case. Tharsetics, as a discipline, belongs to the first pole's dubitative or inquisitive impulse and its critical activity: *doubt's tharsetics*. The tharsetic discipline operates as the interaction of two dynamic phenomena: first, the ground of the courage or confidence from which the aporetic impulse of this method originates, the SBC's historic biblical perspectives or even the history of the SBC's interpretation of the biblical traditions (similar to the *fides quae creduntur* or the faith that is believed); and, second, the actual courage and confidence that emboldens, supports, and informs the dubitative impulse, the line of critical inquiry, or the aporetic dynamic in this method (similar to the *fides qua creduntur*, the faith by which it is believed). Through this tharsetics of doubt, I confidently and systematically question the *RPTSC*. Nonetheless, only by a corresponding and constant return to the ground (the SBC's historic perspectives and commitments themselves) from which the aporetic impulse originates, can genuine confidence accompany

---

[30]*BI (1963)*, 37 (5.9).

[31]Liddell and Scott, eds., *Greek-English Lexicon*, s.v. "θαρσέω" and "θάρσος." Also see Berry, *Classic Greek Dictionary*, 312.

this critical line of inquiry. Thus, the tharsetic source always elicits, encourages, and emboldens the aporetic impulse. Without a tharsetic ground, the aporetic impulse remains purely reductive.

The doubt or the aporetic impulse constantly returns to its source, remembers its origins, confidently and courageously pursuing its line of critical inquiry empowered with and by those resources. With such commitment, this doubt resists the aporias and distortions in everything proposed to faith itself, including proposals like the *RPTSC*. With the tharsetic pole of this method, then, I faithfully and systematically return to the SBC's historic biblical perspectives for resources with which to resist the distortions promoted and the manipulation exercised by the *RPTSC*. As a result, this pole of the dialectical method again resembles the other dynamic of Ricoeur's own dialectical hermeneutics: his hermeneutical trust, recollection, or restoration. Ricoeur confidently expects to receive meaning from the objects of his hermeneutical labors and, hence, discovers within those objects the resources with which to resist distortions within those objects themselves and to liberate meaning from such distortions.[32]

A tharsetics of doubt, therefore, operates with a priestly and conservative impulse. Yahweh often reminded the Hebrew people to remember their own history with God, God's labors with the people and for them, as the firm ground upon which to stand against distortions of their present and future relationships with Yahweh.

> Hear, O Israel: The Lord is our God, the Lord alone. You shall love the Lord your God with all your heart, and with all your soul, and with all your might. Keep these words that I am commanding you today in your heart. Recite them to your children and talk about them when you are at home and when you are away, when you lie down and when you rise. Bind them as a sign on your hand, fix them as an emblem on your forehead, and write them on the doorposts of your house and on your gates.
>
> When the Lord your God has brought you into the land that he swore to your ancestors, to Abraham, to Isaac, and to Jacob, to give you—a land with fine, large cities that you did not build, houses filled with all sorts of goods that you did not fill, hewn cisterns that you did not hew, vineyards and olive groves that you did not plant—and when you have eaten your fill, take care that you do not forget the Lord, who brought you out of the land of Egypt, out of the house of slavery (Deuteronomy 6:4-12 NRSV).

---

[32]Again, see the following examples: Ricoeur, *Freud and Philosophy*, 28-32; idem, *Conflict of Interpretations*, 331-32; idem, *Lectures on Ideology and Utopia*, 307.

So I led them out of the land of Egypt and brought them into the wilderness. I gave them my statutes and showed them my ordinances, by whose observance everyone shall live (Ezekiel 20:10-11 NRSV).

In this respect, a tharsetics of doubt always operates through the Christian community's remembrance of its foundations as the basis for its self-criticism. Again, the SBC has, at least until recently, consistently employed this priestly principle, as also seen for example in its *Baptist Ideals*: "The procedure in this report will be to state, first, those principles or 'ideals' which in combination give to Baptists their distinctive position; and, second, to show their relevance to our continuing task." The *BI (1963)* understands an individual's genuine criticism of her community as originating from that person's deep commitment and loyalty to the community's historic perspectives and commitments.[33]

The tharsetic ground of this method's dubitative impulse, then, represents doubt's critical, suspicious, and profane trust, confidence, or courage. The critical questions with which I will examine the *RPTSC* will always proceed on the basis of this priestly principle, this tharsetic ground, on the basis of a confidence in the SBC's broader historic perspectives and with a courage to restate those perspectives in the face of extensive reductive forces in the SBC.

With this dialectic between an aporetics of faith and a tharsetics of doubt, I utilize a method that resembles Ricoeur's theory of interpretation. David Tracy has described this approach as "retrieval through suspicion." As Tracy expresses this elsewhere, "sometimes the best road to hermeneutical retrievals of tradition is through critique and suspicion."[34] To represent my own dialectical method more accurately, however, I

---

[33]*BI (1963)*, 5, 37-38 (intro., 9; 5.9).

[34]See David Tracy, *Plurality and Ambiguity: Hermeneutics, Religion, Hope* (San Francisco: Harper & Row Publishers, 1987) 112; idem, *Dialogue with the Other: The Inter-Religious Dialogue*, vol. 1, Louvain Theological and Pastoral Monographs (Louvain: Peeters Press, 1990; Grand Rapids: William B. Eerdmans, 1991) 6. Obviously, my dialectical method also relies on Langdon Gilkey's understanding of the Christian community's dual role in public life, a dual role arising from the Christian community's nature as the union of Catholic substance and the Protestant principle: a priestly role and a prophetic role. The two roles or tasks of the Christian community work together and dialectically. Without fulfilling both roles, in relation both to itself and to the larger public world of its context, the Christian community forfeits its authentic character (see, e.g., Langdon Gilkey, *Through the Tempest: Theological Voyages in a Pluralistic Culture*, ed. Jeff B. Pool [Minneapolis: Fortress Press, 1991] 135-39, 167-78).

must describe it as both *retrieval through suspicion* and *suspicion through retrieval.* With the latter formulation, I mean the following: I suspect the presence of distortion and manipulation in the *RPTSC* primarily because I have already appropriated or retrieved much of the SBC's broader historic perspectives, because I began my study with the SBC's historic perspectives as presuppositions. Thus, this method operates as the dynamic tension between a hermeneutic of trust and a hermeneutic of suspicion, between priestly and prophetic principles, between a tharsetics of doubt and an aporetics of faith.[35] On that basis, then, I can reappropriate the SBC's broader perspectives through, as well as beyond, my exposure of and resistance against the *RPTSC*'s distorted and manipulative perspective.

B. Path of Inquiry

My use of the previous method to study the *RPTSC* both suggests and guides this book's specific path of inquiry and, therefore, supplies its larger structure as well. In this study, I have attempted to disclose, on the one hand, the genuine substance of the Presidential Theological Study Committee's activity in its formulation and propagation of the *RPTSC* (the *what*) and, on the other hand, the actual rationale for that activity and accomplishment (the *why*). These two efforts have generated five elemental questions about this document. (1) What situation provoked the production of the *RPTSC*? (2) What end has motivated the writing and publication of this document? (3) Who authorized and produced this document? (4) What strategies operate within the *RPTSC* to attain the document's goal? (5) What actual results have this document's situation, purpose, authors, and strategies produced? By asking these questions, during careful analysis of the *RPTSC*, I have discerned a network of alarming problems in this document.[36] By investigating these problems,

---

[35]According even to R. Albert Mohler, Jr., "seminaries are supported financially by the churches, charged by the churches to train their ministers, and expected to fulfill *a ministry* to the churches that is *both prophetic and priestly*" (Mohler, "Has Theology a Future in the Southern Baptist Convention? Toward a Renewed Theological Framework," in *Beyond the Impasse? Scripture, Interpretation, and Theology in Baptist Life*, ed. Robison B. James and David S. Dockery [Nashville: Broadman, 1992] 104; emphasis mine). Nevertheless, my own interpretation of that dual theological task differs dramatically from Mohler's fundamentalist perspective. Also see Nancy Ammerman's excellent interpretation of the dialectic between priestly and prophetic ministries (Ammerman, "Priests and Prophets," in *Proclaiming the Baptist Vision: The Priesthood of All Believers*, ed. Walter B. Shurden [Macon GA: Smyth & Helwys, 1993] 55-62).

[36]The five stages in this procedure follow the pattern identified by Kenneth Burke in

I aim both *to unmask or expose dangers* for the distinctive emphases in Baptist life promoted by the *RPTSC*'s camouflaged credalism and *to suggest legitimate Baptist lines of resistance* to those threats.[37]

The following studies fulfill this dual aim in reference to several major problematic features of the *RPTSC*, features corresponding respectively as answers to the five previous questions: (1) an implicit network of questionable assumptions upon which the committee apparently has formulated this document; (2) a masked purpose for this document's formulation and use; (3) the dangerously noncongregational source of this document's authorization and production; (4) a deceptive rhetoric operative in this document; and (5) several major, specific, reductive, and distorted doctrinal perspectives. In part one of this book, entitled "Manipulative Methods," I examine in four chapters my answers to the first four questions. In part two of this book, entitled "Distorted Doctrines," I also examine in four chapters my answer to the fifth question.

---

his investigations into the attribution of motivation (Burke, *A Grammar of Motives* [Berkeley: University of California Press, 1945] xv-xxiii). Thus, although some overlap occurs among the eight chapters in this book, those chapters correspond generally to the categories for attributing motives, as identified by Burke, in the following ways: Burke's notion of *scene* corresponds to my study of the assumptive network in the *RPTSC*'s background argument (chap. 1); Burke's concept of *purpose* corresponds to my study of the *RPTSC*'s masked intentions (chap. 2); Burke's understanding of *agent* corresponds to my study of false authority in the *RPTSC* (chap. 3); Burke's concept of *agency* also corresponds to my own study of the deceptive rhetoric employed in the *RPTSC* (chap. 4); and, finally, Burke's notion of *act* corresponds to my study of the Presidential Theological Study Committee's formulations of doctrinal norms in the *RPTSC* (chaps. 5-8). See a similar study, utilizing this Burkean pentad, of the homiletical rhetoric employed by three television preachers: James Vincent Dupree, "A Burkean Analysis of the Messages of Three Television Preachers: Jerry Falwell, Robert Schuller, and Jimmy Swaggert" (Ph.D. diss., Pennsylvania State University, 1983).

[37]Howard Wayne Smith, then managing editor of the Baptist periodical, *The Chronicle*, near the end of World War II published similar suspicions about the use of a confession in the Northern Baptist Convention, as a "prerequisite to membership in the 'Conservative Baptist Foreign Mission Society.' " According to Smith, because "Baptists have never been friendly to creeds, . . . this formal statement both . . . is camouflaged as a 'Confession of Faith' or a 'Statement of Doctrine,' " which "is meant to cloak the real character of the document," and "is, when shorn of all fine words, nothing but a creed used as a test of orthodoxy" (Smith, "Baptists and Creeds," *The Chronicle* 7 [April 1944]: 49). Other Baptists in the SBC have similarly encouraged resistance to all forms of credalism. For example, G. Thomas Halbrooks encourages Baptists in the SBC to "resist any effort in church or denomination to lead them into submission to or dependence upon any elected or self-proclaimed leaders or any doctrinal formulations or statements" (Halbrooks, "Trust Is Foundational to the Baptist Spirit," in *Defining Baptist Convictions: Guidelines for the Twenty-First Century*, ed. Charles W. Deweese [Franklin TN: Providence House Publishers, 1996] 101).

In all eight chapters, both the aporetics of faith and the tharsetics of doubt will operate with varying degrees of intensity. Both exposure of and resistance to the *RPTSC*'s distortions and manipulation will operate in every chapter.

Part One

Manipulative Methods

The LORD sets the prisoners free.
(Psalm 146:7c NASB)

Introduction to Part One

To Control Baptist Christians

In part one, I identify and examine methodological issues, questions, and problems related primarily to the *RPTSC*'s own "Part I." Nonetheless, I will also often refer to examples from the other portions of the document, in order to strengthen various claims about these methodological concerns.

As noted previously, with this part of the study, I will ask and answer four basic questions about the *RPTSC*. First, what situation provoked the production of the *RPTSC*? Second, what end has motivated the writing and publication of this document? Third, who authorized and produced this document? Finally, fourth, what strategies operate within the *RPTSC* to accomplish the document's goal? With these questions, I seek to discover the rationale of and for the *RPTSC*, its *why*.

I have discovered a network of disturbing answers to these questions. In chapter 1, I answer the first question: the *RPTSC* implies a network of questionable assumptions on the basis of which the committee formulated the *RPTSC*, as the situation that provoked the *RPTSC*'s production. Chapter 2 contains my answer to the second question: indicators in the *RPTSC* suggest that those who produced this document intend to use it as a tool with which to control thought and behavior both within the SBC and in churches that participate in the SBC. Chapter 3 addresses the third question: building on the previous evidence, the *RPTSC* discloses the document's noncongregational origin, its source in an elite group of leaders within the SBC. With chapter 4, I answer the fourth question: this analysis uncovers the operation of a deceptive rhetoric as fundamental to the strategies used by the committee to realize the *RPTSC*'s aims.

When the previous very general answers emerge together, the *RPTSC*'s dangerous rationale discloses itself: broadly construed, on the basis of dubious assumptions, a self-appointed and self-perpetuating group of elite leaders in the SBC has produced prescriptive doctrinal formulations and has employed manipulative rhetorical strategies with which to enforce adherence to those doctrinal norms or to control Baptist Christians in the SBC and, thus, the SBC itself. In this light, I have designated part one as "Manipulative Methods."

Chapter 1

Dubious Network of Veiled Programmatic Assumptions

And as Pharaoh drew near, the sons of Israel looked, and behold, the Egyptians were marching after them, and they became very frightened; so the sons of Israel cried out to the Lord. Then they said to Moses, "Is it because there were no graves in Egypt that you have taken us away to die in the wilderness? Why have you dealt with us in this way, bringing us out of Egypt? Is this not the word that we spoke to you in Egypt, saying, 'Leave us alone that we may serve the Egyptians'? For it would have been better for us to serve the Egyptians than to die in the wilderness." (Exodus 14:10-12 NASB)

. . . clouds without water, carried along by winds. . . . (Jude 12 NASB)

Introduction

My effort to answer one basic question guides this first chapter's line of inquiry: what situation provoked the production of the *RPTSC*? My analysis of the *RPTSC* has yielded the following answer to that question: the *RPTSC* implies a network of questionable assumptions on the basis of which the committee formulated the *RPTSC*, as the situation that provoked the *RPTSC*'s production. Following from the previous question, then, what assumptions does the *RPTSC* imply on the basis of which it promotes its formulations? Although the formulations contained in the *RPTSC* disclose numerous assumptions, in consideration of this first problematic feature, I will examine only those major questionable assumptions that constitute this document's programmatic foundations. This document's authors have predicated their entire document on a network of questionable assumptions.

Even with solid evidence from the document itself, however, identifying *implicit* assumptions and presuppositions will be difficult. For that reason, in every case, I have traced from specific statements in this document to assumptions either suggested or acknowledged by those statements themselves. Numerous assumptions remain for examination. Although I will not examine all of them, later in this study other assumptions will emerge as I scrutinize other problematic or questionable features in the *RPTSC*.

I. First Assumption. On Assailment of Baptist Doctrine

The *RPTSC* openly assumes the existence of "the pressing need for a *positive* biblical witness on basic Christian beliefs." Few, if any, Baptists would disagree with this as a perennial Christian assumption in a sinful and wounded world. This document assumes that this "pressing need," in the form of a particular challenge, presently confronts "that people of God called Southern Baptists." The *RPTSC* initially describes this challenge as "the decision *either* to reaffirm 'the faith which was once delivered unto the saints' (Jude 3 [KJV]) *or* to lapse into theological unbelief." Later, this report refers to the problem as "unique and pressing challenges to faithfulness which demand attention and test the integrity of our conviction."[1] Later still, in its doctrinal formulations, the *RPTSC* briefly names some of those "challenges to faithfulness." I will consider the *RPTSC*'s identification, treatment, and assessment of those issues in later chapters of this study.

Beneath this assumption, however, rests another and more dubious implication. The SBC requires this "positive biblical witness on basic Christian beliefs," because *the SBC previously has attested or presently attests negatively or deficiently to basic Christian doctrines*. Both prior to and after listing five basic Christian doctrines (initially referring to them as "major doctrinal concerns," "several issues of contemporary urgency," and "emphases"), the *RPTSC* more explicitly announces this assumption in the committee's declaration for itself: "This report addresses several issues of contemporary urgency in a spirit of pastoral concern and a commitment to the unity of our Baptist fellowship as well as the integrity of our doctrinal confession"; and "we reaffirm our commitment to these great theological tenets since they are assailed, in various ways, by subtle compromise, blatant concession, and malign negligence."[2] By its vagueness, the *RPTSC*'s first assumption elicits at least two critical questions.

A. Which Persons or Categories of Persons Assail Baptist Doctrines?

Does the document refer to non-Christians? The *RPTSC* does declare the necessity for the SBC to "bear a faithful gospel witness to *a culture*

---

[1]*RPTSC*, 113 (1.1, 5); emphasis mine.
[2]*RPTSC*, 112, 113 (intro.; 1.5); emphasis mine.

in decline" and to "be the salt and light in *a society which has lost its moral compass."*[3]

Still, while the committee did also assume the decline of culture (Western?) or society's (the United States's?) loss of moral compass, the committee probably does not refer to persons from the broader public, since non-Christians cannot *compromise* doctrines of a faith to which they do not adhere, although they can resist or attack such doctrines. Less obviously, perhaps, the *RPTSC* probably does not refer to other Christian denominations or groups, since any doctrinal compromises, concessions, and negligence of such groups officially have realized and presently realize neither governing nor widespread doctrinal influences on the SBC. Among possible assailants, whom does this leave, as the principal culprits, subtly to compromise, blatantly to concede, and malignantly to neglect basic Christian beliefs?

The committee, very simply, has implicated Baptists in the SBC themselves as the assailants of the very doctrines that they cherish.[4] In its

---

[3]*RPTSC*, 113 (1.2); emphasis mine.

[4]I intentionally use such phrases as "Baptists in the SBC" and "Baptists of the SBC," rather than the phrases used by the *RPTSC*, such as "Southern Baptists" or "the people of God called Southern Baptists" (e.g., *RPTSC*, 112, 115 [intro.; 2.1.7]), insofar as those latter phrases indicate more than a geographical designation in the United States. George W. McDaniel, president of the SBC for three years (1924–1926), published a significant historical precedent for both my refusal of the *RPTSC* at this point and my alternative proposals, as well as especially for the theological conviction that sustains these actions. McDaniel embraced all Baptist accomplishments, including those prior to, external to, and contemporary with the SBC and its accomplishments. Furthermore, he perceived the SBC as a geographic designation, not as an ideological and political label for identification. On this basis, he speaks about "the people called Baptists" (McDaniel, *The People Called Baptists* [Nashville: BSSB, 1919] 31-32). With this emphasis, I intend to accentuate a very important historic Baptist principle, a principle that the framers of the *RPTSC* (as well as the present leaders of the SBC who motivate them) have apparently forgotten or have chosen to ignore. "Missionary and other religious associations and conventions are not ecclesiastical bodies. They are simply voluntary bodies for coöperative purposes. Churches are not subject to the authority of these or any other organizations" (*Fraternal Address of Southern Baptists* [SBC, n.d.] 9; hereafter cited as *FASB [1920]*). Although this address includes in its title the phrase "Southern Baptists," given the theology of this confession of faith, the committee of the SBC that produced the document clearly used the phrase in a geographical sense. While most often this confession of faith refers simply to "Baptists," even the greeting's introductory remarks expressly indicate the distinction that I have made: "The Southern Baptist Convention, composed of 4200 messengers, in annual session, May, 1919, in Atlanta, Ga., U.S.A., and representing 3,000,000 Baptists in the Southern States of America . . . " (*FASB [1920]*, 4).

On this point, I share the sentiments of L. R. Scarborough, former president of SWBTS: "There is no such thing as 'The Baptist Church' meaning an ecclesiastical unit own words, then, the *RPTSC explicitly assumes* that someone or some group assails these "theological tenets," yet, *less openly and implicitly assumes* that Baptists of the SBC have assailed the very doctrines to which they have attested with both the *BFM (1963)* and their own interpretations of that confessional statement.[5] This first and very presumptuous programmatic assumption, then, invites a second question.

---

composed of a group of Baptist Churches. . . . I never like to hear a Baptist speak of 'The Church,' unless he means some local Baptist Church" (Scarborough, "The Independence and Inter-Dependence of Baptist Churches," in the L. R. Scarborough Collection, SWBTS, Roberts Library Archives, Fort Worth TX, file 390:2). Further, "there is no such thing as the 'Southern Baptist Church,' 'Northern Baptist Church,' the 'Baptist Church of America,' etc. There are tens of thousands of Baptist churches in America. Each local Baptist assembly is a seperate [*sic*], complete church unit. No two of them can be federalized, and no inter-ecclesiastical connection can be established between them" (idem, "Baptist Churches and Other Ecclesiastical Bodies," in the L. R. Scarborough Collection, file 386:1-2). The SBC declared similarly for itself, when the Convention declined to accept an invitation to join the World Council of Churches (WCC) in 1940. "Our Convention has no ecclesiological authority. It is in no sense the Southern Baptist Church. The thousands of churches to which our Convention looks for support of its missionary, benevolent and educational program, cherish their independence and would disapprove of any attempted exercise of ecclesiastical authority over them" ("Reply to World Council of Churches," in *Annual of the SBC* [1940]: 99; hereafter I will refer to this document as *RWCC [1940]*). Both George W. Truett (chairperson) and L. R. Scarborough participated on the committee that composed the SBC's reply to the WCC.

[5]In another essay, Mohler more openly indicates his view: the necessity for both "SBC conservatives" and "moderates" to recognize that a "theological crisis" among Baptists, initiated by Baptists, has generated the conflict within the SBC. "SBC conservatives, who have justified their political takeover of the denomination on the basis of theological compromise among denominational officials and seminary faculties, must broaden and deepen their concern to reflect a more comprehensive theological crisis. Moderates, who have largely resisted the very notion of a theological crisis, must come to see the real gravity of the current hour, both in terms of specific issues of concern and, more importantly, the generalized atheological ethos prevalent within the Convention" (Mohler, "Has Theology a Future in the Southern Baptist Convention?" in *Beyond the Impasse?* ed. James and Dockery, 98-99). Given the origin of the *RPTSC* in such circumstances and its composition by authors with such agendas and credendas, Edward B. Pollard's comments about credal statements contain insights appropriate to the SBC's present situation. "If the creed be born in *polemics* it is *lopsided*; dealing fully with the disputed, and leaving the undisputed, however vital, untouched. Should it, perchance, have its birth, as some creeds have, in an effort *to reconcile* parties, that they may stand upon a common platform, the result is *compromise*, and hence it cannot be really representative of any" (Pollard, "What Shall We Think of Creeds?" 43; emphasis mine).

B. To What Extent Does This Assumption
Indict the Baptist Heritage of the SBC?

Just how deeply into the tree of Baptist history and heritage does the *RPTSC* assume that the rottenness of "subtle compromise, blatant concession, and malign negligence" extends? Apparently, given the *RPTSC*'s various affirmations of the *BFM (1963)*, key distinctive Baptist perspectives, and comments by several Baptist theologians, this assumption does not implicate the entire Baptist heritage.

If this alleged assailment of basic Baptist doctrines, according to the *RPTSC*, does not appear among Baptists before the formation of the SBC in 1845, then, does the *RPTSC* assume that doctrinal compromises, concessions, and negligence have characterized the SBC since the Convention's birth? Again, can the committee possibly assume this for the entire history of the SBC? More than likely, the *RPTSC* refers to Baptists in the SBC's most recent internal conflicts, Baptists who have *purportedly* compromised or neglected Baptist doctrines. Such a reference certainly could imply *either* persons from the aggressive right wing in the SBC *or* persons from the so-called moderate center, although the document cites absolutely no evidence for such implications. Given the content in the remainder of the *RPTSC*, however, this document apparently refers only to persons from the second category. If this is the case, why did the *RPTSC* not more honestly identify the specific assailants to whom this document refers?

On the basis of these very simple questions, this first assumption invites refusal as one component of the *purportedly descriptive basis* upon which the *RPTSC* has submitted its formulations to the SBC. Without identifying the alleged assailants of Baptist doctrine and without citing examples to sustain such indictments, those who formulated this document have neglected relevant evidence for this first assumption upon which they have predicated the need for this document. This implicit logical fallacy seems to function in the *RPTSC* as a device with which to ignore, to minimize, or even to suppress obvious counterexamples to this first assumption.[6] Furthermore, this first programmatic assumption

---

[6]Without examples to support this assumption, the *RPTSC* commits at least two and perhaps three statistical fallacies: (1) the fallacy of insufficient sample; (2) the fallacy of unrepresentative statistics; and (3) the fallacy of false precision. This criticism, of course, extends to all components in the *RPTSC*'s assumptive network or background arguments.

misrepresents Baptist history through an intentional vagueness. Did the committee intentionally inscribe such vagueness into the *RPTSC* in order to alarm Baptists about alleged dangers? This false and veiled assumption (whether or not its framers, with its vagueness, *intentionally* misrepresented Baptist history to alarm Baptists in the SBC) deserves nothing less than complete resistance and rejection by Baptists in the SBC who remain committed to truth and honesty.

II. Second Assumption. On Failed Consensus in the SBC

A second programmatic assumption extends the previous assumption. The *RPTSC* asserts that "we seek to move beyond the denominational conflict of recent years toward a new consensus rooted in theological substance and doctrinal fidelity."[7] Certainly, the reference to moving *beyond denominational conflict* both accurately describes the central feature of the SBC's recent history and apparently states a worthy aim. Nonetheless, according to the document, the committee also seeks to move "toward a *new* consensus *rooted in theological substance and doctrinal fidelity*." Most assuredly, Baptists of the SBC require "a new consensus" among themselves. The committee's formulation, however, seems to imply at least one of two programmatic assumptions, each having other implications. These two broad possibilities raise several questions.

On the one hand, the statement from the *RPTSC* may assume that, prior to the SBC's most recent internal conflicts, Baptists in the SBC had *not rooted* their consensus "in theological substance and doctrinal fidelity." This assumption may even imply that, prior to the recent conflict, Baptists in the SBC *lacked* "theological substance" and *violated* "doctrinal fidelity" in the very consensus through which they actually and successfully pursued evangelism and missions. With this assumption, the *RPTSC* may further imply that previous consensus in the SBC failed precisely because that consensus possessed no rootage in an *adequate* theological substance and doctrinal fidelity—if it possessed any theological rootage or had maintained any doctrinal fidelity at all.

On the other hand, however, perhaps behind the *RPTSC*'s statement lies the assumption that, prior to the most recent struggles in the SBC, Baptists in the SBC *had rooted* their consensus in a dense theological soil that has subsequently eroded. This assumption first implies an original

---

[7]*RPTSC*, 113 (1.2).

theological uniformity or conformity among Baptists that led to the SBC's formation and growth. As a second implication, then, various forms of infidelity (or increasing diversity within the SBC) have eroded this common theological ground among Baptists in the SBC. In light of the SBC's history, however, the two previous, possible assumptions and their implications invite several serious questions.

A. Did an Original Theological Uniformity Produce the SBC?

I begin with a question concerning the second broad possibility. Did a consensus in theological perspectives among Baptists produce the SBC? The *RPTSC* builds its assertions on the unstated myth of *theological uniformity and conformity in the SBC*. In his own writings, Timothy George, cochairperson of the Presidential Theological Study Committee (PTSC), clearly and openly states this myth about the SBC's history: "Despite diversity within and adversity without, by mid-nineteenth century Baptists in America had developed a remarkable unity of purpose and vision, a theological consensus which even cut across the seismic fault line produced by slavery and the Civil War." A second myth, then, accompanies this first myth. George openly declares this aspect of the assumption as well: for a variety of reasons, some internal and some external to the SBC, the solid and fertile ground of *this theological consensus among Baptists in the SBC eroded.*[8]

To the contrary, on this point, Baptist historians commonly agree: the issues of slavery and missions divided Baptists in the northern United States from Baptists in the southern United States, thereby giving birth to the SBC. As a slight qualification of this claim and as I have noted previously, however, while the issue of slavery certainly occasioned the SBC's birth, the violation of the Triennial Convention's polity through the imposition of an antislavery policy on missionary candidates, a move that the Baptists of the South interpreted as the enforcement of a creed, actually caused the division between the northern and southern Baptists. From the beginning, *theological homogeneity did not establish the basis for consensus among Baptists in the SBC.* Furthermore, almost immedi-

---

[8]Timothy George, "Southern Baptist Theology: Whence and Whither?" *Founders Journal* 19/20 (Winter/Spring 1995): 24-26. Similarly, see the thematic statement for this same issue of the intentionally Calvinistic *Founders Journal*: Thomas Ascol, "Southern Baptists at the Crossroads: Returning to the Old Paths," *Founders Journal* 19/20 (Winter/Spring 1995): 1-5.

ately, and throughout the Convention's history, sharp theological differences produced numerous conflicts in the SBC.[9]

B. Was Previous Doctrinal Consensus in the SBC Inadequate or Simply Absent?

Baptists in the SBC, prior to the conflict of the two previous decades, most assuredly shared a consensus deeply rooted in faithfulness to God through Christ. Baptists of the SBC faithfully attested to the shared experience of their consensus with the theologically substantial doctrinal statements formulated in the *BFM (1963)*. Certainly, different interpretations of that document have appeared since both that document's original adoption in 1925 and its subsequent revision in 1963. Such differences do not necessarily indicate either an absence of theological substance or a betrayal of Baptist doctrines, even if they do indicate a lack of *theological* consensus. To the contrary, those differences indicate the wealth in diversity. Rather than paucity of theological substance and infidelity to Baptist beliefs, differing interpretations of (and even disagreements with) the *BFM (1963)* suggest the denomination's health and vitality, its intense desire to understand its experience with God through Jesus Christ.

C. Did Doctrinal Inadequacy Cause the Failure of Previous Consensus in the SBC?

Did the SBC's previous consensus fail, as the *RPTSC* further implies, due to either absent or inadequate doctrinal commitment and depth? Since

---

[9]For example, at its inception, the SBC acknowledged that the division between Baptists in the Northern U.S. and those in the Southern U.S. originated from conflict about the slavery issue as related to missions, even though the issue of credalism lurked within this conflict as foundational (*SBCBUS [1845]*, 17-18). Also see William Wright Barnes, *The Southern Baptist Convention: 1845–1953* (Nashville: Broadman, 1954) 12-42; Robert A. Baker, *The Southern Baptist Convention and Its People, 1607–1972* (Nashville: Broadman, 1974) 148-77; Jesse C. Fletcher, *The Southern Baptist Convention: A Sesquicentennial History* (Nashville: Broadman & Holman, 1994) 9-41. A comment by H. Leon McBeth accentuates my point, by restating the SBC's founding purpose. "In passing, let me reaffirm that the SBC was formed to elicit, combine, and direct efforts to propagate the gospel. We have been at our best when we have done that. The Convention was *not formed to monitor doctrine, control theological issues, or police the faith and morals of Southern Baptists.* When the Convention has gone beyond its constitutional purpose, it has created more problems than it has solved" (McBeth, "Cooperation and Crisis as Shapers of Southern Baptist Identity," *Baptist History and Heritage* 30 [July 1995]: 38; emphasis mine).

the PTSC may have submitted the *RPTSC* as its own effort to supply the grounds for "an explicit doctrinal standard" with which to check lapses "into theological unbelief," or to eliminate "doctrinal minimalism and theological revision,"[10] the committee may also have assumed that such offenses led to the collapse of consensus within the SBC, to the "denominational conflict of recent years."[11]

If I have accurately reconstructed this second programmatic assumption, then, the PTSC has committed another logical fallacy in its background argument: the fallacy of *non causa pro causa*, mistakenly identifying a false cause as the real cause of a given effect. Additionally, even if doctrinal inadequacy played a role in the failure of consensus among Baptists in the SBC, that factor alone did not cause such massive problems. To suggest otherwise, as the *RPTSC* appears to do, causally oversimplifies complex sociopolitical and theological dynamics. If the previous consensus really failed, however, evidence from numerous documents in the SBC's history indicates clearly that the absence of theological substance and infidelity to doctrines among Baptists did not play a significant role as that failure's cause. Rather, that consensus began to fail due to Baptist fears and refusals of the rich diversity among Baptists in the SBC. The previous consensus collapsed, finally, due to the desire of some Baptists to eliminate diversity and to legislate uniformity in every way. Without an extensive study, here even my own claim stands as a hypothesis awaiting inductive confirmation. The remainder of this study, however, at least partially corroborates my claim. Hence, although my counterclaim awaits empirical support, the *RPTSC* does not in any way substantiate its implicit assumption about the doctrinal source for the collapse of consensus in the SBC.

---

[10]*RPTSC*, 113, 114 (1.1, 8, 10).

[11]In Timothy George's efforts elsewhere to emphasize the Reformation (especially Calvinistic) theological heritage of Baptist religious identity, George lists several factors contributing to the obscuration of "the evangelical Calvinism" that "has shaped Baptist identity," among which doctrinal and theological problems figure foundationally for George: "the routinization of revivalism, the growth of pragmatism as a denominational strategy, an attenuated *doctrine* of the Holy Spirit, and a *general theological laxity* which has resulted in *doctrinal apathy*" (Timothy George, "The Reformation Roots of the Baptist Tradition," *Review and Expositor* 86 [1989]: 16; emphasis mine).

D. Can Baptists Restore and Maintain Consensus
in the SBC with Doctrinal Precision?

Perhaps this second major assumption also implies that the SBC both can restore denominational consensus and can avoid denominational conflict, if the SBC *mandates* an adequate rootedness in proper theological substance and *enforces* conformity to precisely defined doctrinal formulas. Can Baptists restore and maintain denominational consensus by formulating precise doctrinal guidelines and requirements for all Baptists in the SBC? In an article published in 1992, R. Albert Mohler, Jr., a member of the PTSC, hypothesized similarly about the SBC: the "common vision of ministry and purpose," upon which the SBC bases its "convictional cooperation," originates in "theological consensus."[12]

To the contrary, the formulation and disciplinary application of more narrow doctrinal statements will not reestablish the consensus for which this document yearns, despite the committee's prayer that its doctrinal statement "will lead to healing and reconciliation throughout the Southern Baptist Convention and, God willing, to a renewed commitment to our founding purpose of 'eliciting, combining, and directing the energies of the whole denomination in one sacred effort, for the propagation of the gospel,' " even though the *RPTSC* describes "sound doctrine" as one of the "indispensable elements of true revival and genuine reconciliation among any body of Christian believers."[13] Some of the most influential Baptist leaders and theologians, such as Francis Wayland and Edwin C. Dargan, have consistently perceived the failure of doctrinal statements to secure Christian unity.[14]

---

[12]Mohler, "Has Theology a Future in the Southern Baptist Convention?" 109.

[13]*RPTSC*, 113, 114 (1.2, 10).

[14]Wayland, Baptist minister and president of Brown University, identified two major reasons why creeds and confessions neither create nor preserve unity: (1) "where a creed is most strictly imposed, and even established by law, *there* is the divergence in sentiment from it the most remarkable"; and (2) "this very absence of any established creed is in itself the cause of our unity," because (since the Bible has been designed "for every individual man, and intended to be understood by every man") "the greatest amount of unity attainable among men of diversified character, will be produced by allowing every one to look at it [the Bible] and study it for himself" (Francis Wayland, *Notes on the Principles and Practices of Baptist Churches* [New York: Sheldon, Blakeman, and Co., 1857] 15). Arising from his opposition to Wayland's perspective on creeds, Mohler declares, either ignorantly or as an intentional misrepresentation, that "Wayland was not a Baptist figure who was greatly marked by definite theological convictions" (Mohler, "To Train

Insofar as doctrine articulates a Christian community's experience with God through Christ, the *renewal of an experiential consensus* necessarily precedes any common doctrinal confession. Behind my claim operates a more substantial assumption, one that the history of the SBC alone corroborates: consensus in the SBC involved a *discovery* of doctrinal similarities among its constituents, but the SBC *never achieved* consensus in its endeavors on the basis of doctrinal precision or explicit doctrinal standards.[15] To suggest otherwise, as the *RPTSC* does, dishonestly engenders and flagrantly appeals to unrealistic hopes in Baptist hearts, hopes based on the use of precise doctrinal statements to which Baptists must conform—false hopes, since such devices more completely dissolve the genuine distinctive perspectives for consensus among Baptists in the SBC. To renew an experiential consensus requires at least three preliminary steps for Baptists in the SBC: first, rediscover the principle of unity in diversity; second, overcome fears of and cease

---

the Minister Whom God Has Called: James Petigru Boyce and Southern Baptist Theological Education," *Founders Journal* 19/20 [Winter/Spring 1995]: 39). Dargan, former professor at SBTS and president of the SBC for three consecutive years (1911–1913), later advocating a similar perspective, clearly perceived the mistake in such aims for Baptists as those expressed by the *RPTSC*. "Unity of doctrine can never be forced upon Baptists by any external ecclesiastical authority—that would be the idlest of idle dreams. It is to be a unity of the spirit, of freedom, or none at all" (Dargan, *Ecclesiology: A Study of the Churches*, 2nd ed. [Louisville KY: Charles T. Dearing, 1905] 222).

[15]In one sense, the SBC only *discovered* a global Baptist doctrinal consensus, rather than attempting to *produce* such a consensus, through efforts to renew its international Baptist relationships following the First World War. Toward this end, in 1919, by adopting a resolution submitted by J. F. Love, corresponding secretary of the SBC's Foreign Mission Board, the SBC authorized and selected a committee to "prepare" and "promulgate" a message entitled "Fraternal Greetings to Baptists of the World." The committee, which composed this address following the adjournment of the SBC's annual meeting in 1919, included E. Y. Mullins (chairperson), L. R. Scarborough, J. B. Gambrell, Z. T. Cody, and William Ellyson (*Annual of the SBC* [1919]: 75, 83-84, 106). The committee later published this address in Baptist state newspapers as well: e.g., "Fraternal Address of Southern Baptists," *Baptist Standard* 32 (26 February 1920): 5, 20, 24; "Fraternal Address of Southern Baptists," *Baptist Courier* 51 (25 March 1920): 1-2. By the time of the SBC's annual meeting in May 1920, the SBC's FMB had distributed 54,800 copies of this confession of faith (J. F. Love, "Appendix A: Seventy-Fifth Annual Report of the Foreign Mission Board," in *Annual of the SBC* [1920]: 196). As one further support for the validity of my evaluation, the *FASB (1920)* received a generally positive global response from Baptists (e.g., "Response of the Baptist Union of Ireland to the Fraternal Address of Southern Baptists," *Religious Herald* [15 July 1920]: 11).

rejecting the actual and rich diversity once gathered under the SBC's large umbrella; and, third, lovingly embrace that diversity.[16]

---

[16]As a related aside, according to J. F. Love, although the FMB produced and unanimously adopted a confession of faith, entitled "A Statement of Belief," during its previous annual meeting (in June 1919), its own "much briefer" statement "will be found *to be in accord with the Fraternal Address. . . .*" Furthermore, the FMB had produced and adopted its own confessional statement "with the purpose of promoting unity on the mission fields" (Love, "Seventy-Fifth Annual Report of the Foreign Mission Board," in *Annual of the SBC* [1920]: 196, 199; emphasis mine). Jesse C. Fletcher mistakenly asserts that the FMB's confessional statement claims "to be an expanded version of the E. Y. Mullins's Committee's Fraternal Address produced in response to the J. F. Love motion in 1919. . . . " Although not a serious mistake, this error then led Fletcher to evaluate as ambiguous the relationship between these two important documents, thus misinterpreting motivations. According to Fletcher, "the claim to have been inspired by Mullins's Fraternal Address was patently false since a letter by Mullins to Love in the fall of 1919 referred to a copy of the Foreign Board's [*sic*] statement and indicated that the Fraternal Address had not yet been prepared." Fletcher cites this letter as follows: "E. Y. Mullins to J. P. [*sic*] Love, June 18, 1919, Mullins Collection, #753" (Fletcher, *Southern Baptist Convention*, 140-41, 415n.81). Actually, in the letter to which Fletcher refers, J. F. Love had written to E. Y. Mullins on June 16, rather than on June 18, as Fletcher records: see J. F. Love to E. Y. Mullins (16 June 1919), in the E. Y. Mullins Collection, SBTS, James P. Boyce Library, Special Collections, Louisville KY, file 753. As I have noted earlier in this discussion, in the FMB's report from 1920, Love only described the FMB's statement as "in accord with," but neither as "inspired by" nor as "an expanded version of," the *FASB (1920)*. Thus, the FMB's report from May 1920 remains consistent with the situation reflected in the letter from Love to Mullins in June of 1919.

Love had written his letter to Mullins as a request for a copy of "the Seminary's Articles of Faith," SBTS's "Abstract of Principles" ("Abstract of Principles," from "Recommendation No. 3: Charter of the Southern Baptist Theological Seminary," in *Annual of the SBC* [1954]: 38-39; hereafter cited as *AP [1858]*). "A few days" previously, Love had requested the same from SBTS, so as "to get those articles before our Board met," yet without response from SBTS. Love posed an interesting question to Mullins in this letter: "Will you also kindly inform me whether members of your Faculty sign the Articles of Faith when their services are contracted for?" Love, then, both expressed good wishes to Mullins in his work on the *FASB (1920)* (obviously not yet completed, since the FMB later distributed the document; and, hence, Love would have had knowledge of it already had Mullins's committee already finished the *FASB*) and enclosed with his letter to Mullins a copy of "A Statement of Belief," "which was unanimously adopted by the Foreign Mission Board" (apparently just prior to the writing of this particular letter). In his letter, Love refers to the reason for his request as "a matter which concerns one of our schools," in the consideration of which SBTS's *AP (1858)* would serve "as a guide" to the FMB (J. F. Love to E. Y. Mullins [16 June 1919]). According to the ninth fundamental law of SBTS's charter, "all persons accepting Professorships in this Seminary, shall be considered, by such acceptance, as engaging to teach in accordance with, and not contrary to, the Abstract of Principles hereinafter laid down, a departure from which principles, on his part, shall be considered ground for his resignation or removal by the Trustees" ("Recommendation No. 3: Charter of the Southern Baptist Theological Seminary," in *Annual of the SBC* [1954]: 37).

Upon recommendation by the SBC in 1962, Herschel Hobbs, then president of the SBC, served as chairperson of a committee composed of those persons then "serving as presidents of the various state conventions," "to present to the Convention" in the following year a statement similar to the *BFM (1925)*, both to serve "as information to the churches" and possibly to function "as guidelines to the various agencies of the Southern Baptist Convention."[17] In his presidential address during the Southern Baptist Convention in 1962, Hobbs declared that, before Baptists of the SBC can attest effectively to the gospel and thereby represent a people of hope within the crises of the twentieth century, "they must first resolve any problems within their own theological position."[18] Among his major proposals, on the basis of which to resolve such problems, Hobbs suggested a step still remarkably relevant as a response to the majority of voices that formulated the *RPTSC*: "Southern Baptists must recognize and practice the principle of unity in diversity."[19]

Additionally, the FMB, to aid in the realization of its broader purpose for "A Statement of Belief," used the document to fulfill two other goals: (1) "to facilitate the examination of the frequently large numbers of applicants in the midst of crowded Board sessions"; and (2) "to satisfy the Board that it is not sending to the field those who will inject discord into their stations, or promulgate on the field doctrines which are not acceptable to the churches at home which support the work." Despite its concern for acceptable doctrines among its appointees to mission fields, in two important ways, the FMB tried to qualify the credal tendency suggested by its own formulation of a doctrinal statement. First, in its report from 1920, the FMB positioned its doctrinal standard within its call for "A Baptist World Program," in which the FMB enthusiastically confessed its desire for "a universal Baptist alliance," as the vehicle for the SBC's missionary enterprises. Second, although the FMB required all volunteers for mission service prior to their appointments to see the document and "to respect it in their teaching and practice on the mission field," the FMB did not require anyone to sign it (Love, "Seventy-Fifth Annual Report of the Foreign Mission Board," in *Annual of the SBC* [1920]: 194-200). Apparently in an effort to dispel all suspicions of credalism, the Committee on the Report of the Foreign Mission Board described "A Statement of Belief" as "*a brief and cautious statement of beliefs* held in common by Southern Baptists," a statement "*not in any sense offered as a creed,*" but "*intended to represent the general viewpoint of Southern Baptists.*" Furthermore, this committee reported its distinct understanding "that *neither present nor prospective missionaries are expected to sign this statement, but to recognize it as embodying our general interpretation of New Testament teaching*" ("Report on Foreign Mission Board," in *Annual of the SBC* [1920]: 43; emphasis mine). William R. Estep helpfully yet briefly discusses several contextual and social factors related this document's production (Estep, *Whole Gospel—Whole World: The Foreign Mission Board of the Southern Baptist Convention: 1845–1995* [Nashville: Broadman & Holman, 1994] 203-204).

[17]*Annual of the SBC* (1962): 64 ("Recommendation 14").

[18]Herschel H. Hobbs, "Crisis and Conquest," in *Annual of the SBC* (1962): 84, 85.

[19]Hobbs, "Crisis and Conquest," 85.

Accordingly, Hobbs wisely identified, rather than "a creedal statement binding upon all Southern Baptists," the "time-honored principle of unity in diversity" as "the cohesive force which holds Southern Baptists together doctrinally."[20]

III. Third Assumption. On the Clarity and Adequacy of the *Baptist Faith and Message (1963)* and Differing Interpretations of That Confession

The *RPTSC* implies a third dubious programmatic assumption. Referring to the five doctrinal areas which this document will later list and elaborate, the *RPTSC* announces its intent with those particular emphases "to illuminate articles of *The Baptist Faith and Message,* consistent with its intention and content."[21] This statement seems to suggest, at least, a twofold assumption: (1) that the *BFM (1963)* itself needs clarification or illumination; and (2) that previous or existing and differing interpretations of the *BFM (1963)* do not interpret that document in ways consistent with that confession's intention and content. Consequently, this serious twofold assumption also requires close scrutiny.

A. Is the *BFM (1963)* an Unclear or Doctrinally Insufficient Document?

Did the authors of the *BFM (1963)* produce an unclear or a doctrinally insufficient document? When the SBC adopted the committee's report on *The Baptist Faith and Message* in 1963, did Baptists of the SBC unwittingly adopt a deficient account of their faith?[22] The *RPTSC* implicitly answers these questions affirmatively.

Although an implicit as well as invalid assumption in the *RPTSC,* one member of the PTSC, R. Albert Mohler, Jr., previously in his fourteen "Imperatives for a Renewed Theological Framework," has openly registered this same assumption about the *BFM (1963).* As his first imperative for a "renewed theological framework," Mohler declares that "*the Southern Baptist Convention must achieve a common recognition of theological crisis and decline.*" This necessary "common recognition" includes acknowledging with Mohler the *BFM*'s lack of both complete

---

[20]Ibid., 85.

[21]*RPTSC*, 113 (1.5). I examine this intention itself through part two of this book.

[22]*Annual of the SBC* (1963): 63.

clarity and comprehensive vision. Such acknowledgment of "theological crisis and decline" in the SBC supplies the foundation for Mohler's second imperative for a renewed theological framework: *"Southern Baptists must strive with intentionality and dispatch toward a new theological consensus."*[23] Thus, acknowledging the deficiencies of the *BFM (1963)* prepares the way for the production of a new doctrinal statement: one with greater clarity, more comprehensive vision, one less open to divergent interpretations; a doctrinal statement *pre*scribing rather than *de*scribing the new theological consensus. Has Mohler employed his participation on the PTSC as a privilege to identify, despite his misrepresentations and misunderstandings, his own negative assessment of the *BFM (1963)* with the actual situation?

Even in 1965, two years after the adoption of the revised *BFM* (ample time for the SBC to reconsider and to study more carefully this document in light of these questions), Wayne Dehoney, then president of the SBC, stated the following: "The *theological guidelines* for our schools and agencies *were clearly defined* at Kansas City by the Articles of Faith."[24] While the committee certainly inscribed into the *BFM (1963)* tensions that reflect the diversity among Baptists in the SBC, given the widespread consensus in the perception of this document by Baptists in the SBC, perhaps the Committee on Baptist Faith and Message *intentionally formulated*, and the SBC *intentionally adopted*, those inscribed tensions. Baptists of the SBC have used the *BFM (1963)* successfully and confidently since its adoption. Thus, if the revised *BFM* has not changed since its adoption, then its intention and content remain as clear now as on the day of that confession's adoption.

B. Are Diverse Interpretations of the *BFM (1963)* Inconsistent with the Document?

Continuing the previous line of inquiry, have previous or existing, differing or divergent understandings of the *BFM (1963)* (especially concerning its article on the Christian scriptures) misinterpreted or misrepresented this document? Have Baptists of the SBC interpreted the *BFM (1963)* in ways not consistent with that document's intention and content?

---

[23]Mohler, "Has Theology a Future in the Southern Baptist Convention?" 98-99, 105, 106.

[24]Wayne Dehoney, "Issues and Imperatives," in *Annual of the SBC* (1965): 95; emphasis mine.

No doubt, some interpretations of that document may have erred in these ways. The PTSC, however, has not demonstrated, nor can it demonstrate, that the majority of the *BFM*'s Baptist interpreters have misconstrued or misinterpreted the *BFM* since 1963. Neither has the PTSC, with any sort of empirical evidence, validated its claim that most Baptists of the SBC share the *RPTSC*'s interpretation of the *BFM*'s intention and content. To identify any divergent perspectives on the *BFM (1963)* would first require the existence of a normative interpretation of that document, a result only genuinely validated by examining relevant data. In the *RPTSC*, this committee has not even supplied the rationale for its implied claim to have located *the normative interpretation* of the *BFM (1963)* among Baptists.[25]

While the *RPTSC* linguistically "affirms and honors" the *BFM (1963)* "as the normative expression of Southern Baptist belief," as well as claiming "to illuminate" articles in the *BFM (1963)* "consistent with its intention and content,"[26] the *RPTSC* actually and practically distorts the *BFM*'s understanding of confessions through the *RPTSC*'s incomplete representation of the *BFM*'s understanding of confessional statements among Baptists in the SBC. Although the *RPTSC* affirms a few emphases on confessional statements from the *BFM (1963)*, the *RPTSC* conveniently omits foundational components from the *BFM*'s conception of confessions in general and, by implication, about both itself and the *BFM (1963)* in particular, such as the following: (1) that confessions "constitute a consensus of *opinion* of some Baptist body"; (2) that Baptists "do *not* regard" confessions "as *complete statements* of our faith, having any

---

[25]Walter B. Shurden has accurately perceived this hermeneutical conflict over the *BFM (1963)* in the SBC. "So just as the groups differ on how they interpret the Bible, they also differ on how they interpret the BFM. More significantly, however, they differ on how they would utilize the document in denominational activities. Fundamentalists want to impose *their interpretation* of the document on all denominational employees, seminary professors, and others who work for the denomination. Moderates believe that such use is a misuse of the document, turning a 'confession of faith' that was intended to be non-binding into a 'creed' that straps the conscience. To say it another way, fundamentalists desire to use the BFM to 'control' biblical and theological interpretation, while moderates want to use it to guarantee freedom of interpretation" (Shurden, "Major Issues in the SBC Controversy," 8; emphasis mine).

[26]*RPTSC*, 113 (1.4, 5).

quality of *finality* or *infallibility*"; and (3) that "confessions are *only guides in interpretation*, having *no authority over the conscience*."[27]

Implicitly, the *RPTSC* suggests that Baptists require definitive and infallible confessions or interpretations of confessions, documents with the status of creeds. The *BFM (1963)* itself, to the contrary, acknowledges its own incompleteness of expression, admits both its lack of finality and its openness to elaboration, defines its own role as a guide in interpretation not as a standard of orthodoxy, and claims no authority for itself over the consciences of those who affirm or do not affirm it. Consequently, rather than requiring one normative interpretation of itself, given its own conception of the nature and function of confessions, the *BFM (1963)* certainly expects or recognizes and even appears to encourage diverse or divergent interpretations of itself.

IV. Fourth Assumption. On Challenging Baptists to Reaffirm Faithfulness to Doctrine

The authors of the *RPTSC* tightly link a fourth assumption to the previous assumptions. I summarize those assumptions again. First, Baptists have assailed their own doctrines through "subtle compromise, blatant concession, and malign neglect." Second, because of resulting inadequate or absent doctrinal bases, previous consensus in the SBC failed; Baptists, however, can restore and maintain a "new consensus" through new doctrinal and theological precision. Third, Baptists will realize such precision only with another doctrinal formulation, since the *BFM (1963)* and its previous interpretations remain unclear or doctrinally insufficient. Therefore, the *RPTSC* implies a fourth assumption in its programmatic foundation.

On the basis of the previous assumptions, a fourth assumption operates behind the *RPTSC*: Baptists of the SBC must either "reaffirm 'the faith which was once delivered unto the saints' (Jude 3 [KJV])," in the form of an additional and more precise doctrinal statement, or "lapse into theological unbelief."[28] Again, when the *RPTSC* claims that "each generation of Southern Baptists faces unique and pressing challenges to faithfulness which demand attention and test the integrity of our conviction," this assumption implies that reaffirmations of faithfulness to

---

[27]*BFM (1963)*, 269, 270; emphasis mine.
[28]*RPTSC*, 113 (1.1).

God in Christ must take linguistic form in an "explicit doctrinal standard."[29] If I have accurately discerned the basic features both of the previous assumptions and of this fourth assumption, then, this basic alternative expresses the central assumption in, or the key to, the *RPTSC*'s background argument or programmatic foundation. For the PTSC, the phrase from Jude 3 functions as the biblically authoritative, thematic basis (or rationale, very loosely conceived, and quite obviously undeveloped) for the *RPTSC*'s declarations.[30]

---

[29]*RPTSC*, 113, 114 (1.5, 10).

[30]For its programmatic use of Jude 3, the PTSC apparently took as its model, or at least considered as a powerful historical precedent for its own work, the following book: James Marion Frost, ed., *Baptist Why and Why Not: Twenty-five Papers by Twenty-five Writers and a Declaration of Faith* (Nashville: BSSB, 1900). This book includes position papers describing Baptist polity, doctrinal perspectives, and distinctive emphases. The various writers develop a series of apologies for both being and becoming a Baptist, as distinct from other Christian denominational perspectives and communities. While the essays address the issue of Baptist identity, generally, the book *describes* Baptists for non-Baptists. The book includes a reference to Jude 3 in its dedication: "Dedicated to the Baptists of the World in Their Contending for the Faith Once for All Delivered to the Saints." Further, the page preceding the book's introduction (by James Marion Frost) contains two quotations, as epigrams, from the Christian scriptures: Matt 28:20 and Jude 3 (*Baptist Why and Why Not*, 8). In its section on the Christian scriptures, the *RPTSC* contains a quotation from Frost's introduction (*RPTSC*, 114 [2.1.1]). In an essay of his own, one cochairperson of the PTSC, Timothy George, interprets the doctrine of the priesthood of all believers in light of Jude 3 as well. "Religious liberty guarantees the ability of every congregation to order its own internal life, its doctrine and discipline, in accordance with its own perception of divine truth. . . . Practically, this means that heresy is always possible and that spiritual vigilance is a constant necessity. Thus, priesthood of believers does not mean, 'I am a priest. I can believe anything I want to.' It means rather, 'As a priest in a covenanted community of believers, I must *be alert to keep my congregation from departing from* "the faith once and for all delivered unto the saints" ' (Jude 3)" (George, "Priesthood of All Believers and the Quest for Theological Integrity," 286-87; emphasis mine). Paul Basden and David Dockery later included George's essay, under a slightly different title, in a book of ecclesiological studies (George, "The Priesthood of All Believers," in *People of God*, ed. Basden and Dockery, 87). In another essay, George discusses five doctrinal "concerns," as his sense of "an urgent agenda for Baptist theology," under a heading obviously inspired by this same text from the book of Jude: "The Faith Once Delivered" (George, "The Renewal of Baptist Theology," in *Baptist Theologians*, ed. George and Dockery, 19-24). More than likely, the PTSC, under the dominating influence of George and Mohler, also intentionally used this text, since one of their Calvinistic heros, Boyce, used his similar interpretation of it to justify his own theological program to the trustees of Furman University (James P. Boyce, *Three Changes in Theological Institutions: An Inaugural Address Delivered before the Board of Trustees*

Unfortunately, the PTSC has predicated the *RPTSC* on another logical fallacy, the fallacy of false alternatives. The committee has wrongly assumed both that these are the only two alternatives and that one alternative is necessarily true. The committee has intentionally ignored other options. Certainly, Christians communicate their fidelity to God and to neighbors with doctrinal and theological discourse. Doctrinal and theological expressions of faithfulness to God, however, neither exhaustively express Christian faithfulness nor necessarily represent the primary or even sufficient expressions of fidelity to God. According to the gospels, even demons and unclean spirits could accurately articulate precise theological truths about Jesus of Nazareth.[31] Linguistic or doctrinal forms of Christian faithfulness necessarily arise from prior loving interactions between the human and the divine in daily experience, prayer, worship, decision, and interaction with others. The *RPTSC* seems to reduce Christian faith to cognitive responses and linguistic precision. Nonetheless, without the necessary conditions for those linguistic formulations, an "explicit doctrinal standard" will not guarantee either genuine revival or reconciliation among Baptists in the SBC. Thus, the real challenge, not the challenge either of assenting to specific and precise doctrinal formulations or of betraying Christian doctrines (or even of abandoning theological substance in doctrinal faithfulness), applies as well to those who might seek to legislate certain cognitive claims for all Baptists as tests of Christian faithfulness.

V. Fifth Assumption. On the Role of the *RPTSC*'s Interpretation of the *BFM (1963)*

Also following from the previous assumptive network, especially from the third and fourth assumptions, the *RPTSC* implies a fifth assumption. The authors of the *RPTSC* seem to assume, in light of the document's own language, that this document constitutes both *the* authoritative interpretation of the *BFM (1963)* and, therefore, the definition through which to issue the *challenge* for doctrinal purity to Baptists of the SBC. The fourth assumption implies that, among Baptists of the SBC, someone or some group has a privileged vantage point from

---

of the Furman University [Greenville SC: C. J. Elford's Book and Job Press, 1856] 34).

[31]Such as, "Son of God," "the Holy One of God," and "Son of the most high God" (Matt 8:29; Mark 1:23-24; 3:11; 5:1-7; Luke 8:27-28).

which both to confront Baptists of the SBC with this version of the contemporary challenge and to decide whether or not Baptists have adequately met this particular challenge. Rather than issuing a *descriptive report*, the committee has delivered a set of *prescriptive criteria*. In light of this fifth assumption, then, I continue the line of inquiry that I initiated concerning the third assumption.

A. Do Baptists Require One Official and Definitive Interpretation of the *BFM (1963)*?

Even if the *RPTSC*'s implicit identification of the need for a document consistent with the *BFM*'s intention and content should imply that previous interpretations of the *BFM (1963)* have misinterpreted that intention and content, would such misinterpretations, however, necessitate or even legitimize the promotion of an official and a definitive interpretation of the *BFM (1963)*, a guide with which to understand the *BFM (1963)*, even assuming the possibility of a definitive interpretation? Based upon the theological rationality of the SBC's historic perspectives themselves, Baptists have responded and continue to respond with resounding refusals to such proposals. Even Herschel Hobbs, the chairperson of the committee that produced the *BFM (1963)*, after writing his own interpretation of that document, later expressed this very conviction: "It is not an *official* interpretation, of course, which would be contrary to the nature and purpose of the statement."[32]

According to the *BFM (1963)* itself, as it concurs with (while also quoting from) the introductory statement in the *BFM (1925)*, Baptists historically have understood confessions as documents which "constitute a consensus of opinion of some Baptist body, large or small." Nonetheless, the *BFM (1963)* continues, "we do not regard them as complete statements of our faith, having any quality of finality or infallibility." Rather, "confessions are only guides in interpretation, having no authority over the conscience," since "the sole authority for faith and practice among Baptists is Jesus Christ whose will is revealed in the Holy Scriptures."[33] Since confessions (as two steps removed from Jesus Christ himself, the sole authority for faith and practice among Baptists in the

---

[32]Hobbs, "Southern Baptists and Confessionalism: A Comparison of the Origins and Contents of the 1925 and 1963 Confessions," *Review and Expositor* 76 (Winter 1979): 67. Also see Hobbs, *The Baptist Faith and Message* (Nashville: Convention Press, 1971).

[33]*BFM (1963)*, 269, 270.

SBC) possess only a derivative authority, *interpretations* (for example, the *RPTSC*) *of confessions* (for example, the *BFM [1963]*), as guides to the guides, have an even more dubious status.

Furthermore, given the first half of the committee's stated purpose, "to *examine* those biblical truths which are most surely held among the people of God called Southern Baptists,"[34] the *RPTSC* itself appears to violate its own limitations. The *RPTSC* moves beyond examination, study, and description of "those biblical truths" held by Baptists of the SBC. The *RPTSC* uses language with which to *prescribe* proper interpretations of those biblical truths that Baptists believe. Apparently, for the majority of members on the committee, this document constitutes at least the first or the most decisive of the final words about proper, normative, or acceptable Baptist doctrines. The *RPTSC* demonstrates this attitude about itself when, in defining its theory of scripture, it approvingly quotes James M. Frost's hermeneutically naive pronouncement: "'More and more we must come to feel as the deepest and mightiest power of our conviction that a "thus saith the Lord" is the end of all controversy.' "[35]

---

[34]*RPTSC*, 112 (intro.); emphasis mine.

[35]*RPTSC*, 114 (2.1.1). Although the committee does not identify the source of this quotation in the *RPTSC*, it comes from Frost ("Introduction" in *Baptist Why and Why Not*, 12). In another publication, Mohler cites a portion of the text by Frost, as quoted in the *RPTSC* (Mohler, "Has Theology a Future in the Southern Baptist Convention?" 111n.5). Mohler also quoted this text, and mentioned Frost no less than three times, in his sermon during the SBC's annual meeting in 1995 (R. Albert Mohler, Jr., "What Mean These Stones: Convention Sermon," Southern Baptist Convention, Atlanta [Wednesday morning, 21 June 1995], 2, 4; also see *Annual of the SBC* [1995]: 93). In other writings, George also quotes the text by Frost as included in the *RPTSC*: George, "Conflict and Identity in the SBC: The Quest for a New Consensus," in *Beyond the Impasse?* ed. James and Dockery, 196; idem, "Introduction" to *The Bible Doctrine of Inspiration* by Basil Manly, Jr., Library of Baptist Classics, ed. Timothy George and Denise George (Nashville: Broadman & Holman, 1995) 13; cf. idem, "The Southern Baptist Wars: What Can We Learn from the Conservative Victory?" *Christianity Today* 36 (9 March 1992): 24-25. Because of George's high evaluation of Frost's influence on the SBC, George has edited a volume of writings that Frost either edited or wrote himself. George entitled this collection *Baptist Why and Why Not*, even though George's collection includes less than half of the chapters from the book by the same title that Frost edited (Frost, *Baptist Why and Why Not*, Library of Baptist Classics, ed. Timothy George and Denise George [Nashville: Broadman & Holman, 1996]). In a reference to Frost's concept of biblical inerrancy, even Richard D. Land quotes this text from Frost's writings (Land, "Southern Baptists and the Fundamentalist Tradition in Biblical Interpretation, 1845–1945," *Baptist History and Heritage* 19 [July 1984]: 31). George, even more importantly, clearly per-

The *RPTSC*—as I will show later by studying its rhetoric—arrogantly (although with carefully veiled strategies) pretends to pronounce its own doctrinal "thus saith the Lord," toward the end thereby of terminating doctrinal and theological tensions (and, therefore, controversy?) by eliminating, as improper interpretations of the *BFM (1963)*, all viewpoints other than those formulated in the *RPTSC*.

To promote an official interpretation of the *BFM (1963)*, as an effort to release the theological tensions reflected in the *BFM (1963)*, by norming one pole of the polarity that generates the theological tensions, actively and intentionally imposes a credal document on noncredal people. In his presidential address to the SBC in 1963, Herschel Hobbs boldly declared the following about theological tension in the SBC.

> We are not without tension in our theology now, nor should we ever be. When a muscle loses its tension, it loses its effectiveness. Theology is the muscles of our denomination. We should not be using these muscles to bash in one another's heads.[36]

Hobbs realized that the loss of theological tension can encourage credalism—a destructive tendency, a force that leads to the atrophy of a Baptist community's vital faithfulness to God. In his previous presidential address to the SBC in 1962, Hobbs, speaking against the imposition of creeds upon Baptists, used an even more powerful metaphor to emphasize this same point: while previously "Southern Baptists were not willing, nor are they now, to wear a blind bridle, so today I do not believe that they are ready to wear a theological straight jacket."[37] As Hobbs rightly observed, creeds that coerce beliefs prevent healthy exercise and movement; imposed and enforced doctrinal formulas discourage creative theo-

---

ceives both Frost's statement and the entire book in which it appears as significant Baptist historical precedents to legitimize the polemical work of both himself and other leaders of the so-called "conservative resurgence" or the domineering right wing of the SBC. Elsewhere, George also appeals to a portion of this same text by Frost to substantiate his claim that Baptists in the SBC have used the term "inerrancy" long before the most recent of the SBC's controversies about theories of the Christian scriptures (George, "Priesthood of All Believers and the Quest for Theological Integrity," 283; idem, "Reformation Roots of the Baptist Tradition," 21-22n.27). In light of Mohler's, George's, and Land's participation on the PTSC, both their appreciation for Frost's theory of inspiration and their need to find Baptist authorities in the SBC to legitimize their agenda at least partially explain the prominence given to Frost's text in the *RPTSC*.

[36]Hobbs, "God and History," in *Annual of the SBC* (1963): 92.

[37]Hobbs, "Crisis and Conquest," 85.

logical exploration and, thereby, contribute significantly to the loss of theological vitality. From its inception in 1845, the Southern Baptist Convention has resisted credalism: "We have constructed for our basis no new creed; acting in this matter upon a *Baptist aversion for all creeds but the Bible*."[38]

B. Do Baptists Require an Elite Group of Leaders to Interpret the *BFM (1963)* for All Baptists?

Closely related to the previous concerns—if one assumes that the *BFM (1963)* needs clarification—do Baptists of the SBC also require for themselves a special committee to interpret, to clarify, or to illuminate that document? Moreover, has the SBC authorized any person or group of persons to compose criteria on the basis of which to decide which interpretations of the *BFM (1963)* have been formulated in ways consistent with this confession's intention and content?

If the Baptist belief in the priesthood of all believers sufficiently authorizes each Baptist Christian to interpret the Christian Bible as the Holy Spirit leads her or him to do, then certainly this same principle authorizes each Baptist freely to interpret the *BFM (1963)* without an official, ecclesiastically designed and imposed, interpretive guide to that

---

[38]*SBCBUS (1845)*, 19; emphasis mine. The SBC passed a resolution instructing William Bullein Johnson, the first president of the SBC, R. Fuller, T. F. Curtis, and C. D. Mallory to form "a committee to prepare an address to the public, setting forth the reasons which have led to the formation of the Southern Baptist Convention, and giving an exposition of its principles and objects" (*Proceedings of the SBC* [1845]: 14). So strong has the aversion to creeds remained among Baptists in the SBC that, despite its overwhelmingly positive reception by Baptists around the world, even the carefully designed *FASB (1920)* elicited some resistance and misunderstanding by well-intentioned and intelligent readers. For example, Edward B. Pollard kindly responded in the public forum about the *use* (not the content) of this document, based on his outspoken opposition to creeds (e.g., Pollard, "What Shall We Think of Creeds?" 40-54), perceiving this address as the SBC's effort to divide Northern Baptists and to draw the more orthodox among them into the SBC (Edward B. Pollard, "An Open letter to Dr. Love," *Religious Herald* [29 January 1920]: 3). Pollard's letter generated a public discussion: e.g., J. F. Love, "Dr. Pollard's Personal Letter," *Religious Herald* (5 February 1920): 11; E. Y. Mullins, "Dr. Pollard and the Fraternal Address," *Religious Herald* (12 February 1920): 12; (editor), "Fraternal Address," *Western Recorder* (26 February 1920): 9; Edward B. Pollard, "From Dr. Pollard," *Western Recorder* (25 March 1920): 10. See James E. Carter's more recent discussion of this confession and its effects: Carter, "The Fraternal Address of Southern Baptists," *Baptist History and Heritage* 12 (October 1977): 209-18.

confession. As Hobbs surmised, "it is not likely that Southern Baptists will *knowingly* and *willingly* relinquish this cherished principle" (the priesthood of all believers). As Hobbs also postulated as a possibility for Baptists, however, the authors of the *RPTSC* have "unwittingly" relinquished this principle "in their zeal for the faith."[39] This assumption requires little further elaboration and critique at this stage, since, if I have correctly identified and expressed it, this fifth assumption obviously contradicts a variety of distinctive Baptist emphases.

Analogue. Episode One

After the Hebrew people had cried to Yahweh for liberation from the severe labors with which the Egyptians afflicted them, Yahweh sent Moses to request their release from Pharaoh. Instead, Pharaoh intensified his oppression of the people. For this increase in their oppression, the people's leaders blamed Moses and Aaron, refusing to listen to Yahweh through them and unable to acknowledge or unwilling to bear the costs to themselves even through divine deliverance. Regardless of these past events, after Yahweh had broken Pharaoh's grip on the people, as the Hebrew people camped beside the sea, when the pursuing Egyptian army neared the Hebrews, the people in their renewed fear complained again to Moses. Through their complaints, they revised their own genuine recent history with Yahweh: denying that they had desired liberation from their slavery; declaring, to the contrary, that they had told Moses to leave them alone; even asserting that they had preferred to serve the Egyptians.[40]

Similarly, the *RPTSC* implies a network of dubious assumptions about, or a distorted hermeneutical perspective on, the SBC's history as the background or situation in and to which the PTSC has addressed the *RPTSC*. Rather than perceiving the various perspectives and differences among Baptists in the SBC as divine gifts and as the risk of freedom in Christ, the *RPTSC* construes the presence of different perspectives in the SBC's recent history as an aberration in the SBC's entire history, even as the assailment of some previous theological uniformity, and especially as the cause of collapsed consensus and conflict within the SBC. Thus, the *RPTSC* implies the need for a return to a situation that never existed

---

[39]Hobbs, "Crisis and Conquest," 85; emphasis mine.
[40]Exod 1:8-22; 2:22-25; 3:1-12; 4:27-31; 5:19-21; 6:9; 14:10-12.

within the SBC, a situation in which doctrinal and theological uniformity supposedly characterized the SBC's participating Baptists. Most certainly, in times of uncertainty and ambiguity, one can understand the fear that motivates such historical revision. Nonetheless, not only does such a revisionist interpretation of the SBC's history misrepresent the actual situation from and to which the *RPTSC* responds, but the *RPTSC*'s call upon Baptists in the SBC to return to such a chimerical situation represents a tactic to control Baptists in the SBC with Christian doctrine.

It appears that the PTSC developed its own goals, and envisioned the purpose for the *RPTSC*, on the basis of the implicit assumptive network that I have exposed in this chapter. My attribution to the committee of the arguments expressed through this network of assumptions, as the committee's background understanding and programmatic foundation, may seem to assess the *RPTSC* too harshly or even unfairly. An examination of the intentions, purposes, and goals communicated by that document, however, will support my preliminary answers to the previous line of inquiry.

Chapter 2

Masked
and Questionable Intentions

*And why is the Lord bringing us into this land, to fall by the sword? Our
wives and our little ones will become plunder; would it not be better for us
to return to Egypt?* (Numbers 14:3 NASB)

*. . . wandering stars, for whom the black darkness has been reserved
forever.* (Jude 13 NASB)

Introduction

A second question focuses this chapter's analyses of the *RPTSC*: what
end, purpose, aim, or intention has motivated the writing and publication
of this document? Generally, indicators in the *RPTSC* suggest that those
who produced this document intend to use it as a tool with which to
control thought and behavior both within the SBC and within churches
that participate in the SBC. In this second chapter, then, I also pursue the
dual aim of these studies, both to unmask threats to distinctive Baptist
perspectives and to suggest legitimate lines of Baptist resistance to those
threats, with reference to this second problematic feature of the *RPTSC*.
Several aspects comprise this questionable feature of the *RPTSC*.[1]

---

[1]In the following interpretation, with my concerns about intention, I may seem to risk
committing the intentional or psychological fallacy. I understand the intentional fallacy,
following W. K. Wimsatt and Monroe C. Beardsley, as the mistaken hermeneutical identification of a text's meaning, almost if not exclusively, with its extratextual origin in the
author's mental intention (Wimsatt and Beardsley, "The Intentional Fallacy," in *Critical
Theory since Plato*, ed. Hazard Adams [New York: Harcourt Brace Jovanovich, 1971]
1015-22). Nonetheless, I aim also to avoid the "fallacy of the absolute text: the fallacy
of hypostasizing the text as an authorless entity," as Paul Ricoeur describes it (Ricoeur,
Interpretation Theory: Discourse and the Surplus of Meaning [Fort Worth: Texas Christian University Press, 1976] 30). With Ricoeur, while acknowledging the "semantic
autonomy of the text," I also acknowledge that the text's style, as a literary genre's individuality, "retroactively points to its author" (Ricoeur, *Interpretation Theory*, 30; idem,
"The Hermeneutical Function of Distanciation," *Philosophy Today* 17 [Summer 1973]:
139). Ricoeur identifies Friedrich D. E. Schleiermacher as among the first scholars to per-

I. Origin and Task
of the Presidential Theological Study Committee

The origin of the committee that formulated the *RPTSC* discloses the first questionable aspect of this document's purpose. The president of the SBC in 1992, H. Edwin Young, appointed this committee. According to the *RPTSC* itself, Young appointed the Presidential Theological Study Committee as a "study group" with the following dual "purpose": (1) "to examine those biblical truths which are most surely held among the people of God called Southern Baptists"; and (2) "on this basis, to re-affirm our common commitment to Jesus Christ, the Holy Scriptures, and the evangelical heritage of the Christian church."[2]

In spite of the positive appearance of the committee's stated purpose, *only the president of the SBC* in 1992 created and empowered the committee, *not the SBC itself.* Unlike the committees formed in 1924 and 1962 to study doctrines held by Baptists in the SBC,[3] no annual session

---

ceive style as the link between a text's language and the author's project or mental intention (Ricoeur, "Schleiermacher's Hermeneutics," *The Monist* 60 [April 1977]: 188).

[2]*RPTSC*, 112 (intro.). During his recent interview of Paige Patterson, Walter Carpenter disclosed that Young originally intended for the PTSC "only to address the nature of Scripture." According to Carpenter, "those on the committee in academia told those of us outside academia that we really didn't understand what was happening today and that it was imperative that this platform be used to deal with these incipient heresies" (Carpenter, "Conversations with Evangelicals," *Texas Baptist* 2 [July 1995]: 7). Apparently, at least George, Land, and Mohler pushed the committee to produce a more comprehensive doctrinal statement.

[3]Regardless of the decisions with which the SBC has demonstrated its concern for adequate doctrine in its missionary enterprises, the SBC as a whole has consistently resisted formulating and adopting explicit doctrinal standards as criteria by which to test the beliefs of its membership. Such consistent resistance to credalism characterized the annual meeting of the SBC in 1924, even though that year the SBC commissioned the first committee to study (and during the annual meeting of 1925 to report on) the Baptist faith and message. In the afternoon session on Wednesday, 14 May 1924, during the SBC's annual meeting, C. P. Stealey, from Oklahoma, introduced a resolution on a doctrinal statement for the Convention. The Convention referred this resolution to the Committee on Resolutions for consideration. On Thursday afternoon, May 15th, Stealey made a motion, which the Convention so ordered, to instruct the Committee on Resolutions "to report out today or tomorrow the resolution offered by him yesterday afternoon." R. K. Maiden, from Missouri, also submitted a resolution concerning "Modernism" to the Convention, following Stealey's motion; the Convention also referred this motion to the Committee on Resolutions. When the Committee on Resolutions reported on Friday afternoon, May 16th, it

of the SBC formed and commissioned the PTSC. In itself, this executive initiative by Young both represents serious irregularities in the SBC's polity and, consequently, raises suspicions about this committee's actual purpose.

The wording of the committee's stated purpose itself should alert Baptists to the heart of the problem. For whom does this committee examine the biblical truths held by Baptists in the SBC? As a committee commissioned by one Baptist minister, who also happened to be the

---

did not recommend the passage of either Stealey's original resolution or Maiden's resolution. The committee rather appealed to two previous documents authorized by the SBC: (1) the "Fraternal Greeting" (or *FASB [1920]*), commissioned by the Convention in 1919; and (2) from E. Y. Mullins's presidential address of 1923 ("Present Dangers and Duties"), the section entitled "Science and Religion," adopted by the Convention in 1923 "as the belief" of the SBC, printed in the annual that year as well as published and distributed by the BSSB (*Annual of the SBC* [1923]: 19-20; hereafter cited as *SR [1923]*).

The Committee on Resolutions used the following grounds for appeal to those two documents: first, the SBC in 1919 authorized and distributed globally the *FASB (1920)* "as a circular of information"; and, second, since the SBC in 1923 had "unanimously endorsed and broadly published" the statement on Baptist beliefs, entitled "Science and Religion," the Committee considered that statement to be "sufficiently comprehensive and definite" as well as "accessible for all who seek to be informed of the fundamental beliefs commonly held by the Baptist churches and people of the South." The Convention adopted the first report of the Committee on Resolutions. Despite the work of the Committee on Resolutions to that point during the meeting in 1924, during the Saturday morning session on May 17th, Stealey introduced another resolution, pressing the Convention to consider it immediately. Although the vote against its immediate consideration was very close, the SBC again referred the resolution to the Committee on Resolutions. Later that morning, during its report, the Committee refused to recommend consideration of Stealey's second resolution, since the second resolution contained essentially the same substance as the first resolution. As part of that same report, however, the Committee on Resolutions presented an alternative recommendation. The Committee recommended "that the following brethren be appointed to consider the advisability of issuing another statement of the Baptist faith and message and to report at the next Convention: E. Y. Mullins, Chairman, L. R. Scarborough, C. P. Stealey, W. J. McGlothlin, S. M. Brown, E. C. Dargan, R. H. Pitt." The Convention adopted the recommendation from the committee's second report as well (*Annual of the SBC* [1924]: 24, 49, 70-71, 80, 95).

Although the Committee on Resolutions had recommended, and the SBC had subsequently appointed, Stealey to the Committee on Baptist Faith and Message, when the latter committee reported during the annual meeting in 1925, Stealey's name did not appear among the signatures of the committee on the document. Instead, Stealey, still not fully satisfied, moved to amend the report's article on the human creation and fall into sin. His motion to amend the report failed and the Convention adopted the report of the Committee on Baptist Faith and Message (*Annual of the SBC* [1925]: 70-76).

president of the SBC in 1992, in constitutional terms, the committee does not represent the SBC in its efforts; the committee legitimately can speak only for itself and, perhaps, for Young. In the second aspect of the purpose with which he commissioned the committee, however, Young calls upon his committee "to reaffirm" three of "our common" commitments. Does this committee reaffirm the common commitments of its own members, when it refers to "*our* common commitment to Jesus Christ, the Holy Scriptures, and the evangelical heritage of the Christian church," or to the common commitments of all Baptists in the SBC, or to those of all evangelical Christians?[4] In this second part of the committee's commission, clearly, on the basis of the committee's examination of the biblical truths held by Baptists in the SBC, Young has called upon this committee to "reaffirm" for all Baptists in the SBC their "common commitment" to the three items named. Even if most Baptists in the SBC would reaffirm their commitments to those things, no committee of appointed inquisitors and legislators has the authority to speak for any other Baptist individual or group, unless so authorized by that individual or group—in this case, unless authorized by the Baptists in the SBC.

II. Purpose in Publication of the *RPTSC*

The questionable origin of the PTSC affects and, therefore, especially impugns even the purpose for which the committee published the *RPTSC*. According to the document itself, "in light of the pressing need for a positive biblical witness on basic Christian beliefs, this report is published not as a new confession of faith, but rather as a reaffirmation of major doctrinal concerns set forth in the *Baptist Faith and Message* of 1963."[5] This statement invites two major questions and corresponding critical observations.

A. Is the *RPTSC* a New Confession of Faith?

First, the committee explicitly denied any intent to publish the *RPTSC* as a new confession of faith. Presumably, with this comment, the committee aimed to alleviate any concerns among Baptists in the SBC

---

[4]Although my question may appear rhetorical, I ask it quite seriously without intending to suggest any irony, since, in the remainder of the *RPTSC*, a subtle oscillation in referentiality occurs in the document's use of first-person-plural pronouns. I will discuss the *RPTSC*'s rhetoric later in this study.

[5]*RPTSC*, 112 (intro.).

that the *RPTSC* would eclipse or replace the *BFM (1963)*. The committee also assumed a very specific situation as the motivation for its publication of the *RPTSC*: "the pressing need for a positive biblical witness on basic Christian beliefs." The assumed situation, however, raises questions about this motive for the report's publication. Did the committee assume that the SBC does not possess "a positive biblical witness on basic Christian beliefs" in the *BFM (1963)*, its existing and Convention-authorized confession of faith? If the *BFM (1963)* does supply such a witness, then why did the committee produce, publish, and promote the *RPTSC*, assuming that the committee did not publish the *RPTSC* as a new confession of faith?

I suspect, to the contrary, that the PTSC has produced this document precisely not as a new confession, but as a protocreed for a new SBC.[6] Two other slippery comments in the *RPTSC*, somewhat even at cross-purposes with one another, deepen this suspicion.

On the one hand, the *RPTSC* "affirms and honors" the *BFM (1963)*, "as the normative expression of Southern Baptist belief," and "declines to recommend any new confession or revision of that statement."[7] Yet,

---

[6]I refer here to the plan for the complete restructuring of the SBC. Not coincidentally, one of the members from the PTSC, R. Albert Mohler, Jr., also participates on the Program and Structure Study Committee (Mark Wingfield, "Major Overhaul of SBC Agencies Proposed," *Western Recorder* 169 [28 February 1995]: 1, 10; idem, "States Offered More Control of Home Missions Work," *Western Recorder* 169 [28 February 1995]: 11). Although perhaps a little early to claim with certainty, the radical right-wing leaders in the SBC probably produced the *RPTSC* in order to function as one of the (maybe even *the* central) SBC-endorsed theological tools for both the political reconstruction and the subsequent control of the SBC's agencies and institutions. The editor of *Texas Baptist* (also a member on the PTSC and, therefore, one of the signatories to the *RPTSC*), J. Walter Carpenter, elsewhere more openly admits the credal status of the *RPTSC*. According to Carpenter, "in the very serious matter of who is 'in our [*sic*] out,' we should recognize that a confession with teeth in it in the most practical way acts as a creed." Apparently, Carpenter perceives the *RPTSC* as the credal "teeth" of the *BFM (1963)*: "Adopting the *Report of the Theological Study Committee* in the states **would** give an adequate definition of what it means to be a Southern Baptist." Furthermore, even more explicitly according to Carpenter, "by assuming that we can call a Southern Baptist one who subscribes to *The Baptist Faith and Message* of 1963 as that is understood by the *Report of the Theological Study Committee* of 1994, affirmed by the 1994 session of the SBC, we can have a working definition from which to proceed" (J. Walter Carpenter, "Are Southern Baptists Evangelicals?" *Texas Baptist* 2 [January 1995]: 6).

[7]*RPTSC*, 113 (1.4).

the very next sentence in the following paragraph of the *RPTSC* begins
with the word, "however." The *RPTSC* qualifies its acceptance of the
BFM (1963), by assuming that the *BFM (1963)* requires illumination and
clarification "consistent with its [the *BFM*'s] intention and content."
Continuing to weaken the normative status of the *BFM (1963)*, the
RPTSC commends its own interpretations of basic beliefs, those already
yet not so narrowly formulated in the *BFM (1963)*, to the SBC.[8]

On the other hand, immediately following its thin affirmation of the
BFM (1963), similar to the way in which an arrogant younger soldier
might honor a presumably now ineffective old combat veteran from a
previous war, the *RPTSC* establishes the basis upon which to affirm the
committee's right to produce its own confessional statement. The *RPTSC*
contains five small though weak paragraphs through which it outlines the
committee's perception about the authority and function of confessions
among Baptists in the SBC.[9]

By abbreviated though grave qualifications of several distinctive Baptist perspectives (such as the priesthood of all believers, the autonomy of
the local church, and even the scriptures as the norm for faith and practice), the *RPTSC* then states that "none of these principles . . . is violated
by voluntary, conscientious adherence to *an explicit doctrinal standard*."[10]
The committee carefully avoids explicit references to the *RPTSC* as a
confession or a creed. Yet, after partially affirming the nature and function of confessions among Baptists, masked as the spirit of confessionalism (more accurately, as I will demonstrate subsequently, with the
spirit of oppressive credalism), the committee commends its own "report"
to the SBC. In its article on the church, the *RPTSC* further reinforces a
suspicion about the most serious danger: that the committee perceives
and seeks to use the *RPTSC* as a standard by which to measure orthodoxy in the SBC and, therefore, as a tool for disciplinary control of Baptists in the SBC. For example, according to the *RPTSC*, "the doctrine of

---

[8]*RPTSC*, 113 (1.6-10).

[9]*RPTSC*, 113-14 (1.5).

[10]*RPTSC*, 114 (1.10). Timothy George appears to consider his own perspective as the
norm for Baptists in the SBC, since this phrase and emphasis come directly from his own
publications: "the idea that *voluntary, conscientious adherence to an explicit doctrinal
standard* is somehow foreign to the Baptist tradition is a peculiar notion not borne out by
a careful examination of our heritage" (George, "Conflict and Identity in the SBC," 203;
emphasis mine).

religious liberty, far from implying doctrinal laxity or unconcern, guarantees the ability of every congregation and general Baptist body to determine (on the basis of the Word of God) its own doctrinal and disciplinary parameters."[11] Does the committee not understand, however, that this claim to some extent conflicts with the document's own prior declaration: "Since God alone is Lord of the conscience, the temporal realm has no authority to coerce religious commitments?"[12] The "temporal realm" still includes "every congregation and general Baptist body." In its various comments, without openly admitting its intention, the committee endeavors indirectly to confer a confessional (more accurately, even a credal) status on the *RPTSC* for both the committee and those to whom the committee addresses this document.

B. Is the *RPTSC* a Reaffirmation or a Revision of the *BFM (1963)*?

Second, then, in the *RPTSC*, does the committee genuinely reaffirm "major doctrinal concerns set forth in the *Baptist Faith and Message* of 1963?" According to the *RPTSC* itself, the PTSC explicitly "declines to recommend any . . . revision of that statement."[13] Uncritical readings of both the *BFM (1963)* and the *RPTSC* might permit an affirmative though

---

[11]*RPTSC*, 118 (2.4.6); emphasis mine. Again, this substantially repeats a sentence from an article by Timothy George: "Religious liberty guarantees the ability of every congregation to order its own internal life, its doctrine and discipline, in accordance with its own perception of divine truth" (George, "The Priesthood of All Believers and the Quest for Theological Integrity," 286).

[12]*RPTSC*, 117-18 (2.4.6).

[13]*RPTSC*, 113 (1.4). During the annual meeting of the SBC in 1994, when the SBC adopted the *RPTSC*, Richard Tribble, Jr. also introduced a motion entitled "On *The Baptist Faith and Message*": "I move that the president of this Convention be requested to call a meeting of those now serving as presidents of the various state conventions to present to the Convention in Atlanta, Georgia, in 1995, an official review and updating of the *Baptist Faith and Message* which shall serve as information to the churches and which may serve as guidelines to the various agencies of the Southern Baptist Convention." The Committee on Order of Business referred this motion to the Executive Committee for consideration (*Annual of the SBC* [1994]: 35, 75). During the SBC's annual meeting in 1995, in response to Tribble's motion from the previous year, the Executive Committee declined "to recommend an official study review and updating of the *Baptist Faith and Message* because of recent reviews and affirmations of the *Baptist Faith and Message* by the Southern Baptist Convention" ("Sixty-Eighth Annual Report of the Executive Committee," in *Annual of the SBC* [1995]: 36, 111). Presumably, the Executive Committee referred primarily to the *RPTSC* in its own report on Tribble's motion from the SBC's previous meeting.

qualified response to the previous question. Broadly considered, the *RPTSC* does interpret five major Christian doctrinal areas.

Posing the previous question from other slightly more specific perspectives, however, clears the way for very different responses. Are the doctrinal formulations in the *RPTSC* "consistent" with the "intention and content" of the *BFM (1963)*? Do the doctrinal "emphases" in the *RPTSC* actually "illuminate" or "clarify" the *BFM (1963)* or, rather, do they *subtly alter* or *revise* the *BFM (1963)* and its doctrinal perspectives?[14] Elsewhere in the *RPTSC*, the committee has placed the burden of proof on the *RPTSC* with its promises to accomplish the goals of illuminating and clarifying the *BFM (1963)*.

When responding to this question (in its different forms), however, both by reconsidering the assumed situation that motivates the committee's publication of the *RPTSC* and by critically comparing the doctrinal formulations in the *BFM (1963)* and the *RPTSC*, the possibility of a positive response to this question rapidly diminishes. I contend, to the contrary, that, rather than a hermeneutical reaffirmation of doctrinal formulations in the *BFM (1963)*, the *RPTSC* actually reductively reconstrues or revises key doctrines in the *BFM (1963)*. Furthermore, such intentionally reductive misreadings of the *BFM (1963)* actually obfuscate the *BFM*'s clearer and much broader doctrinal formulations. I will temporarily postpone, however, my specific comments about some of the *RPTSC*'s hermeneutically reductive doctrinal formulations until part two of this study. For this reason, an empirical confirmation of my present claim awaits those brief comparative analyses.

Insofar as the *RPTSC* suggests the need for a reconstrual of the *BFM (1963)* and then actually attempts one, the PTSC has implied, at least, that the *BFM (1963)* does not supply an adequate "positive biblical witness on basic Christian beliefs." Can Baptists in the SBC really consider such an implication by the *RPTSC* as a genuine reaffirmation of the *BFM*

---

[14]See *RPTSC*, 113 (1.5). Timothy George elsewhere quite clearly perceives the theologian's responsibility to interpret historical documents honestly and carefully: "It is always proper and necessary to rethink and reformulate the classic expressions of the faith; but we must do so in a way that does not do violence to the intention of those expressions, insofar as they faithfully reflect the primary witness of Scripture itself" (George, "Dogma beyond Anathema," 700). Unfortunately, the PTSC appears to withold this commitment from its own strange interpretation of the *BFM (1963)*.

(1963)? Can Baptists in the SBC perceive such misreadings as anything less than subtle revisions of historic, distinctive Baptist principles?

For now, I will also assume that my later examinations of the *RPTSC*'s doctrinal formulations confirm the high probability of my present claim: that the *RPTSC* has misinterpreted and, therefore, not clarified, not illuminated, and not reaffirmed, but has actually revised, the *BFM (1963)*. According to the *RPTSC* itself, the committee that formulated the *RPTSC*, with "commitment" to both "the unity of our Baptist fellowship" and "the integrity of our doctrinal confession" as well as "in a spirit of pastoral concern," sought to promote reconciliation and unity through "holy living and sound doctrine."[15]

Insofar as the PTSC has *reductively misconstrued* the *BFM (1963)* through the formulations of the *RPTSC*, however, it has distorted the sound Baptist doctrine transmitted by the *BFM (1963)*. Furthermore, insofar as this committee has *intentionally misrepresented* the doctrinal intention and content of the *BFM (1963)*, the committee has even mocked holy living. By the committee's own unfaithfulness to those realities that it has designated as "indispensable elements of true revival and genuine reconciliation among any body of Christian believers," the committee has eliminated the very conditions through which it claims to realize the kind of unity that it purportedly desires.[16] Thus, in light of its own ecclesiological statements, when the committee decries "all efforts to weaken our denomination and its cooperative ministries,"[17] the committee should first apply its disparagement or condemnation of such activity to its own efforts.

Analogue. Episode Two

The majority of Hebrews who reconnoitered Canaan returned with an ambiguous report for the people. On the one hand, they brought evidence of the land's riches and fruitfulness. On the other hand, they accentuated the strength and ferocity of the land's inhabitants, while they stressed the Hebrew people's inability successfully to engage those inhabitants. This report frustrated and frightened the Hebrew tribes. They lamented before Yahweh and grumbled to Moses, indicating their preferences for death in

---

[15]*RPTSC*, 113, 114 (1.5, 10).
[16]*RPTSC*, 114 (1.10).
[17]*RPTSC*, 117 (2.4.5).

Egypt or even in the wilderness itself, rather than destruction through struggle with the inhabitants of Canaan. In their fear, they ignored their priestly calling from Yahweh as a people, their calling to be a community of ministers to the world. Instead, they considered that which they might lose in this terrible challenge, that which their freedom must risk in order to fulfill their purpose with Yahweh. Once again, then, the people remembered and desired the security of their bondage in Egypt. Hence, their fear led to their refusal to face the challenge. The people's longings for Egypt, and especially their fears of death in war and the enslavement of their women and children, indicate the people's intention to protect or to secure their lives and belongings even at the cost of faithfulness to their calling and guidance by Yahweh, even if it meant refusing to trust Yahweh's sufficiency rather than their own abilities during the struggle.[18]

Similarly, in the *RPTSC*, the PTSC has crystallized its fear of theological diversity in the SBC, its fear of the ability of the SBC's historic diversity successfully to engage the contemporary issues, problems, and plurality of the larger social reality in which the SBC finds itself. Thus, this committee has produced the *RPTSC* as an instrument to protect its own interests, to allay its own fears, to immure itself from attack, rather than genuinely to remember its divine calling and actually to exercise that calling in ministry to and with others, however different the others might be.

The previous very brief studies and evaluations disclose questionable intentions in the *RPTSC*. Although the intentionalities of that document remain partially veiled, they cannot remain hidden from critical examination. Clearly, the PTSC has submitted the *RPTSC* as its own effort to supply, at least, the grounds for "an explicit doctrinal standard"[19] with which to check the SBC's purported lapse "into theological unbelief" and to eliminate the alleged "doctrinal minimalism and theological revision"[20] that the *RPTSC* claims have produced the conflict of recent years within the SBC.

Nevertheless, given the suspicions raised by the dubious purposes of both the committee and its published report, another concern surfaces for Baptists in the SBC. In 1987, the SBC Peace Committee reported, with a series of recommendations, to the SBC; the SBC in that year adopted

---

[18]Num 13:25-33; 14:1-45; Exod 19:1-6.
[19]*RPTSC*, 114 (1.10).
[20]*RPTSC*, 113 (1.1, 8).

the Peace Committee's report. In its report, the Peace Committee recommended both that the SBC "request all organized political factions to discontinue the organized political activity in which they are now engaged" and that the SBC "request the SBC's Committee on Resolutions to continue its policy of not presenting resolutions that are divisive in Southern Baptist life for *at least* the next three years."[21] Perhaps both the PTSC and the Committee on Resolutions adhered to *the letter* of the law (that is, "the next three years"), since 1990 represented the last year in the legally minimum moratorium on divisive resolutions during the SBC's annual meetings. Both committees, however, apparently ignored *the spirit* of the Peace Committee's recommendations (that is, the "at least"), by introducing another divisive, even explosive, element into the SBC in the form of the *RPTSC*. Certainly even the PTSC can appreciate the irony, and can recognize its own hypocrisy, when the committee simultaneously commends the Peace Committee's report to the SBC and, yet, ignores the complete applicability of the Peace Committee's report to its own activities.[22]

Furthermore, the SBC's Executive Committee in 1994 appointed one of the cochairpersons for the PTSC, Timothy George, also to the Committee on Resolutions.[23] George's participation as a member of the Committee on Resolutions, however, unashamedly indicates another of the now quite common conflicting interests among the leaders of the SBC. This consciously strategic choice by the Executive Committee in 1994 both guaranteed a place on the Convention's agenda for a resolution favoring the *RPTSC* and virtually insured this resolution's unopposed adoption by the SBC.

Such obvious political maneuvering through and manipulations of the SBC's polity render dubious, if they do not flatly discredit, the claims made by the *RPTSC* for itself: (1) the committee's claim to desire "*to move beyond the denominational conflict of recent years* toward a new consensus rooted in theological substance and doctrinal fidelity"; and (2) the committee's claim that it prays for its effort to lead "*to healing and reconciliation throughout the Southern Baptist Convention* and, God willing, to a renewed commitment" to the SBC's "founding purpose of 'eliciting, combining, and directing the energies of the whole denomina-

---

[21]*RPC (1987)*, 241-42; emphasis mine.
[22]*RPTSC*, 115 (2.1.8).
[23]"Proceedings," in *Annual of the SBC* (1994): 33.

tion in one sacred effort, for the propagation of the gospel.' "[24] A purpose motivated the production and adoption of the *RPTSC* beyond the stated purposes for the committee and the publication of its report. Obviously, such activities of deception and subterfuge do not even fulfill "the central purpose of the church" as described by the *RPTSC* itself: "to honor and glorify God."[25]

---

[24] *RPTSC*, 113 (1.2); emphasis mine.
[25] *RPTSC*, 117 (2.4.2).

Presumptuous and Reductive Uses of Authority

But the men who had gone up with him [Caleb] said, "We are not able to go up against the people, for they are too strong for us." So they gave out to the sons of Israel a bad report of the land which they had spied out, saying, "The land through which we have gone, in spying it out, is a land that devours its inhabitants; and all the people whom we saw in it are men of great size." "There also we saw the Nephilim (the sons of Anak are part of the Nephilim); and we became like grasshoppers in our own sight, and so we were in their sight." (Numbers 13:31-33 NASB)

So they said to one another, "Let us appoint a leader and return to Egypt." (Numbers 14:4 NASB)

. . . wild waves of the sea, casting up their own shame like foam; . . . (Jude 13 NASB)

Introduction

In this chapter, I answer the third elemental question in these studies: Who authorized and produced the *RPTSC*? As I stated in the prologue, building on the previous evidence, careful study of the *RPTSC* discloses the document's dangerously manipulative, noncongregational origin, with its source in an elite group of leaders within the SBC. This is the *RPTSC*'s third major problematic feature. I will expand my answer to this question about the *RPTSC*'s origins, through a threefold analysis of the *RPTSC*'s understanding and use of authority to legitimize the agents who produced the document: (1) its sense and exercise of its own authority; (2) its theory of biblical authority and its use of scripture as authority; and (3) its choices and uses of extrabiblical authorities, both Baptist and non-Baptist.

I follow this threefold analytical order, not because either I or most Baptists theoretically endorse this particular structure of authority, but because the *RPTSC* (despite its rhetoric) implies this structure through its actual theory and uses of authority among Baptist Christians. This chapter, then, constitutes a *nomology* of the PTSC's efforts, a study of the principles and processes by which this committee has produced its normative understanding of Christian teachings, its *theological laws* for all Baptists in and institutions of the SBC, its authorizing basis or source.

I. *RPTSC*'s Presumptuous Sense and Exercise of Its Own Authority

Initially, and perhaps most threateningly, a problem arises about the *RPTSC*'s veiled sense of its own authority. This document's presumed authority also implies something about *the committee's* sense of its own authority. By implication, then, the committee's sense of its own authority communicates something equally as problematic about *Young's* sense of his own authority and mission, as the president of the SBC who commissioned the committee that produced the *RPTSC*.

A. Originated in Transgression of Presidential Authority

As I have noted previously, the SBC did not instruct Young to commission such a committee; in this sense, both the committee (The *Presidential* Theological Study Committee) and the document itself ("Report of the *Presidential* Theological Study Committee") have received the appropriate names. Perhaps Young understood Morris Chapman's presidential address of 1992 as the directive for Young to authorize this enterprise.

In that address, Chapman called upon Baptists of the SBC "to take the high ground," citing a lengthy list of names from the SBC's history, to which he added this exclusion: "Those who would use these names for some other movement pay us the ultimate compliment—**but they cannot and will not hijack our heritage.**" Chapman followed his veiled reference to the Cooperative Baptist Fellowship (and other groups of Baptists that oppose the fundamentalist subjugation of the SBC) by referring to the *Fraternal Address of Southern Baptists* (*FASB [1920]*), as authorized in 1919 and distributed by the SBC in 1920, as an authoritative document with which to support his own doctrinal and moral challenges to the churches in the SBC: a challenge to take "the high ground" of refusing to "join or approve those who would reject clear biblical teachings"; a challenge to "protect the purity" of their congregations; and a challenge to "place a premium on holy living." According to Chapman, in the *FASB (1920)*, "Southern Baptists expressed their doctinal [*sic*] commitments and confessed the 'faith once received,' " thus alluding to the phrase from Jude 3, a text later to exercise such a central role in the

RPTSC.[1] Several of the phrases and watchwords used by Chapman later reappear in the *RPTSC*.

Perhaps Chapman himself considered his own declarations as the implementation of the long-standing *suggestion*, submitted in 1984 by James T. Draper, Jr., one of the Baptist leaders in the initial vanguard of the so-called "conservative resurgence": "I would suggest that the Southern Baptist Convention, at one of its annual meetings, *delegate to someone the authority* to appoint a *blue ribbon committee* which would draw up such a set of *parameters*, and then present it for *convention debate* and *possible adoption.*"[2] At that time, at least Draper suggested that the Convention itself authorize such a process.

The president of the SBC, nonetheless, is not the Convention itself; the president of the SBC, rather, represents the will of the Baptists who comprise the SBC. Historically, when the SBC has adopted confessional statements, the SBC itself has authorized and commissioned committees to study and to produce such documents.[3] In both their churches and their ecclesially derived organizations, Baptists practice congregational polity, not episcopal (or even presbyterial) polity: for Baptists, Jesus Christ guides the churches and their organizations through the decisions made by all members of the body of Christ, the entire congregation, not through a bishop or pastor (or even a group of elders) alone. Constitutionally, the Convention itself, which is neither a church nor *the* Southern Baptist Church, only authorizes an *Executive Committee* to act for the Convention between annual sessions. According to the SBC's bylaws, the SBC authorizes the Executive Committee (in which the president of the SBC has membership), however, to act only in *advisory* roles toward both the agencies of the SBC and their boards of directors or trustees.

---

[1]Chapman, "It's Time to Move," 99, 100, 101.

[2]James T. Draper, Jr., *Authority: The Critical Issue for Southern Baptists* (Old Tappan NJ: Fleming H. Revell Co., 1984) 108; emphasis mine.

[3]Perhaps not coincidentally, both the commissioning and the membership of the PTSC parallel in significant ways the origin and character of the Committee on Baptist Faith and Message in 1925. Have the executive leaders of the SBC and their advisors envisioned the PTSC as the SBC's contemporary equivalent (from the standpoint of the so-called "conservative resurgence") to the original Committee on Baptist Faith and Message? As I have noted previously, in terms of origin, these two committees differ drastically from one another in numerous ways: perhaps most importantly, the SBC itself, in session, authorized the committee of 1925, whereas only the president of the SBC commissioned the PTSC in 1992.

"The Executive Committee shall not have authority to control or direct the several boards, agencies, and institutions of the Convention. This is the responsibility of trustees elected by the Convention and accountable directly to the Convention."[4] In subtle ways, Young overstepped his constitutional authority as president of the SBC.

B. Empowered by Manipulation of the SBC's Committee on Resolutions

Beyond Young's display of an episcopal authority in commissioning the PTSC, a more sinister factor in the committee's origin emerges through a brief study of the recent history of one dynamic mechanism that operates during the SBC's annual sessions. I refer to the mechanism through which the SBC considers and adopts resolutions during its meetings. I contend that, by manipulating this particular mechanism, leaders from the right wing in the SBC both have generated much of the momentum for Young's appointment of his Theological Study Committee and have produced many of the building blocks for the committee's formulations in the *RPTSC* itself.

In the SBC's annual sessions, the Committee on Resolutions both holds a central place of responsibility for the Convention and exhibits the considerable power invested in this responsibility through its influence on the course of the SBC's annual deliberations themselves. Through its operations, the Committee on Resolutions recommends the theological and ethical components of the SBC's annual public voice.[5]

Especially since 1988, the Committee on Resolutions has recommended several resolutions with which to articulate and to promote, as the voice of the entire SBC, the social-ethical-political agenda and theological credenda of extreme right-wing leaders in the SBC. I note only a few of the most prominent resolutions, and only some of those most pertinent to the formulations contained in the *RPTSC*, among those both recommended (and subsequently adopted by the SBC) and not recommended for adoption by the Committee on Resolutions.

---

[4]*Annual of the SBC* (1994): 14.

[5]"It shall be the duty of the Committee on Resolutions at each annual meeting of the Convention to prepare and submit to the Convention resolutions *which the Committee deems appropriate for adoption*, and to report on all matters submitted to it by the Convention, with or without recommendation or amendments" (*Annual of the SBC* [1994]: 15 [bylaw 22]; emphasis mine).

In 1988, Fred Wolfe, a member of the Committee on Resolutions, recommended that the SBC adopt (and the SBC did adopt) "Resolution No. 5—On the Priesthood of the Believer." This resolution intentionally minimized the Baptist understanding of the common priesthood and substantially inflated the importance of a faulty concept of pastoral authority.[6] Yet, in 1989, Mark Coppenger, chairperson of the Committee on Resolutions, recommended that the SBC take no action related to four proposed resolutions concerning the priesthood of all believers.[7] In addition, during the SBC's annual meetings in 1990 and 1991, the Committee on Resolutions refused to recommend the adoption of three similar proposed resolutions.[8]

In 1992, R. Albert Mohler, chairperson of the Committee on Resolutions, introduced a motion to adopt seven resolutions, among which three pertain especially to this study: "Resolution No. 1—On God the Father"; "Resolution No. 4—On the Autonomy of Baptist Churches and General Baptist Bodies"; and "Resolution No. 7—On Christian Witness and Voluntary Associations."[9] The SBC adopted these resolutions as well. The first of these three resolutions supplies a theological argument for the

---

[6]*Annual of the SBC* (1988): 68-69. When the Convention released the results of the vote on this resolution, however, the SBC had adopted this resolution only by 10,950 (54.75%) votes for it to 9,050 (45.25%) votes against (*Annual of the SBC* [1988]: 69, 72). In 1979, however, the SBC had adopted "Resolution No. 21—On Disavowing Political Activity in Selecting Officers," presented by Ernest White, in which the SBC resolved both to "go on record as disavowing overt political activity and organization as a method of selection of its officers" and to "urge its messengers and churches to pray *for guidance in the priesthood of the believer* in all matters of decision and to exercise distinctly Christian actions in all deliberations" (*Annual of the SBC* [1979]: 33, 58; emphasis mine). The SBC's resolution on the common priesthood from 1988 so distorted both the factual history and the SBC's historic understanding of this doctrine that several state Baptist conventions later passed resolutions as forceful correctives to that distortion of history and doctrine. For example, see "Resolution VIII Priesthood of the Believer," in *Texas Baptist Annual* (1988): 73. Also see the forceful resistance to the SBC's denigration of the common priesthood in 1988 by a Baptist deacon from a church that participates significantly in the SBC: e.g., Timothy D. Jenkins, *Southern Baptists at the Crossroads* (Canyon TX: Crucible Press, 1988) 54-56, 81-82.

[7]Hugh Wamble, Herbert Wilson, William V. Johnson, and David B. Hardesty submitted these resolutions (*Annual of the SBC* [1989]: 40, 46, 48, 58).

[8]Bill Dudley submitted the proposed resolution in 1991 (*Annual of the SBC* [1991]: 38). Both G. Hugh Wamble and Lamar Wadsworth submitted proposed resolutions on the common Christian priesthood in 1990 (*Annual of the SBC* [1990]: 43).

[9]*Annual of the SBC* (1992): 86-88, 89-90.

defense of gender-specific (masculine-only) language for God, while the latter two resolutions suggest implicit drives toward doctrinal precision and purity in local Baptist churches.

In 1993, Timothy George, member of the Committee on Resolutions, moved that the SBC adopt "Resolution No. 1—The Finality of Jesus Christ as Sole and Sufficient Savior."[10] This resolution, while purportedly addressing issues such as cultural relativism and universal salvation, effectively implies penal-substitutionary atonement as the only legitimate Christian understanding of Christ's death on the cross.

During the SBC's annual meeting in 1994, as well as moving that the SBC adopt "Resolution No. 3—On the Presidential Theological Study Committee," the Committee on Resolutions also introduced a motion to adopt "Resolution No. 5—On Southern Baptists and Roman Catholics." Although Tommy D. Lea (chairperson for the Committee on Resolutions in 1994) introduced the motion for "Resolution No. 5," Timothy George, again a member of the Committee on Resolutions, argued for adoption of the resolution.[11] This last resolution functioned as an apology for the conservative ecumenical document "Evangelicals and Catholics Together: The Christian Mission in the Third Millennium" (ECT [1994]).[12] On the one hand, this resolution clarifies the ECT's intent: to endorse cooperation in the public sphere about social and moral issues, on which both conservative Catholics and fundamentalist Evangelicals espouse similar views. On the other hand, this resolution softens the impact of the Foreign Mission Board's (FMB's) vehemently negative response to the document and, by implication, the FMB's reprimand of the two SBC-employed signatories to the document: Richard Land, executive director of the Christian Life Commission; and Larry Lewis, president of the Home Mission Board.[13]

---

[10]"Resolution No. 1—The Finality of Jesus Christ as Sole and Sufficient Savior," in *Annual of the SBC* (1993): 33, 94.

[11]*Annual of the SBC* (1994): 102, 106.

[12]"Evangelicals and Catholics Together: The Christian Mission in the Third Millennium," *First Things* 43 (May 1994): 15-22; hereafter cited as *ECT (1994)*.

[13]Apparently, however, "Resolution No. 5—On Southern Baptists and Roman Catholics" did not pacify aggressive fundamentalist critics of Land's and Lewis's actions. On 7 April 1995, Land and Lewis issued a joint statement in which, on the one hand, they removed their names from the document (*ECT [1994]*) to dispel the perception that their agencies had endorsed the document and, on the other hand, they disputed the criticisms of the document by their fundamentalist supporters ("Lewis, Land Bow to

My brief glance at this short series of selected resolutions also discloses an illuminating yet disturbing pattern in the composition of the membership of the Committee on Resolutions. From 1989 to 1994, one prominent person, whom Young either would eventually appoint, or had already appointed, to the PTSC in 1992, served each year on the Committee on Resolutions: *Mark Coppenger* in both 1989 and 1990; *R. Albert Mohler* in both 1991 and 1992; *Timothy George* in both 1993 and 1994. Two of these three persons, Coppenger and Mohler, served respectively as chairperson for the Committee on Resolutions in 1989 and 1992.[14] The year of Mohler's service as chairperson for the Committee on Resolutions, of course, ran concurrently with Timothy George's service as cochairperson for the PTSC in 1992.

Although this pattern of shared members between these two committees cannot *conclusively establish* either a direct link between the work of the two committees or even a presidential agenda behind these various committee assignments, the appearance of this pattern strongly suggests a high probability for both possibilities. The Committee on Resolutions, through the vested interests of at least three members on that committee as annually expressed in the committee's recommendations to the SBC, has worked patiently and consistently to establish the precedents in the SBC's recent history with which to support and to structure future credal proposals to the SBC, to produce the theological and political authority with which to legitimize the work of the PTSC and/or other similar politicotheological tactical mechanisms.

Criticism, Drop Signatures," *The Baptist Standard* 107 [12 April 1995]: 3-4; "SBC Leaders Defect from Accord," *The Christian Century* 112 [10 May 1995]: 505). Even evangelical Calvinists both rejected this document and reprimanded its evangelical signatories. "These evangelical men, some of whom we esteem so highly, are trifling with the very word God has revealed to us to take to the world, a message which has been utterly distorted by the Roman Church. This document will be no help to us at all, certainly not to evangelicals, nor to our Catholic friends" (Geoff Thomas, " 'Evangelicals and Catholics Together,' " *Founders Journal* 17 [Summer 1994]: 29).

[14]*Annual of the SBC* (1989): 29; *Annual of the SBC* (1990): 31; *Annual of the SBC* (1991): 30; *Annual of the SBC* (1992): 60; *Annual of the SBC* (1993): 33; *Annual of the SBC* (1994): 33.

C. Expressed with an Assumed Episcopal and Patriarchal Authority

By extending both the presidential transgressions and the manipulative use of the SBC's Committee on Resolutions, the PTSC apparently has also operated—as indicated by the language it uses in the *RPTSC*—with a pretentious, though mistaken, understanding of its own authority. Furthermore, the *RPTSC*'s language even exceeds the descriptive task with which, according to the document itself, Young supposedly commissioned the committee.

First, moving beyond both *examining* "those biblical truths" held by Baptists in the SBC and *reaffirming* three of its (or the SBC's?) "common" commitments, sliding from *reporting* to *advising or even admonishing*, the committee seems to adopt condescending and elitist ministerial attitudes when, according to the *RPTSC*, the committee "addresses several issues of contemporary urgency *in a spirit of pastoral concern.*"[15] When did the SBC call this committee as its pastor? In various portions of the *RPTSC*, the language shifts from describing to prescribing Baptist beliefs.[16] Yet, the SBC has not authorized any committee to *prescribe* standards for doctrinal consensus among Baptists participating in the SBC. Rather, Baptists of the SBC have previously only instructed the SBC to *describe* those elements (doctrinal and otherwise) already constituting the consensus that originally produced and has continued to sustain the SBC. As H. W. Tribble emphasized, since the Holy Spirit teaches "the meaning of the Scriptures" to Christians, Baptists "do not need a hierarchy, or bishop, or even the church to exercise authority over the individual in matters of belief."[17] Yet, as following chapters will demonstrate, much of the *RPTSC*'s content

---

[15]*RPTSC*, 113 (1.5).

[16]For example, "*Baptists must join* with all true Christians in affirming the substitutionary nature of Christ's atonement and reject calls—ancient and modern—for redefining Christ's reconciling work as merely subjective and illustrative" (*RPTSC*, 117 [2.3.9]; emphasis mine). I later clarify my claim with a more detailed analysis of the document's rhetoric.

[17]Tribble, "Individual Competency and Use of Creeds," 93. Tribble, a student of E. Y. Mullins and graduate with the Th.D. degree from SBTS, taught systematic theology there for many years. During the latter years of his career, Tribble served first as president of Andover Newton Theological School and then as president of Wake Forest College.

suggests a departure from congregational Baptist polity and a promotion of episcopal authority in the SBC.

Second, not only does the *RPTSC* express an episcopal authority. Such authority entirely operates with male rationality and dominance. While I will not examine every hint from the *RPTSC* of this problem in the present chapter, I note here only the most obvious display of this patriarchal bias. Young only appointed males to the PTSC. The very composition of the committee suggests the patriarchal attitudes and authority of the *RPTSC* itself. Young has minimized the perspectives of Baptist women, has ignored the significant differences between women's and men's experience, and has implicitly supported a patriarchal concept of authority by his exclusion of women from the PTSC. Additional aspects of the *RPTSC*'s patriarchal attitude will appear as my studies of the *RPTSC* progress.

II. Reductive Theory
and Use of Christian Scriptures as Authority

The agents who produced the *RPTSC*, by manipulating the SBC's institutional mechanisms, also employed the Christian Bible as a tool with which to promote the committee's extreme right-wing agenda and to accomplish its credal aims. A very specific selection of Christian scriptures helped to authorize those who have formulated and promoted the *RPTSC*. More importantly, however, the PTSC supported its own authority and task more with its *theory about* the nature of the Christian scriptures than with the *actual use of* the Christian scriptures themselves.[18]

In its first paragraph, the *RPTSC* announces the first half of the committee's dual purpose: "to examine those *biblical truths* which are most surely held among the people of God called Southern Baptists." This document also describes the Christian Bible as "the *sole authority for faith and practice among Baptists*," "the supreme standard" by which to test "all creeds, conduct, and religious opinions," including, of course, Baptist "statements of faith."[19] Because the *RPTSC* supposedly fulfills the

---

[18]Genuine Baptists in the SBC continue to expose this fundamentalist strategy. For example, "the inerrancy message is a thinly disguised version of 'you may not disagree with me.' The issue is power, control and the right to dictate who may do what and when. This is so foreign to the message of Christ that it should shock all true Christians" (Steven D. Falkenberg, "Inerrancy First?" *Western Recorder* 170 [28 May 1996]: 5).

[19]*RPTSC*, 112, 113-14 (intro.; 1.9); emphasis mine.

former aim, and by implication under the latter conviction about itself, the committee gives doctrinal prominence to its *theory of scripture and its authority*, both explicitly and implicitly in the *RPTSC*. Thus, both its *theory* of the scripture's authority and its *use* of scripture as authority require critical examination.

In the *RPTSC*'s first article, entitled "Holy Scripture," the committee formulated its own understanding of the nature and authority of the Christian scriptures. In an effort to emphasize the divine origin of the Christian Bible, the *RPTSC* construes "the divine inspiration and truthfulness of Holy Scripture" in terms that completely ignore or avoid the issues of human participation in the processes involved in writing, transmitting, and translating the Christian scriptures: "We believe that *what the Bible says, God says.*"[20] The *RPTSC* does not acknowledge in any way the human role in those processes. To the contrary, the *RPTSC* contains proof texts from the *BFM (1963)*, as well as from the writings of James M. Frost and Herschel Hobbs, to support the imbalance of the previous conviction with authorities from Baptist traditions.

Although the *RPTSC* includes a quotation from the *BFM (1963)* on the nature of Christian scriptures, the *RPTSC* formulates a dangerously

---

[20]*RPTSC*, 114 (2.1.1); emphasis mine. The italicized portion of this quotation from the *RPTSC*, as well as most of the two following sentences, appears to be slightly modified quotations from a publication by Timothy George himself. "Let us affirm clearly: *what the Bible says, God says*; what the Bible says happened, happened—every miracle, every event in every book of the Old and New Testaments is altogether true and trustworthy" (George, "Renewal of Baptist Theology," 21; emphasis mine). Of course, George takes this thought (and most of the wording) from the third section (entitled "Exposition") of "The Chicago Statement on Biblical Inerrancy," the final line of the document: "We affirm that what Scripture says, God says" ("The Chicago Statement on Biblical Inerrancy," *Journal of the Evangelical Theological Society* 21 [December 1978]: 296; hereafter cited as *CSBI*). The *RPTSC* also relies on and endorses the *CSBI*'s younger textual sister, that is, "The Chicago Statement on Biblical Hermeneutics," *Journal of the Evangelical Theological Society* 25 (December 1982): 397-401; hereafter cited as *CSBH*. As one of two cochairpersons on the PTSC, George's presence apparently dominates. George has conflated *his own perception* of (and *commitments* to) "the great theological themes which press for clarification and restatement" with those doctrines that Baptists actually affirm. According to George, "Baptists cannot avoid the issues raised by the current debate over biblical inerrancy. The question is not whether the word *inerrancy* should be used to describe the Bible, but rather to what extent one can appropriate the 'advances' of modern biblical scholarship while still remaining faithful to the historic Baptist confidence in the Bible as the totally true and authoritative Word of God" (George, "Renewal of Baptist Theology," 20, 21).

incomplete theory of scripture and its authority. Furthermore, with its only quotation from the *BFM*'s article on the Christian scriptures, the *RPTSC* even misrepresents the *BFM*'s understanding of scripture. According to the *RPTSC*, the *BFM (1963)* declares "that the Bible 'has God for it [*sic*] author, salvation for its end, and truth without any mixture of error, for its matter.' "[21] While the *RPTSC* correctly quotes a portion of the *BFM (1963)*, it misrepresents that document's concept of scripture by omitting the first statement about the Christian scriptures in the *BFM (1963)*: "The Holy Bible was *written by men* divinely inspired and is *the record* of God's revelation of Himself to man."[22] Furthermore, both the *BFM (1925)* and the "New Hampshire Confession, 1833," historical confessions on which the SBC based the *BFM (1963)*, begin their statements on the Christian scriptures with the same phrase: "The Holy Bible was *written by men* divinely inspired. . . . "[23] Even the "Chicago Statement on Biblical Inerrancy" (*CSBI*) acknowledges a modest human participation in the writing of the Christian scriptures.[24] With tactical selectivity, therefore, the PTSC has intentionally distorted the vital understanding of the Christian scriptures, as documents produced through the dynamic interactions between God and humanity in the midst of creation's history with all of its ambiguities, affirmed so boldly and honestly by the SBC through its adoption and seventy-year use of the *BFM*.[25]

---

[21]*RPTSC*, 114 (2.1.2). This sentence, of course, originally appeared in the *New Hampshire Confession (1833)*. The authors of that confession, however, may have borrowed this directly from the philosopher John Locke. The exact words appear in his correspondence with a young inquirer. "You ask me, 'what is the shortest and surest way, for a young gentleman to attain a true knowledge of the christian religion, in the full and just extent of it?' For so I understand your question; if I have mistaken in it, you must set me right. And to this I have a short and plain answer: 'Let him study the holy scripture, especially the New Testament.' Therein are contained the words of eternal life. It has God for its author; salvation for its end; and *truth, without any mixture of errour, for its matter*" (John Locke, Oates, "A Letter to the Reverend Mr. Richard King," 25 August 1703, in *The Works of John Locke*, 11th ed. [London: W. Otridge and Son, 1812] 10:306; emphasis mine).

[22]*BFM (1963)*, 269 (1.1); emphasis mine.

[23]Ibid.; "The New Hampshire Confession, 1833," in *Baptist Confessions of Faith*, rev. ed., ed. William L. Lumpkin (Valley Forge PA: Judson Press, 1959) 361 (1.1); hereafter cited as *NHC (1833)*.

[24]E.g., *CSBI*, 291 (articles VII and VIII).

[25]Cf. James Leo Garrett, Jr., "Biblical Authority according to Baptist Confessions of

Presumably, on the basis of the *RPTSC*'s own claims, this document's theory of biblical authority possesses biblical authority itself only insofar as the scriptures available to Christians authorize this particular theory. This raises at least four related questions. While the PTSC would probably answer all of the following questions affirmatively, Baptists in the SBC can legitimately and should vehemently challenge those answers.

A. Does the *RPTSC*'s Theory of Biblical Authority Originate from *Sola Scriptura*?

If the Christian Bible is the sole authority for faith and practice, does the *RPTSC*'s theory of biblical authority itself originate from that source alone? Did the PTSC really develop its theory of biblical authority only from the scriptures themselves, or *sola scriptura*, to use one of Martin Luther's emblematic phrases? Despite its frequent and vehement claims about scripture's authority, the *RPTSC* contains more quotations from extrabiblical sources, as authorities to support the *RPTSC*'s various claims, than from the scriptures themselves.[26] For example, although the *RPTSC* sometimes alludes generally to the Bible and specifically to various events or narratives attested in scripture, it cites no biblical texts to support its claims about the doctrine of God.[27]

More importantly for my present claim, however, the *RPTSC* cites only one biblical text to support its theory of biblical authority, a theory

---

Faith," *Review and Expositor* 76 (Winter 1979): 43-54; Estep, "Baptists and Authority: The Bible, Confessions, and Conscience in the Development of Baptist Identity," 600-601; idem, "Biblical Authority in Baptist Confessions of Faith, 1610–1963," 157.

[26]On the one hand, the *RPTSC* quotes only eight very short biblical texts in the following order: Jude 3; 2 Tim 3:16; 2 Cor 5:19; Eph 5:25; Phil 3:20; 1 Thess 1:8; Rev 20:14-15; and 2 Peter 3:11 (*RPTSC*, 113, 114, 116, 117, 118 [1.1; 2.1.2; 2.3.1; 2.4.1; 2.4.2; 2.5.4; 2.5.6]). On the other hand, the *RPTSC* several times refers to and quotes from the *BFM (1963)* (*RPTSC*, 112, 113, 114, 115 [1.1; 1.4; 1.5; 1.6; 2.1.2; 2.1.6]), once quotes from the work of James M. Frost (*RPTSC*, 114 [2.1.1]), once quotes from comments by Herschel Hobbs (*RPTSC*, 114 [2.1.2]), once quotes from the *Glorieta Statement* (*RPTSC*, 114 [2.1.4]), three times refers to the *RPC (1987)* (two quotations, one not acknowledged as such, and two references to the document itself: *RPTSC*, 114, 115 [2.1.2, 5, 8]), once refers to the New American Commentary (*RPTSC*, 114 [2.1.6]), twice refers to the *CSBI* (*RPTSC*, 114, 115 [2.1.6, 8]), once refers to the *CSBH* (*RPTSC*, 115 [2.1.8]), once quotes from the writings of Norvell Robertson (*RPTSC*, 115 [2.2.4]), and once quotes comments by E. Y. Mullins, as adopted by the SBC in 1923 in *SR (1923)* (*RPTSC*, 118 [2.5.3]).

[27]*RPTSC*, 115-16 (2.2.1-13).

built upon various claims about "absolute inerrancy" and "infallibility." The biblical text quoted in part by the committee in the *RPTSC* (2 Timothy 3:16), however, attests to scripture's divine inspiration without using terms such as "inerrant" or "infallible." Furthermore, that particular text declares scripture's divine inspiration, not for the sake of inciting debates among the people of God about the nature of scripture itself, but in order to emphasize the practical purposes of and to promote actual specific uses of scripture: to guide, to train, and to equip the people of God for loving service in life. Apparently, the *RPTSC* imports into its use of this single biblical text extrabiblical issues and nonbiblical authorities to encourage the furtherance of those issues. To the contrary, however, as the SBC attested in 1938, because Christ's "word and will, as revealed in the holy Scriptures, is the unchangeable and only law of his reign," "whatever is not found in the Scriptures, cannot be bound on the consciences of men"; "therefore, neither tradition nor customs, nor councils, nor expediencies can be allowed to modify or change the Word of God."[28]

Again, since the *RPTSC* suggests that this particular text affirms the "infallibility" and "inerrancy" of the Bible, when the biblical text itself only affirms scripture's divine inspiration, the *RPTSC* attempts to make normative (as well as infallible and inerrant) only one *interpretation* of this particular text. Even assuming an accurate interpretation, however adequate an interpretation may be to the text interpreted, no interpretation of a biblical text carries the authority of the biblical text itself.[29]

---

[28]"Report on Interdenominational Relations," in *Annual of the SBC* (1938): 24 (esp. point 3); hereafter cited as *RIR (1938)*.

[29]Obviously, the agenda of the extreme right-wing or fundamentalist faction in the SBC has included the following goal: to require Baptists in the SBC to adopt as *the orthodox* Baptist view only one interpretation of scripture's divine inspiration. J. Walter Carpenter, a member of the PTSC, discloses this quite plainly, especially in his definition of inerrancy: "Inerrancy is the view that 1. when all the facts are known, 2. they will demonstrate that the Bible in its autographs 3. *and correctly interpreted* 4. is entirely true 5. in all that it affirms" (Carpenter, "Biblical Hermeneutics for Amateurs," *Texas Baptist* 2 [January 1995]: 13; emphasis mine). Although Carpenter's point applies to the whole Bible, he clearly includes correct interpretation within his definition of inerrancy; therefore, *his interpretation* of the Bible's attestation to its own inspiration (presumably *the correct* interpretation) assumes canonical status as well. Carpenter goes much farther, however, by canonizing certain hermeneutical methods to support the weak definition of scripture's inspiration as inerrancy. According to Carpenter, demonstrating the validity of his definition of inerrancy depends on possessing scripture's autographs. Carpenter acknowledges the historical processes involved in the transmission and translation of the

While the PTSC quotes only one biblical text in its first article, entitled "Holy Scripture," that article also contains numerous extrabiblical quotations about scripture's inspiration. The *RPTSC* identifies the sources for several of these quotations: from James M. Frost and Herschel Hobbs, the *BFM (1963)*, the "Glorieta Statement," the "Report of the SBC Peace Committee" (*RPC [1987]*), and the New American Commentary. The *RPTSC*'s first article, however, also borrows quotations, not identified as such in or by the *RPTSC*, from (1) the "Report of the SBC Peace Committee" and (2) the writings of Timothy George (cochairperson of the PTSC).[30] Apparently, given both the single biblical text quoted and the numerous extrabiblical sources quoted or used, the *RPTSC* does not construct its theory of the Bible's authority on the basis of the Christian Bible alone.

B. Does the *RPTSC* Employ the Central Biblical Texts about Scripture's Authority in Its Own Theory of Biblical Authority?

Beyond the previous and less central question, a second and more basic question surfaces. If one were to assume, in spite of evidence to the contrary, that the *RPTSC*'s theory of biblical authority only originates from the Christian scriptures, have its formulators developed their theory from the most essential biblical texts about the scripture's nature and

---

scriptures. According to Carpenter, however, recovery of scripture's autographic texts depends on the human science of textual criticism and learning all of the facts (as if the latter is possible) (Carpenter, "Biblical Hermeneutics for Amateurs," 13). Such a position disintegrates the purportedly "high view of Scripture" and its inspiration as expressly affirmed by the *RPTSC*, since, finally, human work alone can validate the theory of divine inspiration of scripture as inerrancy. Carpenter essentially, though not as eloquently, repeats the *CSBI*'s position that "inspiration, strictly speaking, applies only to the auto-graphic text of Scripture" (*CSBI*, 291 [article X]), yet, implicitly, denies one other and utterly crucial affirmation: "that a person is not dependent for understanding of Scripture on the expertise of biblical scholars" (*CSBH*, 399-400 [article XIV]). The theory of biblical inerrancy essentially depends on its own criteria for determining the proper interpretations of the Christian scriptures, without which criteria the theory's practical significance and even its validity completely evaporate. See David S. Dockery, *Christian Scripture: An Evangelical Perspective on Inspiration, Authority and Interpretation* (Nashville: Broadman & Holman, 1995) 65, 149-76; L. Russ Bush and Tom J. Nettles, *Baptists and the Bible: The Baptist Doctrines of Biblical Inspiration and Religious Authority in Historical Perspective* (Chicago: Moody Press, 1980) 408-21.

[30]*RPTSC*, 114 (2.1.2) (from *RPC [1987]*, 234, second paragraph); and *RPTSC*, 114 (2.1.1) (from George, "Renewal of Baptist Theology," 21).

authority? To be sure, many Baptists have used the same biblical text cited in the *RPTSC* as the basis upon which to discuss the inspiration and authority of the Christian scriptures. In response to this second question, despite any apparent continuity with Baptist history at this point, the *RPTSC* has not formulated the most adequate biblical and Baptist theory of scripture's authority.

The PTSC has not grounded its theory of scripture's authority most sufficiently in scripture's own attestations to the nature and authority of scripture. Unfortunately, in the *RPTSC*, the PTSC has not employed or referred to a single biblical text from the gospels, as taught by Jesus himself, on the basis of which to formulate the *RPTSC*'s theory of scripture and its authority. Despite this omission, the *RPTSC* rightly attests to the authority of Jesus Christ in several important respects: (1) describing Jesus Christ as "the center and circumference of the Christian faith"; (2) announcing that "Scripture bears faithful and truthful witness to Jesus Christ," accurately recording "the words and deeds of Christ"; (3) proclaiming Jesus Christ as the supreme and definitive revelation of God's own self; (4) declaring God's reconciliation with the world through Christ as "the most fundamental truth of Christianity"; and (5) acknowledging Jesus Christ as "the Head, Foundation, Lawgiver, and Teacher of the church."[31]

Nonetheless, despite the stated christocentrism of the *RPTSC*, the PTSC neither perceived the centrality of nor utilized Jesus' own teaching about the scriptures and their authority as the foundation on which to establish the *RPTSC*'s theory of the Christian scriptures and their authority.[32] Even the equally problematic "Chicago Statement on Biblical Inerrancy," commended as a "biblically grounded" and sound guide "worthy of respect in setting forth a high view of Scripture" by the *RPTSC* "to all Baptist educational institutions and agencies," perceptively registers the importance of Jesus' own teaching for a theory of scripture's

---

[31]*RPTSC*, 116, 117 (2.3.1, 4; 2.4.1).

[32]From a perspective identical to the *RPTSC*'s viewpoint, David Dockery, by contrast, establishes a broader biblical foundation than the biblical basis established by the *RPTSC* (with its virtually exclusive dependence on 2 Tim 3:16) for its theory of inerrancy. Nonetheless, despite his attestation that Christ "binds and unites everything in Scripture," even Dockery fails to assess the significance of Jesus' teaching about the nature of scripture, its authority, and its proper use for Dockery's own theory of biblical authority (Dockery, "A People of the Book and the Crisis of Biblical Authority," in *Beyond the Impasse?* ed. James and Dockery, 19-22).

authority.[33] Since, according to Jesus, the scriptures themselves attest to Jesus as the Christ, certainly people who trust Jesus as the Christ for salvation would need to develop their theory of scripture on the basis of their savior's own understanding of scripture and its authority.[34] For Jesus, scripture possessed real not theoretical authority: empowerment for actual living in the world, for human life actualized as authentic love toward both God and creaturely neighbors. In this light, all other claims about the Bible's inspiration and authority should serve this foundational understanding of scripture.[35] The *RPTSC*'s theory of scripture and its authority, however, do not do that.

C. How Does the *RPTSC* Employ Specific Biblical Texts as Authorities?

The previous inquiries elicit a third question as well. In what ways has the committee derived authority from the few biblical texts that it employs in the *RPTSC*? Although further studies yield similar conclu-

---

[33]*RPTSC*, 115 (2.1.8). See *CSBI*, 292 (article XV).

[34]John 5:30-47; cf. Luke 24:13-35. Utilizing this Christological criterion similarly, R. Alan Culpepper also discloses several of these foundational weaknesses in the theory of biblical inerrancy (Culpepper, "Jesus' View of Scripture," in *Unfettered Word,* ed. James, 26-38).

[35]According to the Gospel of Matthew, Jesus used the phrase, "the Law and the Prophets," to describe the entire corpus of scriptures, even to refer to the entire revelation from God (Matt 7:12; 22:40; cf. Gal 5:14; Rom 13:8-10; 1 Cor 12:31–13:13). Although Jesus did not intend to abolish the divine revelation, he did reinterpret the scriptures on the basis of the authority he had received from his divine Creator, with variations on the following formula: "you have heard that it was said, . . . but I say to you" (Matt 5:17-48). Despite the sincere desires and conscientious efforts of the scribes and Pharisees to obey the teachings of the scriptures, Jesus required the faithfulness of his own disciples to surpass the righteousness of the scribes and Pharisees, through living perfectly like their divine Creator (Matt 5:20, 48). Furthermore, according to the Matthean evangelist, *Jesus* himself completely fulfilled the entire disclosure of divine purpose as attested by the scriptures. In this light, then, how did Jesus construe the content of the scriptures and their claims on or authority for human life? The synoptic gospels supply a clear answer to this question. Jesus summarized the entire divine gift of scripture as dependent on the double divine claim on human life: God created humans (1) to love God with their entire selves and (2) to love their neighbors as themselves (Matt 22:34-40; Mark 12:28-31; Luke 10:25-37; cf. John 13:34-35; 14:15-31; 15:1-17). Similarly, of course, Jesus also condensed "the Law and the Prophets" to the claim commonly designated as the "Golden Rule" (Matthew 7:12; cf. Luke 6:31). See Eduard Schweizer's discussions of Jesus' summary and fulfillment of God's revelation to Israel (Schweizer, *The Good News according to Matthew,* trans. David E. Green [Atlanta: John Knox Press, 1975] 103-38, 174-75).

sions about the *RPTSC*'s use of other biblical texts, to initiate a partial answer to this question, I briefly consider only one example of this document's employment of scripture: Jude 3, the text used as the programmatic biblical basis of support for the *RPTSC*.

The *RPTSC* contains a short phrase from Jude 3 as its first quotation from the Christian scriptures. "In every generation, the people of God face the decision either to reaffirm '*the faith which was once delivered unto the saints*' (Jude 3) or lapse into theological unbelief. Precisely such a challenge now confronts that people of God called Southern Baptists."[36] Both the specific use of a biblical phrase and the reference to its biblical source illustrate several of the tactics operative in the *RPTSC*'s specific references to Christian scriptures as authority for the *RPTSC*'s claims.

First, when the *RPTSC* does not contain the complete biblical thought, but includes only this short phrase while citing its biblical reference, the PTSC has used *Christian scripture as a proof text*. Citing this brief phrase from one verse in the book of Jude denies to readers all actual content and any sense of literary or historical context for this citation. This use of a biblical text intends to place the stamp of biblical authority on the committee's assessment, without providing readers of the *RPTSC* with any real biblical basis for the claim. Such employment of Christian scripture manipulates a reader's genuine confidence in the authority of scripture, with the goal of soliciting the reader's emotional approval for the *RPTSC*.

Second, by its use of the phrase from and the citation of Jude 3, the committee *both* implies that the *RPTSC* itself represents a biblically mandated reaffirmation of the Baptist understanding of Christian faith *and* authoritatively supports the *RPTSC* as such. As I have shown previously, and subsequently will further demonstrate with my brief comments on the *RPTSC*'s doctrinal reformulations, rather than reaffirming the *BFM (1963)*, the *RPTSC* actually weakens confidence in that document. As a document authorized by the scriptures themselves, the *RPTSC* supersedes the *BFM (1963)*. Thus, here the *RPTSC* clearly misleads with its reference to this biblical text.

Third, with its use of this biblical text, the committee mistakenly suggested an identity between "the faith" to which the book of Jude attests and the *statements of beliefs* contained in Baptist doctrinal

---

[36]*RPTSC*, 113 (1.1); emphasis mine.

confessions, most importantly, of course, the statement of beliefs comprising the *BFM (1963)* itself. On the basis of this implication, the PTSC implied also that the *RPTSC* represents *the most sufficient or only orthodox reaffirmation* of both "the faith" and, on that basis by implication, the *BFM (1963)* as well. This phrase from Jude 3, however, most certainly neither addresses nor promotes either of these two suggestions in the *RPTSC*'s use of this biblical text.

Fourth, with the tactical function of this biblical text, the *RPTSC* defines the alternatives as two radically opposed positions. According to the *RPTSC*, in order to reaffirm "the faith" or to maintain "doctrinal fidelity," Baptists in the SBC must *either* adhere to the *RPTSC*'s doctrinal formulations *or* "lapse into theological unbelief." The *RPTSC* does not offer a third alternative to Baptists in the SBC. As expressed by the *RPTSC*, Baptists in the SBC cannot maintain doctrinal fidelity, unless they accept doctrine as understood by the PTSC. Hence, the committee has used this biblical text to intimidate Baptists in the SBC who may hold different or alternative, yet genuine and hermeneutically legitimate, Christian interpretations of Christian doctrines. Nonetheless, Jude does not describe the two mutually exclusive alternatives announced by the *RPTSC*.

Fifth, following from the previous comments and perhaps most importantly, the PTSC quite clearly employed the phrase from Jude 3 about "the faith" as a biblical reference to doctrinal purity or precision. Yet, when studied within its context in Jude, this biblical text plainly refers to relational and volitional not cognitive or doctrinal fidelity, to human trust of and trustworthiness *toward* the divine covenant partner not to ideas *about* that partner.[37] This awareness, derived from the book of Jude itself,

---

[37]For example, Jude 5-23. Richard J. Bauckham argues for a similar interpretation of the book of Jude. "The case for classifying Jude as 'early Catholic' usually rests largely on v 3, understood to refer to a fixed body of orthodox doctrine, passed down from the apostles, which only has to be asserted against heresy. . . . But this is a misinterpretation of v 3, which refers simply to the gospel itself, not to any formalized and unalterable 'rule of faith,' and which, in opposition to deviant teaching, urges its readers to remain faithful to the gospel which they received at their conversion. This is exactly the tactic which Paul used against false teaching (Gal 1:6-9; Rom 16:17). The 'early Catholic' interpretation of v 3 is peculiarly inappropriate since the dispute between Jude and his opponents was not concerned with orthodoxy and heresy in belief, but with the relationship between the gospel and moral obligation. . . . Since the development of 'early Catholicism,' with its growing insistence on institutional order and on creedal orthodoxy,

unravels the knot tied by the PTSC's manipulative use of this particular biblical text. Rather than cognitive interests, Jude addresses practical, relational, social, and moral concerns.

The PTSC has derived authority from its use of this particular biblical text, then, through suggestion, misrepresentation, innuendo, use of scriptures as proof texts, and inadequate hermeneutics. The employment of scripture through such tactics constitutes the blatant abuse, not the proper use, of Christian scripture's authority.

D. Does the *RPTSC* Properly Emphasize Divine Authority?

The previous questions suggest a fourth line of inquiry into the *RPTSC*'s theory and use of biblical authority. Does the *RPTSC* properly emphasize God's relationship to the scriptures? On the surface, by identifying God's role in the Bible's inspiration, the *RPTSC*'s theory of biblical authority emphasizes one major aspect in the divine relationship to the scriptures. As I have indicated previously, however, by ignoring (or even minimizing) human participation in the production of scriptures (especially by using terms such as "inerrant" and "infallible"), the *RPTSC* has misrepresented both the nature of scripture and the SBC's historic convictions about scripture's historical vitality and dynamics. Most seriously, with such an emphasis, the *RPTSC* has virtually *deified* the scriptures themselves.

However perfectly the Christian scriptures attest to God's purposes and activities within creation, the Bible remains an aspect of creation and is not God. Baptists do not worship the scriptures; rather, Baptists worship the God about whom the scriptures testify. In its preamble, while reaffirming the statement in the *BFM (1925)*, that "the sole authority for

---

is usually attributed in large part to the fading of the imminent eschatology and to the struggle with heresy, it is clear that Jude does not belong to this development at all" (Bauckham, *Jude, 2 Peter*, vol. 50, Word Biblical Commentary, David A. Hubbard and Glenn W. Barker, gen. eds.; Ralph P. Martin, N.T. ed. [Waco TX: Word Books, 1983] 9, cf. 29-41). D. J. Harrington interprets Jude 3 in a way similar to the reading implied by the *RPTSC*: Harrington, "The 'Early Catholic' Writings of the New Testament," in *The Word in the World: Essays in Honor of Frederick L. Moriarty*, ed. R. J. Clifford and G. W. MacRae (Cambridge MA: Weston College Press, 1973) 107. Insofar as the PTSC has assumed the credal character of the book of Jude, then, the committee likewise implicitly (even if ignorantly) supplies grounds to support the argument for the book of Jude as a product of the developing early Catholicism. I am grateful to my former colleague, Alan Brehm, for discussing this possibility with me.

faith and practice among Baptists is the Scriptures of the Old and New Testaments," the *BFM (1963)* rightly supplements the conviction from the *BFM (1925)* with the more powerful and accurate attestation: "the sole authority for faith and practice among Baptists is Jesus Christ whose will is revealed in the Holy Scriptures." Furthermore, in its first article, the *BFM (1963)* more boldly declares the following: "The criterion by which the Bible is to be interpreted is Jesus Christ."[38] Since the Christian Bible is not God, Baptists cannot legitimately elevate it above the role with which God has commissioned it: as a library of witnesses to God's interaction with creation and to Jesus as the Christ.[39] For Baptists in the SBC, where does the ultimate authority for faith and practice reside? As H. W. Tribble responded to a similar version of this question, Baptist Christians identify as the ultimate authority for life neither the church nor even the scriptures themselves. Rather, Baptists in the SBC express a very different conviction, one which "places the Scriptures and the church under the Lordship of Christ, and places the Christian in a position of reliance upon the Scriptures and allegiance to the church."[40] Quite plainly, *ultimate* authority for faith and practice among Baptists resides in God alone: the divine Creator, Redeemer, and Sanctifier to whom the Christian scriptures attest. The Christian scriptures possess a derivative and secondary authority, an authority derived from the living God. By deifying the Bible, however, the *RPTSC* changes the understanding of Christian life *from* a trusting interactive journey with the living God *to* tedious and anxious legal transactions with a book. Rather than "people of the book," Baptists in the SBC are *the people of God with the book.*

III. Manipulative Selection and Use of Extrabiblical Authorities

Finally, through the committee's impressment of numerous extrabiblical authorities into service for the *RPTSC*, a third major problem emerges. Using manipulative tactics, through its careful selection and use of extrabiblical authorities in the *RPTSC*, the PTSC has intentionally misrepresented both the SBC's historic perspectives and broader Christian heritages, with a goal toward securing support and affirmations from

---

[38]*BFM (1963)*, 269, 270.
[39]Again, I refer to Johannine testimony (John 5:19-47).
[40]Tribble, "Individual Competency and Use of Creeds," 94-95.

Baptists in the SBC for both this document and the credal or dogmatic impulses that it expresses. Some of the extrabiblical sources cited as authorities in the *RPTSC* agree with various perspectives in this document. Some of those extrabiblical authorities, however, clearly differ in numerous ways from several positions elaborated in the *RPTSC*. In either case, nonetheless, through its use of these sources to formulate the *RPTSC*, the committee has construed all of these extrabiblical authorities as fully supportive of the perspectives expressed in the *RPTSC*. Several examples illustrate my claim.

A. Use of the *BFM (1963)*

Among Baptist extrabiblical authorities selected to legitimize the *RPTSC*'s claims, the document cites the *BFM (1963)* more often than *any other authority* (including the Christian scriptures) to which the *RPTSC* appeals.[41] As I have shown previously, while repeatedly citing the *BFM (1963)* as the primary extrabiblical authority for the *RPTSC*'s claims, the PTSC subtly undermined the *BFM (1963)*. The committee attempted to mislead those Baptists who adhere faithfully both to the *BFM (1963)* and to the distinctive Baptist perspectives that the *BFM (1963)* affirms. The committee employed phrases from and references to the *BFM (1963)* to authorize the *RPTSC*'s modifications of the *BFM*'s doctrinal positions, such as its reference to the *BFM*'s theory of scripture's divine inspiration. The committee used the *BFM (1963)*, despite the glaring differences in both attitudes and perspectives between the *RPTSC* and the *BFM (1963)*, to suggest that the *RPTSC* re-presents doctrines held and affirmed by Baptists in the SBC. As a rhetorical use of the *BFM (1963)*, the *RPTSC* misrepresents the *BFM*'s various positions by its surgically strategic use of selected quotations from and references to the *BFM (1963)*.

B. Use of Baptist Theologians

The *RPTSC* explicitly includes quotations from four Baptist theologians: James M. Frost, designated *by the committee* as "the first president of the Baptist Sunday School Board"; Herschel Hobbs, described as "the chairman of the committee who drafted" the *BFM (1963)*; Norvell Robertson, claimed by the committee as "one of our earliest Southern Baptist theologians"; and E. Y. Mullins, not explicitly identified in the *RPTSC* with any office or role.[42] Despite the apparent

---

[41]*RPTSC*, 112, 113, 114, 115 (1.1, 4, 5, 6; 2.1.2, 6).
[42]*RPTSC*, 114, 115, 118 (2.1.1; 2.1.2; 2.2.4; 2.5.3). Unfortunately, the PTSC did not

honor given to these four significant leaders in Baptist history by the *RPTSC*'s references to their work, the PTSC exhibited, through its use of their names and writings, very little actual understanding of, much less significant and genuine sensitivity to or respect for, the breadth and complexity of their theologies and biographies. I briefly elaborate only the following examples.

1. *James M. Frost.* First, the *RPTSC* contains a strong quotation from the writings of James M. Frost, in which Frost used language, such as "infallible" and "absolute inerrancy," to refer to the Christian scriptures, language in which Frost refused to tolerate even the slightest difference from his own position about the scriptures, and in which Frost emphasized "a 'thus saith the Lord' " as "the end of all controversy."[43] By the use of this text, the committee endeavored to support the *RPTSC*'s emphasis solely on the divine activity in the production of the scriptures.

Elsewhere in his own works, however, Frost honestly represented human participation in the writing of the Christian scriptures. "A man's individuality under the power and spell of inspiration was no more interfered with, than when he is the subject of regeneration, which is of the same power, and is even more radical and revolutionary in heart and mind." Frost, nonetheless, considered the Bible to be "indispensable to the church as its guide and its one source of infallible instruction," with "God for its Author." Even so, according to Frost, "it need not concern us as to *how* God inspired men," since "we serve and worship not the Bible as a book, but the God of the Bible as our light and salvation."[44]

Furthermore, as a historical note, the PTSC mistakenly identified Frost as the "first president of the Baptist Sunday School Board." As Frost himself recounted, in his first report as corresponding secretary of the SBC's then newly reconstituted Sunday School Board (BSSB), earlier in its history, the SBC had organized a first Sunday School Board,

---

supply bibliographic information for these sources. The *RPTSC* contains a minor inaccuracy in its quotation from Robertson's book. According to the book itself, Robertson writes as follows: "The word of God is truth. What He says of Himself is truth, though it may not entirely coincide with our views of what He ought to be; but He alone knows Himself" (Norvell Robertson, *Church-Members' Hand-Book of Theology* [Memphis TN: Southern Baptist Publication Society, 1874] 9).

[43]*RPTSC*, 114 (2.1.1). See this text in Frost, "Introduction," *Baptist Why and Why Not*, 12.

[44]James M. Frost, *Our Church Life: Serving God on God's Plan* (Nashville: BSSB, 1909) 53, 57, 58, 65.

naming Basil Manly, Jr. as its first president and John A. Broadus as its first corresponding secretary.[45] The SBC organized its first Sunday School Board in 1863 and, due largely to financial reasons, abolished it in 1873. In his own study of the SBC's Sunday School Board, Frost narrated his own role in the new board's history. Although Frost became the first *acting* corresponding secretary of the new BSSB, following the SBC's adjournment in 1891, the BSSB had initially elected Lansing Burrows to that office. When Burrows declined the invitation, however, the BSSB elected Frost, who accepted the position on 1 July 1891.[46] The BSSB had also elected W. R. L. Smith, then pastor of First Baptist Church in Nashville, as its first president.[47] Only after Frost resigned as corresponding secretary to become the new pastor of Nashville's First Baptist Church, did the BSSB elect him as president of the BSSB. Frost held office as the second president of the newly reconstituted BSSB for three years (1893–1895), until he resigned from First Baptist Church in Nashville to assume again the role as the BSSB's corresponding secretary in 1896, a position in which he continued until his death on 30 October 1917.[48] Baptist historians have carefully documented and narrated this history.[49] This rather glaring, though perhaps insignificant, historical mistake in the *RPTSC* may help as well to explain the committee's inaccurate and reductive theological construals or revisions of Baptist doctrines. The PTSC's concern for the Baptist heritage extended only as far as Baptist traditions advanced the committee's own agenda and credenda.

2. *E. Y. Mullins and Herschel H. Hobbs.* Second, while the works of both Norvell Robertson and James M. Frost seem to espouse perspectives very similar to those expressed in the *RPTSC*, the larger works of both Mullins (president of the SBC in the years 1921, 1922, and 1923) and Hobbs (also president of the SBC, in the years 1962 and 1963), both chairpersons of the respective SBC-appointed committees that produced

---

[45]James M. Frost, "Appendix C. First Annual Report of the Sunday School Board," in *Proceedings of the SBC* (1892): LVI.

[46]James M. Frost, *The Sunday School Board, Southern Baptist Convention: Its History and Work* (Nashville: BSSB, 1914) 21, 24. Also see Frost, "Appendix C. First Annual Report of the Sunday School Board," LV-LVI.

[47]*Proceedings of the SBC* (1892).

[48]Frost, *Sunday School Board*, 24, 92, 94; *Proceedings of the SBC* (1893); *Proceedings of the SBC* (1894); *Proceedings of the SBC* (1895); *Proceedings of the SBC* (1896); *Annual of the SBC* (1917): 359-69, 470.

[49]E.g., Baker, *SBC and Its People*, 231-32, 244-46, 270-76.

the original (1924–1925) and revised (1962–1963) versions of the *BFM*, differ adamantly from the spirit and intentions, as well as from much of the content, expressed both by individual members of the PTSC and in the *RPTSC* itself.[50] I have previously supplied examples for my claims from the works and service of both Hobbs and Mullins. Apparently, the PTSC employed comments by and the names of both Mullins and Hobbs as devices with which to engender among Baptists in the SBC an *emotional sense* of return to familiar doctrines and, on this basis, to motivate Baptists in the SBC *to volunteer their political support* for the *RPTSC*'s adoption by the SBC.

Recent events corroborate this assessment, especially in reference to the attitudes of the most powerful members of the PTSC toward the influence of Mullins in the SBC's history. For example, in Mohler's keynote address during the thirteenth annual Founder's Conference (an annual assembly of Calvinists in the SBC), Mohler described Mullins as "the pivotal figure" who "paved the way for true liberalism to enter the SBC."[51] Given Mohler's objectionable evaluation of Mullins, only one

---

[50]The PTSC used the following comment by Mullins to lend authority to the committee's perspective on Jesus' parousia: "As E. Y. Mullins put it, 'He will come again in person, the same Jesus who ascended from the Mount of Olives' " (*RPTSC*, 118 [2.5.3]). Mullins made this comment in his presidential address, entitled "Present Dangers and Duties," to the SBC in 1923: specifically, this comment appeared in the section of his address entitled "Science and Religion" (*Annual of the SBC* [1923]: 20). The Committee on Baptist Faith and Message in 1925, noting the importance of clarifying the SBC's perspective on the relation between religion and science, appended this portion of Mullins's presidential address from 1923 to its own report, which included the *BFM* (1925). In a brief preface to the statement, however, the Committee on Baptist Faith and Message significantly qualified the status of its own use of that statement: "matters of science have no proper place in a religious confession of faith" (*Annual of the SBC* [1925]: 75-76). The PTSC took the quotation on scripture by Hobbs from comments made by him during the meeting of the SBC in 1981. During that meeting, Hobbs introduced a motion with two major components: (1) to reaffirm the Christian scriptures as "without error"; and (2) to reaffirm the *BFM (1963)*. Later, when the Convention considered his motion, in his clarification of the motion, Hobbs made the comment later used by the PTSC. After Hobbs had spoken and the SBC had adopted his motion with an "enthusiastic standing vote," Adrian Rogers asked the SBC to request that the recording secretary "place in the record the preceding remarks by Hobbs" (*Annual of the SBC* [1981]: 35, 45). In 1987, the SBC's Peace Committee also quoted this comment by Hobbs in its report: *RPC (1987)*, 234. I will discuss the content of the comment by Hobbs when I examine the *RPTSC*'s doctrinal statement about scripture in chapter 5 of this study.

[51]Keith Hinson, "Calvinists Seek Return to 'Orthodoxy' of SBC Founders," *Western*

explanation can account for the *RPTSC*'s minor use of comments by Mullins: the committee's efforts, by whatever means necessary (even appearing to value the comments of a theologian, when the committee actually did not value the thought of Mullins), to capture the allegiance of all Baptists in the SBC for the *RPTSC*, by a rhetorical invocation of the highly respected name and reputation of E. Y. Mullins.

Although the PTSC used comments by these persons as authorities, this committee did not consistently handle them honestly, fairly, or accurately. Does the SBC's heritage truly have authority for both this committee and the leadership of the SBC that this committee represents, or does that heritage only function as a tool to enable those persons to realize another component in their distorted right-wing agenda and credenda? Given the committee's loose, careless, and manipulative employment of these sources in the *RPTSC*, the latter alternative seems more accurately to characterize the attitude expressed therein.

C. Use of Documents Produced in the SBC's Recent History

The PTSC appealed to other theories of scripture's authority, as formulated in recent historical documents (produced during the SBC's most recent controversies and adopted by the SBC), to support or to legitimize the *RPTSC*'s theory about the authority of Christian scriptures.[52] As the *RPTSC*'s most extensive and significant appeal to and use of Baptist extrabiblical documentary authorities, I will examine only the PTSC's unusual tactical use of the report from the Southern Baptist Convention's Peace Committee (*RPC [1987]*).

Referring to the content of the *RPC* as the most prominent example of "recent developments in Southern Baptist life" that "have underscored the importance of a renewed commitment to biblical authority in every area of our denominational life," the PTSC formulated the following statement.

Recorder 169 (8 August 1995): 2.

[52]The PTSC refers to the very specific content in three of the SBC's documents and publications: the *Glorieta Statement*, produced by the six presidents of the SBC's seminaries in 1986; the *RPC (1987)*, which also includes the *Glorieta Statement*; and the New American Commentary, authorized by the BSSB in 1987, with the first volumes published in 1991 (*RPC [1987]*, 234-35, 237; "Editors' Preface," in *Mark*, by James A. Brooks, vol. 23, New American Commentary, ed. David S. Dockery [Nashville: Broadman Press, 1991] 8).

In 1987, the SBC Peace Committee called upon Southern Baptist institutions to recruit faculty and staff who clearly reflect the dominant convictions and beliefs of Southern Baptists concerning the factual character and historicity of the Bible in such matters as (1) the direct creation of humankind including Adam and Eve as real persons; (2) the actual authorship of biblical writings as attributed by Scripture itself; (3) the supernatural character of the biblical miracles which occurred as factual events in space and time; (4) the historical accuracy of biblical narratives which occurred precisely as the text of Scripture indicates.[53]

This statement from the *RPTSC* contains the substance, but not in every case the exact wording, of a text from the *RPC (1987)*. Nevertheless, at least three major problematic characteristics of the *RPTSC*'s statement deserve critical scrutiny.

1. *Collapsing Distinctions in the RPC (1987)*. First, the PTSC has construed a text from the *RPC*'s second section, entitled "Findings," as the substance of the *RPC*'s recommendation to the SBC in 1987. Although the SBC adopted the *RPC (1987)* without amendment (despite three excellent motions to amend the document), the Peace Committee clearly distinguished from one another the several components included in its report to the Convention: (1) "Sources of the Controversy"; (2) "Findings"; (3) "Conclusions"; (4) "Recommendations"; and (5) "Acknowledgements."[54] The Peace Committee clearly perceived the functional differences between the descriptive or informative status of its *findings* and the advisory role of its *recommendations*. Among its "recommendations" to the SBC, the Peace Committee did not include the statement quoted by the PTSC in the *RPTSC*. Instead, the quotation included in the *RPTSC* from the *RPC (1987)* occurs only in the *RPC*'s second section, "Findings."[55] As a portion of the fifth *recommendation* in its report to the SBC, the Peace Committee produced only the following statement with which to describe the Christian scriptures.

The Bible is a book of redemption, not a book of science, psychology, sociology, or economics. But, where the Bible speaks, the Bible speaks truth in all realms of reality and to all fields of knowledge. The Bible, when properly interpreted, is authoritative to all of life.

---

[53]*RPTSC*, 114 (2.1.5).
[54]*Annual of the SBC* (1987): 56-57; *RPC (1987)*, 232-42.
[55]*RPC (1987)*, 237.

In the *RPC (1987)*, the Peace Committee followed the previous description with the following plea.

> We *call upon* Southern Baptist institutions *to recognize* the great number of Southern Baptists who believe this interpretation of Article I of the Baptist Faith and Message Statement of 1963, and, in the future, *to build* their professional staffs and faculties *from those* who clearly reflect such dominant convictions and beliefs held by Southern Baptists at large.[56]

With both its selection and its framing of the statement from the *RPC*'s "Findings," the PTSC has intentionally misrepresented the function of that particular text in the *RPC (1987)*. Despite the descriptive and advisory functions of the Peace Committee's statements, as perceived and advanced by the Peace Committee itself, the *RPTSC* suggestively endows its own paraphrase from the *RPC*'s "Findings" with a prescriptive authority that the *RPC (1987)* never claimed for its own statement. Through his service on the Peace Committee, Herschel Hobbs (although others contributed significantly as well) successfully helped to prevent the inclusion in the *RPC*'s "Recommendations" of the more specific description of scripture restricted finally to the *RPC*'s "Findings."[57] Unfortunately, even as a senior participant on the PTSC, even though

---

[56]*RPC (1987)*, 241; emphasis mine. The *RPC (1987)* also contains the basic substance, almost word for word, of this plea in its "Findings," with two differences, a minor one and a major one, from its plea in its "Recommendations." First, as the minor difference, the "Findings" substitute the phrase, "this interpretation of our confessional statement," for the phrase, "this interpretation of Article I of the Baptist Faith and Message Statement of 1963." Second, as the major difference, the "Findings" include the more detailed interpretation of the *BFM*'s first article that the PTSC has included in its document, rather than the more general description in the "Recommendations" (*RPC [1987]*, 237).

[57]According to Hobbs's autobiographical reflections on the circumstances related to this particular portion of the *RPC 1987*, when one committee member (not named by Hobbs: was it Adrian Rogers?) suggested that the Peace Committee move this text from "Findings" to "Recommendations," Hobbs vehemently resisted the move. "I said, 'No, sir! I voted to put it in "Findings." If you move it to "Recommendations" I want to be recorded as voting against both motions.' " Furthermore, Hobbs clearly perceived the credal weight that the statement would have gained as one of the *RPC*'s "Recommendations." "Another person said, 'If it is true, then we should have the guts [his word] to move it over to "Recommendations." ' I replied, 'It isn't a matter of "guts" but of brains. Where it is, it is "Findings." If we move it to "Recommendations," it becomes creadal.' The matter was dropped" (Hobbs, *My Faith and Message: An Autobiography* [Nashville: Broadman & Holman, 1993] 262, 263).

himself keenly aware of the Peace Committee's perception of the *RPC*'s distinction between findings and recommendations, and despite his instrumentality in the successful implementation of that distinction in the *RPC (1987)*, Hobbs did not prevent the PTSC's misrepresentation of the *RPC (1987)* on this particular point.

The PTSC clearly perceived this distinction. One of the most influential participants among this committee's majority, R. Albert Mohler, Jr., certainly knew about this distinction. Concerning the Peace Committee's work in addressing the issue of "regulative theological parameters," Mohler wrote the following: "Conservatives, frustrated that their quest for some enforceable doctrinal specificity had been met with great resistance, were successful in detailing four very specific theological determinations, but were unsuccessful in their effort to move the issues from the 'findings' section to 'recommendations.' "[58] From his forefathers in the SBC's so-called "conservative resurgence," Mohler obviously received instruction about the strategic significance of this issue. That which the Peace Committee had failed to accomplish, Mohler and the majority of participants on the PTSC indirectly and deceptively attempted to realize with an intentional misconstrual of the *RPC (1987)* in the *RPTSC*. Although Mohler rightly observed, prior to the *RPTSC*'s adoption by the SBC, that "theological issues are often reduced to the level of individual preference or whimsy, with *little regard* for the most basic issues of truth and falsehood,"[59] his participation on the PTSC apparently contributed nothing to promote such *regard* with respect to the committee's use of the *RPC (1987)*.

2. *Ignoring Incongruities in the RPC (1987)*. Second, the PTSC's misleading use of the *RPC (1987)* intentionally ignores the incongruities in the *RPC (1987)* itself. By ignoring these incongruities, even regarding the example herein under consideration (the question concerning the most characteristic theory about the nature and authority of Christian scriptures held among Baptists in the SBC), the *RPTSC* implies a strength of consistency in the *RPC (1987)* that simply does not exist. A comparison of the various texts from the *RPC (1987)* clarifies my claim.

---

[58]R. Albert Mohler, Jr., "A Call for Baptist Evangelicals and Evangelical Baptists: Communities of Faith and a Common Quest for Identity," in *Southern Baptists and American Evangelicals,* ed. Dockery, 233.

[59]R. Albert Mohler, Jr., "A Response," in *Beyond the Impasse?* ed. James and Dockery, 245; emphasis mine.

In the section of the *RPC (1987)* entitled "Sources of the Controversy," the Peace Committee stated that "we have found *significant theological diversity* within our seminaries, *reflective of the diversity within our wider constituency.*" Following that paragraph, the Peace Committee cited, as examples of the diversity, two very different perspectives on the very issues listed in the text taken by the *RPTSC* from the *RPC*'s "Findings." Yet, later in the *RPC*'s "Findings" (in the very paragraph from which the PTSC took the text that it paraphrased in the *RPTSC*), the Peace Committee narrowed its portrayal of that diversity: "We as a Peace Committee, have found that *most Southern Baptists* see 'truth without any mixture of error for its matter,' as meaning. . . . " Following this statement, then, appears the text that supplies the substance of the *RPTSC*'s interpretation of the *RPC (1987)* on this issue. Further, when the Peace Committee finally introduced its "Recommendations" in the *RPC (1987)*, it had reduced the length of its statement about the scriptures, and had even modified its perception about the extent of the view on scripture described by its "Findings," as the interpretation held by "most Southern Baptists": "We call upon Southern Baptist institutions to recognize *the great number of Southern Baptists* who believe . . . " the interpretation of scripture's nature and authority contained in the *RPC*'s fifth recommendation.[60] Clearly, the *RPC (1987)* oscillates from identifying the reality of "significant diversity" as reflected "within our wider constituency," to describing the beliefs of "most Southern Baptists," and finally back again to recommending a recognition of "the great number of Southern Baptists." By its selectivity, the PTSC masked the inconsistency of the *RPC (1987)* itself and ignored the problems produced by the *RPTSC*'s unqualified affirmation of the

---

[60]*RPC (1987)*, 234, 237, 241; emphasis mine. Oddly enough, however, the PTSC did not explicitly appeal to "Resolution No. 16—On Doctrinal Integrity," adopted without amendment by the SBC in 1980, which resolved to "exhort the trustees of seminaries and other institutions affiliated with or supported by the Southern Baptist Convention to faithfully discharge their responsibility to carefully preserve the *doctrinal integrity* of our institutions and to assure that seminaries and other institutions receiving our support *only employ, and continue the employment of,* faculty members and professional staff who believe in the divine inspiration of the whole Bible, infallibility of the original manuscripts, and that the Bible is truth without any error" (*Annual of the SBC* [1980]: 50-51; emphasis mine).

RPC (1987) as one of the "biblically grounded and *sound guides worthy of respect* in setting forth a high view of Scripture."[61]

3. *Narrowly Interpreting the RPC (1987)*. Third, according to the *RPTSC*, the Peace Committee "called upon Southern Baptist institutions *to recruit* faculty and staff *who clearly reflect* the dominant convictions and beliefs of Southern Baptists concerning the factual character and historicity of the Bible . . . " in terms of the more narrow interpretation of the first article of the *BFM (1963)*. The *RPC (1987)*, however, in both its "Findings" and its "Recommendations" expresses this "call" in a significantly different way: "we call upon Southern Baptist institutions . . . *to build* their professional staffs and faculties *from those* who clearly reflect such dominant convictions and beliefs held by Southern Baptists at large."[62] In the text from the *RPC (1987)*, the preposition "from" indicates two possible interpretations of the Peace Committee's "call" for the SBC's institutions to build (or to employ) institutional staffs and faculties: either (1) to employ persons *also from* that group of Baptists who interpret the scriptures in the terms outlined by the *RPC*'s "Findings," as an effort *also to include* the perspective most acceptable to Baptists of the so-called "conservative resurgence"; or (2) to employ persons *only from* that group of Baptists who interpret the scriptures in the terms outlined by the *RPC*'s "Findings," as an effort *to exclude* all perspectives differing from the viewpoint most acceptable to Baptists of the so-called "conservative resurgence."

The PTSC, with its omission of the preposition "from," obviously has interpreted this statement from the *RPC (1987)* in its second sense, its most restrictive and most exclusive sense. Even though many members of the Peace Committee also obviously interpret the *RPC*'s "call" in the way that the *RPTSC* paraphrased it, the *RPTSC*, however implicitly, leads Baptists falsely to conclude that the *RPTSC*'s paraphrase accurately represents the only possibility for understanding the *RPC*'s position—the most exclusive interpretation. In its use of the *RPC (1987)*, then, the PTSC has committed the logical fallacy of accent, because the *RPTSC* communicates, as the *RPC*'s meaning, a meaning not necessarily intended by the *RPC (1987)* itself. Furthermore, this example illustrates that the PTSC also used the fallacious technique of slanting, in order to suggest

---

[61]*RPTSC*, 115 (2.1.8); emphasis mine.
[62]*RPTSC*, 114 (2.1.5); *RPC (1987)*, 237, 241; emphasis mine.

a distorted perspective on the actual context both in which the Peace Committee produced the *RPC (1987)* and to which that committee addressed the *RPC (1987)*.

While the *RPC (1987)* and other recent Baptist documents reflect similar theological positions, like the *RPTSC*, they also reduce and minimize the historic diversity among Baptists in the SBC on Christian doctrines. Additionally, the sociopolitical processes contributing especially to the production of those documents both suggest explanations for such theologically and socially reductive documents and, therefore, render dubious the appropriateness of their subsequent adoption by the SBC. Hence, insofar as the credibility of those recent Baptist historical documents dissolves under careful study, despite their linguistic and theological superiority to the *RPTSC*, so too their capacity to legitimize or to authorize the *RPTSC* in any genuine sense dissolves.

D. Use of Non-Baptist and Neo-Evangelical Credal Statements

In the *RPTSC*, the committee has also appealed to non-Baptist, neo-Evangelical credal statements: the "Chicago Statement on Biblical Inerrancy" (1978; *CSBI*) and the "Chicago Statement on Biblical Hermeneutics" (1982; *CSBH*). The *RPTSC* does not contain explicit quotations from these documents, but does contain its own formulations of the same content. The two Chicago statements, though not explicitly quoted in the *RPTSC*, supply the elaborate theoretical substance underlying the *RPTSC*'s theory of biblical authority. These documents definitely assume credal shape and status, as their consistent affirmations and denials demonstrate. The two Chicago statements do not express their convictions on the basis of the SBC's historic perspectives. Yet, according to the *RPTSC*, the editors of the BSSB's New American Commentary adopted the *CSBI* "as a guideline more fully expressing for writers the intent of Article I of *The Baptist Faith and Message*." A careful comparison of the *BFM (1963)* and the two Chicago statements, however, obviously invalidates such claims, especially in light of the *BFM*'s emphatic refusal of all creeds, credalism, and credal functions for itself. Finally, the *RPTSC* even commends both the *CSBI* and *CSBH* to the SBC as standards for the proper and more elaborate form of the theory of biblical authority promoted by the *RPTSC* itself.[63] In light of

---

[63]*RPTSC*, 114-15 (2.1.6-7, 8). Walter Carpenter enthusiastically endorses the two

the *BFM*'s abhorrence for creeds, the *RPTSC*'s commendation of two obviously credal, non-Baptist documents (as "more fully expressing" "the intent" of the *BFM*'s first article) clearly and completely misrepresents the *BFM*'s intention and content in all of its articles of belief, especially in the *BFM*'s article on scripture.

Analogue. Episode Three

Following Israel's reconnaissance of the promised land, as the Hebrews fearfully resisted the commencement of struggle to realize Yahweh's purposes for them, they aimed to protect themselves by returning to the security of Egyptian bondage. As the first step in their efforts to return to Egypt, the Hebrews sought to appoint a leader for themselves in this self-serving enterprise. When Joshua and Caleb (the only two persons from the team that reconnoitered the promised land who brought a positive report about Israel's possibilities in the approaching struggle) tried both to reassure the people about Yahweh's ability to protect them in the accomplishment of this task and to persuade them not to betray Yahweh with distrust, the people prepared to stone these two true witnesses. Ironically, the only two persons from that exploratory team who spoke against the people's efforts to return to Egypt, the very voices that the people intended to silence with death, would eventually lead the people into the promised land. Furthermore, those from the reconnaissance group who spoke with consensus, as the majority of authorities or experts, against entering the struggle for the promised land (and, thereby, encouraged the people to return to Egypt) would die from a plague before the people moved from that very place. The people both trusted in false authorities and mistreated the genuine authorities among them. Therefore, by acting on that basis, the people acted unfaithfully toward God.[64]

Similarly, the *RPTSC* originates from the fears of various leaders in the SBC. The *RPTSC* itself represents a distorted and inaccurate assessment both of the situation in the SBC and of the contemporary obstacles that the SBC faces. Yet, the PTSC submits this document as an authoritative and accurate description of the SBC's circumstances. Furthermore,

---

Chicago statements. Even Carpenter perceives, and approvingly describes, the credal purpose of those documents (Carpenter, "Biblical Hermeneutics for Amateurs," 13).
    [64]Num 13:25-33; 14:1-10, 26-38.

not only does this document even utilize various voices within and actions of the SBC itself as the authorities to support the return to a credal security or protection, but it also enlists the Christian scriptures themselves to aid in the realization of this purpose.

As the previous discussions demonstrate, one cannot easily answer the basic question addressed by this chapter: Who authorized and produced the *RPTSC*? One president of the SBC authorized the committee that produced this document. Yet, through the SBC's Committee on Resolutions, a strategy had operated for several years with which the fundamentalist leadership of the SBC had constructed various credal components that the SBC subsequently adopted. Hence, building with many of those components, the PTSC formulated the *RPTSC* to recommend to the SBC for adoption. In order to convince the SBC to adopt this credal statement, the committee carefully manipulated and misrepresented a variety of authorities, ranging from the Christian scriptures, through Baptist theological writings and documents already adopted by the SBC since 1979, to non-Baptist credal documents. At its basis, however, even though the authorizing agent appears finally to be the SBC or the assembly itself, actually agents operating through a noncongregational theory of the SBC's polity authorized and produced the *RPTSC*.

Chapter 4

Deceptive Rhetoric

Now Korah the son of Izhar, the son of Kohath, the son of Levi, with Dathan and Abiram, the sons of Eliab, and On the son of Peleth, sons of Reuben, took action, and they rose up before Moses, together with some of the sons of Israel, two hundred and fifty leaders of the congregation, chosen in the assembly, men of renown. And they assembled together against Moses and Aaron, and said to them, "You have gone far enough, for all the congregation are holy, every one of them, and the Lord is in their midst; so why do you exalt yourselves above the assembly of the Lord?"

(Numbers 16:1-3 NASB)

These are grumblers, finding fault, following after their own lusts; they speak arrogantly, flattering people for the sake of gaining an advantage.

(Jude 16 NASB)

. . . mockers, following after their own ungodly lusts. (Jude 18 NASB)

Introduction

This chapter answers a fourth question: What strategies operate within the *RPTSC* to accomplish that document's goal? Generally, the *RPTSC* employs a deceptive and manipulative rhetoric as the basic strategy to realize the document's purpose. In various ways, this fourth problematic feature of the *RPTSC* has emerged repeatedly throughout the previous line of inquiry. The *RPTSC*, when not linguistically effusive or even slovenly, most broadly utilizes deceptive rhetorical strategies with which to elicit support for itself as well as for the leadership that both envisioned and produced the document. More specifically, the *RPTSC* camouflages its credal intentions with anticredal linguistic and theological resources from the SBC's anticredal heritage itself. Because the *RPTSC* contains such numerous deceptive rhetorical devices, I have selected only a few examples with which to substantiate this claim: consistent obscuration of the *RPTSC*'s genuine voice; shifting understanding of the document's literary genre; tendency to swing from the indicative mood toward the imperative mood; evaporation of distinctive Baptist perspectives; and demonization of diversity.

I. Obscuration of the *RPTSC*'s Genuine Voice

The PTSC intentionally obscured the distinction between the voice articulated through the *RPTSC* (the committee's voice as the voice of the SBC's fanatical, right-wing, politicotheological power-block) and the numerous voices of all other Baptists in the SBC. Although other examples appear as well, I examine only the most obvious linguistic device used by the committee to obscure this distinction. More often than not, by trading on *equivocations in its uses of first-person-plural pronouns* in the *RPTSC*, the committee intentionally obscured the distinction between its own voice and the voices of all Baptists in the SBC.

Equivocation, one of the logical fallacies of ambiguity, occurs in the discourse of a given communication, when a word used more than once within that communication oscillates between two or more meanings, whatever the sphere of linguistic meaning: either the discourse's sense, reference, or significance.[1] The *sense* of discourse concerns the relations between the signs, grammar, and sentences immanent to the discourse itself. Discourse's *referential* meaning describes the object or that about which the discourse speaks or that to which the language refers. Finally, discourse's meaning as *significance* designates the discourse's meaning for the audience, hearer, or partner in dialogue.

When using first-person-plural pronouns (such as, "we" or "our") in the *RPTSC*, the PTSC did not equivocate through its grammatical usage of these words: the committee properly communicated the *sense* of the first-person-plural pronouns used in the *RPTSC*. Nonetheless, as the committee used these pronouns, the committee equivocated on the referential meaning of these pronouns. Through its equivocation in the referentiality of its first-person-plural pronouns, the *RPTSC* also generates equivocation in the significance of these pronouns.

I approach this issue more concretely by responding to a very simple line of investigation. With whose voice did the PTSC speak when using

---

[1]See Gerald Runkle, *Good Thinking: An Introduction to Logic*, 2nd ed. (New York: Holt, Rinehart, and Winston, 1981) 26-28. I follow Paul Ricoeur's use of a distinction between three forms of linguistic meaning: Ricoeur, *Interpretation Theory: Discourse and the Surplus of Meaning* (Fort Worth: TCU Press, 1976) 19-23; idem, "Naming God," trans. David Pellauer, *Union Seminary Quarterly Review* 34 (Summer 1979): 217; cf. David Tracy, *Blessed Rage for Order: The New Pluralism in Theology* (New York: Seabury Press, 1975) 75-78.

these pronouns in the *RPTSC*? When the *RPTSC* contains the pronouns "we" and "our," to which group or groups of people do these pronouns refer? The PTSC often used first-person-plural pronouns equivocally, sometimes referring to Baptists in the SBC and sometimes referring to the members of the committee themselves. Numerous examples from the *RPTSC* corroborate this claim.

Even in its introductory paragraph, the *RPTSC* equivocates when it declares the committee's twofold purpose: "The purpose of *this study group* was to examine those biblical truths which are most surely held among the people of God called Southern Baptists and, on this basis, to reaffirm *our* common commitment. . . . "[2] The *RPTSC* begins by referring to the purpose of the PTSC as the purpose of "this study group": first, "to examine" and, second, "to reaffirm." When the *RPTSC* describes the second half of its purpose, however, the committee has used the pronoun "our." This pronoun suggests that, as the second half of the committee's purpose, the committee should "reaffirm" *the committee's* own commitment. Instead, the pronoun "our" in this first example seems to refer to Baptists in the SBC. If the study group's purpose was to reaffirm the commitments of Baptists in the SBC, then, the committee's purpose has certainly transgressed Baptist limits. In terms of the SBC's historic perspectives, no person or group of persons can make theological and doctrinal commitments for other persons or groups of people.

The *RPTSC* repeatedly employs the pronoun "we," speaking as, and therefore referring to, "the people of God called Southern Baptists." Often in the same paragraphs, without clarification, the *RPTSC* will then use the pronoun "we" to refer collectively to the members of the PTSC. As another example, speaking as the voice of Baptists in the SBC, the *RPTSC* declares the following: "As *we* approach the 150th anniversary of the founding of the Southern Baptist Convention, *we* are presented with unprecedented opportunities for missionary outreach and evangelistic witness at home and abroad." Later, in the fifth sentence of the same paragraph, the *RPTSC* changes its voice to the collective voice of the committee itself and back again to the voice of Baptists in the SBC: "*We* pray that *our* effort will lead to healing and reconciliation throughout the Southern Baptist Convention and, God willing, to a renewed commitment to *our* founding purpose of 'eliciting, combining, and directing the ener-

---

[2]*RPTSC*, 112 (intro.); emphasis mine.

gies of the whole denomination in one sacred effort, for the propagation of the gospel.' " Numerous examples of such equivocations occur throughout the *RPTSC*.[3]

Given the academic credentials of the members of the PTSC, why does the *RPTSC* contain such first-person-plural, pronominal, referential equivocations? By no means has the PTSC simply produced a sloppy document in its pronominal referential oscillations. To the contrary, the committee has used this deceptive rhetorical device to shift the significance of the *RPTSC* for Baptists who read this document. Rather than openly admitting that this document principally describes the committee's own doctrinal commitments, irrespective of any investigation into the beliefs of most Baptists in the SBC, the committee has used first-person-plural pronouns to suggest to readers that the committee speaks with the voice of the readers, as the collective voice of all or most Baptists in the SBC. Thus, this equivocation subtly leads Baptist readers of this document to identify with or to assent to, without consciously considering the real and often unstated issues, the doctrinal commitments espoused by the PTSC itself.

II. Shifting Understanding of the *RPTSC*'s Literary Genre

A. Report?

Similarly, the PTSC has inscribed an oscillating understanding of this document's function, or literary genre, into the *RPTSC* itself. Because this committee quite consciously understood its own *official* status, as evidenced by its designation as a "study group," it used language in the *RPTSC* to reinforce this particular image of itself for the *RPTSC*'s readers. Most obviously, the committee refers to the document that it has submitted as a "report."[4] In most cases, reports principally exhibit descriptive characteristics. According to the *RPTSC* itself, Young commissioned the PTSC as a "study group" with a twofold task: (1) "to examine those biblical truths which are most surely held among" Baptists in the SBC; and (2) "to reaffirm our common commitment to Jesus Christ, the Holy Scriptures, and the evangelical heritage of the Christian church." This purpose

---

[3]*RPTSC*, 113 (1.2); emphasis mine. Similar problems appear in the following examples: *RPTSC* 113, 114, 115, 116, 117, 118 (1.5; 1.7-9; 2.1.1; 2.1.3; 2.1.7-8; 2.2.2; 2.2.4-13; 2.3.6; 2.4.1; 2.4.3-7; 2.5.1; 2.5.4; 2.5.6).

[4]E.g., see *RPTSC*, 112, 113, 114 (intro.; 1.5; 1.10).

clearly endows the PTSC with a descriptive function: *examination* of those biblical truths *already held* and *reaffirmation* of those commitments *already affirmed* in the *BFM (1963)* by Baptists of the SBC.

B. Confession?

Despite the committee's descriptive mask in the *RPTSC*, however, this document's various linguistic and literary strategies suggest that the committee has intended to do far more with this document than to report, to examine, to describe, or even to reaffirm. Although the committee claims not to publish the *RPTSC* "as a new confession of faith," "declines to recommend any new confession," and declines to recommend even a "revision" of the *BFM (1963)*,[5] the committee has constructed the heart of the *RPTSC* around five sections or articles: "Article One" on "Holy Scripture"; "Article Two" on "The Doctrine of God"; "Article Three" on "The Person and Work of Christ"; "Article Four" on "The Church"; and "Article Five" on "Last Things."[6] Obviously, the committee's use of the noun "article" to describe these central sections of the *RPTSC* iterates the designations employed historically in confessions, most importantly, even in the *BFM (1963)*. Even though such designations could simply represent wooden repetitions of the *BFM*'s form and content, closer scrutiny of the committee's actual doctrinal formulations in each of these articles discloses subtle modifications of the *BFM*'s doctrinal statements. This suggests, then, that the committee has *reformulated rather than reaffirmed* the *BFM*'s doctrinal concerns for all Baptists in the SBC. I will examine several examples to support this claim in part two of this book.

C. Creed?

Despite the PTSC's disclaimers (that the *RPTSC* does not represent a new confession of faith; that the committee declines to recommend any new confession of faith; that the committee declines to recommend even a revision of the *BFM [1963]*), observable emphases in the *RPTSC* yield significant evidence to the contrary. Consider the emphases to which I refer.

First, the *RPTSC* builds a case for *producing or writing new confessional statements*. In the *RPTSC*'s preamble (or "Part I") to its doctrinal

---

[5]*RPTSC*, 112, 113 (intro.; 1.4).
[6]*RPTSC*, 114, 115, 116, 117, 118.

formulations, the committee affirmed its own minimal construal of "the historic Baptist conception of the nature and function of confessional statements" for Baptists in the SBC. In this section of the *RPTSC*, the committee rightly identified the production of confessions as a Baptist exercise of religious liberty: "Any group of Baptists, large or small, has the inherent right to draw up for itself and to publish to the world a confession of faith whenever it wishes."[7] Despite the truth of the committee's affirmation, if the *RPTSC* itself does not represent a new confession of faith, if the *RPTSC* does not even recommend a new confession of faith, why did the PTSC develop its own concept of confessions and their functions among Baptists? If this emphasis functions subtly to legitimize the production of the *RPTSC* itself, then, it appears that, the committee's disclaimer to the contrary, the PTSC has submitted the *RPTSC* to the SBC either as a new confession of faith or, at least, as the first major step toward a future call for some sort of new doctrinal statement.

Second, the *RPTSC* develops its case further, by invoking the historic Baptist freedom to *revise existing Baptist confessions*. Since Baptists attest to the Christian Bible as "the sole authority for faith and practice" and, therefore, accept it as "the supreme standard by which all creeds, conduct, and religious opinions should be tried," the committee repeated another component in the SBC's historic posture about confessions: "As in the past so in the future, Baptists should hold themselves *free to revise* their statements of faith in the light of an unchanging Holy Scripture."[8] Again, the PTSC rightly affirms this historic Baptist prerogative. Nonetheless, if the committee did not intend to revise (or even to recommend the revision of) the *BFM (1963)* as it claims, and if the *RPTSC* does not represent a revision of the *BFM (1963)*, then why did the committee reintroduce this historic perspective at all? This emphasis, to reiterate, appears indirectly to legitimize the *RPTSC* either as a revision of the *BFM (1963)* or as an official step toward some future call for revising the *BFM*. Efforts to revise doctrinal statements signal the most serious shift among Baptists in the SBC. Despite Mullins's later participation on the committees that produced the *PCU (1914)*, the *FASB (1920)*, and the *BFM (1925)*, as he previously had reminded Baptists in 1908, because Baptists consider all persons to be directly responsible to Christ, trust the scriptures sufficiently to disclose Christ's will, authorize no proceedings

---

[7]*RPTSC*, 113 (1.7).
[8]*RPTSC*, 114-15 (1.9); emphasis mine.

for heresy trials, and consider the local church competent to address such matters without external interference, Baptists *"have never lost any time or energy over the question of creed revision."*[9] Unfortunately, with the *RPTSC*'s appearance, as many Baptists in the SBC still need to understand, the statement by Mullins accurately reflects neither the motivating dynamics among nor the goals of the present leadership in the SBC.

Third, the *RPTSC* significantly *alters the historic Baptist perspective on the function of confessions* within Baptist Christian communities. In its preamble or "Part I," the *RPTSC* claims that *"voluntary, conscientious adherence to an explicit doctrinal standard"* does not violate historic Baptist principles. Later, in its "Article Four" on ecclesiology, the committee employed the historic Baptist commitment to the autonomy of local churches in order to intensify this emphasis: to support and even to justify its aims with the *RPTSC*. "Under the Lordship of Christ, such a body is free *to order its own internal life* without interference from any external group. This same freedom applies to all general Baptist bodies, such as associations and state and national conventions." Finally, the committee extended this emphasis still further, with its claim that "the doctrine of religious liberty, far from implying doctrinal laxity or unconcern, guarantees the ability of every congregation and general Baptist body *to determine* (on the basis of the Word of God) its own *doctrinal and disciplinary parameters*."[10] The appearance of disciplinary

---

[9]E. Y. Mullins, *The Axioms of Religion: A New Interpretation of the Baptist Faith* (Philadelphia: Judson Press, 1908) 146; emphasis mine. See "Report of Commission on Efficiency to the Southern Baptist Convention," the third section, "Pronouncement on Christian Union and Denominational Efficiency," in *Annual of the SBC* (1914): 69, 75-76; hereafter cited as *PCU (1914)*. See the debates even occasioned among Baptists by the SBC's adoption of the *PCU (1914)*, a document that some Baptists in the SBC defended as necessary and others perceived as a dangerous precedent (J. B. Gambrell, "Notes on the Great Convention," *Baptist Standard* [21 May 1914]: 1; "The Discussions at Nashville," *Baptist World* [28 May 1914]: 16; "Good as Far as It Goes," *Religious Herald* [28 May 1914]: 10; R. H. Pitt, "A Word of Supererogation," *Religious Herald* [11 June 1914]: 10; M. Ashby Jones, "Committee on Efficiency and Doctrinal Statement," *Baptist World* [2 July 1914]: 10-11; "The Convention and the Doctrinal Deliverance," *Baptist World* [2 July 1914]: 16). As James E. Carter notes, "this initiated a discussion which arrayed the *Baptist Standard* and *The Baptist World* [both of which approved the *PCU (1914)*] against the *Religious Herald* [which rejected the *PCU (1914)*]" (Carter, "Southern Baptists' First Confession of Faith," 38).

[10]*RPTSC*, 114, 117, 118 (1.10; 2.4.5; 2.4.6); emphasis mine. A similar tactic appears even in the *RPC (1987)*: "Although the Baptist Faith and Message Statement of 1963 is

concerns in connection with doctrinal formulations signals the committee's alteration of the SBC's historic conception of a confession's function: the shift from descriptive to prescriptive discourse, the shift from nonbinding statements of faith to coercive and enforceable formulas.

To justify this suspicion, as I have previously noted, according to J. Walter Carpenter, a member of the PTSC, "a *confession with teeth in it* in the most practical way acts as a creed."[11] For Carpenter, the *RPTSC* probably represents the "teeth" of the *BFM (1963)*, thereby establishing the possibility for the credal use of the *BFM (1963)*.

Had the PTSC openly identified the *RPTSC* (1) as a *new* confession, (2) as the *recommendation* for a new confession, or even (3) as the *revision* of the SBC's existing confession (*BFM [1963]*), then the committee would have mitigated at least to a small degree the dubiousness of both its labors and the *RPTSC*. Such an honest approach to a still volatile subject would have eliminated the deeper suspicion among Baptists in the SBC: the suspicion that this committee has sought to establish the basis for both the production of a creed among Baptists and its application to the entire SBC—agencies, commissions, and possibly even participating churches (at such time, of course, as the leadership has also emplaced the political mechanisms to make such application possible).

These three major emphases in the *RPTSC* encourage me to submit four counterclaims to the committee's disclaimers. First, the *RPTSC* actually does represent a revision of the *BFM (1963)*. Second, as a revision of the *BFM (1963)*, the *RPTSC* communicates something very different from the *BFM (1963)* and, thereby, qualifies itself as a new confession of faith. Third, since the *RPTSC* commends itself to Baptists in the SBC, the committee has actually recommended a new confession of faith to the SBC with this document. Finally, as such a different confession, the *RPTSC* operates on the basis of a significantly different conception of the confession as a genre: confession as creed. Russell H. Dilday, Jr. similarly observed, as long ago as 1982, that "to make a statement of faith a criterion of orthodoxy or a rule for doctrinal purity would indeed

---

a statement of basic belief, it is *not a creed*. Baptists are non-credal, in that they do not impose a man-made interpretation of Scripture on others. Baptists, *however*, declare their commitment to commonly held interpretations which then become *parameters for cooperation*" (*RPC [1987]*, 240; emphasis mine).

[11]Carpenter, "Are Southern Baptists Evangelicals?" 6; emphasis mine.

be creedalism and violate the historic Baptist tradition of freedom." He also inscribed a prophetic warning through his concern: "there are grave indications that a creed might become a substitute for the Bible—the only creed which Baptists consider authoritative."[12] Although numerous documents have appeared in the SBC since 1982 to deepen such suspicions and concerns, the *RPTSC* more than all other such documents combined has begun explicitly to fulfill Dilday's prophetic insight.

III. Dangerous Mood-Swing

Not only the previous clues about the *RPTSC*'s genre, but also the verbs used by the committee illuminate the credal tendencies within this document. Although the *RPTSC* does not contain verbs explicitly expressing the imperative mood, many of its verbs in the indicative mood, and certainly many of its verbs in the subjunctive mood, convey an imperatival sense or posture.

A. Indicative Mood

Obviously, one can grammatically classify as descriptive much of the language used by the PTSC in the *RPTSC*. The *RPTSC* contains numerous verbs in the indicative mood, some of which actually *describe*, however reductively, historic Baptist commitments or beliefs.[13] Nonetheless, some of the document's indicative verbs carry credal associations and, thereby, communicate an implicit imperative mood or operate with an imperatival attitude.

Similar to both "The Chicago Statement on Biblical Inerrancy" and "The Chicago Statement on Biblical Hermeneutics," with their "Articles of Affirmation and Denial," the *RPTSC* contains its own, while less systematic and even somewhat sporadic, series of affirmations and rejections or denials. A few of numerous examples illustrate this rhetorical pattern: "Baptists *affirm* that God is one, and that he has revealed Himself as a Trinity of three eternally coexistent persons, Father, Son, and Holy Spirit"; "and we *reject* any attempt to minimize or compromise this aspect of God's self-disclosure."[14] As descriptive statements,

---

[12]Russell H. Dilday, Jr., *The Doctrine of Biblical Authority* (Nashville: Convention Press, 1982) 28.

[13]For example, "Southern Baptists *have affirmed* repeatedly and decisively . . . " and "*The Baptist Faith and Message affirms* . . . " (*RPTSC*, 114 [2.1.1; 2.1.2]); or, "Baptists *confess*" or even "we *believe*" (*RPTSC*, 114, 118 [2.1.1; 2.5.1]); emphasis mine.

[14]*RPTSC*, 115-16 (2.2.8); emphasis mine. Compare this with other similar examples

the committee has formulated relatively accurate, even though consistently insufficient, accounts of that which many Baptists in the SBC affirm
or reject. Insofar as the committee has written highly specific dogmatic
formulations, with polemical postures toward alternative perspectives, and
as if all Baptists (or even all true Christians or all faithful Baptists)
espouse these perspectives, however, then the *RPTSC* begins to express
or to suggest normative claims. Occurrences of credal discourse, such as
the terms "affirm" and "reject," indicate the committee's aim to establish
its formulations as norms to which all Baptists (at least, those Baptists
employed by the SBC's institutions) must conform. The committee's use
of other phrases even more substantially supports this intuition: for
example, referring to alternative interpretations of the "biblical doctrine
of God" that allegedly reject biblical teachings, the *RPTSC* declares that
"Southern Baptists *cannot* follow this course."[15] By using the verb
"cannot," does the *RPTSC* mean that Baptists in the SBC do not have the
capacity or that they do not have permission to follow that course?

B. Subjunctive Mood

More problematically still, the committee has intensified its communication of a normative sense through the *RPTSC*'s frequent use of
verbs in the subjunctive mood. I refer specifically to the *RPTSC*'s use of
the modal auxiliary verb "must" to communicate necessity, requirement,
and obligation regarding very specific interpretations of various basic
Christian doctrines. Speaking for all Baptists in the SBC, the committee
formulated a variety of requirements: "we *must bear* a faithful gospel
witness . . . ; we *must be* the salt and light in a society which has lost its
moral compass"; "we *must* also *pass on* to the rising generation the
fundamentals of the Christian faith and a vital sense of our Baptist
heritage"; "as a fellowship of evangelical Christians we *must recommit*
ourselves to the eternal truths concerning God . . . "; "we *must submit*
ourselves to the knowledge God has imparted concerning Himself and
His divine nature"; "Baptists *must reject* any effort to deny the true
nature and identity of Jesus Christ or to minimize or to redefine His
redemptive work"; "Baptists *must reject* any and all forms of universalism and bear faithful witness to salvation in Jesus Christ, and in Him

---

in this document (*RPTSC*, 113, 114, 115, 116, 117, 118 [1.5; 1.6; 1.7; 1.8; 1.10; 2.2.2,
3, 6-11; 2.4.5; 2.5.2]).
    [15]*RPTSC*, 115 (2.2.4); emphasis mine.

alone"; "Baptists *must join* with all true Christians in affirming the substitutionary nature of Christ's atonement and *reject* calls—ancient and modern—for redefining Christ's reconciling work as merely subjective and illustrative."[16]

Despite the partial truths expressed through these skeletal summaries of divine claims on human life and on Baptists in particular, this language signals the more obvious swing from descriptive statements to prescriptive criteria, criteria with which someone or some group of people can decide whether to retain or to exclude anyone from the larger Baptist community. While most Baptists in the SBC undoubtedly adhere to various interpretations of the doctrines addressed in the previous examples from the *RPTSC*, nothing requires any Baptist Christian to adhere to the implied perspectives of the previous examples in order to remain either Christian or Baptist. Yet, the *RPTSC*'s language implies something to the contrary.

C. Imperative Mood?

Admittedly, the *RPTSC* does not grammatically address its readers with verbs in the imperative mood; this document does not explicitly command adherence or obedience to its doctrinal perspectives. Nonetheless, this document does employ verbs, in both indicative and subjunctive moods, that extend beyond mere description of the status quo toward prescriptive standards supposedly contrary to fact or different than prevailing commitments in the present situation. In its oscillations, then, the *RPTSC* swings dangerously from the genre of report to the genre of creed, from a descriptive document to a prescriptive code, from invitation to command, from indicative to imperative, even from grace to law. Such language announces the adoption and promotion of a credal spirit, the shift from the more ontological posture historically characterizing confessions in the SBC to the most deontological attitude and demeanor of some credal Christian communities.[17]

---

[16]*RPTSC*, 113, 115, 117 (1.2; 2.2.4; 2.2.5; 2.3.9); emphasis mine.

[17]In the language of Paul Tillich, this represents the flight from *theonomy* into *heteronomy* (Tillich, *Systematic Theology* [Chicago: University of Chicago Press, 1951] 1:83-86, 147-50; idem, *Systematic Theology* [Chicago: University of Chicago Press, 1963] 3:249-75). Elsewhere, Mohler more accurately labels the mood of his efforts as "imperative": e.g., "Imperatives for a Renewed Theological Framework" (Mohler, "Has Theology a Future in the SBC?" 98-110).

IV. Subtle Evaporation of Distinctive Baptist Perspectives with the Conjunctive Adverb "However"

The PTSC used a fourth rhetorical technique with which to manipulate the sentiments of the *RPTSC*'s readers and to enlist their support for the credenda proposed in that document: through substantial qualifications, the committee evaporated or significantly compromised central distinctive Baptist doctrinal perspectives. This technique appears forcefully in some of the *RPTSC*'s characteristic linguistic patterns. I will examine, nevertheless, only one of the most important among those patterns: a pattern repeating itself in several places, a pattern in which the use of the word "however," as a conjunctive adverb, plays a vital role. While the word "however" can mean either "to whatever degree" or "in whatever manner," the *RPTSC* uses this word several times to communicate its sense as "in spite of that."

A. Evaporating the Foundational Baptist Emphasis on Individual Human Competency

This pattern appears initially in "Part I" of the *RPTSC* and concerns the *BFM (1963)* itself. According to the *RPTSC*, the committee "affirms and honors" the *BFM (1963)* as adopted by the SBC and even "declines to recommend any new confession or revision of that statement." Yet, the *RPTSC*'s next paragraph qualifies the committee's allegiance to the *BFM (1963)*: "*However*, each generation of Southern Baptists faces unique and pressing challenges to faithfulness which demand attention and test the integrity of our conviction." In this latter paragraph, the committee claims, with the *RPTSC*, "to illuminate" or "to clarify" "articles" of the *BFM (1963)* (or "our historic Baptist commitment" to the *RPTSC*'s version of five doctrinal topics or "emphases") "consistent with its [the *BFM*'s] intention and content."[18]

As I have noted previously, this stance implicitly communicates distrust of the *BFM (1963)*, and raises doubts about its original value and adequacy, despite the *RPTSC*'s explicit praise of the *BFM (1963)* to the contrary. Thus, even though the *RPTSC* records an acknowledgment of the *BFM*'s status as "the normative expression of Southern Baptist belief," the *RPTSC* begins to undermine this allegedly normative

---

[18]*RPTSC*, 113 (1.5).

foundation by looking beyond the text itself for the real meaning and intention of the *BFM*'s content.[19] Later, the *RPTSC* commits the intentional fallacy, as the *RPTSC* discovers the *BFM*'s meaning (rather than through the stylistic clues to be found in the text itself) in its origins: such as, either in the psychology of its authors (see, for example, the *RPTSC*'s appeal to the extraconfessional exegesis of the *BFM (1963)* by Herschel Hobbs) or in the past sociotheological situations in the SBC that produced the Committee on the Baptist Faith and Message.[20] As W. K. Wimsatt and Monroe C. Beardsley have perceived, with regard to texts, "critical inquiries are not settled by consulting the oracle."[21]

Furthermore, and most importantly, the use of the conjunctive adverb to weaken confidence in the *BFM (1963)* indicates the *RPTSC*'s refusal of one significant aspect of the *BFM*'s normative status: the creative ambiguity inscribed into that document at its inception. The inscription of this creative ambiguity into the SBC's most recent statement of faith conserves a fundamental and historic Baptist conviction: *the utterly central role of the human individual in Christian experience.*

While every major confessional statement adopted by the SBC explicitly or implicitly expresses this conviction in numerous ways, none more forcefully declares this belief than the SBC's "Statement of Principles" (*SP*) from 1945 and 1946. According to the *SP*, Baptists in the SBC hold as their "distinctive belief" the "Doctrine of Man in the personal order of life, that is, what God says concerning man." The *SP* follows this attestation with a fourfold summary of a Baptist theological anthropology: (1) the eternal value placed by God on the human individual as the "focal unit" for God's interactions with humanity; (2) the human endowment, from the divine Creator, with "competence" to deal properly with both God and other humans; (3) the "rights and privileges" given by God to all humans and not to be violated by any form of coercion; and (4) the human's "responsibility" to realize fully its divinely given and proper possibilities. Most surprisingly, according to the *SP*, "*out of this doctrine of the individual grows the Baptist conviction concerning all aspects of religious experience and life*": (1) the "religious experience of regeneration and conversion" as the "prerequisite to church membership"; (2) the local church as a "voluntary" communion

---

[19]*RPTSC*, 113 (1.4).

[20]See, e.g., the *RPTSC*'s article on the Christian scriptures (*RPTSC*, 114-15 [2.1.2, 6]).

[21]Wimsatt and Beardsley, "Intentional Fallacy," 1022.

of "baptized believers," led by Christ, composed of "equally free and responsible participants," operating with democratic polity, and choosing its own "divinely called ministry" through "the guidance of the Holy Spirit"; (3) "the New Testament," "the one and only authority in faith and practice," as "the divinely inspired record and interpretation of the supreme revelation of God through Jesus Christ as Redeemer, Saviour, and Lord"; (4) the "separation of church and state"; and (5) "religious liberty" for all humans.[22]

In summary, through its use of the conjunctive adverb "however," the *RPTSC* weakens confidence in the *BFM (1963)* on the basis of the creative ambiguity therein inscribed. By implicitly devaluing the creative ambiguity of all previous Baptist confessions in general, the *RPTSC* weakens or evaporates the distinctive Baptist emphasis on the competency and responsibility of individual humans, both as writers and as readers or interpreters of those confessional statements. From the weakening of this foundational Baptist conviction, arises the *RPTSC*'s weakening of other distinctive Baptist beliefs.

B. Evaporating the Baptist Affirmation of Religious Liberty

Through another appearance of the previous pattern, the *RPTSC* evaporates the historic Baptist affirmation of religious liberty. Initially, the *RPTSC* favorably restates in familiar language the SBC's historic commitment: "Since God alone is Lord of the conscience, the temporal realm has no authority to coerce religious commitments." Employing the word "however" as a conjunctive adverb, the *RPTSC* follows the previous declaration with a serious qualification, as the committee's conclusion to

---

[22]"Statement of Principles," in *Annual of the SBC* (1946): 38-39 (emphasis mine); also in *Annual of the SBC* (1945): 59-60; hereafter cited as *SP* followed by either *(1945)* or *(1946)*. J. B. Lawrence, a member of the Committee on Statement of Principles, later developing the principles of the confessional statement itself, considered "the primary and fundamental belief of Southern Baptists in the integrity of the individual as a person before God and man" to be "fundamental in Baptist denominational cooperation": Lawrence, *Cooperating Southern Baptists* (Atlanta: Home Mission Board, SBC, 1949) 12. As an additional illustration of the human individual's importance for Baptists in the SBC, following its annual meeting in 1936, the SBC held a joint meeting with the Northern Baptist Convention, specifically on the topic of the human individual's competency before God as the historic Baptist principle ("The Soul's Competency in Religion under God: The Historic Baptist Principle for Today" [St. Louis: 18-19 May 1936] in *Annual of the SBC* [1936]: 108-15).

its interpretation of this particular Baptist conviction: "*However*," or in spite of that, "the doctrine of religious liberty, far from implying doctrinal laxity or unconcern, guarantees the ability of every congregation and general Baptist body to determine (on the basis of the Word of God) its own doctrinal and disciplinary parameters."[23]

Obviously, as it stands, the *RPTSC*'s qualification avoids direct disputation. Nevertheless, why has the committee emphatically qualified religious liberty in this particular way? Seemingly, with this qualification, the PTSC attempted to restrict the scope of *individual* human religious liberty. Although affirming the religious freedom of all humans outside the Christian community as well as affirming the religious freedom of Christian communities as social groups, from the standpoint of the individual Christian, the *RPTSC* disendows the individual Christian of full and basic religious liberty in the Christian community itself and requires the individual Christian to submit to the corporate will or personality, to find therein alone the range of one's freedom. From the standpoint of the Christian community as a whole, then, the *RPTSC* redoubles the strength of the corporate will or personality, the social group, by emphasizing the community's freedom to determine its own parameters with which to regulate and to control the individual human liberties included within the community itself.[24]

C. Evaporating the Baptist Belief in the Priesthood of All Christians

With an additional use of the word "however" as a conjunctive adverb, the *RPTSC* evaporates a more specific form of religious liberty: Christian freedom, a freedom conceived by Baptists as the central feature in the priesthood of all Christians. Again, the *RPTSC* repeats the same pattern. First, "every Christian has direct access to God through Jesus Christ, our great High Priest, the sole mediator between God and human beings." Second, the *RPTSC* utilizes its conjunctive adverb to qualify its own reaffirmation of this Baptist conviction. "*However*," or in spite of that, "the priesthood of all believers is exercised within a committed community of fellow believers-priests [*sic*] who share a like precious

---

[23]*RPTSC*, 117-18 (2.4.6); emphasis mine.

[24]Elsewhere concerning related issues, I have described this as Baptist infidelity to "internal ecclesial religious liberty," or "freedom of conscience and expression within the Baptist communities of faith themselves": Jeff B. Pool, "Baptist Infidelity to the Principle of Religious Liberty," *Perspectives in Religious Studies* 17 (Spring 1990): 20.

faith. The priesthood of all believers should not be reduced to *modern individualism* nor used as a cover for *theological relativism*. It is a spiritual standing which leads to ministry, service, and a coherent witness in the world for which Christ died."[25]

Again, few Baptists would disagree with the *RPTSC*'s qualification in itself. The context of the qualification (within its article on ecclesiology), however, suggests that the committee aims to weaken the Baptist emphasis on the common Christian priesthood rather than to emphasize its value.[26] Similar to the way with which it qualifies the broader commitment to religious liberty, the *RPTSC* also qualifies the more specific Baptist belief in the priesthood of all Christians. Rather than affirming that the church derives its character (both as a voluntary association of Christians and as an autonomous local group) from the priesthood of all Christians, like the majority of the SBC's previous confessional statements,[27] the *RPTSC* construes this distinctive Baptist emphasis as subservient to, determined by, and controlled through the Christian community. The *RPTSC* thus reverses the relationship, as historically conceived by Baptists, between the priesthood of all Christians and the Christian community as a whole.

D. Evaporating Baptist Commitment to the Autonomy of Local Churches

In a fourth use of the word "however" as a conjunctive adverb, the *RPTSC* also evaporates the distinctive Baptist emphasis on the autonomy of local churches. This veiled qualification by the PTSC occurs in "Part I" of the *RPTSC*, within the context of the committee's affirmation of

---

[25]*RPTSC*, 117 (2.4.4); emphasis mine. Apparently, Timothy George has slightly altered a portion from one of his own articles to include here in the *RPTSC*: "let no one trivialize" the meaning of the common Christian priesthood "by equating it with *modern individualism* or *theological minimalism*" (George, "Priesthood of All Believers and the Quest for Theological Integrity," 294; idem, "Priesthood of All Believers," 93).

[26]Of course, others have used this tactic and have produced similar and related positions, in reference to the priesthood of all believers: most explicitly, during the meeting of the SBC in 1988 ("Resolution No. 5—On the Priesthood of the Believer," in *Annual of the SBC* [1988]: 68-69).

[27]See the following examples: *PCU (1914)*, 69, 75-76 (esp. point 4); *FASB (1920)*, 8, 11, 13, 14 (esp. §5, "A Church: Its Form, Functions and Limitations," and §7, "The Rights and Responsibilities of the Individual Soul" and "Baptists and Christian Union"); *RIR (1938)*, 24-25 (esp. points 4 and 5); and *SP (1946)*, 38-39.

"the historic Baptist conception of the nature and function of confessional statements in our religious and denominational life," most specifically, in the *RPTSC*'s affirmation of a confession "as a statement of our religious convictions." Once again, the *RPTSC* repeats the same pattern. First, "we *affirm* the priesthood of all believers and the autonomy of each local congregation." Second, "*however*, doctrinal minimalism and theological revision, left unchecked, compromises [*sic*] a commitment to the gospel itself. Being Baptist means faith as well as freedom. Christian liberty should not become a license for the masking of unbelief."[28]

Although the *RPTSC* targets the doctrine of the common priesthood in this qualification as well as the doctrine of the local congregation's autonomy, because I have previously noted the committee's evaporation of the Baptist belief in the common Christian priesthood and because I will return again to that doctrine in connection with a later discussion of the *RPTSC*'s more extensive ecclesiological comments, I will focus here only on the second target of the *RPTSC*'s qualification: *local ecclesial autonomy*. Nonetheless, as I have previously shown, for Baptists in the SBC, the doctrine of the shared Christian priesthood establishes the basis for the doctrine of the local church's autonomy. On the basis of this factor, the *RPTSC*'s qualification of local ecclesial autonomy applies as well to the doctrine of the shared Christian priesthood.

The *RPTSC*'s comments seem to operate on the basis of an implicit fear: perhaps the committee itself perceived the autonomy of local Baptist churches as a threat to the authority of Baptist doctrinal commitments and statements, such as the *BFM (1963)*, as formulations or documents produced by larger Christian communities. This may explain the *RPTSC*'s contrast between "faith" and "freedom." Of course, numerous problems attend such a contrast, among which two problems tend to predominate. First, one cannot properly describe *Christian faith* primarily (and certainly not only) as a cognitive experience; Christian faith initially arises (and also sustains all dimensions, including the cognitive, of human life from this basis) as faithfulness, as a restored relationship of trust and trustworthiness between the divine and the human.[29] Second,

---

[28]*RPTSC*, 113 (1.8); emphasis mine.

[29]Elsewhere, of course, Mohler weakly (even if "eagerly" by his own claim) acknowledges my claim about the nature of Christian faith. "Jesus Christ and our knowledge of Him are not in any sense coextensive. But one cannot have a relation with Him without knowledge, and that knowledge represents incipient doctrine. . . . If one does

one cannot properly construe *Christian freedom* as void of cognitive content. Hence, the *RPTSC*'s contrast falsely reduces faith to cognitive specificity or knowledge and freedom to volitional tasks or actions.

Here, I specifically refer to the *RPTSC*'s understanding of *the local church's*, or communal rather than individual, expressions of faith and freedom. The *RPTSC* seems to imply the necessity for some mechanism, presumably in the form of a doctrinal or confessional statement, with which to prevent "compromises" of "a commitment to the gospel itself": compromises such as "doctrinal minimalism" and "theological revision." Of course, any such mechanism applied from an external perspective would radically violate local ecclesial autonomy. If the *RPTSC* actually proposes what the document seems to imply, then the *RPTSC* certainly weakens one of the SBC's foundational and historic commitments. Obviously, the autonomy of local churches holds numerous risks; even faithful freedom always entails risks. Does not the *RPTSC*'s implied confessional reduction or limitation of local ecclesial autonomy, however, realize exactly the two major compromises that the *RPTSC* identifies as major threats to Christian fidelity: (1) *theological revision* of this historic and biblical Baptist doctrine; and (2) retention of only a narrow version of this doctrine or *doctrinal minimalism*?

In the cases that I have examined, the *RPTSC*'s uses of the word "however" as a conjunctive adverb function to evaporate, or to qualify reductively, at least the four areas in Baptist beliefs as identified. Characteristically, however, the *RPTSC* does not specify carefully or openly its suggestive reductionism. As a consequence, my own assessments of the *RPTSC*'s evaporation of distinctive Baptist beliefs, through its use of "however" as a conjunctive adverb, cannot conclusively claim a definitive status and possess only the accuracy of probabilities—probabilities based on solid evidence, nonetheless.

---

not believe the truths concerning the Christ as revealed in Holy Scripture, one *cannot* have any authentic relationship with Him. Doctrine, we eagerly concede, does not in itself save" (Mohler, "Response," 249). Other Baptists also more accurately describe faith as trust or faithfulness. See Charles H. Talbert, "The Bible's Truth is Relational," in *Unfettered Word*, ed. James, 39-46; G. Thomas Halbrooks, "Trust Is Foundational to the Baptist Spirit," in *Defining Baptist Convictions: Guidelines for the Twenty-First Century*, ed. Charles W. Deweese (Franklin TN: Providence House Publishers, 1996) 95-102.

V. Demonization and Excommunication of Theological Diversity

As a fifth rhetorical technique, the *RPTSC* uses language with which to demonize and to excommunicate all perspectives at variance either with the viewpoints espoused in this document itself or with those held by the committee members who composed it. More specifically, the *RPTSC* demonizes and, therefore, excommunicates the perspectives of those Baptists in the SBC with whom it vehemently disagrees, construing those persons as the roots of the SBC's most urgent problems.

A. Describing the Problem as Baptist Doctrinal Infidelity

This tendency initially and most often appears in the *RPTSC*'s estimation and characterization of the serious circumstances in which the SBC finds itself. Generally, expressions of this rhetorical technique intensify gradually from the beginning to the end of the *RPTSC*. First, the *RPTSC* announces and characterizes these dire straits as "the *pressing need* for a *positive* biblical witness on basic Christian beliefs," suggesting (but not explicitly stating) the lack of such a positive witness among and by Baptists themselves. Second, the *RPTSC* describes this "pressing need" as "*unique and pressing challenges to faithfulness*" or *tests* for "*the integrity of our conviction*," implying, much more seriously, that certain Baptists in the SBC may have engineered these very challenges to or tests of Baptist fidelity. Third, the *RPTSC* characterizes this problem more intensely as "*several issues of contemporary urgency*," identified within the same paragraph as the SBC's need for the clarification of five central doctrines: on the Christian scriptures, God, Christ, the church, and last things. By the end of that paragraph, the *RPTSC* fanatically intensifies the assessment, describing the problem as the *assailment* of these doctrines "in various ways, by *subtle compromise*, *blatant concession*, and *malign negligence*." Of course, if the *RPTSC* does refer to specific Baptists in the SBC as those responsible for this "pressing need for a positive biblical witness on basic Christian beliefs," for these "unique and pressing challenges to faithfulness," or for these "several issues of contemporary urgency," then this latter statement begins to demonize those responsible parties as the assailants of those doctrines cherished by Baptists in the SBC. For the *RPTSC*, at least by implication, such assailants do not *really* belong to the Baptist community, do not *really* identify with the SBC, are not *really* Baptists in any sense, or

perhaps do not even *actually* belong to Christ: such as, according to the
RPTSC, either (1) those who utilize the doctrine of the shared priesthood
"as a *cover for theological relativism*," or (2) those who claim "Christian
liberty" as a "*license* for the *masking of unbelief*," unbelievers who
pretend to be Christian. More destructively, the *RPTSC* implies that those
with different theological perspectives in the SBC not only assail the
"great theological tenets" held by Baptists in the SBC, but also both have
produced "the denominational conflict of recent years" and presently
represent "efforts to weaken" the "denomination and its cooperative
ministries." Whatever the extent of this alleged unbelief, although this
assailment of basic Christian beliefs occurs through "subtle compromise,"
"blatant concession," and "malign negligence," the *RPTSC* tends to identify *doctrinal or theological compromise* both as the determining factor
in this assailment and as an attestation in those who supposedly
compromise to the absence of genuine or salvific faith and commitment
to the gospel. The *RPTSC* formulates five doctrinal *interpretations*, from
the committee's perspective about the most critical issues or "contemporary compromises" with respect to those particular doctrinal areas, to
dissent from which automatically defines dissenters as non-Baptist, non-
Evangelical, or more than likely non-Christian. Referring to the doctrine
of God, for example, the *RPTSC* claims that its statements about God,
"based upon Scripture and undergirded by historic Baptist confessions,
force our attention to contemporary compromises which threaten the
fidelity and integrity of our faith."[30]

B. General, Denigrating Designations for Opponents

In its demonization of the theological diversity that supposedly produced "the denominational conflict of recent years," the *RPTSC* variously
labels the general culprits to which the *RPTSC* opposes itself. Although
the *RPTSC* does not define its designations for its opponents, these labels
condemn by denigration those interpretations that differ from the
RPTSC's doctrinal formulations, through a network of loose and
supposedly implicit perceptions about the meaning of these labels. The
RPTSC tends to use these caricatures or labels interchangeably, as if all
of these labels refer to the same thing. In spite of their usage by the
RPTSC, however, these caricatures fit on a spectrum, perhaps progressing

somewhat as follows: (1) from "theological revision"; (2) through "doctrinal minimalism"; (3) through "theological relativism"; (4) through "doctrinal laxity or unconcern"; and, finally, (5) to "theological unbelief."[31] Nonetheless, the *RPTSC* does not specify the differences between these different labels. Furthermore, the *RPTSC* explicitly clarifies very little of the meaning with which the committee has endowed these labels. As a consequence, numerous problems arise in their actual usage.

I will consider some of the problems in only one example. The *RPTSC* condemns "theological revision," but does not define the label. First, by virtue of the *RPTSC*'s own claim, Baptists remain free *to revise* their theological (as well as confessional) statements in light of the Christian scriptures. With the *RPTSC*, the PTSC *has revised*, through reformulation (and even misrepresentation), the doctrines expressed in the *BFM (1963)*, without adequate biblical support. In addition, although suggestively equated with the other labels, such theological revision hardly qualifies as "theological unbelief," "doctrinal laxity," or "doctrinal unconcern." The *RPTSC*'s theological revision itself represents energetic and neurotic if dogmatic doctrinal efforts, expresses rigidly formulated if inadequate theological beliefs, and remains piously if misguidedly concerned.

Thus, with these designations the PTSC endeavored to render dubious all theological reinterpretation other than that which harmonizes or agrees with the formulations contained in the *RPTSC* itself. With these labels, however, the *RPTSC* contends against another more basic opponent than the opponents described by these denigrating caricatures: *religious liberty* within the church (the danger in which the *RPTSC* alarmingly announces as *doctrinal laxity or unconcern*); even more specifically, *Christian freedom* (the danger in which the *RPTSC* suspiciously identifies as the license to mask *unbelief*); and most specifically, *the priesthood of all Christians* (the danger in which the *RPTSC* fearfully perceives as *theological relativism*). Thus, rather than continuing *to risk* improper expressions of these various liberties, as most previous confessions of the SBC have confidently done, the *RPTSC* demonizes theological diversity in order to dull or to inhibit the operations of these dimensions of Christian liberty.

---

[31]*RPTSC*, 113, 117, 118 (1.1; 1.2; 1.8; 2.4.4; 2.4.6).

C. Unfair Representation
of Specific Contemporary Theological Alternatives

The *RPTSC*'s tendency to demonize theological diversity also erupts in its actual statements about the several specific viewpoints, movements, or doctrines opposed by the writers of this document. The *RPTSC* contains a variety of examples with which to substantiate this claim.[32]

Although the *RPTSC* attacks only a few emphases from both Process and Feminist theologies, the document casts suspicion on every perspective in these movements, by calling on the SBC to "beware lest revisionist views of God," as developed by these movements, "compromise our faithful commitment to biblical truth." With this approach, the *RPTSC* errs in two major respects.

First, the *RPTSC* does not treat these theological perspectives fairly. All Feminist and Process theologies do not share uniform perspectives even on the concerns noted by the *RPTSC*. Furthermore, even these theological perspectives have not developed devoid of all truth. In light of their other writings, key members of the PTSC even acknowledge these claims. For example, in his less ideological and more scholarly moments, even Mohler distinguishes between "evangelical" and "radical" feminists, admonishing theologians in the former group "to make their evangelical affirmations clear and plain."[33] As a consequence, despite any genuine concerns, use of such labels in the *RPTSC* indicates their purely rhetorical function, their employment to alarm the *RPTSC*'s readers. Second, the *RPTSC* obviously ignores the doctrinal distortions in the classical Christian traditions themselves, distortions requiring unmasking

---

[32]*RPTSC*, 116, 117, 118 (2.2.9; 2.2.13; 2.3.9; 2.4.4; 2.5.5).

[33]Mohler, "Response," 248. In another publication, Timothy George, following his own critique of feminist theology, wisely qualifies his assessment: "This is not to say that all Feminist theologies are equally destructive, nor is it to deny that there are 'elements of truth' (Newport) in the feminist critique of sexism both in society and the church" (George, "Conflict and Identity in the SBC," 210). In addition, David Dockery, former dean of the School of Theology at SBTS and one of Mohler's more irenic colleagues in the project of redefining Baptist identity, supplies an even more discriminating approach to feminist thought with his threefold typology of feminist theologies: "(1) rejectionist or post-Christian; (2) reformist or liberation; and (3) loyalist or evangelical" (Dockery, "People of the Book," 38n.49). Nonetheless, on the basis of his typology, even Dockery appears unable to acknowledge that an evangelical approach might also require reformist or liberation orientations and efforts in both contemporary global contexts and the SBC itself.

both through alternative theological methods and in light of the Christian scriptures. The *RPTSC*'s myopia at this point may arise from the theological naïveté of its authors: no theological or confessional perspective represents the final or definitive interpretation of Christian doctrines. Just as the contemporary Christian community must proclaim the gospel within its own time and place, so must every contemporary Christian community reinterpret Christian life with God for its own unique position in history.

Similarly, the *RPTSC* indiscriminately attacks both annihilationism and universalism. Regarding the former, according to the *RPTSC*, "nowhere does the Bible teach the annihilation of the soul or a temporary purgatory for those who die without hope in Christ."[34] Obviously, some evangelical and Baptist Christian scholars have affirmed various concepts of annihilationism or conditional immortality on solid biblical grounds.[35]

---

[34]*RPTSC*, 118 (2.5.5).

[35]For example, on the basis of carefully developed biblical studies, the evangelical, John Stott offers a nicely measured statement. "I do not dogmatise about the position to which I have come. I hold it tentatively. But I do plead for frank dialogue among Evangelicals on the basis of Scripture. I also believe that the ultimate annihilation of the wicked should at least be accepted as a legitimate, biblically founded alternative to their eternal conscious torment" (John Stott, "John Stott's Response to Chapter 6," in *Evangelical Essentials: A Liberal-Evangelical Dialogue*, by David L. Edwards and John Stott [Downers Grove IL: Intervarsity Press, 1988] 320; similarly, see Edward Fudge, "The Final End of the Wicked," *Journal of the Evangelical Theological Society* 27 [September 1984]: 325-34). More accurately, many Christians understand their own viewpoints as "conditional immortality" and not under the often pejorative designation of "annihilationism" (e.g., John Wenham, *The Goodness of God* [Downers Grove IL: Intervarsity Press, 1974] 34-41). Contemporary Baptist theologians also develop similar viewpoints (Clark Pinnock, "Fire, Then Nothing," *Christianity Today* 31 [20 March 1987]: 40-41; idem, "The Destruction of the Finally Impenitent," *Criswell Theological Review* 4 [Spring 1990]: 243-59; idem, "The Conditional View," in *Four Views on Hell*, ed. William Crockett [Grand Rapids: Zondervan Publishing House, 1992] 135-78; Dale Moody, *Apostasy: A Study in the Epistle to the Hebrews and in Baptist History* [Greenville SC: Smyth & Helwys, 1991] 67-73; idem, *Hope of Glory* [Grand Rapids: Eerdmans, 1964] 94-112).

Various concepts of conditional immortality or annihilationism have appeared earlier in Baptist history as well. Several examples illustrate this claim. General as well as particular Baptists developed versions of annihilationism or conditional immortality. Among particular Baptists, see the work of Samuel Richardson, one of the signatories to the "First London Confession" (1644, 1646): Richardson, *Of the Torments of Hell, with the Foundations and Pillars Thereof Discovered, Shaken, and Removed* (London: 1658) 135-36. Even

Consequently, such a claim in the *RPTSC* only asserts the dogmatic position of the committee itself, rather than either noting the biblical bases for the concept of annihilationism (however debatable) or reviewing the works of Baptists who have shared or presently hold this perspective.

Also, the *RPTSC* never explicitly defines the term "universalism." The *RPTSC* leaves readers puzzled about the meaning with which it endows the concept of universalism. Certainly, according to the *RPTSC*, only humans who receive Christ experience salvation from sin; presumably, for the *RPTSC*, "universalism" refers to teachings about the salvation of all humans regardless of their responses to Christ. Still, the *RPTSC*'s statement about universalism contains more ambiguity than the *BFM (1963)*, which the *RPTSC* supposedly clarifies on this point. If, as the *RPTSC* claims, "all human beings—*in all places and of all ages*—are lost but for salvation through Jesus Christ,"[36] then did no human experience salvation prior to the birth of Jesus? Does the *RPTSC* mean to imply, on the one hand, that no Jews experienced salvation prior to Jesus of Nazareth? In such a perspective, not even Abraham received salvation. Does the *RPTSC* mean to imply, on the other hand, that, prior to God's becoming human as Jesus of Nazareth, the Christ appeared on the earth in some form to the humans who did experience salvation? If so, then, a host of other problems arise, not the least of which is the dehistoricization of biblical faith.

---

one early General Baptist statement of beliefs may have accommodated this viewpoint ("The Standard Confession of 1660," in *Baptist Confessions of Faith*, ed. W. J. McGlothlin [Philadelphia: American Baptist Publication Society, 1911] 118-19 [article 22]). Also, see the works of William Whiston (1667–1752) and Richard Wright (1764–1836), both of whom also were General Baptists who shared this perspective (Whiston, *The Eternity of Hell-Torments* [1740]; Wright, *An Essay on Future Punishment* [1846]). In 1878, some English Baptists formed the Conditionalist Association. George A. Brown, an English Baptist pastor, hosted this conference and later edited the journal of this association, entitled *Bible Standard*. Other Baptist ministers from this period held this viewpoint as well: Henry Hamlet Dobney, an English Baptist (Dobney, *The Scripture Doctrine of Future Punishment* [1846]); and Henry Grew, an English immigrant to the United States and pastor of First Baptist Church in Hartford, Connecticut (Grew, *The Intermediate State* [1835]; idem, *Future Punishment, Not Eternal Life of Misery* [1844]). I especially thank Rick Willis, recent graduate from SWBTS, for much of this information from his dissertation (Willis, " 'Torments of Hell': Conditional Immortality and the Doctrine of Final Punishment among Seventeenth-Century English Baptists" [Ph.D. diss., SWBTS, 1995]).

[36]*RPTSC*, 116-17 (2.3.5); emphasis mine.

Employment of rhetorical techniques to demonize differing perspectives arises from and incites social polarizations: *us*-versus-*them* or *insider*-versus-*outsider* attitudes and behavior. The *RPTSC*'s tendency toward these polarizations, and its effort to realize them, especially disclose themselves in two examples. The first example occurs in the *RPTSC*'s article on Christology. According to the *RPTSC*, "Baptists must join with *all true Christians* in affirming the substitutionary nature of Christ's atonement." The second example initiates the *RPTSC*'s eschatological formulations: "with *all true Christians everywhere*, Baptists confess that 'Christ has died, Christ is risen, Christ will come again.' "[37] In these examples, with the phrase "all true Christians," the *RPTSC* includes within the *true* community of God all persons who affirm this document's Christological and eschatological formulations, but implicitly defines as *false* Christians (including those who pretend to be Christians or those who wrongly think that they are Christians) all persons who might disagree with the *RPTSC*'s interpretations (or actually hold alternative Christological and eschatological formulations). The *RPTSC*'s formulations represent criteria by which the formulators of that document can identify their own and even Christ's own people; according to this document, persons espousing alternative perspectives, consequently, are not truly Christians. Given this situation, a question once asked by John Leland deserves both boldly to be posed and conscientiously to be answered again today by Baptists in the SBC: since Jesus himself did not leave a confession of faith or "a system of religion" for his followers, "why should a man be called a heretick [*sic*] because he cannot believe what he cannot believe, though he believes the Bible with all his heart?"[38] The *RPTSC*'s comportment, if not yet explicitly, certainly prepares the way for the excommunication of dissenters, of those who disagree with the official doctrinal formulations. Such an attitude reverses the evangelistic impulse of God's community, arrogantly withdrawing from others rather than offering life together in mutuality, reciprocity, and humility.[39]

---

[37]*RPTSC*, 117, 118 (2.3.9; 2.5.1); emphasis mine; cf. similarly, in the article on the doctrine of God, the phrase "all evangelical Christians" (*RPTSC*, 115 [2.2.2]).

[38]Leland, "Virginia Chronicle," 114n.*

[39]The authors of the *RPTSC* would benefit by heeding the wisdom in another observation by John Leland: "I have generally observed, that when religion is lively among the people no alienation of affection arises from a difference of judgment; and

As ambiguous as it is, the *RPTSC* contains numerous statements about those things against which it stands, or which its formulators and all real Christians do not believe. In this respect, the PTSC again has departed from the healthiest Baptist concepts of religious confessions. As Scarborough noted about confessions following the adoption of the *BFM (1925)*, "a declaration of faith is a declaration of *what you do believe* and is *not a disclaimer nor a declaration of what you do not believe.*"[40]

Analogue. Episode Four

When Korah, with Dathan, Abiram, On, and the 250 leaders from the people conspired against Moses and Aaron, they pretended to speak for all the Hebrews, as the voice of the entire assembly. These usurpers abused their legitimate roles of leadership, popular renown, and functional authority, rejecting the leadership of Moses and Aaron. Although appearing to describe the situation, insinuating that Moses and Aaron had abused their own leadership roles, this group of self-appointed leaders actually issued orders to the legitimate leaders of the people (Moses and Aaron) for their resignations. Dathan and Abiram even refused to meet with Moses, referring in their refusal to Egypt itself as a land flowing with milk and honey from which Moses had taken the people. Furthermore, by describing the holiness of every Hebrew person, this group of leaders flattered the people and, with that flattery, enlisted the people in this struggle, as the support for securing their own places as leaders of the people in the return to Egypt. Nonetheless, even though the Levitical leaders who initiated this rejection of Yahweh's purpose gained a temporary advantage with their rhetorical tactics, the absence of adequate ground upon which they could stand finally and terrifyingly surprised them.[41]

With the *RPTSC*, the PTSC has employed similar rhetorical tactics. As this chapter has shown, the committee often has articulated its own

---

whoever considers that the Devil is orthodox in judgment, and that the Bible is not written in form of a system, will surely be moderate in dealing out hard speeches towards his heterodox brother" (Leland, "Letter of Valediction, on Leaving Virginia, in 1791," in *Writings of John Leland*, 172).

[40]L. R. Scarborough, "Southern Baptists Lift up a Great Doctrinal Standard," in the L. R. Scarborough Collection, Fort Worth TX, SWBTS, Roberts Library, Archives, file 509:2.

[41]Num 16:1-4, 12-14, 19-35.

agenda and credenda as the voice of all Baptists or as the voice of the SBC itself. Thus, this committee and the group of leaders that it represents have subtly manipulated and controlled the majority of Baptists in the SBC. Furthermore, although this committee has disguised its document as a report, elements of its language betray its credal character and intent. Similarly, although the document contains a large percentage of descriptive language, other linguistic elements in the *RPTSC* disclose the committee's imperatival or normative posture toward Baptists in the SBC. Among other efforts, in an additional attempt to cast suspicion on divergent perspectives in the SBC as the source of the SBC's problems, the *RPTSC* even demonizes specific theological perspectives. Thus, the *RPTSC* operates with the rhetoric and rationality of conquest, assimilation, and domination, not with the rhetoric and rationality of recognition and alterity.[42] With these and other rhetorical devices, certain leaders in the SBC have enlisted a majority of Baptists to follow them, adopting their credenda and agenda without question.

---

[42]See Johann-Baptist Metz's distinction between a "logic of domination," "assimilation," or "transformation" and a "logic of otherness" or "recognition" (Metz, "Freedom in Solidarity: The Rescue of Reason," in *Faith and the Future: Essays on Theology, Solidarity, and Modernity*, by Johann-Baptist Metz and Jürgen Moltmann, Concilium Series [Maryknoll NY: Orbis Books, 1995] 72-73).

Part Two

Distorted Doctrines

The LORD opens the eyes of the blind.
(Psalm 146:8a NASB)

Introduction to Part Two

To Revise and Prescribe Baptist Doctrines

Completion of my resistance to the *RPTSC*'s reductive approach to Baptist Christian experience requires an answer to the fifth question with which I began this study: What actual results have this document's assumed background arguments, veiled intentions, illegitimate authorization, and deceptive rhetorical strategies produced? In answering this question, I arrive at the heart of the *RPTSC*'s substance, the document's more explicit theological formulations: (1) on the Christian scriptures; (2) on God; (3) on Christ's person and work; (4) on the church; and (5) on last things. Again, several problems appear in the formulations themselves, as very specific *reductively distorted doctrinal perspectives*.

In my analyses of these doctrinal problems, I will again follow the double pattern of my overarching aim: *first, to unmask dangers* for distinctive perspectives in Baptist experience promoted by the *RPTSC*'s camouflaged credalism in these distorted doctrinal formulations and, *second, to suggest legitimate Baptist lines of resistance* to those credal threats. Because I have previously examined several doctrinal issues and formulations in connection with other questions in this study, my analyses of each doctrinal article in the *RPTSC* will neither exhaust the areas needing careful study nor will always gather or repeat the features of my previous conclusions about the problems peculiar to each doctrinal formulation. For that reason, I will not devote additional study in part two of these studies to the *RPTSC*'s article on eschatology. I have considered some of the most problematic features of that formulation previously in other connections. In that which follows, nonetheless, I have engaged with several of the central problems inscribed into the *RPTSC*'s first four major doctrinal statements.

Prior to examining each doctrinal perspective separately, a more general and introductory line of inquiry emerges. First, in order to delineate even more specifically the *RPTSC*'s intentionality, with what rationale has the Presidential Theological Study Committee chosen its particular doctrinal emphases? Second, which doctrinal areas has the committee chosen on which to focus its interpretive attentions, and why has the committee omitted other equally crucial doctrinal areas of concern for contemporary Baptist communities?

I. Revisionist and Prescriptive Motives

Regarding my first question, according to the *RPTSC*, the committee's choices and formulations arose as responses to urgent issues or needs in the contemporary situation of both the broader society and the SBC itself, specifically, various challenges to or attacks against essential Baptist and evangelical Christian doctrines. As I have already tried to demonstrate about the *RPTSC*'s background argument or network of assumptions, this document construes the principal enemies of the SBC's doctrinal fidelity and theological substance as Baptists within the SBC's own membership. I have also endeavored to illustrate from the SBC's broader heritage that the *RPTSC*'s perspective actually narrows a much larger and more diverse range of Baptist traditions to its own emaciated set of perspectives, as the definitive set of criteria by which to measure all Baptists in the SBC.

Generally, the *RPTSC*'s promotion of its interpretation of a dichotomized SBC discloses the *RPTSC*'s explicit concern with the *doctrinal* identity of Baptists in the SBC. Without explicitly inquiring in this way, the *RPTSC purportedly* seeks to answer the following or a similar question: who *are* Baptists theologically or what *are* the essential Baptist doctrines? In its purported effort to answer this kind of question, however, *rather than describing* the ranges of interpretation actually present among Baptists,[1] the *RPTSC* has *produced a prescriptive document* on Baptist identity, formulating doctrinal norms for all Baptists in the SBC. The *RPTSC*'s answer in its doctrinal formulations, thus, really implies a rather different question to which the committee responded with the document: to which doctrinal standard and theological perspective *should* all Baptists in the SBC adhere, in order by which both to measure themselves and to be regarded as faithful Baptists? The *RPTSC*, consequently, represents the committee's response to what it perceived as a *crisis of doctrinal and theological identity in the SBC.*

---

[1]For a superb example of a *genuinely descriptive* approach to Baptist doctrinal and theological identities, in stark contrast to the *RPTSC*, see James Leo Garrett's recent convocation speech to the Baptist World Alliance–Eastern Orthodox Conversations in Instanbul, Turkey, 22 October 1994: James Leo Garrett, Jr., "Major Emphases in Baptist Theology," *Southwestern Journal of Theology* 37 (Summer 1995): 36-46.

Various other published writings by members of the Presidential
Theological Study Committee, in addition to published statements by
major theological and political architects of this so-called "conservative
resurgence," corroborate this claim.[2]

In light of Timothy George's role as cochairperson of the Presidential
Theological Study Committee, his publications have great importance for
understanding the *RPTSC*'s agenda and credenda. In a recent manifesto
of his own, Timothy George has submitted an "agenda" for "the renewal
of Baptist theology" with "five major components."[3] A brief glance at
George's agenda explains many of the factors also behind much of the

---

[2]See the following examples from the writings of George and Mohler. In his constant
efforts to identify Baptists solidly with "the larger family of evangelical Christianity" (as
the rightful heir to the Reformation's heritage), George refers to a "new identity crisis"
for Baptists in the SBC, a distinctly theological and doctrinal crisis (George, "Reformation
Roots of the Baptist Tradition," 19; also see idem, "Conflict and Identity," 195-213).
Elsewhere, George assesses the "crisis in Baptist life today" as "a crisis of identity rooted
in a fundamental theological failure of nerve." More specifically, he describes "the
burden" of his essay with one sentence: "The crisis of Baptist identity is closely related
to the loss of a defining theological vision epitomized by the coinherence of intellect and
piety" (George, "Renewal of Baptist Theology," 13, 19). Among Mohler's own efforts
to pull Baptists of the SBC into the evangelical community, he also assesses the SBC's
most recent and continuing political and theological struggles as an "identity crisis": "This
most recent identity crisis is the underlying dynamic in the current Southern Baptist controversy" (Mohler, "Call for Baptist Evangelicals and Evangelical Baptists," 227). David
Dockery, in concert with Mohler and George, construes this crisis of identity more
specifically as "a crisis of biblical authority," "a crisis of piety," and "a crisis of
theology," then supplies his own confessional statement "as a place to begin to develop
a common consensus grounded in Holy Scripture" (Dockery, "A Response," in *Beyond
the Impasse?* ed. James and Dockery, 223, 225). Behind the perspectives of George,
Mohler, and Dockery, of course, statements by Adrian Rogers and Paige Patterson remain
strategically and politically important for this movement. For example, Rogers affirms the
traditional Baptist commitment to unity-in-diversity, but qualifies it substantially in terms
consistent with the previous perspectives. Rogers affirms "functional diversity" in terms
of worship, for example, but refuses theological diversity: "But I think we will always be
eccentric if our unity is not in doctrine and in truth" (Rogers, "Southern Baptist Theology
Today: An Interview with Adrian Rogers," *Theological Educator* 37 [Spring 1988]: 12).
Patterson, much more combatively, emphasizes this as well in comments about the
concept of biblical authority: "The fatuous assumption that good education does not
indoctrinate not only fails to understand the basic meaning of 'indoctrinate' but also is
patently and logically absurd" (Patterson, "Beyond the Impasse—Fidelity to the God Who
Speaks," in *Beyond the Impasse*, 163).
[3]George, "Southern Baptist Theology," 22-31.

RPTSC's vagueness. Referring to his five components as "benchmarks for shaping Baptist theological identity," as "classic principles," or as "identity markers," George develops his "mosaic" with its five components in the following order: (1) "Orthodox Convictions," (2) "Evangelical Heritage," (3) "Reformed Perspective," (4) "Baptist Distinctives," and (5) "Confessional Context."

Regarding his first benchmark for shaping Baptist identity, however, George's orthodox convictions include, among other similar elements, the ancient Catholic dogmas of conciliar consensus, Calvinistic strands in Baptist confessional traditions, the narrow doctrinal dogmas from early twentieth-century Fundamentalism, and even an appeal to the *RPTSC*. As his second benchmark, identity-marker, or classic principle, George construes contemporary Evangelicalism as the legitimate heir of both classical Christian orthodoxy and the sixteenth-century Protestant Reformation. Becoming more specific, George derives the third component in his agenda for the renewal of Baptist theology from the Reformed heritage of the Reformation, the traditions developed from the teachings of John Calvin in particular. Most specifically, George claims the Reformed scholastic, Calvinistic, theological heritage as adopted by one Baptist, James Petigru Boyce.[4] As the fourth component of his agenda,

---

[4]Without a doubt, as the SBC's president for nine years of its history (1872–1879, 1888), Boyce contributed significantly, even though he seemed *only to tolerate* the SBC's genuine theological diversity, conceding compromises only as required to attain institutional goals in the SBC. See his rationale for writing a new doctrinal statement at the establishment of Southern Baptist Theological Seminary (SBTS), rather than arguing for the adoption of either the *New Hampshire Confession* or the *Philadelphia Confession*, since neither of those confessions then satisfied all Baptists in the South. Boyce conceded to expediency in the following way, however, subsequently citing the prevalence of Landmarkism in the West as an example of the need for such concessions: "While, however, it was deemed essential to avow distinctly and unreservedly the sentiments universally prevalent among us, both as to doctrine and practice, it was equally important that upon these questions upon which there was still a difference of opinion among Southern Baptists, the Seminary articles should not bind the institution" (James P. Boyce, "The Two Objections to the Seminary," *Western Recorder* 40 [20 June 1874]: 2). Nonetheless, Boyce clearly interpreted the *AP (1858)* for SBTS from a decidedly Calvinistic perspective: for example, "Election is God's eternal choice of some persons unto everlasting life—not because of foreseen merit in them, but of His mere mercy in Christ—in consequence of which choice they are called, justified and glorified" ("Abstract of Principles," from "Recommendation No. 3, Charter of the Southern Baptist Theological Seminary," in *Annual of the SBC* [1954]: 38-39). In addition, Boyce considered two

George adds only a dash of historic Baptist emphases. Astonishingly, however, George discusses only two items under this fourth heading: Baptism and the Lord's Supper. Furthermore, he interprets these two ordinances entirely in line with a Calvinistic perspective, eliminating almost everything genuinely and distinctively Baptist from these two ordinances.[5] As a consequence, in this connection, George entirely omits any references to the central, historic Baptist principles: such as, Baptist perspectives on religious liberty, the separation of church from state, the priesthood of all Christians, and the autonomy of local churches. As a fifth identity-marker, George places all of the previous markers within a

---

significant streams of theological diversity among Baptists in the SBC as perils for "the sound doctrine of our Churches," perspectives dangerous enough to legitimize "the adoption of a declaration of doctrine to be required of those who assume the various professorships" of the SBC's first theological seminary: "Campbellism" and "Arminianism" (Boyce, *Three Changes in Theological Institutions*, 33). Despite Boyce's Calvinistic influence on the theological education of ministers in the SBC, however, Z. T. Cody later answered the following question with a firm negative: "Are Baptists Calvinists?" Although not quite as prominent as Boyce, Cody served as vice president of the Foreign Mission Board in 1898; later, as editor of the *Baptist Courier*, the SBC appointed him to its Committee on Fraternal Greetings, on which committee he served with Mullins, and which committee composed the SBC's second (omitting the *AP [1858]* as a document adopted for only one institution or agency) convention-wide confessional statement: the *FASB (1920)* (the SBC's first confessional statement was the *PCU [1914]*; also see Carter, "Southern Baptists' First Confession of Faith," 24-28, 38). Cody described the "so-called 'five points of Calvinism' " as "the essential doctrines of the system": (1) "particular predestination," (2) "limited atonement," (3) "natural inability," (4) "irresistible grace," and (5) "perseverance of the saints." According to Cody, "now if this is the system that constitutes Calvinism it is again very certain that Baptists are not Calvinists." Cody perceived a difference between Calvinists and Baptists over the concept of religious liberty: "Calvinists loved freedom for themselves—for the elect; Baptists loved freedom for every one." Furthermore, for Calvinists, freedom originated in the election of a few to rule over the rest, while, for Baptists, freedom originated in the Spirit whom God poured on all flesh, thus producing "modern democracy and congregationalism" (Z. T. Cody, "Are Baptists Calvinists?" in *Christian Union Relative to Baptist Churches*, ed. James M. Frost [Nashville: Sunday School Board, SBC, 1915] 33-34).

[5]In this respect, George has even more thoroughly narrowed his acceptance of Baptist distinctives than he had in his study, from 1989, of the Reformation theological heritage of Baptist doctrine. Then, at least, George discussed the priesthood of all Christians in that connection, even if as a support for his understanding of its use in the defense of doctrinal purity (George, "Reformation Roots of the Baptist Tradition," 17; similarly, cf., idem, "Priesthood of All Believers and the Quest for Theological Integrity," 283-294; idem, "Priesthood of All Believers," in *People of God*, 85-95).

confessional context, in which he tends to affirm the coercive role of creeds within the churches. In his statement about confessions, George actually summarizes the major points outlined in the *RPTSC*'s concept of confessions. By following precisely the *RPTSC*'s statement, George likewise omits several important facets of the concept of confessions developed in the *BFM (1963)*. In this regard, George relies almost exclusively on the *RPTSC* rather than on the SBC's official, historic, and greatly superior confession.[6]

Although George published his discussion of these benchmarks for Baptist identity after the SBC's adoption of the *RPTSC*, clearly these components formed the foundation of the rationale with which the Presidential Theological Study Committee chose and then shaped its particular doctrinal emphases. With the resources of this rationale, therefore, this committee has formulated its normative concerns about specific Christian doctrines, with a goal toward revising and prescribing rather than describing Baptist doctrines.

II. Doctrinal Concerns

In reference to my second question, then, on the basis of the prescriptive concerns noted previously, the Presidential Theological Study Committee selected five major Christian doctrinal themes or *loci* on which to focus its interpretive energies: (1) the nature of the Christian scriptures; (2) the concept of God; (3) Christology and soteriology; (4) ecclesiology; and (5) eschatology. Comparison of the *RPTSC*'s content with prior publications by the architects of the SBC's so-called "conservative resurgence" indicates that key members of the Presidential Theological Study Committee have merely developed the legacy, the long-standing yet vehemently denied agenda and credenda, from the *fathers* of that militant, right-wing movement.[7]

For example, James T. Draper, Jr., as early as 1984, called for "a consensus among Southern Baptists as to *the irreducible minimum theology* that a person *must subscribe to* in order *to be acceptable* as a professor at one of our schools, or as a worker, writer, or policymaker

---

[6]George, "Southern Baptist Theology," 22, 26-31. On George's fifth principle or identity-marker, see *RPTSC*, 113 (1.6-9).

[7]For example, "there is no 'takeover agenda' by which certain people are being promoted to key positions with definite and specific instructions for actions on their part" (Draper, *Authority*, 93-94).

[*sic*] in one of our agencies." Draper helpfully stated those minimal "*theological parameters*," those "most basic fundamentals, *beyond which a person really ceases to affirm the Christian faith*": (1) the "hypostatic union" of Christ's divinity and humanity; (2) the penal-substitutionary interpretation of Christ's atonement; (3) the "literal, bodily" resurrection, ascension, and return of Jesus Christ; and (4) the "doctrine of justification by God's grace through faith." In the same chapter, in a partial qualification of his extreme judgment, Draper retreated enough from his claim to import some ambiguity into his initial pronouncement: "if a person does not subscribe to these doctrines then he really is not an *evangelical* Christian; he is not a *biblical* Christian."[8]

The content of the *RPTSC* itself suggests that key members of the Presidential Theological Study Committee chose particular doctrines, negotiated which ones to include or exclude, and produced specific interpretations of them prior to the formation of the committee itself. Comparison of the *RPTSC* with writings by George and Mohler suffice as a foundational, even if partial, demonstration of this claim.

A. Mohler's Agenda and Credenda

Mohler, first, has openly articulated his own theological agenda and credenda for the SBC. According to Mohler, the SBC "has no hope of reclaiming its denominational equilibrium," unless it overcomes the most significant impasse in the SBC's recent controversies, the theological impasse. In order to overcome the SBC's disequilibrium, Mohler proposes a reclamation and restatement of "a shared theological framework," even though, by his own assessments, both the *BFM (1963)* and the *RPC (1987)* failed "to establish consensus"; and, therefore, their failure "indicates that even less can be assumed, and more must be articulated." Quite pointedly, Mohler continues, "the process of developing a *new theological consensus* must be accompanied by the *drawing of articulated theological parameters* which are *commonly understood and affirmed* by the seminaries, agencies, and institutions of the SBC."[9]

---

[8]Ibid., 105-106, emphasis mine; similarly, see Paige Patterson, "My Vision of the Twenty-First Century SBC," *Review and Expositor* 88 (Winter 1991): 37-52.

[9]Mohler, "Has Theology a Future in the Southern Baptist Convention?" 91, 106, 107; emphasis mine. This language, of course, closely resembles statements in the *RPTSC* itself: "we seek to move beyond the denominational conflict of recent years toward a new consensus rooted in theological substance and doctrinal fidelity" (*RPTSC*, 113 [1.2]).

Among his series of fourteen "imperatives for a renewed theological framework," Mohler identifies the rough contours of his understanding of doctrinal fidelity and theological substance: (1) reaffirmation of biblical authority, as understood through the theory of inerrancy; (2) reaffirmation of biblical theism, while undefined, yet still contradistinguished from revisionist, Process, and Feminist theologies; and (3) reaffirmation of specific Christological and soteriological positions (Christ as *fully human and fully divine*, "justification through faith," "salvation through Jesus Christ's substitutionary and sacrificial life, death, and bodily resurrection," and "salvation through Jesus Christ alone"), as contradistinguished principally and explicitly from universalism.[10]

B. George's Agenda and Credenda

Second, prior to serving as the first dean of Samford University's Beeson Divinity School, Timothy George taught historical theology. George, however, construes the essential role of historical theology as more *normative* than *descriptive*, that is, more as the transmission of ecclesiastical dogma (or what Christians *should* believe) than as the history of Christian beliefs (or what Christians *do* believe and *have* believed). For example, according to George, "we must not simply repeat the classical doctrines of the faith with precision and clarity; we must also reflect upon these doctrines in such a way that *we can expound them as our own*." More pointedly, when George does historical theology, he does not begin "from a neutral standpoint"; but, as "*deeply rooted in the community of faith itself*" or engaged in "a species of *fides quaerens intellectum*," he labors "toward the *recovery of dogma*."[11] On the basis of George's understanding of historical theology, only theologians who espouse the faith of the community whose theology they study can produce genuine historical theology. George's particular stance, therefore, characterizes his concept of this discipline primarily as *dogmatics* rather than as history: ecclesial dogmatics served by history, rather than the

---

[10]Mohler, "Has Theology a Future in the Southern Baptist Convention?" 100, 101, 102.

[11]George, "Dogma beyond Anathema," 693, 703; emphasis mine. George similarly emphasizes this in his study of sixteenth-century reformers. "We must ask not only *what it meant* but also *what it means*. How can the theology of the reformers challenge and correct and inform our own efforts to theologize faithfully on the basis of the Word of God?" (George, *Theology of the Reformers* [Nashville: Broadman Press, 1988] 309).

history of ecclesiastical dogmas. Because George openly identifies these normative concerns of his own work, the status of his historical assessments and evaluations of both doctrine and theology in Christian history should alert readers to consider cautiously any *purportedly descriptive claims* in the *RPTSC* which he has affirmed by his signature on this document.

Efforts to accentuate, to discover, or even to rediscover the heritage of the sixteenth-century Protestant reformations (particularly, the inheritance from Calvin and, selectively, from the Reformed traditions arising as Calvin's legacy) in the history of Baptist experience and theology characterize George's theological preoccupations and labors, as his identity-markers for Baptist identity forcefully indicate. In this connection, in 1989, he outlined five major areas in Baptist theology in which he considered the Reformed heritage significantly determinative, in the following order: (1) the doctrine of God, emphasizing both "the *absoluteness* of God" and the Trinity; (2) the doctrine of Christ, emphasizing both "the Chalcedonian description of Jesus Christ as 'one in person, two in nature,' " and salvation through Christ alone; (3) the doctrine of "Holy Scripture," as "what God had once and for all said (*Deus dixit*)," with a reference to the "dispute over inerrancy" in the SBC as addressed by the "Chicago Statement on Biblical Inerrancy"; (4) the doctrine of salvation, with negative evaluative references to Arminian Baptist interpretations of this doctrine, through references to the polemical Calvinism of Boyce; and (5) the doctrine of the church, with a strong emphasis on the regulative character of the community as a whole over individual Christians.[12]

In 1990, however, George identified and discussed five "great theological themes which press for clarification and restatement" in the immediate future of Baptists, five (almost, although not altogether, identical with those stated previously) "concerns" that "constitute an urgent agenda for Baptist theology." George approached these concerns, however, in a noticeably different order from his previous list: (1) the

---

[12]George, "Reformation Roots of the Baptist Tradition," 11-19. Similarly, in his investigations into the theologies of four sixteenth-century reformers, George outlines several doctrinal areas of "abiding significance" for contemporary Christian life and thought: (1) "Sovereignty and Christology"; (2) "Scripture and Ecclesiology"; (3) "Worship and Spirituality"; and (4) "Ethics and Eschatology" (George, *Theology of the Reformers*, 314-23).

"Authority of Scripture"; (2) the "Doctrine of God"; (3) the "Person and Work of Jesus Christ"; (4) the "Ministry of the Holy Spirit"; and (5) the "Church."[13] By 1992, George had affirmed Mohler's "fourteen-point program of theological revitalization" as "worthy of further elaboration and implementation," again emphasizing, as well as "the doctrine of Holy Scripture," both "biblical theism" versus "Process theology" and "salvific particularism" versus various forms of universalism and Feminist theology.[14]

C. The *RPTSC*'s Agenda and Credenda

The previously identified agenda and credenda, as shared by Mohler and George, substantially explain the specific emphases in the *RPTSC*'s theological content: (1) the theory of biblical authority; (2) the doctrine of God; (3) Christology and soteriology; (4) ecclesiology; and (5) eschatology. From one perspective, the *RPTSC*'s emphases merely represent interpretations of several, major, classical, Christian doctrinal topics. I critically qualify this minor affirmation of the *RPTSC* in one essential respect.

While the *RPTSC* attends to several major Christian doctrines, it also almost entirely avoids several fundamental doctrinal discussions, pertinent to issues in contemporary Baptist life and theology: such as, protology (the doctrine of creation), morality (doctrine of the Christian life), and pneumatology (doctrine of the Holy Spirit). Oddly, the *RPTSC* does not devote articles to these doctrinal topics.

Although similar comments apply with various degrees of force to other doctrinal omissions, I will only and briefly consider the omission of pneumatology from the *RPTSC*'s urgent concerns, as a paradigmatic example of this problem in the document. At an earlier stage in his own work, George clearly perceived a need for renewed emphasis on the Holy Spirit in Baptist theology, a perception leading him to emphasize several aspects of the Spirit's work: convicting the human of sin, regenerating the sinner, inspiring the writers of scriptures, illuminating scripture's meaning for the Christian, empowering the Christian for daily living.[15] The *RPTSC*, however, not only does not contain an article on the Holy Spirit, but only refers superficially to the Holy Spirit. The *RPTSC*

---

[13]George, "Renewal of Baptist Theology," 20-24.
[14]George, "Conflict and Identity in the SBC," 207-208, 210.
[15]George, "Renewal of Baptist Theology," 22-23.

describes neither the Holy Spirit's activities in the history of God's relation to creation nor the Holy Spirit's ministries in the present, nor the Holy Spirit's role in the future. The *RPTSC*, however, does discuss the divine origin of scripture, but without any reference to the Holy Spirit, and does mention the Holy Spirit as one member of the Trinity, but without any discussion of the Holy Spirit's place in the Trinity.[16] With the exception of one *implicit* reference to the Holy Spirit's role in the conception of Jesus, no other direct or indirect references to the Holy Spirit occur in the *RPTSC*.[17] For a document that both supposedly acknowledges "the Trinity as essential and central to our Christian confession" and supposedly rejects "any attempt to minimize or compromise this aspect of God's self-disclosure," an embarrassing and serious silence about the Holy Spirit pervades the *RPTSC*. Since the Holy Spirit holds one of the three places within the Trinity, failure to discuss the Holy Spirit appears more as a minimization (or even as a compromise) of this doctrine (the Trinity) than as an affirmation of its essential place within Baptist doctrinal commitments and perspectives.

This problem encourages related observations. The almost complete absence of a discernible pneumatology in the *RPTSC* accentuates this document's almost exclusive concern with divine transcendence, on the one hand, and with absolute epistemological objectivity for its own claims, on the other hand. In the first case, the *RPTSC* characteristically affirms divine sovereignty.[18] This first example discloses an absence of concern for divine immanence, a topic usually discussed most fully in connection with the doctrine of the Holy Spirit. In the second case, the Presidential Theological Study Committee positioned its declarations on biblical authority as the *RPTSC*'s first article. Thus, the Presidential Theological Study Committee elevates the scriptures above the God to whom those scriptures attest. In itself, this move only instantiates and reinforces a form of Protestant scholasticism within Baptist theology, a form of Christian theology far more dependent on the capacities of human reason to deduct propositional truths from scripture than upon the illumination of those texts by the Holy Spirit. This second emphasis,

---

[16]*RPTSC*, 114, 115-116 (2.1.1-2; 2.2.8).

[17]See *RPTSC*, 116 (2.3.3). Edward B. Pollard noticed a similar neglect of reference to the Holy Spirit in both the "Westminster Confession (1646)" and the "New Hampshire Confession (1833)" (Pollard, "What Shall We Think of Creeds?" 43).

[18]E.g., *RPTSC*, 115, 116 (2.2.1; 2.2.10; 2.2.11).

then, tends even to work against the *RPTSC*'s emphasis on the living God's sovereignty.

At this point, another question arises. Given George's acknowledgment of the need for a renewed emphasis on the doctrine of the Holy Spirit in Baptist theology, what has inhibited the appearance of that urgent concern in the *RPTSC*? To this question, I offer no conclusive answer. I can only surmise, on the basis of numerous pieces of evidence, that the most powerful members of the Presidential Theological Study Committee argued strongly for the inclusion in the *RPTSC* of the most important components from their own particular theological perspectives. Obviously, this process required some negotiation. George, however, did not succeed in retaining this aspect of his concern in the document, or else George has become much less comfortable with the unpredictable Holy Spirit. Consequently, the committee's deliberations did not produce an explicit pneumatology.

From the more general questions about the order and topical choices of the *RPTSC*'s doctrinal formulations, I now move to the actual theological content of those formulations: chapter 5 on the *RPTSC*'s theory of scripture; chapter 6 on the document's idea of God; chapter 7 on the *RPTSC*'s concepts of Christ and salvation; and chapter 8 on this document's model of the church. As I have noted previously, not only will I not devote a chapter to the *RPTSC*'s article on eschatology, I will not exhaustively analyze each doctrinal statement. Rather, I will focus my comments on central issues to which I have not yet spoken at length in previous chapters.

The following studies require one additional qualification. Since my studies have focused on the issue of credalism in the SBC (as promoted with the *RPTSC*), with what rationale have I examined the theological perspectives themselves? After all, does not the real issue concern the norming of those particular perspectives, rather than their specific conceptual content? I answer the second question affirmatively. Nonetheless, I have examined the *RPTSC*'s theological formulations primarily because those interpretations of Christian doctrines supply the theological foundations for the *RPTSC*'s camouflaged credal impulse. Illumination of those theological foundations, therefore, will also strengthen the support for my claims about the *RPTSC*'s credalism.

Chapter 5

Fissures
in the Theory of Scripture

And the rabble who were among them had greedy desires; and also the sons of Israel wept again and said, "Who will give us meat to eat? We remember the fish which we used to eat free in Egypt, the cucumbers and the melons and the leeks and the onions and the garlic, but now our appetite is gone. There is nothing at all to look at except this manna."

(Numbers 11:4-6 NASB)

Then they set out from Mount Hor by the way of the Red Sea, to go around the land of Edom; and the people became impatient because of the journey. And the people spoke against God and Moses, "Why have you brought us up out of Egypt to die in the wilderness? For there is no food and no water, and we loathe this miserable food." (Numbers 21:4-6 NASB)

But these men revile the things which they do not understand; and the things which they know by instinct, like unreasoning animals, by these things they are destroyed. (Jude 10 NASB)

Introduction

With this chapter, I initiate more extensive studies of the *RPTSC*'s explicit doctrinal formulations. Specifically, I examine four major fissures in the *RPTSC*'s theory of the Christian scriptures. In reference to the previous discussions of the *RPTSC*'s use of authority, I have already noted several problematic areas in this document's concept of biblical authority. Without entirely reproducing those discussions here, I consider the following four additional issues in the *RPTSC*'s theory of scripture.

I. Inerrancy of Scripture's Original Autographs Alone?

The *RPTSC*, employing a quotation from the writings of James M. Frost, affirms a view of biblical authority as "absolute inerrancy." Besides examples of this theory's application taken by the PTSC from both the "Glorieta Statement" and the section entitled "Findings" in the *RPC (1987)*, however, the *RPTSC* supplies no substantial definition of the term "inerrant." Nonetheless, on the basis of historical precedents in the

SBC, the *RPTSC* does "commend" to the SBC three documents "as biblically grounded and sound guides worthy of respect in setting forth a high view of Scripture," which describe and affirm the theory of biblical inerrancy: the *RPC (1987)*, the *CSBI*, and the *CSBH*.[1]

An initial fissure or theoretical difficulty originates from the previous point of departure. Generally, this first issue arises from the documents affirmed by the *RPTSC* as "biblically grounded and sound guides." I have already examined several of the *RPC*'s problems in this regard. Here, I direct attention to the *RPTSC*'s commendation of the other two credal statements: *CSBI* and *CSBH*. By commending to the SBC these two documents without qualification, the *RPTSC* also affirms their specific contents. Specifically, as a consequence, the *RPTSC* commends several very problematic claims in the *CSBI*, two of the most important of which follow: (1) "that inspiration, strictly speaking, applies *only to the auto-graphic text of Scripture*, which in the providence of God can be ascertained from available manuscripts with great accuracy"; and (2) "that copies and translations of Scripture are the Word of God *to the extent that they faithfully represent the original*." Although the *CSBI* then denies that "the absence of the autographs" invalidates or "renders . . . irrelevant" the theory of "biblical inerrancy," the *CSBI* does no more than declare that utterly necessary element in its position.[2]

Fundamentalist Baptist writers emphatically declare the truth of this claim: "absolute biblical authority strictly applies only to the autographs, which no longer seem to be in existence." Nevertheless, those who share that perspective still affirm the "full truthfulness" of an autograph's copy or translation, but only "to the extent that it is an accurate copy or translation."[3] This sort of claim, however, merely begs the question or

---

[1]*RPTSC*, 114, 115 (2.1.1, 5-8); see the statement employed by the *RPTSC* in the following: Frost, "Introduction," in *Baptist Why and Why Not*, 12.

[2]*CSBI*, 291 (article X); emphasis mine.

[3]Bush and Nettles, *Baptists and the Bible*, 413. Recently, the official news journal of the SBC's Executive Committee published a story about this book, recognizing its significance for the initial stages of the fundamentalist subjugation of the SBC or during the so-called "conservative resurgence" in the SBC: see Dwayne Hastings, "Baptists and the Bible," *SBC Life* 4 (October 1995): 4-5. Also see David Dockery's more recent discussion of this autographic theory of the Christian Bible's authority: Dockery, *Christian Scripture*, 64-65; cf. David S. Dockery, *The Doctrine of the Bible* (Nashville: Convention Press, 1991). As long ago as 1914, B. A. Copass also espoused a version of this theory: see Copass, "Concerning the Baptist Declaration of Faith" ("I. The Scrip-

reasons circularly: only the autographs of the scriptures possess absolute authority; those autographs, however, no longer exist; nevertheless, complete truthfulness and, therefore, authority belong to accurate copies or translations of the autographs; the accuracy of those copies or translations, strictly speaking, one can ascertain with absolute certainty only by comparison with the autographs themselves, which, as the inerrantists claim, no longer exist.

Thus, the *RPTSC* vehemently and unreservedly affirms *a theory about the nature of scripture* on the basis of which to guarantee the complete and inerrant authority of the Christian scriptures. Because the so-called "original autographs" no longer exist, despite inerrantist objections to the contrary, the *RPTSC* has removed *full* authority from the actual scriptures that Baptist Christians really have possessed and do possess. Furthermore, even though one *supposedly* can ascertain "the autographic text of Scripture," according to the *CSBI*, "from available manuscripts with great accuracy," great accuracy does not translate into absolute certainty; rather, only with varying degrees of probability can the results of such textual labors produce and sustain any confidence in the scriptures. Acceptance and promotion of such a theory actually eliminate the basis for unreserved confidence in the very scriptures that Baptists both read in numerous translations and trust on a daily basis.

Since the fundamentalists began their struggle for control of the SBC, many Baptists in the SBC have refused to accept the fundamentalist theory of the Bible's inerrancy, with the claim that the theory differs significantly from the SBC's historic perspectives on the Bible's inspiration and authority.[4] Often, as an effort to refute the previous claim about the SBC's heritage, those who promote the theory of the Bible's inerrancy have ransacked the Baptist heritage to discover historical precedents with which to support their theory. Usually, these Baptist

---

tures"), *Baptist Standard* 26 (11 June 1914): 3.

[4]As examples, see Fisher Humphreys, "Biblical Inerrancy: A Guide for the Perplexed," in *Unfettered Word*, ed. James, 57-58; Philip D. Wise, "Biblical Inerrancy: Pro or Con?" *Theological Educator* 37 (Spring 1988): 37-44. The SBC adopted two of its last healthy statements on the Christian scriptures in 1978 and 1979. The first statement (1978) took the form of a resolution, while the second statement (1979) took the form of a motion by Wayne Dehoney. Both statements reaffirmed the first article of the *BFM (1963)*: "Resolution No. 22—On the Bible," in *Annual of the SBC* (1978): 68; *Annual of the SBC* (1979): 31, 45. The *BFM (1963)* does not contain a theory of biblical inerrancy in the sense implied by the *RPTSC*.

defenders of inerrancy will catalogue a variety of Baptist theologians (not always Baptists from the SBC's history, however) who held some version of the theory of biblical inerrancy. In addition, characteristically, these same defenders of the Bible's inerrancy will enlist support for their theory from Baptist confessional statements, notably the "Second London Confession" (1677, 1688) and the "Philadelphia Confession" (1742), both Calvinistic Baptist doctrinal statements based on the Reformed "Westminster Confession of Faith" (1646).[5] For example, those two Calvinistic Baptist confessional statements begin with the declaration that "The Holy Scripture is the *only sufficient, certain, and infallible rule* of all saving Knowledge, Faith, and Obedience."[6] Dockery incautiously considers the historical results from such methods of research adequate to silence "the repeated charges that the doctrine of biblical inerrancy is a recent innovation in Southern Baptist theology."[7]

Such historical methods, however, gather very little support from the documents actually adopted by the SBC during its own annual sessions, at least prior to 1979 when the fundamentalist subjugation of the SBC officially began. Those who espouse the theory of biblical inerrancy cannot even legitimately establish that either the *BFM (1925)* or the *BFM*

---

[5]Dockery, Bush, and Nettles employ this method in their works, even though they largely demonstrate only that Baptists historically have affirmed the authority of the Bible, a point that opponents of the theory of the Bible's inerrancy never have disputed (Dockery, *Christian Scripture*, 178-81; idem, "A People of the Book," 26-29; Bush and Nettles, *Baptists and the Bible*, 371-95). Although the debate continues among Reformed scholars, the weight of evidence suggests that Calvin held and operated with some version of the theory of biblical inerrancy: see Roger Nicole, "John Calvin and Inerrancy," *Journal of the Evangelical Theological Society* 25 (December 1982): 425-42; B. A. Gerrish, "Biblical Authority and the Continental Reformation," *Scottish Journal of Theology* 10 (1957): 337-60.

[6]"The Assembly or Second London Confession (1677 and 1688)," in *Baptist Confessions of Faith*, rev. ed., ed. William L. Lumpkin (Valley Forge PA: Judson Press, 1959) 248 (1.1); "The Philadelphia Confession (1742)," in *Baptist Confessions of Faith*, ed. Lumpkin, 348-53 (1.1); emphasis mine. Of course, the "Second London Confession" borrowed this phrase, changing it a little, from its predecessor, the "London Confession" (1644): "The Rule of this Knowledge, Faith, and Obedience, concerning the worship and service of God, and all other Christian duties, is not mans [*sic*] inventions, opinions, devices, lawes [*sic*], constitutions, or traditions unwritten whatsoever, but onely [*sic*] the word of God contained in the Canonicall [*sic*] Scriptures" ("The London Confession [1644]," in *Baptist Confessions of Faith*, ed. Lumpkin, 158 [article VII]).

[7]Dockery, *Christian Scripture*, 193.

(1963) endorses or supports that theory. Prior to the fundamentalist struggle to control the SBC, the documents that expressed the SBC's consensus did not use the theory of biblical inerrancy to describe the SBC's understanding of the Christian scriptures and their authority. Not only does the theory of biblical inerrancy not appear in the SBC's broader historic perspectives, neither does the concomitant theory of the scripture's autographic text occur in records of the SBC's official perspectives. Even a brief survey of the SBC's confessional statements corroborates this claim.

The SBC's first confessional statement, the "Pronouncement on Christian Union and Denominational Efficiency" *(PCU [1914])*, does not employ the watchwords of the present fundamentalist leadership in the SBC: words such as, "inerrant," "infallible," or even "original autographs" do not appear in the document. Rather, the SBC formulated its earliest confessional statement on the basis of several assumptions, through two of which the SBC stated its concept of the Christian Bible and its authority: first, "that all true disciples agree in accepting the Lordship of Jesus Christ as supreme and final in all matters of faith and practice"; and, second, "that *in the New Testament alone* do we find the *sufficient, certain, and authoritative revelation of His will*."[8]

This statement contains numerous points for comparison with the previous Calvinistic Baptist understanding of scripture. Three points of difference, however, will suffice. First, the *PCU (1914)* describes the Christian scriptures as the *"revelation"* of God's *"will,"* while the Calvinistic confessions describe the scriptures as the *"rule* of all saving Knowledge, Faith, and Obedience." Second, the Calvinistic confessions consider the entire Bible as the "only" adequate and dependable rule for salvific faith and practice, while the *PCU (1914)* perceives the New Testament "alone" as the adequate and dependable disclosure of the divine intentions. Third, while the *PCU (1914)* describes the New Testament as "sufficient, certain, and *authoritative*," the Calvinistic Baptist confessions of faith describe the Bible as "sufficient, certain, and *infallible*"; the *PCU (1914)* intentionally exchanged the latter statement's term "infallible" for the word "authoritative."[9]

---

[8]*PCU (1914)*, 73, 74; emphasis mine.

[9]With this linguistic substitution, the *PCU (1914)* followed the *AP (1858)*, which introduced this significant linguistic change into the SBC's vocabulary.

The SBC's *FASB (1920)* both describes the authors of the Christian scriptures as "inspired" or "moved by the Holy Spirit" and describes the scriptures themselves as "the *record* of the messages" which these authors "received from God." Furthermore, this important confessional statement also employs the *PCU*'s phrase as a designation for the Bible: "we hold that the Scriptures are the *sufficient, certain, and authoritative* revelation of God in all matters of faith and practice, and that obedience to their teachings is binding upon all men."[10] Nowhere in the *FASB (1920)*, however, do terms like "inerrant," "infallible," and "original autographs" occur. Yet, this document affirms the highest possible view of the Christian Bible, without deifying the Bible itself.

Even the very brief statement of belief adopted by the SBC in 1923, entitled "Science and Religion" (*SR [1923]*), follows the previous pattern: "The Bible is God's revelation of Himself through man moved by the Holy Spirit, and is our *sufficient*[,] *certain and authoritative guide* in religion."[11] Again, this document, originally from a portion of Mullins's presidential address to the SBC in 1923, avoids even the word "infallible," much less any of the other terminology related to the theory of biblical inerrancy. Additionally, while the Calvinistic Baptist confessions refer to the Bible as a "rule," the statement on "Science and Religion" describes the Bible as a "guide."

The SBC's "Statement of Principles" (1945, 1946; *SP*), including elements from the SBC's previous confessional tradition, supplies a similar concept of the Christian scriptures: "the one and *only authority* in faith and practice is the New Testament as the divinely inspired *record* and *interpretation* of the supreme revelation of God through Jesus Christ as Redeemer, Saviour, and Lord."[12] Similar to the SBC's previous statements, while the Calvinistic Baptist confessions employed the word "rule" to describe the Bible, the *SP* described the New Testament as the "*record* and *interpretation* of the supreme revelation of God." Although retaining terms and phrases such as "divinely inspired," "only authority,"

---

[10]*FASB (1920)*, 5, 6; emphasis mine.

[11]*SR (1923)*, 19; emphasis mine.

[12]*SP (1945)*, 59; *SP (1946)*, 38; emphasis mine. Similarly, although employing slightly different language, neither does the SBC's "Report on Interdenominational Relations" (1938; hereafter cited as *RIR [1938]*) utilize the theory of biblical inerrancy with its theory of the Bible's autographic text to express the *RIR*'s equally exalted understanding of the Christian scriptures (e.g., *RIR [1938]*, 24).

and "record" of the "revelation of God," this document stresses the human character of the scriptures even more, with its notion of the New Testament as the "divinely inspired . . . interpretation" of God's "supreme" self-disclosure in Jesus the Christ. Despite its honesty, this confessional statement maintains an extremely exalted view of the Christian scriptures. Nonetheless, it contains none of the terms employed to express the theory of biblical inerrancy.

Both the *BFM (1925)* and the *BFM (1963)* retain some of the linguistic specificity from the SBC's previous confessions of faith: such as "the Bible was written by men divinely inspired." Nonetheless, both versions of the *BFM* largely follow the linguistic formulations of the *NHC (1833)*, rather than employing the linguistic resources of the SBC's previous confessional documents. That change, through both versions of the *BFM*, slightly altered the SBC's confessional posture. For example, in all of the confessional documents of the SBC discussed previously, statements about the Christian scriptures always follow attestations to the relationship either between God and creation or between Christ and the Christian individual or community. In both versions of the *BFM*, however, the article on the SBC's understanding of scripture precedes its article on the doctrine of God. Furthermore, the two *BFM*'s introduce the following phrase that they have borrowed from the *NHC (1833)*, the very source of contention among Baptists in the SBC ever since its introduction, to refer to the scriptures: the Bible has "truth, without any mixture of error, for its matter." Nonetheless, as I have noted previously, despite this very high view of the Christian scriptures, both versions of the *BFM* continue to emphasize the human authorship of the scriptures as well. The *BFM (1963)* even reintroduces concepts from the SBC's previous confessional documents: such as, (1) from both the *FASB (1920)* and the *SP (1945, 1946)*, the Bible as "the *record* of God's revelation of Himself to man"; and (2) adding a sentence that refers to Jesus Christ as "the *criterion by which the Bible is to be interpreted*," thus subordinating the article on scriptures once again to the reality of God in Christ.[13]

---

[13]*BFM (1925)*, 71; *BFM (1963)*, 270; *NHC (1833)*, 361-62; *PCU (1914)*, 73-74; *FASB (1920)*, 5-6; *SR (1923)*, 19; *RIR (1938)*, 24; *SP (1946)*, 38; emphasis mine. Although both the FMB's "Statement of Belief" and SBTS's "Abstract of Principles" place their articles on the doctrine of the Bible prior to their articles on the doctrine of God, neither document develops any version, weak or strong, of the theory of inerrancy or of its companion theory, the theory of the autographic text of the Christian Bible. Furthermore, both

Additionally, neither version of the *BFM* develops the new emphasis
from the *NHC (1833)* into anything resembling the theory of biblical
inerrancy with its concomitant autographic theory of the Bible.[14]

---

confessions of faith, though following the "Second London Confession," replace the term
"infallible" with other terms. In the first case, "I believe that the Holy Scriptures of the
Old and New Testaments were written by men who were divinely inspired and that they
are a *sufficient and final authority* in all matters of religious faith and practice" ("A
Statement of Belief," in "Appendix A. Seventy-Fifth Annual Report of the Foreign
Mission Board," in *Annual of the SBC* [1920]: 197, emphasis mine; hereafter cited as *SB
[1920]*). In the second case, "the Scriptures of the Old and New Testaments were given
by inspiration of God, and are the *only sufficient, certain and authoritative rule* of all
saving knowledge, faith, and obedience" (*AP [1858]*, 38). Even in the *Baptist Ideals*, the
SBC places an article on the lordship of Christ prior to its article on the scriptures; neither
does this document contain any linguistic or conceptual support for any theory of biblical
inerrancy (*BI [1963]*, 6-7 [1.1-2]). More than likely, the SBC's earliest confessional statements borrowed this phrase from the "Second London Confession," via the "Philadelphia
Confession," via its nineteenth-century version in the "Abstract of Principles," however
significantly the SBC's later statements modified the phrase, as the model for their own
statements about the Christian scriptures.

[14]Even the statement from the *NHC (1833)* does not carry the meaning attributed to
it by Baptists in the SBC who espouse the theory of biblical inerrancy. See William L.
Hendricks, "The Difference between Substance (Matter) and Form in Relationship to
Biblical Inerrancy," in *The Proceedings of the Conference on Biblical Inerrancy 1987*,
ed. Michael A. Smith (Nashville: Broadman Press, 1987) 481-89. In the *NHC (1833)* as
well as in both the earlier and revised versions of the *BFM*, consequently, the term
"matter" seems to connote qualities similar to those that John Smyth had earlier associated with the meaning of "the matter or substance of the scripture."

    "Holy Scriptures (as all other writings whatsoever,) consist of two partes: of the tong
& character & of the substance or matter signified by the character.

    "The tong or character hath apertaining to it the grammar & the Rhethorick wherof
the tong or character is the subiect.

    "The matter or substance of the scripture hath in it, Logick, History, Cronology,
Cosmography, Genealogy, Philosophy, Theologie & other like matter.

    "The principall parte of the matter is the Theologie

    "A Translation of the holy originalls may expresse very much of the matter
contayned in or signified by the originall characters: it can expresse also much of the
Rhethorick as Tropes & Figures of sentence.

    "No Translation can possibly expresse all the matter of the holy originalls, nor a
thousand thinges in the Grammar, Rhethorick, & character of the tong. . . .

    "The holy originalle signifie and represent to our eyes heavenly things therfor the
book of the law is called a similitude of an heavenly thing Heb. 9.19-23" (John Smyth,
"The Differences of the Churches of the Seperation: Contayning, A Description of the
Leitourgie and Ministerie of the Visible Church" [1608], in *The Works of John Smyth:
Fellow of Christ's College, 1594-8*, Tercentenary Edition for the Baptist Historical

Finally, despite the absence of complete consistency with the SBC's heritage, however, and perhaps even more problematically in this connection, the *RPTSC* never admits that its concept of biblical inerrancy applies only to the original autographs of the Christian scriptures and not to the Bibles presently or historically in the hands of Baptist Christians.[15] Again, in this obviously intentional move, the PTSC has omitted the most dangerous portion of its theory, in order to enlist support and to avoid questions from Baptists in the SBC who trust the scriptures that really do exist.[16] If nothing else does so, this rhetorical tactic should raise suspicions about the honesty and the moral integrity of those who formulated the *RPTSC*'s doctrinal statements, despite the document's nod to "holy living" as one of the "indispensable elements of true revival and genuine reconciliation among any body of Christian believers."[17] *Probitas laudatur et alget*: virtue is praised and then left to freeze.

II. Deification of the Bible?

The second fissure in the theory of scripture also originates from the *RPTSC*'s enthusiastic embrace of the other Chicago statement, the *CSBH*. The *CSBH* affirms "that as Christ is God and Man in one Person, so Scripture is, indivisibly, God's Word in human language." Elaborating this affirmation, the *CSBH* equates its notion of the Bible's inerrancy with Christ's sinlessness: "We deny that the humble, human form of Scripture entails errancy any more than the humanity of Christ, even in His humiliation, entails sin."[18] By assuming this position in concert with the *CSBH*, the PTSC, by implication, has inscribed two major doctrinal transgressions into the *RPTSC*. The first transgression prepares the way for the second.

Society, ed. W. T. Whitley [Cambridge: Cambridge University Press, 1915] 1:281 [1.8]; emphasis mine).

[15]Ralph H. Elliott makes the same point: see Elliott, *The "Genesis Controversy" and Continuity in Southern Baptist Chaos: A Eulogy for a Great Tradition* (Macon GA: Mercer University Press, 1992) 37.

[16]More recently, Dockery has declared the theory of biblical inerrancy to be "the focus of the developing new theological center in the SBC" (Dockery, *Christian Scripture*, 208).

[17]*RPTSC*, 114 (1.10).

[18]*CSBH*, 397 (art. II).

A. Errancy as Sin

First, such a position confuses the limitations, weaknesses, and vulnerabilities of finitude with sin itself. By implication, according to the *CSBH* and the *RPTSC*, insofar as the latter document follows the former document, any characteristics of the scriptures produced by human limitations or weaknesses would be errors and, therefore, evil or sinful. When the *RPTSC*, along with the *CSBH*, equates errancy with sin, for example, ignorance has received the same status as a lie. This implies that, when God's creatures err, even if solely due to their created limitations and vulnerabilities, they sin.[19] Since ancient times, Christian communities have struggled to affirm the goodness of creation, refusing systems of thought (such as various forms of Gnosticism) that denigrated matter and biological life as evil, due to their very materiality, creatureliness, or finitude. The *RPTSC* initially transgresses doctrinally, then, when it implicitly suggests that the creaturely limitations created by God are evil in themselves.

B. Deifying the Bible, Dehumanizing Christ

Obviously, the *CSBH* uses a simile with which to describe the relation between the divine and human partners in the writing of scripture, comparing the Christian Bible to God's becoming human as Jesus of Nazareth. Nonetheless, the *CSBH*'s additional qualifications indicate far more in this claim than a similitude: an emphasis upon divinity at the expense of humanity in both its doctrine of scripture and its doctrine of Christ.

By affirming the *CSBH* and therefore on the basis of that document's perspective, the *RPTSC* virtually posits the Christian Bible as a second divine incarnation, yet this time as a book, as a collection of human words, rather than as a human. Equally as seriously, this theory tends to posit a God who overrides all limitations of human finitude, as well as human sin, to produce the scriptures: an implication threatening to rival the orthodox Islamic doctrine of the *Qur'an*. In the Johannine gospel, to the contrary, Jesus quite clearly distinguishes between the creaturely char-

---

[19]Perhaps this same confusion of categories also impairs the rigid perspective of Tom Elliff, elected president of the SBC in 1996: "Asked if he had any words for moderates who still identify with the convention, Elliff replied immediately that anyone who 'does not hold to the inerrancy of Scripture' should 'repent' " (Marv Knox, "Elliff Elected President without Opposition," *Western Recorder* 170 [18 June 1996]: 13).

acter and function of the scriptures and his own divine authority: "You search the Scriptures, because you think that in them you have eternal life; and it is *these* that *bear witness of Me*; and you are unwilling to come to Me, that you may have life."[20]

According to William R. Estep, the "Second London Confession" (1677, 1688), following the structure of the "Westminster Confession of Faith" (1646), departs from the structural pattern of previous Baptist confessions, by commencing with an article on the Christian scriptures positioned prior to its article on God, an innovation perpetuated also through the "Philadelphia Confession" (1742).[21] As noted previously, the SBC's earliest confessional statements avoid this dangerous pattern in order, structure, and theological emphasis. Despite the return to this pattern in the *BFM (1925)* through its imitation of the *NHC (1833)*, in 1963 the SBC substantially mitigated that danger, at least by its addition of two elements to the *BFM*'s article on the Christian scriptures: (1) the Christological criterion; and (2) the SBC's older emphasis on the scriptures as the record of divine revelation. To the contrary, however, the *RPTSC*'s article on the scriptures returns to the more dangerous form of this pattern, thus elevating its theory of biblical inerrancy above its understanding of God. This pattern in the *RPTSC* implicitly deifies the Christian scriptures.

This deification of scripture operates simultaneously with an obliteration of the experiences of limitation, vulnerability, and risk for the divine person as the human, Jesus of Nazareth. As a result, the concept of the Christian Bible as essentially a divine book, by implication, works only

---

[20]John 5:39-40 NASB; emphasis mine. According to H. Edwin Young, as he responded to Kenneth Kantzer during the SBC's conference on biblical inerrancy in 1987, "logically, then, whatever Jesus Christ believed about the truthfulness of Scripture must be accepted by every believer" (Young, "Response," in *Proceedings of the Conference on Biblical Inerrancy 1987*, 481-89). Yet, Young appears to do precisely what the Johannine Christ identified as the supreme danger for biblicists. Although in chap. 6 I utilize the narrative of Israel's construction of the golden calf as a metaphor for the *RPTSC*'s understanding of God, Joe Edward Barnhart also rightly applies it to the theory of biblical inerrancy (Barnhart, *The Southern Baptist Holy War* [Austin: Texas Monthly Press, 1986] 135-39).

[21]Estep, "Baptists and Authority," 610. Baptists in the SBC have begun to notice the presence of this dangerous pattern in the message of the fundamentalists who dominate the SBC. For example, "Chapman lists commitment to inerrancy before belief in Jesus Christ. If Chapman had been in the prison at Philippi with Paul when the jailer cried, 'What must I do to be saved?' would he have responded, 'Affirm inerrancy, and believe in the Lord Jesus'?" (Falkenberg, "Inerrancy First?" 5).

as a result of the dehumanization of the Christ himself. Hence, a Gnostic Christ also hides within this doctrinal transgression about scripture.[22]

III. Theory of Biblical Authority above the Christian Bible

A third fissure in the *RPTSC*'s doctrine of scripture dangerously distorts the SBC's historic perspectives on the authority of the Christian scriptures: the *RPTSC* effectively installs *its theory* of the Bible's authority, or the theory of biblical inerrancy, as the regulative principle for scripture itself, for the scripture's illumination by the Holy Spirit, and for all human interpretation of scripture. Thus, nothing proposed either by any human interpreter of scripture, or by the scriptures themselves, or even by the Holy Spirit constitutes a legitimate (perhaps even a Christian) insight or truth claim, if it diverges even slightly from truths explicitly or implicitly allowed by virtue of their consistency with the theory of biblical inerrancy itself. I illustrate this through a brief examination of the PTSC's use of a comment by Herschel Hobbs, a comment quoted in the *RPTSC* as a historical precedent and support, from a known Baptist statesman, for the *RPTSC*'s own theory of biblical authority as inerrancy.

The PTSC quoted from a statement that Hobbs had made during the SBC's annual meeting in 1981. In this particular comment, Hobbs explained a motion that he had introduced during the meeting on the previous afternoon. His motion contained two parts: (1) that "we reaffirm our historic Baptist position that the Holy Bible, which has truth without any mixture of error for its matter, is our adequate rule of faith and practice"; and (2) that "we reaffirm our belief in 'The Baptist Faith and Message' adopted in 1963, including all seventeen articles, plus the preamble which protects the conscience of the individual and guards us from a creedal faith."[23] The following morning, Hobbs discussed his motion, emphasizing his own contextualization of his statement about the scriptures. He began his explanation with the following comments.

> This motion is designed to emphasize that the preamble is as much a part
> of the statement voted by the Convention as any other part. When the
> Convention voted to set up a committee to do the study that resulted in this

---

[22]Charles H. Talbert similarly exposes and criticizes the dehumanization of Christ in the theory of biblical inerrancy (Talbert, "The Bible's Truth Is Relational," in *Unfettered Word,* ed. James, 43-46).

[23]*Annual of the SBC* (1981): 35.

statement, it said that the product *shall* serve as information to the churches and *may*—notice the difference—not shall, *may* serve as guidelines for agencies of the Convention.

Within this context, and only following these initial comments, Hobbs then supplied a commentary to the *BFM*'s affirmation of scripture, the comments actually quoted in the *RPTSC*. "Now I'm reading from the King James version—II Timothy 3:16—'all scripture is given by inspiration of God.' The Greek New Testament reads, 'all'—without the definite article—and that means every single part of the whole is God-breathed. And a God of truth does not breathe error." Upon the request of Adrian Rogers, "by common consent," the SBC placed Hobbs's comments "in the record."[24]

The *RPTSC* rightly acknowledges that, with his comments, Hobbs "explained" a phrase from the first article of the *BFM (1963)*: that scripture has "truth[,] without any mixture of error, for its matter." The *RPTSC*, however, does not indicate the broader and quite significant context in which Hobbs made his own statement. Quite clearly for Hobbs, as evident both in his own motion and in his later explanation of that motion, both the *BFM*'s statement on scripture and, most especially, his own interpretation of 2 Timothy 3:16 function only as *possible guidelines* for understanding *not* as *doctrinal requirements or parameters*. Thus, in light of Hobbs's own claims, even the *BFM*'s theory of biblical authority remains subject to revision, correction, or even refusal in light of the Christian scriptures themselves.

Do the authors of the *RPTSC* envision such a possibility for their own theory of biblical authority? If that possibility does not exist for the *RPTSC*'s theory, then its authors have implicitly declared as infallible their own abilities to interpret and to theorize. The *RPTSC*'s authors, consequently, have emplaced this document and its operative theories above the biblical texts themselves. Given the *RPTSC*'s own commitment in theory to a particular epistemological criterion (supposedly, the

---

[24]Ibid., 45. Hobbs had previously expressed this same point, even more forcefully, in an article. "The preamble is as much a part of this statement adopted by the Southern Baptist Convention as any of the seventeen articles which follow. Without it the statement becomes a creed. And Baptists are not a creedal people. Without this preamble the Convention would not have adopted it. Therefore, no one Southern Baptist or group of such has the right to seek to ignore the preamble in interpreting or applying it" (Hobbs, "Southern Baptists and Confessionalism," 68).

Christian scriptures, as authority for faith and practice among Baptists), refusals to allow the possibility that the *RPTSC*'s theory of biblical authority might be wrong, distorted, or faulty (in light of the scriptures themselves) disclose a commitment to an epistemological criterion other than (and regulative of) the Christian scriptures themselves.[25] With this effort, the PTSC threatens to transform the Christian Bible into a *mare clausum*, a closed sea: bountiful, majestic, dynamic depths, bounded on all sides by a theory with which a few guardians attempt to ration this divine gift's unlimited resources to everyone else at sea with this committee, or even to prevent other fishers from discovering through the Holy Spirit the as yet unknown and unharvested resources there.

IV. Abandonment of Christ
as Criterion for Interpreting Christian Scriptures?

Following from the previous discussions, the PTSC has inscribed into the *RPTSC* one specific theory of biblical authority (inerrancy) as *the criterion by which to interpret* the scriptures. As a fourth fissure in its theory of scripture, consequently, insofar as the *RPTSC* elevates its theory of biblical authority above the Christian scriptures, the *RPTSC* establishes a *deficient criterion* on the basis of which to interpret the Christian scriptures.

The *RPTSC* appeals to "recent developments" in which the SBC has affirmed this theory. As the *RPTSC* acknowledges by its commendation to the SBC of the *CSBI* and the *CSBH*, however, the most scholastic and sophisticated forms of this criterion originated outside the SBC. Nonetheless, on the basis of the SBC's various affirmations of this theory (yet only in its recent history), the *RPTSC* calls upon Baptists in the SBC and the SBC's institutions to shape their attitudes toward scripture, to use scripture in witness to others, to interpret scripture, and to encourage scripture's translation and dissemination solely on the basis of this theory of biblical authority or this criterion.[26] In short, according to the *RPTSC*, as I have noted previously, only interpretations of scripture in harmony with this particular theory have status as authentic (or even Christian)

---

[25]This criticism, of course, resembles in some ways the principles of verifiability and falsifiability in contemporary linguistic philosophy. See Frederick P. Ferré, *Language, Logic, and God* (New York: Harper, 1961; repr., Chicago: University of Chicago Press, 1981) 1-17, 42-57.

[26]*RPTSC*, 114-15 (2.1.3-7).

interpretations or receive approval within the SBC. The *RPTSC* supplies
more than just a general theory, however, giving specific documentary
formulations of this theory by which to measure biblical interpretations:
"the *Report of the Peace Committee* (1987), the *Chicago Statement on
Biblical Inerrancy* (1978), and the *Chicago Statement on Biblical
Hermeneutics* (1982)."[27]

Both the *RPTSC*'s hermeneutical criterion and the recent historical
precedents on the basis of which the *RPTSC* legitimizes the normative
value of its criterion, however, depart fundamentally from the SBC's
historic hermeneutical criterion. As the *BFM (1963)* declares, while the
Christian Bible is "the true center of Christian union, and the supreme
standard by which all human conduct, creeds, and religious opinions
should be tried," "the *criterion by which the Bible is to be interpreted is
Jesus Christ*."[28] For this reason, in 1963, the Committee on Baptist Faith
and Message introduced its entire doctrinal statement with the even more
foundational claim: because Baptists "profess a living faith," a faith
"rooted and grounded in Jesus Christ, . . . the sole authority for faith and
practice among Baptists is Jesus Christ whose will is revealed in the Holy
Scriptures."[29] Because Jesus Christ himself most fully disclosed God in
human history, E. Y. Mullins understood Jesus Christ as "the key" both
"to the interpretation of Scripture" and to the "construction of Christian
doctrine." For that reason, Mullins considered the four gospels to be
"central in our approach to the Bible."[30] Even James Petigru Boyce
understood this: for example, "our salvation does not rest in the belief
that the books of the Bible teach the truth, but in belief of the things
which they teach."[31]

On this basis, historically, the SBC has described both, more broadly,
the whole Christian Bible as "the *record* of God's revelation" of the
divine self to humanity and, more narrowly, even the scriptures of the
New Testament "as the divinely inspired *record and interpretation* of the
supreme revelation of God through Jesus Christ as Redeemer, Saviour,

---

[27]*RPTSC*, 115 (2.1.8).

[28]*BFM (1963)*, 270 (article 1); emphasis mine.

[29]*BFM (1963)*, 270 (preamble).

[30]Edgar Young Mullins, *The Christian Religion in Its Doctrinal Expression* (Philadelphia: Judson Press, 1917) 154, 164, 166.

[31]James Petigru Boyce, *Abstract of Systematic Theology* (Philadelphia: American Baptist Publication Society, 1887) 362.

and Lord."[32] Thus, as a *record* or an *interpretation* of God's self-revelation (supremely realized in Jesus Christ), the Christian Bible itself becomes a *derivative authority*, insofar as the Bible attests to the living God's self-disclosing interaction with and in creation's history. As the *originative revelation and supreme authority*, the *living God through the living Christ* functions as the criterion by which Christians interpret the derivative revelation, the record or interpretation of divine revelation, or the Christian scriptures.

Quite simply, the *RPTSC* avoids reaffirming this foundational belief from the *BFM (1963)*. Does evidence from the *RPTSC* contradict my claim? The *RPTSC* does link Christ to the Christian scriptures in various ways. Nonetheless, the absolute and *a priori* claims comprising the *RPTSC*'s theory of inerrancy do not permit genuine commitment to the living Christ as the criterion by which to interpret the scriptures. Consequently, the *RPTSC* can only refract this radical yet ambiguous hermeneutical criterion into its several less foundational, vague, and scattered commitments: (1) Christ as "the center and circumference of the Christian faith"; (2) Christ as the only one through whom the Christian scriptures, "from beginning to end," proclaim salvation; (3) Christ as the one to whom "Scripture bears faithful and truthful witness"; and (4) Christ as the one "under the Lordship" of whom, and "in full confidence of the truthfulness of His Word," Baptists in the SBC's institutions exercise "firm faith and free research."[33]

Yet, although properly emphasizing that Baptists should research or interpret the scriptures "under" Christ's "lordship," as a noticeable absence, the *RPTSC* does not affirm Christ as the criterion for interpreting the Christian scriptures. Rather, the *RPTSC* accepts a nonbiblical theory, formulated in the documents mentioned above, as the criterion for interpreting the scriptures. With this move, the *RPTSC* even revises the

---

[32]*BFM (1963)*, 270; *SP (1945)*, 59; emphasis mine. Important Baptist theologians, such as Mullins and Tribble, developed this point well. For example, "God thus becomes our supreme authority, and the Bible is recognized as the authoritative *record of his supreme revelation.*" "We have in the Scriptures of the Old and New Testaments the *record of God's revelation of himself* to his people" (Mullins, *Christian Religion in Its Doctrinal Expression*, 41, 142; emphasis mine). "All Christian doctrines are based upon and derived from the revelation of God in Christ. The Bible is the *record of that revelation*" (Harold W. Tribble, *Our Doctrines*, rev. ed. [Nashville: Convention Press, 1936] 14; emphasis mine).

[33]*RPTSC*, 114, 116 (2.1.8; 2.3.1, 2, 4).

BFM (1963). If the PTSC had treated the SBC's history more faithfully, the committee's report would have placed these "recent developments in Southern Baptist life" within the context of the SBC's larger history. Greater fidelity to, and more honest treatment of, the SBC's confessional history would not allow the *RPTSC*'s revisionist departure from Christ as hermeneutical criterion of the Christian scriptures themselves.

Analogue. Episode Five

On more than one occasion, the Hebrews complained in the wilderness about the food with which God had supplied them, and desired something much more substantial, that which they considered themselves able to procure by returning to Egypt. Following their deliverance from Egypt, when the people accused Moses and Aaron of leading them into the wilderness to starve them, Yahweh had sustained and nourished the liberated Hebrew slaves with an unusual food, a food described by Yahweh as "bread from heaven" and named "manna" by the people themselves. Yahweh provided this food every morning, as well as sending quail in the evening. The people gathered as much manna as they needed for each day, except on the sixth day, when they gathered twice as much for that day and the following sabbath. Thus, whenever the people greedily hoarded this daily bread, not depending on Yahweh's promise to provide for their needs, the manna rotted. Despite these regular provisions from Yahweh for their sustenance, the liberated Hebrew people began to loathe the food with which Yahweh had lovingly nourished them. The people remembered the security of Egypt and idealized their experience there. More seriously, the people began to long for the foods that they had eaten in Egypt, disregarding their bondage there, preferring the comfort of rich food over freedom. They desired nourishment that they could not see any longer, yet, in their minds, something more certain and less ambiguous, something more substantial and less evanescent than the actual nourishment provided freely and daily by Yahweh.[34]

Similarly, the *RPTSC* records the dissatisfaction of the PTSC with that which the Christian scriptures state about themselves both explicitly and implicitly. Neither this committee nor the leaders it represents can tolerate the ambiguity and the diversity in the actual scriptures that they

---

[34]Exod 16:2-31; Num 11:4-23, 31-34; 20:1-5; 21:4-9.

read regularly. Thus, the *RPTSC* posits and promotes something more certain and more definite than the scriptures themselves, imagining and trusting something totally other than the scriptures themselves: a *theory about* the scriptures.

Although this chapter has identified and examined four distinct fissures in the *RPTSC*'s theory of the Christian scriptures, those fissures form a tangled web in which different aspects in the *RPTSC*'s theory operate at cross-purposes to one another. As a consequence, for the *RPTSC*, the Bible possesses authority only if the original autographs are inerrant. Furthermore, the inerrancy of even the original autographs depends on a concept of God in which the deity overrides all limitations of finitude and distortions of sin in the human writers of the scriptures, thus effectively deifying the scriptures themselves. Nonetheless, the *RPTSC* subordinates that deified book to the *RPTSC*'s own theory of biblical authority, by denying the truthfulness of, or at least devaluing, any insights or claims that diverge from those allowed by the *RPTSC*'s theory. Consequently, the *RPTSC* also abandons the living Christ (as well as the deified book) as the criterion by which to interpret the Christian scriptures and, instead, embraces its own theory of biblical inerrancy as that criterion.

Chapter 6

Weaknesses
in the Idea of God

Now when the people saw that Moses delayed to come down from the mountain, the people assembled about Aaron, and said to him, "Come, make us a god who will go before us; as for this Moses, the man who brought us up from the land of Egypt, we do not know what has become of him." And Aaron said to them, "Tear off the gold rings which are in the ears of your wives, your sons, and your daughters, and bring them to me." Then all the people tore off the gold rings which were in their ears, and brought them to Aaron. And he took this from their hand, and fashioned it with a graving tool, and made it into a molten calf; and they said, "This is your god, O Israel, who brought you up from the land of Egypt." Now when Aaron saw this, he built an altar before it; and Aaron made proclamation and said, "Tomorrow shall be a feast to the Lord." So the next day they rose early and offered burnt offerings, and brought peace offerings; and the people sat down to eat and to drink, and rose up to play. Then the Lord spoke to Moses, "Go down at once, for your people, whom you brought up from the land of Egypt, have corrupted themselves." (Exodus 32:1-7 NASB)

. . . all the harsh things which ungodly sinners have spoken against Him. (Jude 15b NASB)

Introduction

I have already addressed several problems in the *RPTSC*'s interpretation of the Christian doctrine of God in connection with other issues. As examples, the *RPTSC* exhibits both an almost exclusive concern with divine transcendence and the almost complete absence of pneumatological concerns (despite the document's strong statements about the doctrine of the Trinity). I will not repeat those discussions here. Nonetheless, other weaknesses surface in the *RPTSC*'s idea of God. This chapter addresses three of those problems.

I. Biblical Theism?

First, the *RPTSC* affirms "the centrality of biblical theism" for
Baptists, announces recent compromises of "the biblical doctrine of God,"
and declares that "Southern Baptists cannot follow this course."[1] These
assertions elicit at least two major questions regarding the *RPTSC*'s interpretation of biblical theism.

In one respect, the *RPTSC* seems to construe these alleged compromises of "the biblical doctrine of God" as *external threats* to the biblical
theism affirmed by Baptists, such as threats from "process" theology,
"feminist" theology, and even "the New Age movement."[2] Since the
BFM (1963) clearly summarizes major points of biblical theism, why
does the *RPTSC* raise these issues at all, unless the PTSC really perceived these three specific theological perspectives as threats originating
from Baptists in the SBC? I have tried to suggest some answers to similar questions in my chapter on the *RPTSC*'s rhetorical strategies.

In any case, at this juncture, a more crucial question arises. What
does the *RPTSC* mean by "biblical theism"? Although the *RPTSC*
supplies six basic affirmations about "the biblical God," the document's
specific emphases, in virtually every respect, attempt to bolster an understanding of divine sovereignty as *unqualified transcendence*. Indeed, the
RPTSC's article on the doctrine of God begins with this thesis: "the God
revealed in Holy Scripture is the *sovereign God*. . . . "[3] In light of
Mohler's, Coppenger's, and George's well-known commitments to
Calvinism, the *RPTSC*'s formulations about God seem to suggest a
variety of unstated and background commitments to a Calvinistic doctrine
of God. Several examples disclose the basis for this suspicion.[4]

---

[1] *RPTSC*, 114 (2.2.2, 4). The *RPTSC*, of course, only reiterates Mohler's own naive
demand for a "reaffirmation of biblical theism" (Mohler, "Has Theology a Future in the
Southern Baptist Convention?" 101).

[2] *RPTSC*, 116 (2.2.9, 13).

[3] *RPTSC*, 115 (2.2.1); emphasis mine.

[4] Both George's and Mohler's commitments to Calvinism, of course, extend far beyond the doctrine of God, embracing all of the so-called "doctrines of grace." These two
members of the PTSC represent two of the most vocal members of a militant Calvinistic
Baptist vanguard, a cadre of theologians seeking aggressively and entirely to *re-Calvinize*
the SBC. For example, George considers SBTS's Calvinistic doctrinal statement, the "Abstract of Principles," to be "Southern Baptists' . . . best confessional document" (George,
" 'Soli Deo Gloria!' The Life and Legacy of James Petigru Boyce," in *James Petigru*

As a first example, referring to use of the word "father" as a title for God, the *RPTSC* states that *"God has accommodated Himself* to us by *naming* Himself in human words."[5] Although the concept of divine accommodation in various forms appears in Christian thought prior to Calvin (as in works by Irenaeus, Clement of Alexandria, Origen of Alexandria, John Chrysostom, and Augustine of Hippo), the *RPTSC*'s use of this concept in conjunction with the *RPTSC*'s emphasis on divine

---

Boyce: Selected Writings, ed. Timothy George [Nashville: Broadman Press, 1989] 20).
 Wherever this group has concentrated its efforts, it has produced irresolvable controversy and has seriously threatened the very stability of community itself among Baptists. See Mark Wingfield, "Resurgent Calvinism Renews Debate over Chance for Heaven," *Baptists Today* 13 (16 February 1995): 4; Roy W. Pitchford, " 'Founders' Group Works to Preserve Calvinism in Southern Baptist Life," *Baptists Today* 13 (16 February 1995): 4; Mark Wingfield, "Nothing Comical about Baptist Shift to Calvinism, Scholars Say," *Baptists Today* 13 (16 February 1995): 5; idem, "Scholars Debate Impact of Calvinism on Evangelism and Missions," *Baptists Today* 13 (16 February 1995): 5; "Hobbs Denounces Calvinism," *Western Recorder* 169 (11 April 1995): 11; "Marshall Calls Calvinism 'Irrelevant' & 'Distracting,' " *Western Recorder* 169 (9 May 1995): 2; Bill J. Leonard, "Seminary Crackdown," *Christian Century* 112 (10 May 1995): 500-502; Glenn A. Brown, "Salvation for All or Only for the Elect?" *Baptist Messenger* 84 (1 June 1995): 2; Mark Wingfield, "Mohler Declares His Beliefs in Line with Abstract," *Western Recorder* 169 (27 June 1995): 2, 12; Presnall H. Wood, "Nothing Wrong with 'Whosoever Will,' " *Baptist Standard* 107 (16 August 1995): 6; Henlee Barnette, "Progressive Baptist," *Western Recorder* 169 (29 August 1995): 4; "Vines: Focus on God, Not Man," *Western Recorder* 169 (5 September 1995): 2.
 So convinced of his own perspective's infallibility and identification with God's unalloyed truth, however, during his sermon to the SBC in 1995, Mohler issued his final evaluative pronouncement on those who disagree with him and his aggressive Calvinistic vanguard, those who prefer humbly and tolerantly to account for their lives together with God through love rather than through factiousness: "When a denomination begins to consider doctrine divisive, theology troublesome, and conviction inconvenient, consider that denomination on its way to a well-deserved death" (Mohler, "What Mean These Stones: Convention Sermon," 2; *Annual of the SBC* [1995]: 93; cf. "Mohler: Defend Doctrines, Convictions or Die," *Baptist Standard* 107 [28 June 1995]: 11).
 A denomination may also die from unnecessary doctrinal divisions, troublesome theologians (whether academicians or pastors), and theological convictions without love. Even during the SBC's annual meeting in 1995, following reports from the presidents of the seminaries, David McNair questioned Mohler about Calvinism (*Annual of the SBC* [1995]: 85). Mark Coppenger, member of the PTSC and recently elected president of Midwestern Baptist Theological Seminary, also fully committed to Calvinism, participates wholeheartedly with Mohler and George in this neo-Calvinization of the SBC: see Hinson, "Calvinists Seek Return to 'Orthodoxy' of SBC Founders," 2.
 [5]*RPTSC*, 116 (2.2.9); emphasis mine.

sovereignty suggests the *RPTSC*'s dependence on Calvin's understanding of this idea.[6] The concept of divine accommodation, especially as developed by Calvin and his followers, presupposes a classical theistic framework unmistakably different from biblical theism, despite Calvin's extensive use of the Christian scriptures.[7] For instance, when John Calvin

---

[6]Calvin's theory of divine accommodation applies to every aspect of God's relation to the creation, not merely to God's gift of scripture to disclose the divine self to humans. For example, see John Calvin, *Institutes of the Christian Religion*, ed. John T. McNeill, trans. Ford Lewis Battles, vol. 20, Library of Christian Classics (Philadelphia: Westminster Press, 1960) 1:51-54, 102-103, 120-21, 162-63, 171, 225-27, 433, 451-52, 462-63, 504-505 (1.5.1-2; 1.11.3; 1.13.1; 1.14.3; 1.14.11; 1.17.12-13; 2.10.6; 2.11.2; 2.11.13-14; 2.16.2); emphasis mine. Ford Lewis Battles conclusively demonstrates the accuracy of this claim (Battles, "God Was Accommodating Himself to Human Capacity," *Interpretation* 31 [January 1977]: 19-38).

[7]Classical *Christian* theism belongs to the family of classical theism. Various understandings of classical theism abound, however. Some identify this designation with the convictions of piety, without showing how the beliefs of that piety became intertwined with various categories and concepts from Hellenistic philosophy. Hence, for those espousing this first and rather indiscriminate way of understanding, classical theism describes God with some or all of the following central characteristics or attributes: omnipotence, omniscience, omnipresence, eternity, omnibenevolence, aseity, perfection, and so on (e.g., J. E. Barnhart, *Religion and the Challenge of Philosophy* [Totowa NJ: Littlefield, Adams, and Co., 1975] 61). Of course, the scriptures in many religious traditions, including those originating from Christian piety and reflection, characterize God with most or all of those attributes. Nevertheless, such descriptions do not adequately represent classical theism's entire conceptual network. Other central and even more definitive features of classical theism include technical concepts primarily inherited from Hellenistic philosophies: impassibility, immutability, simplicity, incorporeality, incomprehensibility, indivisibility, and so forth. These latter characteristics or attributes, plus those mentioned previously, more fully reflect the essential characteristics of classical theism's concept of God. Other characteristics become necessary to qualify a belief-system as any particular variety of classical theism: such as classical *Christian* theism. More careful analysts of classical theism perceive, in the history of various religious traditions, phenomena in which the symbols and images of religious piety combine with more refined philosophical concepts. In this respect, see the excellent collection of Jewish, Christian, and Islamic theologies (Philo, Maimonides; Augustine, Anselm, Aquinas, Descartes, Leibniz, Kant, Channing, von Hügel; Al-Ghazzali), and their philosophical precursors (Plato, Aristotle), with which Charles Hartshorne and William L. Reese illustrate various religious traditions in the family of classical theism (Charles Hartshorne and William L. Reese, eds., *Philosophers Speak of God* [Chicago: University of Chicago Press, 1953; repr., University of Chicago Press, 1976] 38-164).

Numerous careful analyses of classical Christian theism address these issues. For example, see Robert M. Grant, *Gods and the One God*, Library of Early Christianity, ed.

discusses biblical references to divine repentance (for example, in Genesis 6:6), he argues as follows.

> Surely its [repentance's] meaning is like that of *all other modes of speaking that describe God for us* in *human terms*. For because our weakness does not attain to his exalted state, the description of him that is given to us must be *accommodated to our capacity* so that we may understand it. Now the mode of accommodation is for him to represent himself to us *not as he is in himself,* but *as he seems to us*.[8]

Although I will address this issue in a different context later, here I emphasize only an epistemological point. Calvin bluntly refuses to attribute any sort of dynamism or change to God, even when the language of the Christian scriptures attributes such qualities to God. Calvin considers such language only as divine accommodation to human perceptions and understanding, and not as a reflection of that which God actually is in God's own self, since such attributions to God would contradict divine immutability and, therefore, dissolve the very deity of God. Hence, behind Calvin's hermeneutical principle of accommodation, with which he interprets such biblical language about God, operate presuppositions about the divine nature that Calvin has not derived from the Christian scriptures themselves. From such presuppositions about the

---

Wayne A. Meeks (Philadelphia: Westminster Press, 1986) 75-83; G. L. Prestige, *God in Patristic Thought*, 2nd ed. (London: S.P.C.K., 1952; S.P.C.K. paperback, 1964) 1-24; J. N. D. Kelly, *Early Christian Doctrines*, rev. ed. (San Francisco: Harper & Row, 1978) 14-28, 83-87. More recently, others have studied the relationship of classical Christian theism to the modern and contemporary worlds: as examples, see Langdon Gilkey, "God," in *Christian Theology: An Introduction to Its Traditions and Tasks*, ed. Peter C. Hodgson and Robert H. King, rev. and enlarged ed. (Philadelphia: Fortress Press, 1985) 88-113; also as "The Christian Understanding of God" in Gilkey, *Through the Tempest*, 69-88. Also see G. A. Cole's careful though brief description of classical theism: "Towards a New Metaphysic of the Exodus," *The Reformed Theological Review* 42 (September-December 1983): 75-76. In addition, see the distinction between classical Christian theism and biblical Christian theism made in excellent, recent Evangelical critiques of classical theism: Clark Pinnock, Richard Rice, John Sanders, William Hasker, and David Basinger, *The Openness of God: A Biblical Challenge to the Traditional Understanding of God* (Downers Grove IL: InterVarsity Press, 1994).

[8]Calvin, *Institutes*, 1:227 (1.17.13); emphasis mine. Calvin takes this same approach in his commentary on Genesis: *Commentaries on the First Book of Moses Called Genesis*, trans. John King (Grand Rapids: Eerdmans, 1948) 1:219. See Calvin's similar statements regarding divine wrath and the atonement (e.g., Calvin, *Institutes*, 1:462-463 [2.11.13]).

nature of God, arises Calvin's hermeneutical theory of divine accommodation. Although elsewhere Timothy George correctly notes that Calvin borrowed the concept of accommodation from classical rhetoric, George fails to discern or conveniently ignores the presuppositions about the divine nature that Calvin also borrowed from classical philosophy via the Christian thought of Augustine among others.[9] These presuppositions clearly determine the operation of and conclusions derived from Calvin's and the *RPTSC*'s hermeneutical principle of divine accommodation.

In a second example, the *RPTSC* vigorously defends the designation of God as "father" against purported attacks in contemporary theology.[10] Again, this emphasis may indicate a solid though unstated reliance on Calvin's concept of God. For Calvin, whatever knowledge of God humans may derive from "contemplating the universe," humans cannot infer thereby that "he is Father." According to Calvin, knowledge of God as father comes only through faith in Christ. A person truly has faith only when "convinced by a firm conviction that God is a kindly and well-disposed Father toward him." Calvin gives an extremely prominent, perhaps the central, place to the image of fatherhood in his doctrine of God.[11] While much of this emphasis mirrors biblical perspectives, several problems accompany the *RPTSC*'s statements about divine fatherhood, especially as contextualized in Calvin's broader doctrine of God. I will address this claim more extensively later.

Although neither of the previous illustrations conclusively demonstrate my claim about the Calvinistic theological assumptions behind the *RPTSC*, I simply note that much of the *RPTSC*'s language about God *suggests* that the document's framers have adopted, though neither openly nor critically, a sixteenth-century Calvinistic interpretation of biblical theism as the only or the normative interpretation of biblical theism. The examples previously supplied merely amplify the *RPTSC*'s unqualified affirmations of divine sovereignty. *Uncritical* receptions of doctrinal perspectives from sixteenth-century reformations (or any other theological tradition) tend to ignore distortions, even distortions in the creative and

---

[9]George, *Theology of the Reformers*, 192-94, 199-213.

[10]*RPTSC*, 116 (2.2.9).

[11]Calvin, *Institutes*, 1:341, 562 (2.6.1; 3.2.16). Brian Gerrish emphasizes this point about Calvin's doctrine of God: *"for faith*, God is above all the benevolent Father"*: Gerrish, *The Old Protestantism and the New: Essays on the Reformation Heritage* (Chicago: University of Chicago Press, 1982) 204.

powerful interpretations of the Christian traditions from that pivotal period of theological suspicion and retrieval. As I examine two related major difficulties in the *RPTSC*'s doctrine of God, this weakness becomes more obvious.

II. Divine Gender?

As I noted previously, a second major difficulty also revolves around the *RPTSC*'s statements about divine fatherhood. The *RPTSC* declares that "God has revealed Himself as the Father of the redeemed." The *RPTSC*, however, both understands the designation of God as "father" to be God's *name* and construes Jesus' model prayer as a mandate for every disciple to use this particular *name* to speak or to refer to God. On this basis, the *RPTSC* launches a very specific attack against feminist theologies: "We have no right to reject God's own name for Himself, nor to employ impersonal or feminine names in order to placate modern sensitivities."[12] Although other issues invite critical scrutiny, I consider only two related questions raised by the *RPTSC*'s unqualified affirmations of divine fatherhood.

A. Does the Term "Father" Name God?

Is the word "father" really a name? In one sense, as a designation for God, the term "father" does name God. Such language, however, operates more to describe a relationship with God or a role assumed by God, than to state an immutable divine name. The prophet Hosea, for example, describes the intimate relationship between God and Israel as a marital relationship, referring to God as husband and to Israel as wife and

---

[12]*RPTSC*, 116 (2.2.9). This emphasis on divine fatherhood in the *RPTSC* incorporates the substance and much of the same wording of a resolution promoted (perhaps written) by Mohler and adopted by the SBC during its annual meeting in 1992. Despite that resolution's admissions "that God is Spirit and beyond any human gender," the resolution with biblical support vehemently defends references to God as "father," declares designations of God as father to be "central and essential to trinitarian faith," and appeals to all Christians "to remain faithful" to this particular biblical language for God. This resolution, however, completely ignores and avoids the multitude of other biblical descriptions of and *actual* names for God. This particular resolution itself both declares a false alternative through its reductionistic construal of the content of the Christian scriptures and, thereby, obscures the biblical witness ("Resolution No. 1—On God the Father," in *Annual of the SBC* [1992]: 86-87). The *RPTSC*, as a consequence, perpetuates the inscription of these distortions.

mother.[13] Yet, few people, if any at all, would describe the term "husband," in the strictest sense, as a name for God. While the prophet does refer to God with this term, the word describes an intimate relationship with God, but in no way functions as God's name. In the same way, when Jesus refers to God as "father," he designates both the intimate relationship with God in which all faithful humans participate and one primary series of roles or functions exercised by God as parent of God's beloved children, but not by any means every divine role, function, or activity. This informal term for addressing God, however, attests to an intimate relationship, not to God's official name or title. Although a child addresses a parent as father or mother, the child invokes and describes a relationship with the parent; yet, the term of endearment does not *name* the parent. While a wife may refer to her spouse as husband, this role, function, or relationship does not represent her spouse's name. One role or function does not exhaustively describe even a human life; much less does one term, role, or type of relationship definitively designate the divine life and activity. Even the *RPTSC* supposedly acknowledges this point: "we affirm that no human words can exhaust the divine majesty."[14]

Following the logic invoked by the *RPTSC*, however, if the term "father" names God in the sense implied by the *RPTSC*, then so too does the biblical designation of God as the husband of God's people. Consequently, both the *RPTSC*'s own understanding of the inspiration of all Christian scriptures and that document's declaration that "we have no right to reject God's own name for Himself" require, or at the very least allow, Baptist Christians to use all of the names for God attested by the scriptures, including the word "husband" as God's name. As I have indicated previously, however, such designations do not name God, even though metaphorically they describe various aspects of the relationship between God and humans.

Nonetheless, the scriptures contain many other actual *names* for God, divine names certainly available for use by Christians. Among those names, for example, the scriptures include the name "El Shaddai," a name based upon a word for a very specific portion of the female anatomy, to refer to God as source and nurturer.[15] For more than a

---

[13]E.g., Hosea 2:1-23. The prophet Ezekiel also refers to God as the faithful yet betrayed husband of Israel (esp. Ezek 6:9; 16:6-63).

[14]*RPTSC*, 116 (2.2.9).

[15]See the appearances of this name for God in the following texts: Gen 17:1-2; 28:3;

century, scholarly consensus has traced the derivation of the name "El Shaddai" from the Akkadian word *shadu*, which means "mountain." Most significantly, in the early twentieth century, the studies of both E. P. Dhorme and W. F. Albright demonstrated that, originally, the word *shadu* meant "breast," and only later signified "mountain." More recently, scholars have discovered perhaps a more probable linguistic origin of the name "El Shaddai" in the Egyptian word *shdi*, which means "to suckle."[16] Thus, if divine functions (such as the divine nursing of human infants) express legitimate names for God, then the scriptures even authorize the use of the words "mother," "breasted one," or "nurse" as proper designations for God. This name for God both represents a powerful counter-example to the *RPTSC*'s claims about the divine name and, consequently, illustrates the *RPTSC*'s reductive approach to the superabundance of meaning in the scriptures. My response to a second question extends the implications of such biblical examples.

B. Do the Christian Scriptures Refer to God Only with Masculine Language?

Do the Christian scriptures, in all such role-designating language about God, exclusively refer to God with masculine terms? According to the *RPTSC*, "we have no right . . . to employ impersonal or feminine names in order to placate modern sensitivities." Yet, by the *RPTSC*'s own guidelines, since the Christian scriptures describe God's activity in terms of feminine roles or with feminine terms, then, given the *RPTSC*'s own claims about biblical authority and that document's own concept of naming, the scriptures themselves have authorized the employment of "feminine names" for God. Even if feminine metaphorical descriptions of God do not name in the strictest sense, as I have claimed, since such

---

35:9-12; 43:14; 48:3-4; 49:25; Num 24:4, 16; Psa 68:14-16.

[16]For the history and current state of this discussion, see the following: Friedrich Delitsch, *Prolegomena eines neuen hebräisch-aramäischen Wörterbuches zum Alten Testament* (Leipzig, 1886) 95-97; idem, *Assyrisches Handwörterbuch* (Leipzig, 1894–1896) 642-43; E. P. Dhorme, "L'Emploi metaphorique des noms de parties du corps en Hebreu et en Akkadien," *Revue Biblique* 31 (1922): 230-31; William F. Albright, "The Names Shaddai and Abram," *Journal of Biblical Literature* 54 (1935): 180-93; Frank Moore Cross, "Yahweh and the God of the Patriarchs," *Harvard Theological Review* 55 (1962): 244-50; idem, *Canaanite Myth and Hebrew Epic: Essays in the History of the Religion of Israel* (Cambridge MA: Harvard University Press, 1973) 52-60; David Biale, "The God with Breasts: El Shaddai in the Bible," *History of Religions* 21 (February 1982): 241-56.

descriptions actually appear in the scriptures, those scriptures still have authorized their use as legitimate discourse with which to describe or to refer to God.

In answer to my question, obviously the Christian scriptures do not describe God exclusively in masculine terms. I cite only a few of numerous examples from the scriptures. In several places, the Hebrew scriptures describe God as a woman giving birth to either the entire creation or to God's people. Even in the Gospel of John, Jesus tells Nicodemus that he must be born again, or from above, born from God the Holy Spirit, in order to experience the kingdom of God.[17] Even the word used to refer to divine compassion for the Hebrew people comes from the Hebrew word *rechem*, which means "womb." In places, the Hebrew scriptures even refer to God as carrying the people in the divine womb.[18] Some Baptists in the SBC have discovered these riches from the Christian scriptures as well.[19]

Why did the framers of the *RPTSC* belittle the use of feminine language to describe God by misrepresenting the contents of the scriptures themselves? Despite the *RPTSC*'s two rhetorical courtesies toward gender inclusiveness,[20] this document's intentional misrepresentation of the Christian scriptures discloses the PTSC's obviously patriarchal attitudes toward women in general.[21] Perhaps the committee also intends,

---

[17]See Deut 32:18; Isa 49:15; 66:7-9; John 3:1-8.

[18]See, as examples, Jer 31:20; Isa 46:3-4.

[19]For example, Paul R. Smith, *Is It Okay to Call God "Mother"? Considering the Feminine Face of God* (Peabody MA: Hendrikson, 1993). Smith serves as minister of Broadway Baptist Church (a local church still participating in the SBC) in Kansas City, Missiouri. See also the excellent work of Jann Aldredge-Clanton in which she recovers the resources in the feminine dimensions of biblical Wisdom-Christology for contemporary Christian theology, spirituality, ethics, and worship (Aldredge-Clanton, *In Search of Christ-Sophia: An Inclusive Christology for Liberating Christians* [Mystic CT: Twenty-Third Publications, 1995]; also see idem, *In Whose Image? God and Gender* [New York: Crossroad, 1990]). An ordained Baptist minister, Jann Aldredge-Clanton has served in Baptist institutions for twenty-five years. By contrast, however, reactionary Baptist responses also continue to appear: for example, see the recent flippant, sarcastic, unkind, and even denigrating, yet virtually uninformed, attack on Christians who explore biblical imagery of God as female: Calvin Miller, "Is God a Girl or Not?" *SBC Life* (February/March 1996): 2 (Miller teaches at SWBTS).

[20]Such as, "the direct creation of *humankind*," "the God of Abraham, Isaac, and Jacob, *of Sarah, and Rachel, and Ruth*" (*RPTSC*, 114, 115 [2.1.5; 2.2.7]; emphasis mine).

[21]Also see further discussion of these issues in Jürgen Moltmann, "The Motherly

with both its apology for masculine God-language and its polemic against feminine God-language, finally to establish conclusively the theological norm with which to legitimize its as yet unstated intention (at least, in the *RPTSC*) to exclude women from pastoral ministries in particular.

Father: Is Trinitarian Patripassianism Replacing Theological Patriarchalism?" in *Concilium: Religion in the Eighties*, vol. 143, *God as Father?* ed. Johannes-Baptist Metz, Edward Schillebeeckx, and Marcus Lefébure (New York: Seabury Press, 1981) 51-56. During its annual meeting in June 1984, the SBC, by adopting a resolution (58.03% in favor, 41.97% against, of the messengers who voted), stated its opposition to the participation of women in "pastoral functions and leadership roles entailing ordination" ("Resolution No. 3—On Ordination and the Role of Women in Ministry," in *Annual of the SBC* [1984]: 60, 65). In August 1984, an advertisement appeared in a newspaper in Louisville, Kentucky. This advertisement, itself written as a confession, expressed disapproval of the SBC's then very fresh resolution against women in pastoral ministry, affirmed the role of women in ministry, and affirmed the autonomy of local churches. Mohler's signature appeared among more than 200 sponsoring signatures on this advertisement, just above the signature of Roy L. Honeycutt (*Courier-Journal* [Louisville], 4 August 1984). Of course, recently, Mohler, as president of Southern Baptist Theological Seminary, has refused to consider David Sherwood as a member of the seminary's faculty, because Sherwood believes that God may call women as well as men to pastoral ministry in local churches. In an interview, Mohler states his own *most recent viewpoint* quite bluntly: " 'I hold to the traditional understanding based on Scripture that women should not serve in the office of pastor. . . . We will not apologize for hiring only . . . persons that reflect this position, but we are not seeking to deny evangelical authenticity to those with whom we disagree on this position' " (Joe Maxwell, "PC Meets CC," *World* 10 [29 April 1995]: 17; cf. Diana R. Garland, "What's Really Going on at Southern Seminary?" *Western Recorder* 169 [18 April 1995]: 7). Similarly, in a sermon during chapel at MBTS on 11 April 1996, Coppenger described the contemporary phenomenon of women ministering in the role of pastor as "one of the raging, raging heresies and confusions of the day," "an affront to the creation order," "an affront to home and family," and "a threat to the order of the home" ("Coppenger: Women Pastors Dangerous," *Western Recorder* 170 [7 May 1996]: 2). In justified responses to Coppenger's preposterous and unverifiable declarations, genuine Baptists correctly assessed the character of Coppenger's remarks: as examples, while one Baptist perceived that the SBC's institutional concept of the Christian Bible's inerrancy "is merely a mask for the suppression of women," another Baptist rightly noted that "the only concept dangerous while looking at women pastors is the time and energy spent debating over it" (John P. Reed, "Male Domination," *Western Recorder* 170 [28 May 1996]: 4; Dawn M. Richardson, "God Has Answers," *Western Recorder* 170 [28 May 1996]: 4).

III. Divine Illimitability?

As a third additional problem in its doctrine of God, the *RPTSC* unqualifiedly affirms Divine illimitability: "God is limitless in power, knowledge, wisdom, love, and holiness." The *RPTSC* rejects "any effort to redefine God as a limited deity."[22] Timothy George, as cochairperson of the PTSC, appears to have reproduced his own perspective in the *RPTSC* once again. George adheres very closely to the theological perspectives of the mainline, Protestant reformers of the sixteenth century, specifically, to Calvin's perspective. Similarly for George, and as he states it, "the Protestant reformers saw themselves in continuity with the Trinitarian and Christological consensus of the early church."[23] Elsewhere, George equates all notions of divine limitation with that which he describes as "the transcendence-starved deity of process theology." In his discussion about the doctrine of God, George reinforces his perspective with two Calvinistic Baptist confessions of faith. As support for his understanding of the "*absoluteness* of God," George quotes a text from the "Second London Confession" of 1677, a confession based upon and, in both form and substance, with some variations almost identical to the Calvinistic "Westminster Confession of Faith": God is "immutable, immense, eternal, incomprehensible, Almighty, every way infinite." According to the fuller text from the "Second London Confession," God is "a most pure spirit, invisible, *without* body, parts, or *passions*, . . . *immutable*, immense, eternal, incomprehensible, Almighty, every way infinite, most holy, most wise, most free, *most absolute*." As easily perceived by comparing the previous and following samples, the "Westminster Confession of Faith" clearly supplied its Baptist imitation with much of its exact wording: God is "a most pure spirit, invisible, without body, parts, or passions, immutable, immense, eternal, incomprehensible, almighty, most wise, most holy, most free, most absolute." While the "Second London Confession" certainly remains part of the larger Baptist heritage, the SBC did not produce this confession, nor any confession fully consistent with it. Moreover, the SBC's confessional statements have never infused the doctrine of God with the meaning ascribed to that doctrine by the concepts of either divine immutability or

---

[22]*RPTSC*, 115 (2.2.6).
[23]George, "Reformation Roots of the Baptist Tradition," 12.

divine impassibility, as confessed by both the "Second London Confession" and its parent, the "Westminster Confession of Faith." George endeavors to support his own concept of complete divine involvement with creation, or his doctrine of providence, by referring to Calvin's notion that "in every one of life's events human beings have direct 'business with God' (*negotium cum Deo*)." As an exposition of Calvin's concept, George quotes a text from Southern Baptist Theological Seminary's confessional statement, the "Abstract of Principles," concerning God's predestination and complete control of creation's processes and events: "God from eternity, decrees *or permits* all things that come to pass, and perpetually upholds, directs, and governs all creatures and all events."[24]

---

[24]George, "Renewal of Baptist Theology," 21; "The Assembly or Second London Confession, 1677 and 1688," in *Baptist Confessions of Faith*, Lumpkin, 252 ("Of God and of the Holy Trinity" [2.1]); "The Westminster Confession of Faith, A.D. 1647," in *The Creeds of Christendom*, vol. 3, *The Evangelical Protestant Creeds*, 6th ed., ed. Philip Schaff and David S. Schaff (New York: Harper & Row, 1931; repr., Grand Rapids MI: Baker Book House, 1990) 606 (chap. II, "Of God, and of the Holy Trinity"); *AP (1858)*, 38 (IV. "Providence"); emphasis mine. Notwithstanding, according to John Calvin, God "repudiates" the distinction between divine "doing and permitting" as a "falsehood" and an "evasion," since humans cannot accomplish anything except by God's "secret command," "secret direction," or previous and eternal decree (Calvin, *Institutes*, 1:228-37 [1.18.1-4]; 1:309-16 [2.4.1-8]; 2:947-64 [3.23.1-14]). Jaroslav Pelikan carefully examines Calvin's rigorous and thorough rejection of the notion of divine permission (Pelikan, *The Christian Tradition: A History of the Development of Doctrine*, vol. 4, *Reformation of Church and Dogma [1300–1700]* [Chicago: University of Chicago Press, 1984] 223-25). The *AP (1858)*, the articles of faith for SBTS, clearly contains an inconsistent modification (although a prudent beginning), at this very point, of Calvin's understanding of God's activity and will. According to the *AP (1858)*, "God from eternity, decrees *or permits* all things that come to pass, and perpetually upholds, directs, and governs all creatures and all events; yet so as not in any wise to be the author or approver of sin nor to destroy the free will and responsibility of intelligent creatures" (*AP [1858]*, 38 [IV. "Providence"]; emphasis mine). Naturally, this emphasis in the *AP 1858* arises from Boyce's influence on this document's content. Boyce held and vehemently defended the notion of divine permission. Unlike Calvin, for whom God's decree prior to creation caused all humans (elect and reprobate alike) to fall into sin (Calvin, *Institutes*, 2:955-56 [3.23.7]), Boyce espoused a milder (though inconsistent) notion: that God permitted sin. "It is neither as an effect of Election or Rejection or of Preterition that man has fallen, or sins, or is condemned, or will be destroyed. The simple effect is that he is not rescued, and consequently is left where he would have been without these acts. They do not lead to destruction. They simply do not rescue from it" (Boyce, *Abstract of Systematic Theology*, 362). According to the stricter Calvinism of John Gill (1697–1771), an English Baptist, while "God pre-

Certainly, like the writers of the *RPTSC, some Baptists* in the SBC have shared and continue to share such perspectives. The *RPTSC*'s formulation essentially reproduces James Petigru Boyce's perspective, however, even using many of Boyce's own linguistic expressions.[25] Nonetheless, although the *RPTSC*'s formulation enlists part of the truth, by ignoring other aspects of the truth, the apparent strength of this perspective intentionally conceals dangerous distortions of biblical perspectives on the divine life and activity.

When the *RPTSC* rejects "any effort to redefine God as a limited deity," the *RPTSC* leads its readers to understand, or implies, that the concept of divine limitation refers only to constraint "by any external force or internal contradiction." The document also implies that Baptists, specifically Baptists in the SBC, have never understood God as limited in any sense.[26] Both of the *RPTSC*'s implications require critical responses.

If the *RPTSC* rejects *any concept of God as limited*, or *"any effort* to redefine God as a limited deity," then that document also rejects the concept of divine *self*-limitation, as a subset within the set of all concepts of divine limitations. Assuming such a posture, consequently, the *RPTSC* also rejects clear teachings from the Christian scriptures, in order to affirm presuppositions from Reformed Protestant scholasticism on which it has established its own idea of God.

For example, although the creator of all that exists and as such the source of all power (omnipotent), God shares power with God's creation, most obviously with the human as the image of God. God did not desire for humans to betray the divine love, but God gave humans freedom to sin. Contrary to the divine desire for human life, humans betrayed God through the very power with which God has endowed them. According

---

determined the fall of Adam," according to the divine decree, God also "permitted or suffered Adam to sin and fall," where Gill interpreted divine permission as "voluntary, wise, holy, powerful, and efficacious," influentially permitted by God only "as a mean of glorifying his grace and mercy, justice, and holiness" (John Gill, *A Body of Doctrinal and Practical Divinity* [London: n.p., 1769; repr., Atlanta: Turner Lassetter, 1965] 319 [3.8.2.2, 3]).

[25]For example, "when we say that God is infinite, we deny to him all limitation in his nature or essence. . . . we deny all such limitation in him, and therefore ascribe to him infinity as to time and space, as well as infinite perfection in his mode of existence, in his power, wisdom, goodness, justice, holiness, and truth" (Boyce, *Abstract of Systematic Theology*, 68).

[26]*RPTSC*, 115 (2.2.6).

to the book of Genesis, prior to the "flood of the world," the pervasive-
ness of human sin grieved God; according to book of Isaiah, Israel's
betrayal of God's loving mercy also grieved God. Even Pauline writings
in the New Testament refer to the abilities of reconciled people to limit
the indwelling Holy Spirit's work: reminding both Thessalonian
Christians not to quench the Spirit and Ephesian Christians not to grieve
the Holy Spirit of God.[27] The scriptures do not describe God as "without

---

[27]Gen 1:26-31; 3:1-24; 6:5-6; Isa 63:7-10; 1 Thess 5:19; Eph 4:30. Both Luther and
Calvin interpreted such biblical texts through the philosophical presuppositions of classical
theism. As Isaak August Dorner insightfully notes, although the sixteenth-century
Protestant reformers developed soteriologies *implicitly* or *latently* containing "a better, yes,
the true concept of God," those soteriologies (including Luther's and Calvin's) and those
of their dogmatic heirs "left standing a doctrine of God which, built up from other
principles, was taken over traditionally from the pre-Reformation church and remained
essentially consonant with the Roman doctrine, as if the purification from non-Christian
conceptions did not have to extend also to this doctrine, whereas in fact the medieval
doctrine of God in large part and clearly goes back to non-Christian sources" (Isaak
August Dorner, "Dogmatic Discussion of the Doctrine of the Immutability of God," in
*God and Incarnation in Mid-Nineteenth Century German Theology: G. Thomasius, I. A.
Dorner, A. E. Biedermann,* ed. and trans. Claude Welch, A Library of Protestant Thought,
ed. John Dillenberger et al. [New York: Oxford University Press, 1965] 116). Luther's
understanding of divine hiddenness (not so much God as veiled in Christ's flesh
[hiddenness 2], but the divine majesty as operative in nature and history [hiddenness 1])
governs his interpretation of language that attributes suffering to God. On Luther's views
about the hiddenness of God, see Gerrish, *Old Protestantism and the New,* 131-59. Luther
understands God "in His essence" as "immutable and unchanging in His counsel from
eternity" and "altogether unknowable." On this basis, with reference to the language about
divine grief in Gen 6:6, Luther contends that "God lowers Himself to the level of our
weak comprehension and presents Himself to us in images, in coverings, as it were, in
simplicity adapted to a child, that in some measure it may be possible for Him to be
known by us." Thus, Luther firmly refuses to attribute any sort of real suffering to God.
"One should not imagine that God has a heart or that He can grieve. But when the spirit
of Noah, of Lamech, and of Methuselah is grieved, God Himself *is said* [emphasis mine]
to be grieved. Thus we should understand this grief to refer to its effect, not to the divine
essence. When, by revelation of the Holy Spirit, Noah and his father and grandfather
perceived in their hearts that God hated the world because of its sins and intended to
destroy it, they were grieved by its impenitence. . . . The inexpressible groanings of these
outstanding men *are assigned to* [emphasis mine] God Himself because they proceed
from His Spirit." Luther continues, "it is unbelievable how much the contemplation of the
wrath of God depresses the heart" (Luther, *Luther's Works,* vol. 2, *Lectures on Genesis:
Chapters 6-14,* ed. Jaroslav Pelikan, trans. George V. Schick [Saint Louis: Concordia
Publishing House, 1960] 45, 49, 50, 54). Also see Luther's similar comments on Isa
63:10: *Luther's Works,* vol. 17, *Lectures on Isaiah: Chapters 40-66,* ed. Hilton C.

. . . passions."[28] Unless God *willed* to grieve or to suffer prior to or regardless of human betrayal, something external to God affected the divine self, even if God had established the very possibilities of such external influences. By giving humans freedom to sin or not to sin, God limited the divine power, since God could have prevented human sin entirely by not giving humans such freedom, by not creating the very conditions of possibility for sin. By giving humans such freedom, then, God risked the suffering inflicted on Godself by human betrayal of God's love. Here the scriptures even challenge the *RPTSC*'s sixth affirmation about God: "that God is *sovereign* over history, nature, time, and space."[29] If God *completely controls* human history, as the *RPTSC*'s use

---

Oswald, trans. Herbert J. A. Bouman (Saint Louis: Concordia Publishing House, 1972) 358. Calvin comments similarly about the language of Gen 6:5-6. Because humans "cannot comprehend him [God] as he is, it is necessary that, for our sake, he should, *in a certain sense, transform himself.* . . . Certainly God is not sorrowful or sad; but remains for ever like himself in his celestial and happy repose: yet, because it could not otherwise be known how great is God's hatred and detestation of sin, therefore the Spirit *accommodates himself to our capacity.* . . . as if he would say, 'This is not my workmanship; this is not that man who was formed in my image, and whom I had adorned with such excellent gifts: I do not deign now to acknowledge this degenerate and defiled creature as mine.' . . . that God was so offended by the atrocious wickedness of men, *as if* they had wounded his heart with mortal grief." According to Calvin, God, "in order more effectually to pierce *our hearts, clothes himself* with *our affections*" (Calvin, *Commentaries on the First Book of Moses Called Genesis*, trans. John King [Grand Rapids: Eerdmans, 1948] 1:219, emphasis mine; also see Calvin, *Institutes* 1.5.1; 1.11.3; 1.13.21; 1.15.5; 1.17.12-14; 2.11.13).

[28]For example, Terence E. Fretheim helpfully demonstrates "how *common understandings* of sovereignty in Exodus (and elsewhere) are subverted by suffering metaphors and an understanding of sovereignty more congruent with the text can emerge" (Fretheim, "Suffering God and Sovereign God in Exodus: A Collision of Images," *Horizons in Biblical Theology* 11 [December 1989]: 32). Walter Brueggemann, citing Exodus 3:7-8a, expresses a similar thought (Brueggemann, "The Rhetoric of Hurt and Hope: Ethics Odd and Crucial," in *The Annual of the Society of Christian Ethics* [1989]: 79). Fretheim helps correct the tendency, often expressed in older theologies of the Hebrew scriptures, to see divine sovereignty as the metaphor for God that concentrates and organizes the entire O.T. As an example, see the neoorthodox perspective of Edmond Jacob: "what gives the Old Testament its force and unity is the affirmation of the sovereignty of God" (Jacob, *Theology of the Old Testament*, trans. Arthur W. Heathcote and Philip J. Allcock [New York: Harper & Brothers, 1958] 37).

[29]*RPTSC*, 116 (2.2.11); emphasis mine. According to the fifth article of the *BFM (1963)*, "Believers may fall into sin through neglect and temptation, whereby *they grieve the Spirit*, impair their graces and comforts, bring reproach on the cause of Christ, and

of the term "sovereign" suggests, then God also causes sin. To the contrary, according to the scriptures, since God does not will evil, then God does not completely control everything done by humans; God does not make humans sin; and, therefore, since only sin separates humans from God, God did not create any human for damnation.

Even though Boyce denied all limitations to God's power, defining God's power as "the effective energy inherent in his nature by which he is able to do all things," nevertheless, he also claimed that God, although not subject to human or creaturely limitations, "is limited in his power." For Boyce, God's limitations "arise, not from without, but from the excellence and perfection of his own nature," limitations "congruent with his will, which can never desire to do what his nature does not permit": limitations such as divine impeccability, impossibility of divine self-contradiction, immutability of the divine nature, decrees, and purposes. In spite of these claims, however, Boyce also affirms human freedom to sin or human fallibility, as something created by God, but denies God's desire for sin itself.[30] Despite the contradictions intrinsic to Boyce's softer Calvinism, even Boyce at least qualified his own affirmation of divine illimitability.

More significantly, E. Y. Mullins bequeathed to Baptists in the SBC a more adequate biblical understanding of God in this regard. Although the *RPTSC* employs a quote by Mullins as an authority for its final doctrinal formulation, the *RPTSC* intentionally avoids references to his understanding of God. According to Mullins, basing his comments on Philippians 2:5-11, one must describe God as a limited God in one sense: the *self-limiting God*. God limited God's own self both when God created all things and when God became human as Jesus of Nazareth. More radically still, due to the limitations peculiar to human creatureliness, "if deity becomes incarnate it can only be under such limitations." In Mullins's understanding, through divine self-limitation, God exercises more power than God does according to either the *RPTSC*'s concept or even Boyce's understanding of God, since the self-limiting God *can do*

---

temporal judgments on themselves, yet they shall be kept by the power of God through faith unto salvation" ("God's Purpose of Grace," *BFM [1963]*, 275; emphasis mine). This affirmation alludes, of course, to Eph 4:30, even though the *BFM (1963)* cites this reference only among the scriptures that follow the third section of the article on the doctrine of God, on "God the Holy Spirit" (*BFM [1963]*, 272).

[30]Boyce, *Abstract of Systematic Theology*, 68, 83, 84, 85, 214, 216.

something more than the absolutely unlimited God can do: the biblical God can even limit (voluntarily or without any compulsion) God's own self, can use divine power to limit God's power. To Mullins, "the capacity for self-limitation is a mark of the infinite perfection of God," not, as the *RPTSC* states, the redefinition of "God as a limited deity."[31]

Even Herschel Hobbs, in his commentary on the *BFM (1963)*, flatly contradicts the *RPTSC* on this point. Although Hobbs also affirms the omnipotence of God, unlike the *RPTSC*, he also qualifies his affirmation: "The only limits to his [God's] power are self-imposed," limitations that function as "evidences of God's power, not of his weakness."[32]

Analogue. Episode Six

Following their deliverance from the Egyptian army, as the liberated Hebrews awaited the return of Moses from the mountain of Sinai, they became impatient. The people desired a tangible and visible not an auditory representation of their God, an image of immediate divine manifestation not an invisible God mediated to them through another human, an ever-present not apparently a sporadically absent God. Thus, they instructed their leader Aaron to construct a god who would lead them. To this end, the people contributed their golden jewelry, perhaps the very treasure that Yahweh had enabled them to plunder from Egypt, to produce this image of God. In a syncretistic impulse, the people represented God as a young bull. Perhaps the people honored the memory of their Egyptian sojourn by constructing an image of the Egyptian god

---

[31]Mullins, *Christian Religion in Its Doctrinal Expression*, 181, 182, 183, 186. In the nineteenth century, the Baptist theologian A. H. Strong also developed the concept of divine self-limitation (Strong, "God's Self-Limitations," *Baptist Quarterly Review* 13 [January 1891]: 521-32). More recently, H. Wheeler Robinson and Paul S. Fiddes, British Baptists, have also advocated divine self-limitation (Robinson, *Redemption and Revelation in the Actuality of History* [New York: Harper & Brothers, 1942] 267; Fiddes, *The Creative Suffering of God* [Oxford: Clarendon Press: 1988] 32-33, 45, 74-75). Warren McWilliams, a Baptist theologian who teaches theology at Oklahoma Baptist University, also embraces the concept of divine self-limitation with his own qualifications (McWilliams, *The Passion of God: Divine Suffering in Contemporary Protestant Theology* [Macon GA: Mercer University Press, 1985] 73-95). Even B. A. Copass supported his own understanding of human freedom with a concept of divine self-limitation (Copass, "Concerning the Baptist Confession of Faith" ["III—Of the Fall of Man"], *Baptist Standard* 26 [25 June 1914]: 7).

[32]Hobbs, *Baptist Faith and Message*, 36.

Apis and, by identifying Yahweh with Apis, also intended to invoke divine power for their return to Egypt. Despite the dynamic reality displayed by this virile image, by representing Yahweh as a golden calf, the people converted the invisibly free and unpredictable God of the wilderness expanses into the manageable and predictable God of a civilization in harmony with and organized strictly according to the world's natural cycles, fixing the active divine presence into a static object of power at the people's disposal. Furthermore, despite any qualities held in common between Yahweh and Apis, the people's representation of Yahweh as one particular creature reduced the infinite qualities in Yahweh's vitality to a single and limited range of qualities and possibilities, in addition to distorting those qualities of power in the divine life actually disclosed, however partially, by this image.[33]

Similarly, the *RPTSC* embraces a concept of divine sovereignty derived mainly from the sixteenth-century theology of John Calvin, a concept of God still remarkably medieval and unreformed (despite the soteriological reformations initiated by Luther and advanced by Calvin) and, hence, still heavily dependent on and distorted by an inheritance from Hellenistic philosophical sources. Certainly, with an emphasis on divine power, the *RPTSC* affirms a legitimate dimension in the Christian understanding of God. Nevertheless, the *RPTSC*, through its unqualified construal of divine sovereignty, by its virtual reduction of the vitality and richness of God to the notion of absolute sovereignty, distorts the fuller reality of God: that divine reality also marked by suffering and weakness even prior to God's becoming human as Jesus of Nazareth. Furthermore, consistent with its credalizing aim, the *RPTSC* declares its own idea of this absolutely sovereign God to be the norm for all Baptists in the SBC.

Did the members of the PTSC truly "submit" themselves, as the *RPTSC* claims, "to the knowledge God has imparted concerning Himself and His divine nature?"[34] Clearly, the *RPTSC* misrepresents both the bib-

---

[33]Exod 3:20-22; 11:2-3; 12:35-36; 32:1-35; cf. Psalm 105:37; Acts 7:39-41; 1 Cor 10:7-8. Also, see the following works for helpful exegetical discussions related to these narratives: Brevard S. Childs, *The Book of Exodus: A Critical, Theological Commentary*, Old Testament Library, Peter Ackroyd, James Barr, John Bright, and G. Ernest Wright, gen. eds. (Philadelphia: Westminster Press, 1974) 552-81; Gerhard von Rad, *Old Testament Theology*, vol. 1, *The Theology of Israel's Historical Traditions*, trans. D. M. G. Stalker (New York: Harper & Row, 1962) 203-19.

[34]*RPTSC*, 115 (2.3.5).

lical bases for the previous divine characteristics and the history of their interpretation among Baptists, with exclusive and unqualified uses of the notions of sovereignty and fatherhood. As Terence E. Fretheim notes, such intentional uses of one metaphorical field to exclude other metaphorical fields in the Bible's language about God, such univocal interpretations of biblical references to divine sovereignty and fatherhood, as examples, qualify as idolatry.[35] These misrepresentations, of course, also have significant ramifications for the *RPTSC*'s remaining theological perspectives, most immediately for its Christology and soteriology.

---

[35]According to Fretheim, "the sovereignty metaphors have commonly been left largely unqualified, with a consequent univocal reading of them. And one way to define idolatry is: a univocal reading of metaphors for God" (Fretheim, "Suffering God and Sovereign God in Exodus," 45). One Baptist theologian, Molly Marshall-Green, has accurately identified this problem in the SBC. "I think the understanding of God which dominates Southern Baptist life today is, to some extent, an elitist view of God. Martin Luther would accuse us of being fascinated with a 'theology of glory.' We have not sufficiently noted the power of the suffering God who stands with marginalized persons and takes suffering up into God's own life in the cross. I think Southern Baptists are often more concerned about God's so-called 'manifest destiny' for themselves than they are concerned about God's self-emptying love for all the world" (Marshall-Green, "Southern Baptist Theology Today: An Interview with Molly Marshall-Green," *Theological Educator* 40 [Fall 1989]: 25).

Chapter 7

Disfigurations in the Concepts of Christ and Salvation

Then they said to Moses, "Is it because there were no graves in Egypt that you have taken us away to die in the wilderness? Why have you dealt with us in this way, bringing us out of Egypt?"   (Exodus 14:11 NASB)

And all the sons of Israel grumbled against Moses and Aaron; and the whole congregation said to them, "Would that we had died in the land of Egypt! Or would that we had died in this wilderness!"

(Numbers 14:2 NASB)

. . . ungodly persons who . . . deny our only Master and Lord Jesus Christ.

(Jude 4d NASB)

Introduction

The Presidential Theological Study Committee produced the *RPTSC*'s Christological and soteriological statements on the basis of traditional Baptist interpretations of these doctrines. Nonetheless, through reductive and biased approaches to these doctrines, this committee also disfigured and inscribed distortions of these central doctrines, as norms, into the *RPTSC*'s Christological and soteriological formulations. The *RPTSC*'s formulations primarily represent the PTSC's responses to three major contemporary theological issues: (1) reaffirmation of the *orthodox* Christian concept of Christ's deity, purportedly as a response both to an overemphasis on Christ's humanity and to denials of *traditional* or *classical* concepts of Christ's deity; (2) reaffirmation of salvation through *Christ alone*, as a response to all concepts of universalism; and (3) reaffirmation of *penal-substitutionary atonement*, as the only legitimate interpretation of the divine effort to save creation, as a response to the committee's narrow construal of alternative Christian theories of atonement. Although the *RPTSC*'s statements imply several other distortions as well, I will examine only the three problematic areas correlative to the *RPTSC*'s three major concerns.

I. Classical Orthodoxy's Christ of Two Natures?

As a first problem, in its Christological language, the *RPTSC* betrays the PTSC's *uncritical commitment* to the ancient conciliar Christological formulations of Christian orthodoxy via their reception and transmission through the orthodox theology of Reformed scholasticism. Two phrases among the *RPTSC*'s Christological statements indicate this document's dependence on the Christology officially and finally adopted by the Council of Chalcedon (451 C.E.): (1) as incarnate, Christ "was the perfect union of the human and the divine"; and (2) Christ "was truly God and truly man."[1]

On the surface and *formally*, these assertions express nothing explicitly inconsistent with historic Baptist commitments to Christ as both divine and human. Linguistically, nonetheless, these statements from the *RPTSC* certainly reflect key formulas from the ancient "Symbol of Chalcedon," rather than biblical language. For example, the Chalcedonian creed refers to Jesus Christ with the following formulations: τέλειον τὸν αὐτὸν ἐν θεότητι, καὶ τέλειον τὸν αὐτὸν ἐν ἀνθρωπότητι, Θεὸν ἀληθῶς, καὶ ἄνθρωπον ἀληθῶς, ... οὐδαμοῦ τῆς τῶν φύσεων διαφορᾶς ἀνῃρημένης διὰ τὴν ἕνωσιν, σωζομένης δε μᾶλλον τῆς ἰδιότητος ἑκατέρας φύσεως.[2] Given the bias or, at least, the penchant of the *RPTSC*'s writers for the Reformed tradition, perhaps the designers of the *RPTSC*'s Christological article shaped these statements with language from Philip Schaff's translation of the Chalcedonian creed: "*perfect in Godhead* and also *perfect in manhood*; *truly God and truly man*, . . . the distinction of natures being by no means taken away by *the union*."[3] Just as probably, and more than likely for the same reason, perhaps the committee used the similar formulations from the "Westmin-

---

[1]*RPTSC*, 116 (2.3.3).

[2]"Symbolum Chalcedonense," in *Enchiridion Symbolorum: Definitionum et Declarationum de Rebus Fidei et Morum*, 33rd ed., ed. Henricus Denzinger and Adolfus Schönmetzer (Freiburg im Breisgau: Verlag Herder, 1965) 301, 302 (108); hereafter, this collection is cited as *DS*.

[3]"Symbolum Chalcedonense," in *The Creeds of Christendom*, vol. 2, *The Greek and Latin Creeds*, 6th ed., ed. Philip Schaff and David S. Schaff (New York: Harper & Row, 1931; repr., Grand Rapids MI: Baker Book House, 1990) 62; cf. different translations, "The Definition of Chalcedon," in *Creeds of the Churches*, 35-36; "Definition of the Two Natures of Christ," in *The Sources of Catholic Dogma*, 30th ed., ed. Henry Denzinger, trans. Roy J. Deferrari (St. Louis MO: B. Herder Book Co., 1957) 60-61; emphasis mine.

ster Confession of Faith" (1646) as the basis for its own Christological statements. This strictly Calvinistic confession, referring to the becoming-human of the Logos, describes a union of the divine and human natures in similar terms: "So that two whole, perfect, and distinct natures, *the Godhead and the manhood*, were *inseparably joined together* in one person"; "which person is *very God and very man*, yet one Christ, the only mediator between God and man."[4]

Even though, formally, these phrases themselves do not necessarily contradict historic Baptist Christological perspectives, insofar as these assertions in the *RPTSC*, beneath the surface and *materially*, reproduce the substance as well as the form of Chalcedonian and Reformed Christologies, the *RPTSC* affirms uncritically an orthodoxy not fully consistent with Baptist interpretations of biblical Christologies. By briefly examining aspects of conciliar Christology's substance, I will clarify this claim.

The critical issues in any appropriation of orthodox conciliar Christology do not revolve so much around the *formal* declaration or acceptance of Christ's divinity and humanity, as much as they revolve rather around two more subtle questions. First, how did this Christology construe or characterize the matter or substance of both the divine and the human natures? Second, how did this Christology conceptualize, on the basis of those characterizations, the relationship between those two natures in the one person of Jesus the Christ? Even though the anthropology of the conciliar tradition contains as many problems in itself, in responding to these two critical questions, I will illustrate my previous claims by considering principally the conciliar tradition's construal of the nature of deity itself as it affects Christology.

The participants in the ancient ecumenical Christian councils shared a common presupposition about the nature of God: immutability and impassibility define the very nature of deity itself. In other words, God can neither change nor suffer in any sense. No representatives during the councils, not even those who finally disagreed with the various conciliar formulations and decrees, neither Apollinaris of Laodicea nor Nestorius as examples, contested the immutability and impassibility of God.[5] For

---

[4]"The Westminster Confession of Faith," in *Creeds of the Churches*, 203-204 (chap. 8.2); emphasis mine.

[5]Apollinaris, "On the Union in Christ of the Body with the Godhead," in *The Christological Controversy*, trans. and ed. Richard A. Norris, Jr., Sources of Early Christian Thought, ed. William G. Rusch (Philadelphia: Fortress Press, 1980) 104, 105,

orthodox and heterodox theologians alike, divine immutability (and, by implication, divine impassibility as well) distinguished God from humans and the rest of creation. When the bishops in council at Chalcedon formulated their creed, describing Christ as truly divine and truly human, they understood both Christ's deity to be impassible like the nature of God the creator and Christ's humanity to be passible like the nature of all humans. Thus, in the orthodoxy of conciliar Christology, during his life and on the cross, only Christ's human nature suffered, but never in any real sense Christ's divine nature. Reformed orthodoxy staunchly maintained this claim, as seen in the "Westminster Confession of Faith."[6] Moreover, the ancient councils, the Council of Chalcedon included, anathematized everyone who believed that Christ's divine nature suffered in any sense.[7] The substance or matter, although not the form, of ancient

---

107; idem, "Fragments," in *Christological Controversy*, 108, 109, 110, 111 (fragments 25, 76, 108, 126); Nestorius, "First Sermon against the *Theotokos*," in *Christological Controversy*, 125, 126, 128-29, 130; idem, "Second Letter to Cyril," in *Christological Controversy*, 136-38. Also see the commitments to divine impassibility and immutability among orthodox victors, such as, Cyril of Alexandria and Pope Leo I: Cyril of Alexandria, "Second Letter to Nestorius," in *Christological Controversy*, 132-34; idem, "Letter to John of Antioch," in *Christological Controversy*, 143, 144; Pope Leo I, "Letter to Flavian of Constantinople," in *Christological Controversy*, 148, 149. Timothy George ignores this shared consensus, between orthodox and heterodox Christians about the nature of God, in his own assessments of ancient conciliar theology and Christology. "The Arian God is static, immobile, autocratic if also bureaucratic (he has lots of creatures who do his bidding). But the God of the Trinitarian theologians is very different. This is a God whose inner being resonates with an eternal dynamism, a reciprocity of giving and receiving, of love and service and self-sacrifice" (George, "Dogma beyond Anathema," 705). Even Boyce perceived and openly accepted the classical theistic notions of divine immutability and impassibility (e.g., Boyce, *Abstract of Systematic Theology*, 73-85).

[6]This Reformed confession both describes God as "*without* body, parts, or *passions, immutable*" and Christ as "of *one substance*, and equal with the Father" ("Westminster Confession of Faith," in *Creeds of the Churches*, 197, 203 [chaps. 2.1; 8.2]).

[7]"The Council of Chalcedon's 'Definition of the Faith,' " in *Christological Controversy*, 157-58. Catholic conciliar decrees have consistently defined divine immutability and impassibility (in regard to every member of the divine Trinity) as ecclesiastical dogmas, anathematizing every person who denies these dogmas. A Latin anathema, upon those who describe Christ's deity as changeable (*convertibilem*) or mutable (*demutabilem*), accompanies the creed formulated by the Council of Nicea (325 C.E.) (*DS*, 126 [53]). "The Creed of Epiphanius" (fourth century) declares both that the divine nature of the Logos did not alter or change during the incarnation and, further, that nothing altered the Holy Spirit (*DS*, 44, 45 [31-32]). One Council of Toledo (400 C.E.) produced a creed in which this council anathematizes those who believe that Christ's divine nature suffered. A later

orthodox Christology, then, leads to the following question about the
RPTSC's allegiance to historic Christian orthodoxy.

A. Do the *RPTSC*'s Authors Affirm the Substance as Well as the Form of Orthodox Christology?

From the *RPTSC* itself, only clues suggest a tentatively affirmative
answer to this question. If the writings of George and Mohler accurately
reflect the dominant influence on the *RPTSC* as I have argued, however,
their theological commitments require a more certain affirmative response
to this question. While the *RPTSC*'s language strongly implies this document's deep dependence upon orthodox Christian traditions, the *RPTSC*'s
principal architects in other publications explicitly, yet still uncritically,
commit themselves to historic Christian orthodoxy with its concomitant

---

Council of Toledo (447 C.E.) slightly emended this creed with an anathema upon those
who believe in the mutability or passibility of Christ's divine nature (*DS*, 196.6; 197.7
[76]). One Lateran Council (649 C.E.) condemns those who do not confess the Trinity's
immutability (*DS*, 501, canon 1 [171]). The Roman Council (860, 863 C.E.) professes that,
during the crucifixion, Christ suffered only in his human flesh and remained impassible
in his deity: "passionem crucis tantummodo secundum carnem sustinuit, deitate autem im-
passibilis mansit" (*DS*, 501, 635). Leo IX (1049–1054) declares, in his "Professio fidei,"
about the Christ: "impassibilem et immortalem divinitate, sed in humanitate pro nobis et
pro nostra salute passum vera carnis passione et sepultum" (*DS*, 681 [225]). The Fourth
Lateran Council (1215) reiterates faith in an unchangeable ("*incommutabilis*") Trinity (*DS*,
800 [259]). The Second Council of Lyons (1274), in its "Professio fidei Michaelis
Palaeologi imperatoris," with slight alterations, reaffirms Leo IX's Christological formulation: "impassibilem et immortalem divinitate, sed in humanitate pro nobis et salute nostra
passum vera carnis passione, mortuum et sepultum" (*DS*, 852 [276]). The Council of
Florence (1438–1445), in its "Decretum pro Iacobitis," both reaffirms an unchangeable
(*incommutabilem*) Trinity and similarly formulates its faith in Christ: "immortalis et
aeternus ex natura divinitatis, passibilis et temporalis ex condicione assumptae
humanitatis" (*DS*, 1330, 1337 [337, 339]). Even in the First Vatican Council (1869–1870),
the Roman Catholic Church reiterates its faith in an unchangeable (*incommutabilis*) divine
creator (*DS*, 3001 [587]). In the twentieth century, however, several Christian communities have authorized doctrinal commissions to study contemporary interests in, testimonies
to, and discussions of divine passibility and impassibility: for example, *Doctrine in the
Church of England: The Report of the Commission on Christian Doctrine Appointed by
the Archbishops of Canterbury and York in 1922* (London: S.P.C.K., 1938; 1982 ed.) 55-
56; Commissio Theologica Internationalis, "Theologia-Christologia-Anthropologia: Quaes-
tiones Selectae. Altera Series (Sessio Plenaria 1981, relatio conclusiva)," *Gregorianum*
64 (1983): 20-24; *We Believe in God: A Report by the Doctrine Commission of the
General Synod of the Church of England* (Wilton CT: Church House Publishing, 1987)
viii-ix, 157-60.

problems. Most generally, both George and Mohler openly affirm the orthodox Christian tradition as the settled and unambiguous deposit of Christian truth which Baptists must affirm or reaffirm and defend against contemporary reinterpretations of Christian doctrines. Yet, they never evaluate critically those equally historically and culturally conditioned orthodox formulations.

George, for example, explicitly affirms the "place in our heritage" of "the classical creeds of the Christian tradition." Furthermore, elsewhere for George, because *"heresy is a possibility," "theological discrimination is a priority."* According to George, however, such theological discrimination requires *"the cultivation of a holistic orthodoxy,"* an orthodoxy that he affirms strictly with support only from orthodox and neoorthodox Reformed Protestant traditions (via John Calvin, Charles H. Spurgeon, and Karl Barth).[8]

Mohler also explicitly yet uncritically reaffirms the "orthodox Christian tradition," specifically as interpreted through Reformed Protestant orthodoxy. Mohler audaciously declares, as one of his fourteen imperatives for "a renewed theological framework," a rule for all Baptists in order to move beyond the present theological impasse in the SBC: *"This new theological consensus must be based on a recovery of the classical Christian paradigm."* Mohler explicitly and accurately interprets "the classical Christian paradigm" as classical Christian orthodoxy via Reformation theological frameworks.

> A model of dynamic orthodoxy *must* be reclaimed within the Baptist tradition. That orthodox tradition *must* be recovered in conversation with Nicaea, Chalcedon, Augustine, Luther, Calvin, and the Protestant confessions—as well as the sturdy confessional tradition of Baptists developed over four centuries. In sum, any new theological consensus *must* be rooted within the *consensus fidei* of the Christian church. Nothing less will suffice.[9]

---

[8]George, "Dogma beyond Anathema," 700, 701; idem, "Conflict and Identity in the SBC," 208-11; emphasis mine. See also, for example, Mohler's various insufficient treatments of both soteriology and the doctrine of the Trinity: Mohler, "Has Theology a Future in the Southern Baptist Convention?" 102; idem, "Response," 248.

[9]Mohler, "Has Theology a Future in the Southern Baptist Convention?" 99; emphasis mine. Not accidentally does Mohler invoke the phrase *consensus fidei*, a concept originally developed in Roman Catholic tradition, between the thirteenth century and the latter half of the sixteenth century, as the *sensus fidei*. The *sensus fidei* contains two dimensions: (1) the internal quality of the believer (the subjective dimension) or the *sensus fidei* proper; and (2) the external reality in which the believer trusts and which the

More particularly, however, striving to validate his claim about the "Reformation roots" (and, indirectly, the orthodox roots) of historic Baptist commitments to both Christ's divinity and Christ's humanity, George stresses the intentional fidelity of both Calvin and Luther "to the Chalcedonian description of Jesus Christ as 'one in person, two in nature.' "[10] Both George and Mohler explicitly adhere to that which they have perceived to be the *substance* of Chalcedonian Christology.

---

believer can grasp (the objective dimension) or the *sensus fidelium*. By subsequently including the notion of universality (the whole church, all Christians), Roman Catholic tradition developed the objective dimension in the concept of the *sensus fidei* into the concept of *consensus fidelium* (*Dictionary of Fundamental Theology*, ed. René Latourelle and Rino Fisichella [New York: Crossroad Pub. Co., 1994], s.v. "Sensus Fidei," by Salvador Pié-Ninot). During the sixteenth century, as part of the Roman Catholic response to the Protestant reformations, the Council of Trent expressed this latter concept as the "universus *ecclesiae sensus*" ("Conc. [oecum. XIX] Tridentinum: Iulius III: 7. Feb. 1550 – 23. Mart. 1555," in *DS*, 1637 [385-86]; "Council of Trent: Julius III 1550–1555, Session XIII [Oct. 11, 1551]," in *Sources of Catholic Dogma*, 874 [266]; also see, in reference to the use of this concept in the Second Vatican Council, Zoltán Alszeghy, "The *Sensus Fidei* and the Development of Dogma," in *Vatican II, Assessment and Perspectives: Twenty-Five Years After [1962-1987]*, ed. René Latourelle [New York: Paulist Press, 1988] 1:138-56). In his catholicizing neo-Calvinization of the SBC, while Mohler seems to find both dimensions of the *sensus fidei* in his notion of the *consensus fidei*, his writings indicate a naive emphasis on the objective dimension, without a corresponding awareness of the contemporary difficulties in such naiveté. Apparently, Mohler aims to establish the new theological consensus in the SBC by legislating the content to which all Baptists "must" consent for inclusion among "faithful" Baptists in the SBC. With such an attitude, Mohler designates himself and other leaders of the SBC and the SBC's institutions (only those leaders, however, who share a fundamentalist vision, and, perhaps more narrowly, a Calvinistic version of this vision) as the present representatives of the new magisterium or the official teaching office for the SBC and its participants. The fundamentalist juggernaut long ago targeted the SBC's institutions of theological education, its six seminaries. According to Mohler, "higher education and the education of ministers will remain the most critical battleground in denominational and parachurch battles" (Mohler, "Call for Baptist Evangelicals and Evangelical Baptists," 236). The identities of executive leaders of the SBC's seminaries, and related theological schools, powerfully illustrate this claim: *Paige Patterson*, president of Southeastern Baptist Theological Seminary; *Mohler*, president of Southern Baptist Theological Seminary; *Mark Coppenger*, president of Midwestern Baptist Theological Seminary; *Chuck Kelley*, brother-in-law of Paige Patterson and president of New Orleans Baptist Theological Seminary; *Timothy George*, Dean of Beeson Divinity School at Samford University; and *Ken Hemphill*, president of Southwestern Baptist Theological Seminary.

[10]George, "Reformation Roots of the Baptist Tradition," 12-13.

Can these architects of the *RPTSC*'s Christology, however, legitimately affirm the *form* of Chalcedonian orthodoxy (Christ as one person
with two natures: divine and human) without affirming its *substance*
(which necessarily includes the impassibility and immutability of Christ's
divine nature)? The various ancient, ecumenical, conciliar decrees
themselves anathematize anyone who attributes suffering to Christ's
divinity, whether or not that person attests to Christ as one person both
divine and human. Surely, Mohler and George perceive this crucial
point.[11] Assuming their awareness of this significant issue, since they
both repeatedly affirm their commitments to historic Christian orthodoxy,
specifically as transmitted through orthodox Reformed Protestantism, they
obviously remain committed to the substance as well as to the form of

---

[11]Boyce himself certainly realized this. According to Boyce, God's nature could not
suffer. Boyce consistently defended a Reformed version of divine impassibility. Although
Boyce claims that Christ "was equally divine when a babe in Bethlehem, when suffering
upon the cross, when ascending from Olivet, and even now, while in human nature, he
rules as Mediatorial King, or makes intercession with the Father as our great High Priest,"
because he also defends God's immutability and impassibility, he emphatically and
unequivocally follows the orthodox Christological position that the divine nature of Christ
does not and cannot suffer in any sense. "And, hanging upon the cross, how amazing the
mystery of contradiction! As God, he enjoys supreme felicity in the unchanged blessedness of his divine nature; as man, he is in vital agony both of body and soul." In the
person of Christ (as seen paradigmatically on Jesus' cross), "there was here, therefore, no
participation of the divine nature in the suffering. . . . It was, therefore, not the human
nature of Christ that was substituted for us, but Christ himself; yet it was not Christ in
his divine nature that suffered, but value was given to the suffering from its being the
suffering of one who also essentially possessed the divine nature" (Boyce, *Abstract of
Systematic Theology*, 79-82, 275, 288, 289, 325). In vivid contrast, W. T. Conner notes
the essential contradiction in Christian concepts of divine impassibility. "One who was
only a man could not do something that would reveal the love of God. This is also con-
tradictory to the idea that it was only the human nature of Christ that suffered, not his
divine nature. In that case, the cross stands for what humanity did, not what God did for
man. . . . The revelation of God as love contradicts the idea that God cannot suffer. A
God who loves must suffer when his world is invaded by sin and men are destroyed by
it. To say that God does not suffer is to say that he does not care. . . . Theologians once
held, perhaps some do yet, that God was impassible. They held that he could not suffer
and be a blessed God, too. This was a strange position for people to hold, the symbol of
whose religion was a cross. The cross stands for what it cost God to save us. He finds
his blessedness in blessing others, even when blessing them means a cross" (Conner, *The
Gospel of Redemption* [Nashville: Broadman Press, 1945] 108, 119, 135; cf. idem, *The
Cross in the New Testament*, ed. Jesse Northcutt [Nashville: Broadman Press, 1954] 135-
36, 176).

Chalcedonian orthodoxy. If this is the case, why did the PTSC avoid clarifying the substance of its attestation to Christ's two natures?

At least three major possibilities appear as answers to this question. First, perhaps the committee left this aspect of its Christology ambiguous to allow for diverse Baptist interpretations of this credal statement: some from the perspective of classical theism, some from other perspectives. Given the PTSC's drive toward greater specificity in doctrinal expression, toward more narrow and rigid interpretations of Baptist doctrines, nothing exists to commend this first possibility. As a second answer, perhaps the committee naively formulated its Christology or approached its task without a thorough knowledge of the essential issues in the ancient Christological controversies. Again, given the academic credentials and positions of the *RPTSC*'s principal architects (George and Mohler, in particular, but not exclusively), this second possibility appears to be unlikely as well.

This leaves a third possible answer. My previous findings about other problems in the *RPTSC* strongly support the high probability for this last possibility. Probably, the *RPTSC* does not contain statements about the substance of its Christology, in order also to camouflage the theological basis of support for the Calvinistic commitments presupposed by the principal writers of this document. Veiled in this way, the *RPTSC*'s Christology does not alarm the block of non-Calvinistic voting Baptists in the SBC. Hence, once again, the architects of this document have manipulated the *RPTSC*'s readers by intentionally avoiding the real issues behind the formulations contained in this document. This problem in the *RPTSC*'s Christology, then, leads to a second critical question.

B. Can Baptists Remain Biblical Christologically without Affirming Orthodox Christology?

Although the following answer to the preceding question invites examination and dialogue, in many ways, when formulating Christology, Baptist Christians can remain most biblical only by refusing to affirm the *substance* of orthodox Christologies. For example, while E. Y. Mullins affirms the form of the Chalcedonian statement, as "the definition which most fully gathers up the statements of the New Testament," he also critically examines that ancient orthodoxy's substance. Mullins identifies in orthodox conciliar Christology the presence of "*certain speculative elements* to which objection has been and may be made." According to Mullins, "the two-nature conception has been made *to dominate too completely* in many efforts to define Christ's person." Mullins senses the implicit dualism residing within conciliar orthodoxy's description of Christ as a *"union"* of two natures. Consequently, perhaps as the almost instinctive reaction of a less dogmatically and more biblically oriented theologian, Mullins reconstrues divine immutability as only "the moral self-consistency of God," not as God's inability to change in any sense whatsoever. To the contrary and paradoxically, for Mullins, the becoming human of God as Jesus of Nazareth or "the self-emptying of Christ in the incarnation," "displays the *infinite mobility* of the divine immutability," "the retention of divine qualities and powers, but *under the restraints and limitations of a human life.*" As Mullins accurately perceives, when God became human, God both changed by assuming creaturely limitations and, as a result, also suffered as a human. In this way, Mullins endeavors to avoid the dichotomies of ancient orthodox Christologies. "In Jesus Christ, God and humanity become one. Humanity finds itself ideally and forever in him. He expresses ideally and forever the inner core of God's heart and life."[12] Such claims obviously remain true to the biblical testimonies to Christ. Nonetheless, Mullins's Christology departs radically from the meaning or substance of the orthodox conciliar Christological formulations.

H. Wheeler Robinson, a British Baptist biblical scholar and theologian, reminds Baptists that "the Chalcedonian doctrine of two distinct natures in Christ" evades concluding that, because God loves like Christ loves, "for God also, love is costly, involving suffering." Robinson notes that, when orthodox theology "denies suffering in God," it usually proceeds by restricting "to the human nature" Christ's "costly love," "whilst the divine does not suffer at all."[13]

Baptists, obviously, can remain biblical in their Christologies, even as they refuse the substance of ancient orthodox conciliar Christologies. This entails, however, the avoidance of two related problems, problems implicit in the *RPTSC*'s own Christology.

First, as I have previously emphasized about the doctrine of God, according to Christian scriptures, God can and does suffer in various ways on the basis of three major creaturely occasions: (1) with grief as

---

[12]Mullins, *Christian Religion in Its Doctrinal Expression*, 178, 183, 184-85, 187; emphasis mine.

[13]H. Wheeler Robinson, *Suffering, Human and Divine* (New York: Macmillan, 1939) 156.

creator, *from* or *due to* human betrayal of the divine love; (2) through self-sacrifice as redeemer, *for* humans, in order to release them from the misery or bondage of their betrayal of God; and (3) in affliction as companion, *with* humans in their fidelity to the God who loves them. Christ, as both human and divine, discloses this claim most poignantly through his crucifixion.[14]

Second, rather than describing Christ as the *union* in one person of two radically different essences, human nature (passible) and divine nature (impassible), the Christian scriptures attest to God's involvement in a process or an event. In this divine activity, the divine Logos *did not unite with* humanity, *did not inhabit* human flesh, *did not put on a cloak* of creatureliness, but rather *became* a human creature. God did something new. God experienced something that God had not experienced previously: divine life as a human creature, as Jesus of Nazareth. According to the Christian scriptures, God had never existed as a human until the Logos became human. In the incarnation, Christ is not divine without being human; Jesus is not human without being divine.[15]

Thus, Baptists most certainly can remain biblical in their Christologies without affirming the traditional Christology of Christian conciliar orthodoxy. More emphatically, Baptists will not remain biblical in the fullest sense, unless they perceive the denial of biblical teaching about the divine nature in the concept of divine impassibility, and unless they refuse the substance of that ancient orthodoxy.

II. Ahistorical Soteriology

A second severe problem emerges in the PTSC's peculiar interpretation of salvation through Jesus of Nazareth alone. Again, the problem lurks beneath the surface of purportedly biblical language. In spite of the *RPTSC*'s desperate concern to affirm the historical accuracy of the scriptures, its vehement assertion of the historicity of all events to which scriptures refer, and its emphatic description of God's becoming-human as "an event in historical space and time,"[16] the PTSC, nevertheless, has enshrined in this document an *ahistorical* soteriology, as most succinctly expressed in the following statement: "From beginning to end the Bible

---

[14]Gen 6:5-6; Exod 3:7; Isa 63:8-10; Matt 26:1-27:66; Eph 4:30.
[15]John 1:1-5, 14-18.
[16]*RPTSC*, 114, 116 (2.1.1-5; 2.3.3).

proclaims salvation through Jesus Christ and no other."[17] However much that declaration may thrill Baptists in the SBC, the *RPTSC*'s soteriological vision at its basis only coheres as a piece of a larger Calvinistic system, most of which system remains veiled in the *RPTSC*. This ahistorical, perhaps even antihistorical, problem contains several aspects, only two of which I will examine here. These two aspects revolve around both hamartiological and Christological ambiguities.

A. Ahistorical Hamartiological Ambiguity

First, the *RPTSC*'s soteriology presupposes a theology of the human plight, a theology of sin, or a hamartiology. According to the *RPTSC*, *"all human beings*—in all places and *of all ages*—are lost but for salvation through Jesus Christ."[18] This phrase contains an ambiguity that suggests at least two possible interpretations, but both of which indicate the severity of the first and foundational aspect to this problem. The ambiguity revolves around the meaning communicated with the phrase "all human beings . . . of all ages."

1. *Humans in All Historical Epochs?* According to the first interpretation of this declaration, no human in any place or time will receive or has received salvation without Jesus. The phrase "all human beings . . . of all ages" refers to all humans in all historical periods or epochs. Such a reference would include all history prior to Jesus' birth and life as well as all history contemporary with his life and subsequent to his death and resurrection.

Understood in this way, consequently, this claim suggests two possibilities, neither of which satisfactorily expresses the meaning of the biblical witness concerning human salvation: either (1) no human being prior to Jesus' birth and life experienced salvation from God in any sense; or (2) any human prior to Jesus' birth and life who did experience salvation only received salvation by trusting in Jesus. The first possibility cannot be correct. According to the Christian scriptures, numerous people prior to Jesus' life received salvation, such as Abel, Enoch, Noah,

---

[17]*RPTSC*, 116 (2.3.2). The exact wording of this quotation, of course, appears also in the resolution promoted (and perhaps written) by Timothy George and adopted by the SBC in 1993, the same year in which the PTSC circulated the *RPTSC* at the SBC's annual meeting: "From beginning to end the Bible proclaims salvation through Jesus Christ and no other (1 Tim 2:5)" ("Resolution No. 1—The Finality of Jesus Christ as Sole and Sufficient Savior," in *Annual of the SBC* [1993]: 94).

[18]*RPTSC*, 116-17 (2.3.5); emphasis mine.

Abraham, Sarah, Isaac, Jacob, Joseph, Moses, Rahab the harlot, Gideon, Barak, Samson, Jephthah, David, Samuel, and the true prophets.[19] The second possibility, however, contradicts itself. Since this latter possibility concerns Christology more directly than hamartiology, I will consider that possibility more carefully, when I examine the second major ambiguity of this ahistorical soteriology, the heart of the problem itself.[20]

2. *Humans in Every Age-Group.* According to the second interpretation of this hamartiological ambiguity, humans in every age-group (adults, children, infants, and even unborn fetuses) are lost, under condemnation, or damned and, hence, cannot receive salvation without Jesus. With this meaning, the phrase, "all human beings . . . of all ages," refers, then, to humans in every age-category: young or old, adult or unborn child. All humans are sinners from the moments of their conceptions. More than likely, the PTSC used the phrase "all human beings . . . of all ages" in this second sense, even though this meaning remains consistent with the first sense as well.

In this second sense, consequently, the committee affirms (and the *RPTSC* contains a truncated version of) a Calvinistic or classical Reformed (and, to some extent, perhaps even Augustinian) doctrine of original sin, a seriously deficient hamartiology even when consistently stated. Some of those deficiencies emerge, for example, by considering the following question. In the *RPTSC*'s hamartiology, what fate awaits unborn fetuses who die prior to their births, or infants, children, and even mentally challenged persons who die prior to the development or maturation in them of the capacity for conscious decision for or against the divine purposes in the creation? According to the *RPTSC*'s hamartiology, because persons in all of these categories are lost in sin, any of

---

[19]Heb 11:1-40.

[20]The PTSC certainly may have aimed to convey this first understanding as the governing sense of its phrase, "all human beings . . . of all ages." Once again, during its annual meeting in 1993, in "Resolution No. 1—The Finality of Jesus Christ as Sole and Sufficient Savior," the SBC explicitly affirmed this meaning, even though its resolution did not contain the exact wording inscribed in the *RPTSC*: "general revelation has been so perverted by sin as to leave *all persons utterly destitute of any hope of salvation outside* of personal repentance and faith in the Redeemer (Rom 1–2)"; "therefore, Be it RESOLVED, That the messengers to the 136th session of the Southern Baptist Convention, affirm biblical teaching concerning the uniqueness of Jesus Christ as the sole and sufficient Savior for *all persons who have lived or ever shall be . . .* " (*Annual of the SBC* [1993]: 94; emphasis mine).

those who die prior to birth or without having the ability (or becoming able) to decide for or against the gospel (like any other person who dies without receiving salvation through Jesus, without salvation from sin) will go to hell: for example, *"all human beings*, marked by original sin and their own individual sins, are utterly helpless before God and *without excuse, deserving of eternal punishment and separation from God"*; *"those who die without hope in Christ"* or *"the lost* shall be forever with the devil in hell, a place of utter darkness and inexpressible anguish."[21]

Does the *RPTSC*'s hamartiology, however, adequately represent biblical portrayals of sin? According to the *RPTSC*, "the redeemed are justified before God by grace *through faith* in Jesus Christ, *trusting* in Him alone for their salvation and *acknowledging* Him as Savior and Lord."[22] Nonetheless, in the *RPTSC*'s theology, God condemns persons to hell who as yet, at least, cannot actively and consciously respond (or perhaps never will be able to do so) to Christ with faith in, trust in, or acknowledgment of God as savior through Christ. Thus, the *RPTSC* leaves a gap in human life uncovered by divine grace or justice, should something happen to prevent the development of the human capacity to decide for or against the gospel: the period of human life between conception and the age when the human at least can make conscious decisions, if not the age of actual human responsibility and accountability for decisions.

The PTSC has not responded explicitly in any way to the obvious dilemma of this hamartiology in the *RPTSC* itself. Nonetheless, the presence of this anthropological gap in the *RPTSC*'s hamartiology supplies an implicit answer. This particular theology of sin works consistently and coherently only within classical Reformed, Calvinistic, or even Augustinian frameworks, whether or not every human becomes a sinner at conception through divine decree (Calvin) or human genes (Augustine). Elsewhere, Timothy George rightly distinguishes Calvin's hamartiology from Augustine's hamartiology, even though George indicates his own preference for Calvin's understanding of sin.[23]

---

[21]*RPTSC*, 116, 118·(2.3.5; 2.5.5); emphasis mine. Coppenger flippantly and uncritically applies the *RPTSC*'s deficient hamartiology to evangelism: see, e.g., "Non-Christians Are 'Bad,' Coppenger says," *Western Recorder* 170 (19 March 1996): 2.

[22]*RPTSC*, 117 (2.3.8); emphasis mine.

[23]George, *Theology of the Reformers*, 213-16.

Without openly expressing it, then, the *RPTSC*'s hamartiology also presupposes a *roughly* Calvinistic theory of the divine decree, the decree whereby God decided before creation both to elect some humans and to reject all remaining humans, wherein God chose both to save some and to damn all others.[24] Of course, this theory of predestination to damnation explains why some persons, without the capacity or opportunity to respond to the Gospel, go to hell when they die: God simply had predestined them for damnation (either actively or passively) in God's eternity, long before creation and their births. Humans will be saved only if called by God, and effectually called only if elected by God. Therefore, those not having the ability or opportunity to respond to a divine call remain lost and, therefore, damned.

Despite the implicit congruence between Calvinistic thought and the *RPTSC* on the doctrine of election, however, orthodox Reformed theologies have addressed the previous problem more openly and consistently. According to Calvin and many branches of the Reformed tradition resulting from his influence, children born to Christian (or elect) parents already participate in the covenant with God and do so from their conceptions in their mothers's wombs. Since God has elected a child's parents, God has also elected the child. For this reason, Calvin vigorously advocated the baptism of infants belonging to Christian parents, as "the sign of regeneration" or the sign of the covenant in which they already participate. Still, even infants require both salvation from sin and regeneration, although they do not yet have the capacity to respond to proclamation. According to orthodox Reformed theology, with "secret workings" the Spirit regenerates elect infants. Thus, in a mode different from the "ordinary arrangement and dispensation of the Lord," God saves elect children who die in infancy or even prior to baptism, by Christ through the Spirit. In the same way, God saves every elect person, however incapable of receiving the divine call. For Calvin, "election remains inviolable, although its signs do not always appear." The basis for this entire qualification, however, rests upon two essential theological commitments: (1) divine election of some persons always produces

---

[24]Calvin, *Institutes*, 2:920-87 (3.21-24); "Canones Synodi Dordrechtanae, The Canons of the Synod of Dort, A.D. 1618 and 1619," in *Creeds of Christendom*, 3:552-56, 582-85 (1.6-16) (hereafter cited as "Canones Synodi Dordrechtanae"); "Westminster Confession of Faith," in *Creeds of Christendom*, 3:608-11 ("Chapter III. Of God's Eternal Decree," 1-8).

salvation, despite the absence of all signs or even outward faith; and (2) divine reprobation of all other persons always produces damnation, despite the presence of any sign or outward faith.[25]

Even some Calvinistic Baptists have also addressed this sensitive issue more openly than the *RPTSC*. According to the Calvinistic "Second London Confession," just as "*elect* Infants dying in infancy, are regenerated and saved by Christ through the Spirit," "so also are all other *elect* persons, who are *uncapable* [sic] *of being outwardly called* by the Ministry of the Word." Even Boyce, in his milder (though often less consistent) Calvinism, considered aspects of this issue. According to Boyce, "regeneration (as in infants) may exist without faith and repentance, but the latter cannot exist without the former." Furthermore, an "appreciable interval" of time may intervene between regeneration (God's preparation or enabling of the human to turn to God) and conversion (the human's actual turning to God). For Boyce, not only must this be "true of all infants and of all persons otherwise *incapable of responsibility*, as for example idiots," but it can also "be true of *some heathen*" or persons with other religious (or non-Christian) commitments.[26]

---

[25]Calvin, *Institutes*, 2:929, 1338–1359 (3.21.5; 4.16.17-32); "Canones Synodi Dordrechtanae," 3:556 (1.17); "Westminster Confession of Faith," in *Creeds of Christendom*, 3:625 ("Chapter X. Of Effectual Calling," 3).

[26]"The Assembly or Second London Confession, 1677 and 1688," in *Baptist Confessions of Faith*, ed. Lumpkin, 265 ("Chap. X. Of Effectual Calling," 3); Boyce, *Abstract of Systematic Theology*, 381; emphasis mine. Boyce's last point about the "heathen" departs significantly from the mainstream of the orthodox Reformed tradition, even as Calvinistic Baptists repeated that theology in their "Second London Confession": "much less can men, not professing the Christian religion, be saved in any other way whatsoever, be they never so diligent to frame their lives according to the light of nature and the law of that religion they do profess; and to assert and maintain that they may is very pernicious, and to be detested; . . . much less can men that receive not the Christian Religion be saved; be they never so diligent to frame their lives according to the light of nature, and the Law of that Religion they do profess" ("Westminster Confession of Faith," 3:625-26 ["Chapter X. Of Effectual Calling," 4]; "The Assembly or Second London Confession, 1677 and 1688," in *Baptist Confessions of Faith*, ed. Lumpkin, 265 ["Chap. X. Of Effectual Calling," 4]). Even John Gill, illustrating his claim that God does not elect persons to salvation based upon a divine foreknowledge of their perseverance, addresses "the case of infants dying in infancy": "now though their election is a secret to us, and unrevealed; it may be reasonably supposed, yea, in a judgment of charity it may rather be concluded, that they are all chosen, than that none are" (Gill, *Body of Doctrinal and Practical Divinity*, 188 [2.2.2]).

Most importantly, as seen in the SBC's confessional statements themselves, the SBC as an entity *has never adopted* either a Calvinistic theory
of election or its concomitant, extrabiblical, hamartiological or soteriological excesses and dilemmas. In connection with explaining the Baptist
rationale for not practicing infant baptism, both the *FASB (1920)* and the
PCU (1914) completely avoid a Calvinistic theory of election with the
same concept and in similar language: (1) "all are equally entitled to
direct access to God"; (2) "*all men* are entitled equally to the direct
access to God." Additionally, the FMB's "Statement of Belief" (*SB
[1920]*) explicitly rejects Calvinistic theories of election in its formulation
of the missionary endeavor's most basic presupposition: "That on
condition of personal repentance for sin and faith in the Lord Jesus Christ
any man can receive the forgiveness of sin and salvation unto everlasting
life." Even the "Statement of Principles" (1945, 1946), the SBC's
response to the social, political, and economic evils following the Second
World War, reiterates this conviction as part of the SBC's foundational
and distinctive belief: "*Every man* is endowed by the Creator with
competence as a person to deal with God and with his fellowmen in all
rightful relations." Both the *BFM (1925)* and the *BFM (1963)* contain
statements about election. Clearly, however, both of these documents
eschew Calvinistic or even more broadly Reformed doctrines of election,
by interpreting both election as "the *gracious purpose* of God" by which
God saves sinners and salvation as "*made free to all* by the Gospel" or
as "*offered freely to all* who accept Jesus Christ as Lord and Saviour."[27]
No confessional document produced by the SBC, however, has ever
affirmed divine reprobation either explicitly or implicitly as the negative

---

[27]"Fraternal Address of Southern Baptists," *Baptist Standard* 32 (26 February 1920):
24; *PCU (1914)*, 74 (point 1); *SB (1920)*, 197; *SP (1946)*, 38; *BFM (1925)*, 72 (arts. 6
and 9, "The Freeness of Salvation" and "God's Purpose of Grace"); *BFM (1963)*, 273,
274-75 (arts. 4 and 5, "Salvation" and "God's Purpose of Grace"); emphasis mine. Even
though the "Declaration of Faith of English People Remaining at Amsterdam in Holland,
1611," evaluated by William L. Lumpkin as "the first English Baptist Confession of
Faith" (*Baptist Confessions of Faith*, ed. Lumpkin, 115), espouses the hereditary or biological sinfulness of humans, that document vehemently opposes the Calvinistic doctrines
of election and reprobation. Accordingly, for this confession of faith, God does not
predestine humans to be sinful and, thus, to be damned; rather, because humans are
sinners, they are damned. God desires salvation from sin for all humans, that none should
perish ("A Declaration of Faith of English People Remaining at Amsterdam in Holland,
1611," in *Baptist Confessions of Faith*, ed. Lumpkin, 117-18 [arts. 4-5]).

side of a Calvinistic theory of the eternal decree—at least not until the *RPTSC*.

Consequently, although the SBC's confessional statements have emphasized, sometimes inconsistently, the human inclination toward sin even from conception, these documents have *generally tended to stress more heavily* that individual human guilt for sin results only from its actualization by humans who possess moral capacity. This emphasis, of course, continued a long tradition among Baptists that originated with the first Baptists and their Anabaptist precursors.[28] In several ways, the *FASB (1920)* explicitly addresses the hamartiological dilemma now appearing in the *RPTSC*: (1) "each soul is responsible directly to God *for sins committed*"; (2) infants are "morally unconscious"; and (3) persons must reach a "suitable age" prior to actual responsibility for sin and response to the gospel. According to the *BFM (1925)*, "humans inherit a nature corrupt and in bondage to sin, are under condemnation, and *as they are capable of moral action, become actual transgressors.*" The *BFM (1963)* clarified and significantly modified the more ambiguous and severe implications contained in the statement from 1925: humans "inherit a nature and an environment inclined toward sin, and *as soon as they are capable of moral action become transgressors and are under condemnation.*"[29] The statement from 1963 interprets condemnation of humans both as the result of actual (not inherited) sin and as a fate possible only for those who have developed the capacity for moral behavior. Prior to the

---

[28]As examples of this hamartiological emphasis among early English Baptists, see the following confessions, among the earliest of which appear confessions from the congregations of John Smyth and Thomas Helwys: "Short Confession of Faith in XX Articles by John Smyth, 1609," in *Baptist Confessions of Faith*, ed. Lumpkin, 100-101 (arts. 5, 8, 9); "A Short Confession of Faith, 1610," in *Baptist Confessions of Faith*, ed. Lumpkin, 103-105 (arts. 4-8); "A Declaration of Faith of English People Remaining at Amsterdam in Holland, 1611," in *Baptist Confessions of Faith*, ed. Lumpkin, 117-19 (arts. 4-5, 7); "Propositions and Conclusions concerning True Christian Religion, 1612–1614," in *Baptist Confessions of Faith*, ed. Lumpkin, 126-28 (arts. 14-26); "The Standard Confession, 1660," in *Baptist Confessions of Faith*, ed. Lumpkin, 225-26, 227-28 (arts. 3-4, 5, 8-10).

[29]"Fraternal Address of Southern Baptists," *Baptist Standard* 32 (26 February 1920): 20, 24; emphasis mine; *BFM (1925)*, 72 (art. 3, "The Fall of Man"); *BFM (1963)*, 273, 274-75 (art. 3, "Man"); emphasis mine. In its article on sin, the *BFM (1925)* substantially follows the *AP (1858)*, using most of the latter confession's language as well: humans "inherit a nature corrupt and wholly opposed to God and His law, are under condemnation, and as soon as they are capable of moral action, become actual transgressors" (*AP [1858]*, 38 ["VI—The Fall of Man"]).

development of moral capacity and its consequent sinful actualization, according to the *BFM (1963)*, humans receive no condemnation for their natural state.

The hamartiology of the *BFM (1963)* has functioned as the normative understanding of sin among Baptists of the SBC for more than three decades. This confession of faith clearly supplies both a more sufficient understanding of sin than previous confessional statements produced by the SBC and a non-Reformed doctrine of sin. Unfortunately, the PTSC has inscribed in the *RPTSC* a very different hamartiology, a Calvinistic doctrine of sin, but one camouflaged as such with an ahistorical ambiguity. The ahistoricity arises in the *RPTSC*'s understanding of sin, because, in this hamartiology, humans inherit sin at conception (in Calvin's scheme, even before the creation of the world in God's eternal decrees), before they ever have the opportunity in history to betray the divine love and purposes for creation.

B. Ahistorical Christological Ambiguity

The first ambiguity leads to the heart of the soteriological problem itself: a correlative Christological ambiguity. The *RPTSC* expresses this problem fully in a parallel Christological statement: "Jesus Christ is the sole and sufficient Savior of *the redeemed* throughout the world and *of all ages*."[30] A similar and related ambiguity appears, naturally, around the phrase "the redeemed . . . of all ages." Again, this ambiguity suggests two possible interpretations. Both interpretations, however, harmonize well with, and result from, the more probable interpretation of the previous hamartiological ambiguity. This situation, consequently, intensifies difficulties in the clarification of this Christological ambiguity. Still, although I will note both interpretations of this second ambiguity, and even how these two interpretations actually cohere with one another, more than likely the second interpretation of this Christological ambiguity most accurately reflects the *RPTSC*'s meaning. Furthermore, identifying this Christological ambiguity and its problems will more fully clarify the

---

[30]*RPTSC*, 116 (2.3.2); emphasis mine. Again, this formulation expresses the substance and much of the exact wording contained in "Resolution No. 1—The Finality of Jesus Christ as Sole and Sufficient Savior": "the messengers to the 136th session of the Southern Baptist Convention, affirm biblical teaching concerning the uniqueness of Jesus Christ as *the sole and sufficient Savior for all persons who have lived or ever shall be*" (*Annual of the SBC* [1993]: 94; emphasis mine).

problems previously discovered in the commitments to orthodox Christology presupposed in the *RPTSC*'s Christological formulations.

1. *The Redeemed in Every Age-Group?* According to the first interpretation of this Christological ambiguity, redeemed humans in every age-group (adults, children, infants, and even unborn fetuses) receive salvation through Jesus Christ. If this Christological statement parallels the *RPTSC*'s previous hamartiological counterpart in meaning, then, with this statement the *RPTSC* describes Jesus Christ as the only savior of redeemed persons in any or every age-category. Of course, as I have previously shown, Christ's salvation of infants and others without the capacity or the opportunity to respond, however, remains problematic unless based upon Calvinistic, orthodox Reformed, Augustinian, or similar theories of election and sin. Although this first possible interpretation of the Christological ambiguity logically coheres with the more probable interpretation of the preceding hamartiological ambiguity, the second interpretation of this Christological ambiguity more adequately expresses the *RPTSC*'s meaning.[31]

2. *The Redeemed in All Historical Epochs.* According to the second interpretation of the Christological ambiguity in the *RPTSC*'s soteriology, the phrase, "the redeemed . . . of all ages," refers to persons in every historical period who have received salvation. In this sense, therefore, the *RPTSC* claims that all persons who have ever experienced salvation from God have only received that salvation through God's activity on their behalf in Jesus of Nazareth. The *RPTSC*, of course, supports this claim with another of its characteristically general appeals to the content of the Bible itself: "*From beginning to end* the Bible proclaims salvation through Jesus Christ and no other."[32] This statement signals several obvious problems. These problems disclose the ahistorical character of the *RPTSC*'s Christology.

First, consider the *RPTSC*'s stated epistemological basis for its soteriological claim about Jesus of Nazareth: "from beginning to end," the Christian scriptures attest only to salvation through Jesus of Nazareth.

---

[31]In addition, if this second interpretation more adequately represents the meaning in the Christological ambiguity of the *RPTSC*'s soteriology, not only has the PTSC camouflaged its soteriology with these two major ahistorical ambiguities, but this committee has also equivocated in its two uses of the phrase "of all ages," thus, more completely confusing or manipulating the *RPTSC*'s readers.

[32]*RPTSC*, 116 (2.3.2); emphasis mine.

The Christian scriptures also include the Old Testament or the Hebrew scriptures as well as the New Testament. From a more obvious perspective, much of the Old Testament contains no messianic references at all. In addition, messianic texts in the Old Testament never refer to the future Messiah with the name "Jesus," only with the name "Immanuel." Furthermore, although the book of Revelation refers to Jesus of Nazareth as the Christ, the book of Genesis does not refer to the Messiah at all (unless *interpreted* allegorically or typologically). Thus, not only *does* the *RPTSC* not *supply* any corroborating textual support for its claim, the *RPTSC cannot legitimately justify* its exaggerated epistemological claim from the scriptures themselves.

More substantively, the *RPTSC*'s claim discloses the genuinely ahistorical perspective dwelling within the *RPTSC*'s Christological formulations. With its claim, the *RPTSC* implies that, to read properly all Old Testament texts about salvation, one must read them as testimonies to God's activity in Jesus of Nazareth. Frankly and hermeneutically, this entails theological eisegesis: *reading* the meaning one wants to find *into* the text, rather than searching for the meaning that the text conveys (exegesis). Theologically, the *RPTSC*'s claim rests upon a concept of Christ that precedes the birth of Jesus in a particular historical place and time, in Palestine during the first century of the common era at Nazareth.

Second, following from the previous point, the *RPTSC* contradicts itself: humans who experienced salvation from God (such as Abraham, Isaac, Jacob, Ruth, Sarah, and Jephthah's daughter) did so only through Jesus of Nazareth who neither had been born yet nor even had been mentioned by the name "Jesus." According to the Christian scriptures themselves, insofar as God became human only once in history, and specifically became Jesus of Nazareth during one particular period of history, no person experienced salvation through Jesus of Nazareth prior to his life. According to the Johannine gospel, the divine Logos (Word) became human, became the human person named "Jesus."[33] God the Logos became finite, became a creature, chose to and came to experience life fully as a human. As the human Jesus, the divine Logos became Christ for humanity. Before the Logos became human, however, Jesus of Nazareth did not exist; only the divine Logos existed in the divine Trinity. The radicality of the Christian story arises from this scandalous

---

[33]John 1:1-5, 14, 18.

claim. God did something new for the divine self as well as for the creation: God became human. This claim attests to the radical historicity of
God's everlasting life, not to the timelessness of a divine eternity. Thus,
although God created from nothing all things through the divine Word or
Logos, Jesus, the human, created nothing. Rather, as Jesus, God
participated with and in the creation as an interdependent creature. God
has taken the divine life as God-become-human (Jesus) more seriously
than has the PTSC in its soteriology.

This awareness leads more deeply into the theological rationale
behind the Christological ambiguity in the *RPTSC*. Again, Calvinist and
Reformed theological paradigms figure prominently in this rationale.
According to the "Westminster Confession of Faith," which substantially
repeats Calvin's own position, even though Christ only accomplished
redemption after his incarnation, God communicated to all "elect"
humans "the virtue, efficacy, and benefits" of that incarnation "in all ages
successively from the beginning of the world," through "those promises,
types, and sacrifices, wherein he was revealed, and signified to be the
seed of the woman which should bruise the serpent's head, and the lamb
slain from the beginning of the world, being yesterday and today the
same and forever."[34] This Reformed theological claim rests entirely on

---

[34]"Westminster Confession of Faith, 1647," in *Creeds of Christendom*, 3:621-22
("Chapter VIII. Of Christ the Mediator," 6). This confession utilizes three biblical texts
explicitly: Gen 3:5; Rev 13:8; and Heb 13:8. The use of the text from Genesis in this
connection demonstrates the eisegetical approach (yielding an allegorical interpretation
at best) toward the O.T. to which I referred previously. Calvin similarly understood the
serpent in this narrative as Satan (Calvin, *Institutes*, 1:174 [1.14.15]). One can translate
differently, however, the Greek of the text from the book of Revelation. The translation
quoted by the "Westminster Confession of Faith" obviously accommodates a Reformed
perspective. The KJV contains that particular translation of the text. Still, Calvin did not
use Rev 13:8 in his *Institutes* to emphasize the retroactive validity or effectiveness of
Christ's crucifixion; rather, Calvin relied more on Eph 1:4 to make that and similar claims
(Calvin, *Institutes*, 1:469, 506 [2.12.5; 2.16.4]). Vernon Storr rightly considers the idea
of "the Lamb slain from the foundation of the world" in Rev 13:8, at least as translated
in the KJV, to be "more characteristic of the Greek Fathers than of the New Testament"
(Storr, *The Problem of the Cross* [London: John Murry, 1919] 49). More recent translations of this text alleviate this problem: "and all who dwell on the earth will worship him,
every one whose name has not been written from the foundation of the world in the book
of life of the Lamb who has been slain" (Rev 13:8 NASB); "and all the inhabitants of the
earth will worship it, everyone whose name has not been written from the foundation of
the world in the book of life of the Lamb that was slaughtered" (Rev 13:8 NRSV).
Recently, Richard Bauckham has similarly translated this text with this latter meaning

Calvin's doctrine of the divine decree. That God would become human as Jesus of Nazareth and suffer the divine punishment against human sin, God had decreed eternally, just as God had chosen some humans for salvation and some for damnation prior to creation. Accordingly, as acknowledged even by Timothy George, "indeed, the Reformation doctrines of justification and election are not only inconceivable apart from the basis of the Trinitarian and Christological consensus of the early church but also are the necessary outcome and application of the latter."[35] Thus, all humans who experienced redemption prior to Christ did so through Christ, because God had foreordained (or willed beforehand) the future birth, death, and resurrection of Jesus. Having predetermined this Messianic future, God saved all elect persons prior to Christ through this ontological and epistemological certainty.

Again, some Baptists have strongly advocated this perspective. "The Second London Confession" duplicates this section from "The Westminster Confession of Faith." Boyce, also quoting Revelation 13:8, holds this same position. "The fact that the Lamb was slain before the foundation of the world, or, in other words, the certainty of Christ's death, makes salvation beforehand possible, and permits God to bestow it. The death of Christ only fulfils what has thus been relied on."[36] Nonetheless, even

---

(Bauckham, *The Climax of Prophecy: Studies on the Book of Revelation* [Edinburgh: T.&T. Clark, 1993] 440). John F. Walvoord, however, accepts the former and Reformed translation, interpreting its meaning as follows. "The simplest explanation here seems the best, namely, that their names were written in the book of life from eternity past. This was made possible by anticipation of the future dying of the Lamb on their behalf" (Walvoord, *The Revelation of Jesus Christ: A Commentary* [Chicago: Moody Press, 1966] 202). Similarly, also see G. B. Caird, *The Revelation of St. John the Divine*, Harper's New Testament Commentaries, ed. Henry Chadwick (New York: Harper & Row, 1966) 168. Although following the Reformed translation of this text, neither Herschel Hobbs nor James T. Draper, Jr. indicate any awareness of this issue or its seriousness (Hobbs, *The Cosmic Drama: An Exposition of the Book of Revelation* [Waco TX: Word Books, 1971] 130; James T. Draper, Jr., *The Unveiling* [Nashville: Broadman Press, 1984] 192). The third text from the Christian scriptures, Heb 13:8, often serves theologians as support for the classical theistic understanding of divine immutability as well. Calvin certainly used this text in that way (e.g., Calvin, *Institutes*, 1:431-32 [2.10.4]).

[35]George, *Theology of the Reformers*, 309.

[36]"The Assembly or Second London Confession, 1677 and 1688," in *Baptist Confessions of Faith*, ed. Lumpkin, 262 ("Chap. VIII. Of Christ the Mediator," 8.6); Boyce, *Abstract of Systematic Theology*, 315. Although the "Second London Confession" follows the "Westminster Confession of Faith" in this respect, the "Westminster

though the supreme moment in God's salvific activity, as Baptists in the SBC have attested historically, Jesus of Nazareth represents only one period of time in the history of God's salvific interaction with the entire creation.[37]

As a consequence, the *RPTSC*'s excessive emphasis on Jesus as the *only* savior merely distorts the biblical witness to the genuine uniqueness of Jesus as the Christ.[38] The uniqueness and radicality of Jesus as the Christ resides in the witness to this person as God-become-human, a

---

Confession of Faith" more carefully distinguishes between two different "dispensations" of one covenant, in which, by God's grace, salvation came through Christ: the "covenant of works," administered "under the law," which instructed and strengthened the elect in "the promised Messiah"; and the "covenant of grace," administered "under the gospel," dispensed through proclamation of the Word, Baptism, and the Lord's Supper, attesting to the accomplished work of Christ ("Westminster Confession of Faith, 1647," in *Creeds of Christendom*, 3:616-18 ["Chapter VII. Of God's Covenant with Man," 1-6]). The "Second London Confession" virtually collapses this distinction: "This *Covenant* is revealed in the Gospel; first of all to *Adam* in the promise of Salvation by the seed of the woman, and afterwards by farther steps, until the full discovery thereof was compleated [*sic*] in the new Testament; and it is founded in that *Eternal Covenant* transaction, that was between the *Father* and the *Son*, about the Redemption of the *Elect*; and it is alone by the Grace of this *Covenant*, that all of the posterity of fallen *Adam*, that ever were saved, did obtain life and a blessed immortality; *Man* being now utterly uncapable [*sic*] of acceptance with *God* upon those terms, on which *Adam* stood in his state of innocency" ("The Assembly or Second London Confession, 1677 and 1688," in *Baptist Confessions of Faith*, ed. Lumpkin, 260 ["Chap. VII. Of God's Covenant," 7.3]).

[37]For example, although the *FASB (1920)* describes God's becoming human in Jesus Christ as "the center of the entire revelation," the "crowning revelation" to which "all the earlier stages" of divine revelation "lead," and "the key to the meaning of all history," this confession, nevertheless, acknowledges quite comfortably, and properly, both that God revealed the divine self to humans "by slow degrees as they were able to receive" the divine self-disclosure and that the scriptures, in both of its large parts (the two testaments), represent "preliminary" and "completed" portions in the "record" of the "revelation of the Gospel of our redemption" ("Fraternal Address of Southern Baptists," *Baptist Standard* 32 [26 February 1920]: 5).

[38]See the *RPTSC*'s numerous phrases and claims to this effect in five short paragraphs on portions of two pages: "the *sole* and sufficient Savior of the redeemed"; "the *unique* and *solitary* Savior in whom *alone* there is redemption and forgiveness of sins"; "salvation through Jesus Christ and *no other*"; "*no other* gospel"; "the *only* hope of salvation and the *only* Savior"; "the gospel of that cross" as "the *only* message which can and does save"; "trusting in Him [Christ] *alone* for their salvation"; "bear faithful witness to salvation in Jesus Christ, and in Him *alone*" (*RPTSC*, 116, 117 [2.3.2, 5, 7, 8, 9]; emphasis mine).

claim which suggests a double implication: (1) by becoming a human creature in and with the rest of creation, God has done something new for the creation, has participated with or alongside humans in their finitude, sin, and misery; and (2) by becoming a human creature, God has done something new for God's own self, for the first time has become finite as well as infinite, creature as well as creator. Nonetheless, God had already and consistently acted to redeem creation prior to becoming human as Jesus of Nazareth. God's salvific activity for the creation neither began nor ended with Jesus' birth, life, death, and resurrection.

Most seriously, the ahistorical character of the *RPTSC*'s Christology implies that God slays Jesus; sinners do not kill Jesus. Since God has predestined everything prior to creation itself, including the life of Jesus as salvation for all elect humans, then God has also predestined Jesus' death. As implied in the *RPTSC*'s Christology, therefore, God causes Jesus to die; God ultimately kills Jesus. This implication in the Christological ambiguity of the *RPTSC*'s soteriology discloses a third major distortion or severe problem in the *RPTSC*'s Christology and soteriology, one also correlated to the PTSC's third major concern.

III. Only Penal-Substitutionary Atonement?

As a third problem in the PTSC's construal of God's soteriological activity in Christ, the *RPTSC* explicitly prescribes the *penal-substitutionary theory* of Christ's death as the only biblical and, therefore, only legitimate soteriological theory for Baptists in the SBC. According to the *RPTSC*, "Christ's redemption was wrought by His atonement which was both *penal* and *substitutionary*. Christ died in our place, bearing in His body the *penalty* for our sin and *purchasing* our redemption by His blood." A concept of divine justice, specifically justice as retribution for offenses, dominates this construal of Christ's death, in spite of this theory's parallel emphasis upon divine mercy and love. In his crucifixion, Christ paid the price of death for elect humans to satisfy divine justice and to appease divine wrath against them as sinners. Consequently, once again, the PTSC has declared another Calvinistic interpretation of Christian doctrine to be normative for all Baptists in the SBC. "The gospel of that cross is the *only* message which can and does save. . . . Furthermore, Baptists *must join* with *all true Christians* in affirming the substitutionary nature of Christ's atonement *and reject calls*—ancient and modern—for redefining Christ's reconciling work as merely subjective and illustrative."[39] Two major problems arise from these soteriological statements.

A. Misleading Standardization of the Penal-Substitutionary Theory

First, the *RPTSC* treats the penal-substitutionary theory of Christ's death as the only legitimate (or biblical) Christian concept of atonement. When the *RPTSC* in any way standardizes or makes normative (whether historically, logically, or both) this particular understanding of Jesus' death, this document falsely construes or misrepresents both biblical interpretations of Jesus' death and the history of Christian soteriology. This misrepresentation has two sides to it.

On the one side, historically, Christian communities and theologians have interpreted the salvific meaning of Christ's death through numerous

---

[39]*RPTSC*, 117 (2.3.6, 7, 9); emphasis mine. This formulation continues to follow the soteriological declarations in "Resolution No. 1—The Finality of Jesus Christ as Sole and Sufficient Savior": "the redeemed are justified by grace through faith in *our Lord* who on the cross personally *bore the penalty of our sin in His body* and *purchased* our redemption by His blood" (*Annual of the SBC* [1993]: 94; emphasis mine). Although I will not examine Calvin's soteriology in detail here, without a doubt, the metaphorical network of human sin/offense-divine wrath/vengeance-penalty/punishment-price/payment-satisfaction/appeasement dominates Calvin's understanding of Jesus' death on the cross (e.g., Calvin, *Institutes*, 1:501-502, 503-12, 528-34 [2.15.6; 2.16.1-7; 2.17.1-6]). Certainly, Calvin registers numerous important differences from Anselm's soteriology; for example, Calvin rejects Anselm's notion of the incarnation's absolute necessity, locating its cause simply in the divine decree (Calvin, *Institutes*, 1:464 [2.12.1]). Nonetheless, Calvin remains fundamentally indebted to Anselm's basic soteriological paradigm: see, for example, Anselm, "Cur Deus Homo," in *Saint Anselm: Basic Writings*, 2nd ed., trans. S. N. Deane, Open Court Library of Philosophy, ed. Eugene Freeman (La Salle IL: Open Court Pub. Co., 1962) 201-38 (1.11-25). Furthermore, Anselm endeavors to avoid the notion that Christ suffered punishment from God for human sin, in order to satisfy the divine honor or justice; that is, Anselm refuses a penal-substitutionary theory, by distinguishing between, on the one hand, Christ's obedience of God or accomplishment of that which God demands from all rational beings (maintaining truth and justice in life) and, on the other hand, Christ's voluntary endurance of that which God does not demand of sinless humans (death) (Anselm, "Cur Deus Homo," 187-201 [1.7-10]). Paul Fiddes supplies brief, but accurate, comparisons of the concepts of justice upon which both Anselm and Calvin developed their theories of atonement: feudal justice (Anselm) and Roman criminal justice (Calvin) (Fiddes, *Past Event and Present Salvation: The Christian Idea of the Atonement* [Louisville: Westminster/John Knox Press, 1989] 96-104). Although Timothy George rightly underscores several points where Calvin's soteriology differs from Anselm's theory of atonement, he mistakenly describes Anselm's soteriology as a "theory of penal, substitutionary atonement" (George, *Theology of the Reformers*, 220).

theories or models with significant support from the Christian scriptures. This situation arose because, as W. T. Conner claimed, "there is no theory of atonement in the New Testament."[40] Most importantly, a committee with such urgent concerns for orthodox pronouncements should know that the ancient, ecumenical, Christian councils never endorsed as orthodox, or officially adopted, any single concept or theory of atonement.[41] Furthermore, in terms of the practical, ecclesial reception and use of an atonement theory, a very different interpretation of Jesus' death predominated in the ancient Christian communities: the model of Christ as the victor in God's conflict with evil, the *Christus victor* theory, convincingly described by Gustaf Aulén as the "classic Christian idea of the Atonement."[42] Nonetheless, John Calvin, and especially subsequent Reformed Protestant orthodoxy and scholasticism, emphasized and developed the very different penal-substitutionary theory most completely, even though it had appeared variously in previous theologies as well.[43]

Certainly, some early Baptist confessions, such as the Calvinistic "Second London Confession," espoused the penal-substitutionary interpretation of Jesus' death.[44] Nonetheless, other (and some earlier) Baptist confessions of faith avoided construing Christ's crucifixion as penal sub-

---

[40]Conner, *Cross in the New Testament*, 124.

[41]Fiddes notes this as well (*Past Event and Present Salvation*, 4-5). Furthermore, Conner drew an even more important conclusion: "So far as I can see there has never been developed any theory of atonement in Christian history that was entirely satisfactory" (*Cross in the New Testament*, 125).

[42]Gustaf Aulén, *Christus Victor: An Historical Study of the Three Main Types of the Idea of the Atonement*, trans. A. G. Hebert (New York: Macmillan, 1969) 4-7. Robert S. Franks quite appropriately notes, of course, that even Aulén's name for this theory begs the question: "The mere fact that this theory was actually developed first in the order of history, does not make it a standard by which other theories are to be tested" (Franks, *The Atonement: The Dale Lectures for 1933* [London: Oxford University Press, 1934] 78-79).

[43]Besides the references from Calvin's *Institutes* cited previously, consider also the following examples as additional support for this claim: John Calvin, "The Catechism of the Church of Geneva (1545)," in John Calvin, *Calvin: Theological Treatises*, ed. and trans. J. K. S. Reid, Library of Christian Classics (Philadelphia: Westminster, 1954) 95-100; "Canones Synodi Dordrechtanae," 586-87 ("Second Head of Doctrine. Of the Death of Christ, and the Redemption of Men thereby," arts. 1-9); "Westminster Confession of Faith," in *Creeds of Christendom*, 3:621, 626-27 ("Chapter VIII. Of Christ the Mediator," 5; "Chapter XI. Of Justification," 3).

[44]"The Assembly or Second London Confession, 1677 and 1688," in *Baptist Confessions of Faith*, Lumpkin, 258-59, 261-63 ("Chap. VI. Of the fall of Man, of Sin, and of the Punishment thereof," 3-5; "Chap. VIII. Of Christ the Mediator," 4-6, 8).

stitution. One Baptist confession of faith, written between 1612 and 1614
in Holland by English Baptists in exile, explicitly resists a penal-substitutionary interpretation of Jesus' death: even though Jesus pleased God in
his crucifixion, Jesus' sacrificial death "doth not reconcile *God* unto us,
which did never hate us, nor was our enemy, but reconcileth *us* unto God
(2 Cor. v. 19), and *slayeth the enmity and hatred, which is in us against
God* (Eph. I. 14, 17; Rom. I. 30)." Furthermore, this latter confession of
faith fully affirms the Christus-victor theory of Jesus' death on the
cross.[45] While stating that Christ "made atonement for our sins by his
death," not even "The New Hampshire Confession" (1833), the confession on which the SBC later based the *BFM (1925)*, describes Jesus'
death or this atonement as penal substitution.[46]

Most importantly, however, in its major confessional statements, the
SBC has never interpreted Jesus' death with terminology either unreservedly or exclusively affirmative of the penal-substitutionary theory.[47]
Although the *FASB (1920)* interprets Jesus' death as *vicarious* atonement
(without using that precise language), the document completely grounds
that interpretation in a broader understanding of Jesus' death *through the
Christus-victor motif.* Thus, for this early confession of faith from the
SBC, Jesus struggled with and conquered sin and death as the enemies
of humanity, thereby liberating humanity from an enslavement, rather
than receiving punishment from God as the vengeful enemy of sinful
humanity or to satisfy an offended divine holiness or justice.[48] In the

[45]"Propositions and Conclusions concerning True Christian Religion, 1612–1614," in
Baptist Confessions of Faith, ed. Lumpkin, 129-30 (arts. 32-34); emphasis mine. Nonethe-
less, see the lingering Calvinism in the soteriologies of earlier Baptist confessions: "Short
Confession of Faith in XX Articles by John Smyth, 1609," in *Baptist Confessions of
Faith*, ed. Lumpkin, 100-101 (arts. 2-4, 6-10); "A Short Confession of Faith, 1610," in
Baptist Confessions of Faith, ed. Lumpkin, 104-106 (arts. 8-10, 12-13).
[46]*NHC (1833)*, 362-64 (arts. 4-6, 9).
[47]Among confessions of faith in use by institutions of the SBC, *only* the explicitly
Calvinistic "Abstract of Principles" (1858) (the articles of belief for only one of the
SBC's institutions, SBTS, not for the entire SBC) uses language fully consistent with and
suggestive of the penal-substitutionary theory of atonement: "Justification is God's gracious and full *acquittal of sinners*, who believe in Christ, from all sin, through the *satisfaction that Christ has made*" (*AP [1858]*, 38 [art. 11, "Justification"]; emphasis mine).
[48]*FASB (1920)*, 5. Although only an institutional confession of faith and not a statement for the entire SBC, the FMB's "Statement of Belief" from 1920 contains very little
about the atonement; in its brief formulation, similarly yet explicitly, that document interprets the crucifixion of Jesus as a "vicarious death" (*SB [1920]*, 197). Four of the SBC's

statement entitled "Science and Religion" (a portion of the president's address by E. Y. Mullins, adopted by the SBC in 1923 "as the belief of this body"), the SBC in a brief formulation also interprets Jesus' death as vicarious (not penal-substitutionary) atonement.[49] In addition, even though the *BFM (1925)* declares that Jesus "made atonement for our sins by his death" and defines justification as "God's gracious and *full acquittal* upon principles of righteousness of all sinners who believe in Christ," bringing believers into "a state of most blessed *peace and favor with God*," this document does not construe the crucifixion of Jesus as the Messiah's penal-substitutionary atonement for sinful humanity.[50] Finally, in its soteriological statements, the *BFM (1963)* supplies even more room to interpret Jesus' death on the cross in terms of the fullest range of scriptural images, metaphors, and models: "in His death on the cross He *made provision for the redemption of men* from sin."[51] The *BFM (1963)*, however, most assuredly does not construe the death of Jesus in terms of the penal-substitutionary theory of atonement.

On the other side of its misrepresentation of Christian history, the *RPTSC* also contains a misrepresentation of the only major interpretation of Jesus' death to which the committee opposes its own formulation, a theory described in the *RPTSC* as a "merely subjective and illustrative" interpretation of Christ's death, a theory that redefines and minimizes "His redemptive work."[52] Although one cannot know with certainty, given the *RPTSC*'s oblique language and lack of citations, probably the *RPTSC* refers to Peter Abelard's interpretation of Jesus' death (as well as to modern or contemporary versions and interpretations of Abelard's theory). If so, then the *RPTSC* has most certainly misconstrued his soteriology.[53] In any case, the *RPTSC* does not clarify adequately or exactly

---

confessional documents do not interpret the nature and meaning of Jesus' death at all: *PCU (1914)*; *RIR (1938)*; *RWCC (1940)*; and *SP (1946)*.

[49]"He died as the vicarious atoning Saviour of the world and was buried" (*SR [1923]*, 19-20).

[50]*BFM (1925)*, 72 (arts. 4 and 5, "The Way of Salvation" and "Justification").

[51]*BFM (1963)*, 271 (art. 2.2, "God the Son"); emphasis mine. See also *BFM (1963)*, 272-75 (arts. 3-5, "Man," "Salvation," and "God's Purpose of Grace"). In his own interpretation of the *BFM (1963)*, nonetheless, Herschel Hobbs does construe the atonement with language from the penal-substitutionary theory, even though he does not use that phrase itself (Hobbs, *Baptist Faith and Message*, 43).

[52]*RPTSC*, 117 (2.3.8, 9).

[53]See Peter Abailard, "Exposition of the Epistle to the Romans (An Excerpt from the

that to which it refers with the phrase "merely subjective and illustrative." Furthermore, if the PTSC has produced the *RPTSC* in order to attend to "unique and pressing challenges to faithfulness" or to address "several issues of *contemporary* urgency,"[54] why has this particular family of ancient soteriologies so alarmed the committee? Why has the PTSC isolated this one interpretation of Jesus' death as an object of rejection, when neither it nor the penal-substitutionary theory appear explicitly in any of the SBC's major confessional statements?

B. Aporias in the Penal-Substitutionary Theory of Atonement

Second, nothing in the *RPTSC* indicates that the PTSC either has acknowledged or even has realized the serious theological aporias in the penal-substitutionary theory itself. Significantly and fortunately, the SBC's confessional statements have rightly avoided this particular soteriology. This theological penology generates internal inconsistencies throughout the theological paradigm in which it operates and, more seriously, undermines the gospel's basic rationale or logic as well. As W. T. Conner emphasized so strongly in the latter part of his career, the penal-substitutionary theory "can hardly be regarded as an adequate interpretation of the redeeming work of Christ." More forcefully, according to Conner, because this theory "abstracts the justice of God from the

---

Second Book)," in *A Scholastic Miscellany: Anselm to Ockham*, ed. and trans. Eugene R. Fairweather, Library of Christian Classics, John Baillie, John T. McNeill, and Henry P. Van Dusen, gen. eds. (Philadelphia: Westminster, 1956) 276-87. Richard E. Weingart has conclusively invalidated such trivial construals of Abelard's soteriology, whether offered by opponents or proponents of his theory of atonement (Weingart, *The Logic of Divine Love: A Critical Analysis of the Soteriology of Peter Abailard* [Oxford: Clarendon Press, 1970]). Perhaps the PTSC aimed its criticism at older interpretations of Abelard's soteriology, such as Hastings Rashdall's understanding of Jesus' death (Rashdall, *The Idea of Atonement in Christian Theology* [London: Macmillan, 1919] 435-64), interpretations certainly at least partially open to the implicit criticisms in the *RPTSC*, yet definitely more nuanced than the *RPTSC*'s caricature suggests. W. T. Conner describes Abelard's soteriology and soteriologies derived from it as "moral influence" theories of atonement. According to Conner, the moral-influence theory "has one thing in its favor. It makes central the idea of the love of God. No theory can be considered Christian that does not do this. In the New Testament, the central thought in the death of Christ is that his death was a revelation of God's love for sinful men. Christ did not die to win for man the love of God but to reveal that love. God does not love us because Christ died for us, but Christ died for us because God loves us. Any theory that obscures that idea is either non-Christian or anti-Christian" (Conner, *Cross in the New Testament*, 151).

[54]*RPTSC*, 113 (1.5); emphasis mine.

other moral qualities in God and makes justice stand out above the others," this theory "becomes a heresy by virtue of an overemphasis."[55]

This understanding of Jesus' death has received numerous and devastating critiques in the history of Christian thought. I repeat here only a few of the most obvious aporias or theoretical difficulties in the penal-substitutionary model. Furthermore, rather than representing merely difficult yet manageable puzzles, these aporias infix insoluble theoretical and, hence, praxiological obstacles into Christian interpretations of the meaning in Jesus' death. These problems issue from conjoining the notion of punishment for sin, where sin is defined as offending God's holiness, honor, or justice, to the idea that the innocent Jesus becomes the sinful human's substitute, receiving someone else's punishment for sin from the offended, righteously indignant, and wrathful deity.

1. *First Aporia.* By emphasizing the satisfaction of divine justice toward human sin through Jesus' punishment on the cross, the soteriology embraced by the *RPTSC* primarily *construes Jesus' crucifixion too objectively*, fundamentally interprets it as a legal transaction between God the father and God the son, as *merely an event between God and God.* God eternally accomplished reconciliation with elect humans on Jesus' cross. Sinful human involvement in God's action through Christ does not play a significant part in this event itself (excluding for the moment, of course, the way in which this Christological model construes the relationship between the divine and human natures in the person of the Christ, and the cross's effects or noneffects on both of them). Only later, sinful humans (and elect humans at that) claim this divine work by faith. Consequently, this understanding misrepresents the *subjective* meaning of Jesus' cross in at least two related respects.

First, the *RPTSC*'s soteriology construes the death of Jesus completely as the intention of God, and fails to acknowledge, with the Christian scriptures, the extent to which sinful humans victimized God in the

---

[55]Conner, *Gospel of Redemption*, 99; idem, *Cross in the New Testament*, 151-52. In the latter stages of Conner's career, he shifted from a penal-substitutionary soteriology to a *Christus victor* model of atonement. From this latter perspective, he directed numerous criticisms against penal-substitutionary soteriologies. Walter D. Draughon III also notes this shift in Conner's soteriology: see Draughon, "The Atonement," in *Has Our Theology Changed? Southern Baptist Thought Since 1845*, ed. Paul A. Basden (Nashville: Broadman & Holman, 1994) 96-104.

crucifixion of Jesus.[56] Second, the process or event of reconciliation or at-one-ment concerns and involves all estranged parties, both victim and victimizers; in the soteriology affirmed by the *RPTSC*, however, only God reconciles with God; God draws sinful humans into this past event only insofar as God has elected any of them in the preceding eternal decree. To the contrary and according to the Christian scriptures, *actual* reconciliation and salvation occur for humans only after they have responded positively, with repentance and faith, to God's offer of that possibility in the crucifixion of Jesus. Atonement, then, names the entire process of restoring relationships between humans and God, neither an event between God and God nor even only an event within God.[57]

2. *Second Aporia.* By examining this theory more closely, a second aporia emerges. Insofar as the *RPTSC*'s soteriology depends fully on its affirmation of orthodox Christology, in this construal of Jesus' death, *God sacrifices nothing as God for human salvation, except the human nature of God the son.* In effect, and despite the dissonance between this and the previous aporia, the penal perspective construes the cross as the work of only the human nature of Christ. God does not actually bear the cost of the cross.[58] Since God in all three persons of the Trinity remains impassible and immutable, only the human nature of Jesus suffers and, therefore, receives the punishment from God for humanity's sin. Hence, only a human repays God for sinful humanity's debts; God does not freely give salvation from the divine self; God requires and receives payment from a creature for sin. For this theory, in Jesus' cross, no divine self-sacrifice produces the possibility of human salvation. In addition, insofar as the commitments that generate this second aporia operate alongside the commitments behind the first aporia, this second aporia also generates an internal conflict between those two sets of commitments.

3. *Third Aporia.* Through the previous difficulties, a third major aporia with two prongs becomes visible. According to the soteriology affirmed by the *RPTSC*, insofar as humans do not victimize Jesus in his

---

[56]Similarly, see Conner, *Cross in the New Testament*, 158-61.

[57]Fiddes argues similarly in *Past Event and Present Salvation*, 99.

[58]W. T. Conner also advanced this criticism about penal theories of atonement: "It has been customary among advocates of the penal view, from the days of Anselm on, to regard the atonement as man's work, not God's, in the sense that it was held that it was the human nature of Christ that suffered, not the divine" (Conner, *Gospel of Redemption*, 118; cf. idem, *Cross in the New Testament*, 135-36).

death and this remains an event between God and God, and inasmuch as only the humanity of the Christ truly bears the punishment on the cross for humans, on the one hand, *God the father victimizes the innocent and faithful divine son*; yet, on the other hand, God the father victimizes *only the humanity* of God the son, the Christ's divine nature remaining impassible like God the father's divinity.

a. The first prong of this third aporia concerns *the innocence or guilt of the Christ who suffers the divine wrath*. Given the concept of justice (as retribution, revenge, or equivalence) operative in this theory, characterized as "an eye for an eye and a tooth for a tooth," only those guilty of sin *must and will* suffer God's wrath: punishment from the God whose laws guilty humans have broken, vengeance from the God whose character the guilty humans have offended. Yet, the only person without sin (according to both the scriptures and the *RPTSC*), Jesus of Nazareth, the only innocent human, suffers punishment from the angry divine father for the sins of others. Whether or not Jesus voluntarily submits to this divine sentence, whether actively or passively a participant in his own victimization, insofar as God exercises *wrath* toward Jesus in the event of his suffering and death, this indignantly righteous God has violated the terms of the divine justice itself. God has punished, tortured, and killed the innocent Christ. In this exercise of divine wrath against the faithful human, God has acted unjustly, has become a criminal against the divine self and the divine laws.[59] In this scenario, only if Jesus had actually sinned, could God the father avoid acting unjustly in the divine punishment of Jesus. Yet, neither scripture nor the *RPTSC* claims that Jesus sinned and, therefore, truly deserved punishment on the cross. Furthermore, then, in the penal-substitutionary theory, God the father's victimization of God the son invalidates, or at least raises perpetual doubt about, every claim concerning God's everlasting fidelity to faithful humanity. In this theory, God the father has victimized and abandoned the only perfectly faithful person, Jesus of Nazareth. As a consequence, God the father has become unfaithful as well as unjust in the penal-substitutionary interpretation of Jesus' death on the cross.[60]

---

[59]Rashdall offers a similar criticism in his *Idea of Atonement in Christian Theology*, 422-23.

[60]Conner argued similarly: "This theory, at least in its more rigid forms, gives an impossible view of substitution. It insists that Christ bore the exact penalty that was due the sinner on account of his sins. . . . The very nature of sin is to alienate from God. But

b. The second prong of the third aporia intensifies that unjust divine victimization of Jesus. *Only the humanity*, not the divinity, *of God the son experiences this fate from God the father*. By victimizing only the innocent humanity of Christ, certainly God the father avoids the charge of masochism (here narrowly defined as receiving pleasure from self-inflicted pain): God does not inflict suffering on the divine nature or on God per se. Nonetheless, given the standards of justice in this theory, this divine punishment of the innocent messianic humanity thoroughly justifies an indictment of the wrathful divine father as sadistic (here

---

Christ was not alienated from God. God was not displeased with him. Some will say that God withdrew his presence as evidenced by the cry of desolation on the cross. This was no doubt a cry of perplexity, perhaps verging on despair, as Jesus realized that God was leaving him in the hands of wicked men to die like a criminal and an outcast. But it is to be noted that Jesus clung to God in faith and did not despair. He committed himself in full trust into the hands of the Father. And where faith is, there God is. Faith cannot exist where God is not. To talk of Jesus as dying in sin in the sense that a sinner dies in sin is to speak of an impossibility; and that is what it would mean if he should bear the sinner's penalty. . . . But in the strict sense of suffering spiritual death as the unrepentant sinner dies under the displeasure of God—in this sense, Jesus did not suffer the penalty of sin" (Conner, *Cross in the New Testament*, 145).

Some theologians interpret Jesus' cry of dereliction, in light of Psalm 22, as indicating both Jesus' struggle not to despair in his pain and God's fidelity toward Jesus in the midst of his victimization by sinful humanity—directly repudiating the claim that God has somehow forsaken the faithful one, Jesus the Christ (e.g., T. Vincent Tymms, *The Christian Idea of Atonement* [London: Macmillan, 1904] 292). Such a perspective interprets the event between God and God on the cross of Jesus as *Deus cum Deo* or God with God, emphasizing God the father's fidelity to God the son. In one version of this interpretation, although Jesus experiences abandonment by God or "loss of God," actually "the absence of God experienced in the abandonment characterizes the loving presence of the Father who gives to Christ the possibility of being fully himself as Son—just as the abandonment experienced by the Son allows the Father to be such" (Gérard Rossé, *The Cry of Jesus on the Cross: A Biblical and Theological Study*, trans. Stephen Wentworth Arndt [New York: Paulist Press, 1987] 111-12, 136). This viewpoint, however, distinguishes itself from the view of Moltmann (and those who follow his line of interpretation) because, by "abandonment," it attempts to emphasize both God the creator's and God-become-human's maintenance of genuine alterity, rather than judgment upon the one who has identified with humans in their sin. Other theologians incorporate fragments of this latter viewpoint somewhat differently. For example, while Paul Fiddes agrees that God did not inflict a penalty upon Christ with the cross, nevertheless, he claims that Jesus vocalizes his loss of meaning in the cry of dereliction—an emptiness left open and unchallenged until the resurrection (Fiddes, *Creative Suffering of God*, 163; idem, *Past Event and Present Salvation*, 194-95).

defined narrowly as receiving pleasure by inflicting pain on others).[61] Defining as good whatever God chooses to do, as a defense of such an understanding of Jesus' death, only begs the question: such an exercise of divine freedom contradicts God's character itself, disclosing an arbitrary and, therefore, thoroughly mutable God as well. Additionally, appealing to the mystery of the divine method in this matter, as a second defense, does even less to alleviate the problem: since the character of Jesus has disclosed the character of God to human experience and knowledge, then, for humans, no doubt remains about the contradiction of that character in such an alleged divine victimization of the innocent Messiah.

4. *Fourth Aporia.* Even though God the father only victimizes the humanity of God the son, the previous difficulty discloses a fourth aporia, one in which the actual character of this Calvinistic event between God and God fully appears: the penal-substitutionary theory construes the event between God and God on the cross of Jesus as *Deus contra Deum* or God *against* God. God the father either inflicts this death upon God the son or flees to remain helpless (even if sorrowful) as sinful humanity victimizes God-become-human. Jesus of Nazareth both suffers wounds

---

[61]Some Calvinist theologians have tried to develop genuine theologies of divine suffering, hence rejecting the classical theistic insistence on the impassibility of the divine nature, at least in terms of the Logos or the second member or expression of the Trinity. For example, George Griffin retains much of the Calvinist dependence upon the classical theistic model, especially in his contention that nothing forces God to suffer against God's will. In support of his contention, Griffin returns to a modified version of the double decree. "The incarnation and sufferings of God the Son were not caused by any change in the eternal counsels. . . . The earliest eternity had registered in its archives the advent and sufferings of the incarnate Deity, and his ascension and ceaseless reign at the right hand of the Highest. We might almost say that, before the worlds were formed, incarnation and suffering were incorporated into his very being among its constituent elements" (Griffin, *The Sufferings of Christ,* 2nd ed. [New York: Harper & Brothers, 1846] 275). "The second person of the Trinity voluntarily became the vicarious Sufferer for the redeemed. The substitution was not to depress the awful standard of retributive justice. The Glory of God was to be maintained; heaven must be satisfied, hell silenced. . . . The redeeming God lacked not capacity to suffer" (Griffin, *Sufferings of Christ,* 50). In this particular mutation of the Christian symbol of divine suffering, however, God appears somewhat *masochistic:* "the Parent of the universe so loved our fallen race that, for their salvation, *he awakened the sword of divine justice to smite his Other Self; his Other Self,* moved by pity known only in the pavilion of the Godhead, *freely bared his filial heart to the descending stroke,* which naught but Omnipotence could have endured" (Griffin, *Sufferings of Christ,* 186; emphasis mine).

inflicted by divine wrath and suffers abandonment by God the creator. In this event between God and God, God combats God. An internal conflict bifurcates God.[62] God as creator becomes an antagonist toward God-become-human, the agonist on the cross. As W. T. Conner noted to the contrary, "no theory of atonement is Christian that runs a line of cleavage between the Father and the Son and looks on Christ as saving us from God."[63]

---

[62]The nineteenth-century, Calvinistic theologian George Griffin perceived in Jesus' cry of dereliction God the father's actual abandonment of God the son, due to Jesus' identification with godforsaken humans (Griffin, *Sufferings of Christ*, 96). As a major source for similar contemporary perspectives, Jürgen Moltmann claims that Jesus died "ultimately because of his God and Father," that on the cross occurred "an event between God and God," "a deep division in God himself, in so far as God abandoned God and contradicted himself" (Moltmann, *The Crucified God: The Cross as the Foundation and Criticism of Christian Theology*, trans. R. A. Wilson and John Bowden [New York: Harper & Row, 1974] 149, 244). Moltmann attempts to ameliorate the implications of his perspective by describing Jesus' experience in the following way. The cross of Jesus is "the experience of abandonment by God in the knowledge that God is not distant but close; does not judge, but shows grace. And this, in full consciousness that God is close at hand in his grace, to be abandoned and delivered up to death as one rejected, is the torment of hell" (Moltmann, *Crucified God*, 148). Nonetheless, even in Moltmann's attempted amelioration of his notion of divine "bifurcation," lurks the still problematic notion of a conflict between wrath/justice/honor and love/mercy/grace within God, a reliance upon residuals from penal-substitutionary or satisfaction theories of atonement. Similarly, according to David E. Jenkins, God's intense identification with humans in Jesus Christ has enabled God to experience for the sake of humans "almost a split personality," that which is at the basis of the mystery in Jesus' cry of dereliction (Jenkins, *Living with Questions: Investigations into the Theory and Practice of Belief in God* [London: S.C.M. Press, 1969] 53). Martin Luther, for whom the tension between divine wrath and divine love determines the entire character of theology, when examining the context of Jesus' cry of dereliction (Matt 27:39, 40, 49) in light of Psalm 22, speaks of God fighting God, "da streydet Got [*sic*] mit Gott" (*D. Martin Luthers Werke: Kritische Gesamtausgabe* [Weimar: Hermann Böhlaus Nachfolger, 1911] 45:370). Kazoh Kitamori, a Japanese Lutheran theologian, radicalizes Luther's notion of conflict in God between wrath and love. For Kitamori, because of their sin, humans deserve divine wrath and cannot be loved. Yet, the pain of God is not grief over human sin, but is rather this conflict between wrath and love—when God loves the undeserving sinner anyway. God can do this only because the divine father causes the divine son's death (Kitamori, *Theology of the Pain of God*, 5th ed., trans. M. E. Bratcher [Richmond: John Knox Press, 1965] 47).

[63]Conner, *Cross in the New Testament*, 144-45. Frank Stagg argues similarly. "The cry of Jesus on the cross: 'My God, my God, why hast thou forsaken me?' is by some taken as an actual abandonment of the Son by the Father, or a giving over of the Son to his fate. Such interpretation suggests the impossible idea of two Gods at Golgotha. It

5. *Fifth Aporia.* Proceeding more deeply into the fourth difficulty indicates a fifth aporia in the soteriology affirmed by the *RPTSC*. The penal-substitutionary theory, thus, relies on a doctrine of God in which a *conflict occurs within God's own self* between two dynamic networks in the divine life: between divine holiness, justice, hate, wrath, or vengeance and divine mercy, grace, love, self-sacrifice, or forgiveness. As Calvin himself says, "in some ineffable way, God loved us and yet was angry toward us at the same time, until he became reconciled to us in Christ."[64] As problematic as the struggle between God the father and God the son may be, this dimension of the conflict more seriously jeopardizes the coherence and credibility of the doctrine of God. This aporia concerns the internal cognitive, emotional, and volitional conflicts in the life of God the father—for that matter, in the life of all three members of the Trinity. In this aporia, God's nature resists itself and contradicts itself. Because humans have broken God's law or dishonored God, God's wrath opposes them in their sin; and God must punish those sinners. Yet, God loves them and wants to release them from this necessary penalty. In this theory of Jesus' death, God operates with a self-imposed double bind: God hates and loves, seeks to punish and longs to forgive sinful humans simultaneously.[65] The Christian scriptures

---

would represent the Son friendly to man and the Father hostile. Such division between Father and Son is forbidden by the New Testament and especially protested in the Fourth Gospel" (Stagg, *New Testament Theology* [Nashville: Broadman, 1962] 131).

[64]Calvin, *Institutes*, 1:530 (2.17.2). Also see Calvin's quotation from Augustine's work on this same point (Calvin, *Institutes*, 1:506-507 [2.16.4]). As Conner noted, "it can be easily seen how this view at times tended to introduce antithesis within the Godhead, the Father being regarded as the embodiment of justice requiring the sinner's punishment and the Son regarded as the embodiment of mercy seeking to save the sinner. . . . The view also—at least, in its more rigorous forms—tended to run a line of cleavage between the justice of God and the mercy of God. . . . God's chief function came to be regarded as the meting out of rewards and punishments to the subjects of his moral government according to their deserts. This was in accord with the emphasis on justice as the chief or supreme attribute in God. It was often said that God *might* exercise mercy, but he *must* punish sin. Mercy on God's part was optional, punishment was obligatory" (Conner, *Gospel of Redemption*, 99).

[65]Numerous theologians have perceived this aporia. See the following examples of responses to this paralyzing problem. "Among the unedifying features of popular Protestant theology which cannot justly be attributed to St. Augustine is the tendency to contrast the mercy and lovingkindness of the Son with the sternness, severity, and unrelenting justice of the Father. The anger of the just Father is propitiated because His anger and resent-

describe human persons with such tendencies as doubleminded. In addition, although the *RPTSC* identifies love as a divine motive, through the *RPTSC*'s acknowledgment that the cross of Christ reveals "God's absolute holiness and infinite love,"[66] as do the major proponents of this particular soteriology, divine love remains fully subservient to the reality of divine justice or holiness. The legal analogies and the corresponding concept of justice as retribution dominate in the penal-substitutionary interpretation of Jesus' death.

6. *Sixth Aporia.* A sixth aporia arises from the concept of divine justice in the penal-substitutionary theory, a problem identified in various ways in my elaborations of the previous aporias: despite this theory's *concern for the individual person*, it promotes an *impersonal relationship between God and the human.*[67] At the most general level, this theory construes justice strictly as a legal category. The relationship between God and sinful humanity becomes thoroughly mechanistic and impersonal. This theory concentrates so heavily on the individual human's standing with God that it almost entirely ignores soteriology's social dimensions. More specifically, this theory understands justice as retribution, as punishment for wrongs done, or, quite bluntly, as "getting even" or vengeance.[68] Sin requires punishment; the offended party in a

---

ment is satisfied by the death of His innocent Son" (Rashdall, *Idea of Atonement in Christian Theology*, 410). "But we cannot accept a battle between the Divine Mercy and the Divine Justice as a serious account of the Atonement. A divided will in God there cannot be" (Franks, *Atonement*, 178). "In the end, however, the theory of penal substitution fails to unify the love of God with his wrath" (Fiddes, *Past Event and Present Salvation*, 103).

[66]*RPTSC*, 117 (2.3.7).

[67]Fiddes argues similarly (*Past Event and Present Salvation*, 99). John McLeod Campbell supplies a related argument. "Another result of that conception of the nature of the atonement, not less conclusive as an argument against it, is the substitution of a legal standing for a filial standing as the gift of God to men in Christ" (Campbell, *The Nature of the Atonement and Its Relation to Remission of Sins and Eternal Life* [Cambridge: Macmillan, 1856] 67).

[68]W. T. Conner strongly emphasized this criticism. "The condemnation of sin in the cross is more than an exhibition of retributive justice. It is a condemnation that grows out of an exhibition of grace that saves. It results from a manifestation of the mercy of God toward the unworthy. Retributive justice measures out to every man rewards and punishment in accordance with his deserts; mercy deals with men better than they deserve. . . . The law method of dealing with sin is the method of retributive justice. Penalty is executed against the sinner. . . . But grace transcends this method. Grace also manifests

broken contractual relationship deserves satisfaction through reciprocal suffering in the offender. In this theoretical framework, God's execution of Jesus reestablishes some mystical equilibrium in God's eternal legal framework or just order. Rather than conceiving justice as the restoration of conditions that promote genuine community or life together, the penal-substitutionary framework construes justice as punishment that enables the holy God, the God who cannot remain in the presence of sin, once again to look upon humans as righteous, yet only through the sinless Christ. This sense of divine justice suggests again a deficient under-standing of God, a god deservingly designated as *deus fastidiosus*—the squeamish god.

7. *Seventh Aporia.* Another aporia in penal-substitutionary soteriology comes to light by examining the way in which this theory addresses the connection between the past event of Jesus' death and contemporary human salvation. The penal-substitutionary construal of Jesus' death links that past event to contemporary human experience through God's eternal decree. Since God from eternity has elected (foreordained to salvation) some persons and reprobated (foreordained to damnation) other persons, and since whatever God wills to do is effectual or occurs, then God has limited the divine activity in Jesus' death as applicable only to those humans whom God had elected to salvation from eternity: or, more simply, Christ died only for elect humans.[69] Again, although several

---

and vindicates righteousness, but it is righteousness that transcends retributive justice. . . . Suffering under law is penal; Christ's suffering was redemptive." According to Conner, in penal-substitutionary soteriology, "justice was also looked on as primarily, if not exclusively, penal in its nature, and was exalted to the supreme place among the attributes of God." "John tells us that God is love (1 John 4:8, 16). This makes love the essence of God's being. The penal view tends to make retributive justice the fundamental or controlling attribute of God. The New Testament makes nothing more fundamental than love in God" (Conner, *Gospel of Redemption*, 94, 99, 116-17; similarly, idem, *Cross in the New Testament*, 84-85).

[69]Robert S. Franks also perceives this problem. "But now, if satisfaction is to be made to a strict penal justice, the rigid logic of the situation requires that it should be the equivalent only of the punishment of those actually saved: otherwise Christ would have suffered for some in vain and unjustly" (Franks, *Atonement*, 89). This idea, although not developed as systematically as in the theologies of his followers, certainly appears in Calvin's theology. Referring specifically to salvation's relationship to election, Calvin says the following. "Whence it comes about that the whole world does not belong to its Creator except that grace rescues from God's curse and wrath and eternal death *a limited number* who would otherwise perish. But the world itself is left to its own destruction,

anthropological problems also arise here, the central aporia at this point concerns the very nature of divine freedom. Calvin particularly emphasizes, as I have mentioned previously, that no necessity produces the atonement through Jesus' death, other than God's eternal decree that salvation should occur in that way. Thus, *although election* (like atonement itself) *occurs* due to God's will alone, only through divine sovereignty, or *only through absolute divine freedom, because God must punish sin, God cannot forgive sin freely*, cannot reconcile with sinful humanity without punishing someone for sin. In this theological penology, God can elect humans arbitrarily, but cannot arbitrarily forgive.[70] Again, an internal contradiction shatters the concept of God presupposed by this construal of Jesus' death: the virtually external or extradivine reality of retributive justice dominates this absolutely free or sovereign God.

    8. *Eighth Aporia.* An eighth aporia emanates from the previous problem in the penal-substitutionary theory. Even though the declaration of *salvation by divine grace alone* accompanies this particular understanding of Jesus' death, *God only forgives following* the satisfaction of divine justice, *after the payment of a debt owed by sinful humanity to God.* Only a punishment of sin received by Jesus, as humanity's substitute, satisfies divine wrath and deflects punishment from sinful humans themselves. This problem extends the previous difficulty. God has not forgiven unconditionally. Rather, God has required a payment for forgiveness. According to this theory, God's wrath spent itself on the substitute victim: therefore, God can forgive. To the contrary, genuine forgiveness entails the cancellation of the debt, not its payment by someone else.[71]

---

to which it has been destined. Meanwhile, although Christ interposes himself as mediator, he claims for himself, in common with the Father, the right to choose." "Hence it is clear that the doctrine of salvation, which is said to be reserved solely and individually for the sons of the church, is *falsely debased when presented as effectually profitable to all.*" "If he willed all to be saved, he would set his Son over them, and would engraft all into his body with the sacred bond of faith" (Calvin, *Institutes*, 2:940, 944, 946 [3.22.7, 10]; emphasis mine). Even the very credalistic Baptist, B. A. Copass, rejected the concept of a limited atonement (Copass, "Concerning the Baptist Declaration of Faith" ["VI—Of the Way of Salvation"], *Baptist Standard* 26 [16 July 1914]: 12).

    [70]Again, see the similar argument by Paul Fiddes (*Past Event and Present Salvation*, 102).

    [71]W. T. Conner forcefully expressed this criticism of penal-substitutionary soteriology. This soteriological theory "insists that God is bound by his own justice to punish sin and

9. *Ninth Aporia*. The previous theoretical difficulties in the penal-sub-stitutionary theory disclose a ninth aporia, an even more serious problem within the divine nature itself. In this theory, despite protestations to the contrary, Jesus' crucifixion does not really portray God's nature as genuine love, as the scriptures attest.[72] Most generally, since God elected some humans and reprobated others from eternity, and decreed this double destiny without regard to human sin or righteousness, God elected any at all, displayed divine mercy to some, *only to bring glory to the divine self.* Any benefits received by humans whom God elected to salvation, therefore, occur only as residual and incidental effects of God's self-love, valuable only as items to glorify God and necessary only for that end. Calvin's doctrine of reprobation even more crudely illustrates this point. According to Calvin himself, "the reprobate are raised up *to the end* that through them *God's glory may be revealed*."[73] Thus, only a self-consumed divine self-love manifests itself through God's election of some humans to salvation in the penal-substitutionary scheme.

Moreover, a Calvinistic theory of election, or election as predetermination, and its corollary in a doctrine of limited atonement do not reveal *the quality of risk* that essentially characterizes divine love itself.[74] In this

---

that he cannot forgive sin without first punishing sin and that he cannot forgive sin without first punishing it. But it is a fair question to ask if punishment and forgiveness are not mutually exclusive. If a sin is punished, is it forgiven! [*sic*] If it is forgiven, is it punished? Or, to use the other figure constantly used by the advocates of this theory, can a debt be forgiven and paid at the same time? If it is paid, the creditor has no further claim on the debtor. Payment and forgiveness exclude each other" (Conner, *Cross in the New Testament*, 143-44). Frank Stagg noted this same point about the soteriology of the Christian scriptures. "God is free to forgive. The Father does not need to punish the Son in order to win the right to forgive. Were the Father paid off, then there would be no forgiveness. God himself forgives, and in so doing he assumes the responsibility for the sinner" (Stagg, *New Testament Theology*, 141).

[72]For example, 1 John 4:8, 16. See John McLeod Campbell's related argument about this theory's failure to reveal God as love (*Nature of the Atonement*, 61-67).

[73]Calvin, *Institutes*, 2:947 (3.22.11); emphasis mine.

[74]During the SBC's annual meeting in 1995, L. D. Brown, Jr. introduced a motion on the atonement entitled "On Our Belief That Christ Died for the Sins of the Entire World," a motion explicitly designed to respond to the encroachment of the doctrine of limited atonement on soteriology in the SBC: "I move that the Southern Baptist Convention affirm our belief that Jesus Christ died for the sins of the entire world and offers salvation to every human being." Nonetheless, the Committee on the Order of Business ruled this motion "out of order" (*Annual of the SBC* [1995]: 87, 94).

theory, since God wills to save some humans prior to creation, and since God accomplishes everything that God wills, then God risks absolutely nothing by offering mercy only to some humans through Jesus' payment on the cross. In this theological penology, God guarantees the salvation of elect humans only with Jesus' death. This divine activity operates with complete efficiency.

In the offer of genuine love to those in need, to the contrary, one cannot accurately calculate the nature of truly free responses to it. Often, although one lovingly endeavors to forgive and to reconcile with an offender or betrayer, the offender may refuse the offer: in that case, one has then sacrificed much in vain. For the penal-substitutionary theory, God acts only efficiently, without wasting any effort, energy, or merit on those creatures to whom God has eternally decreed to refuse divine grace.

10. *Tenth Aporia.* The previous weakness in penal-substitutionary soteriology suggests a tenth major theoretical difficulty. Although this theory explicitly affirms salvation by divine grace through Christ's penal-substitutionary death,[75] this theory's economy and logic of equivalence or retribution dissolve the notion of grace itself *as gift*, as new life and relationship with God *freely given* by God. God received payment for human sin in Christ's death on the cross. Hence, God remits the punishment of sinful humans not with voluntary forgiveness, but in reception, through Christ's death, of that which sinful humanity owes to God.[76] Furthermore, following from the previous aporia also, this theory of Jesus' death thoroughly neutralizes the apostle Paul's logic of the superabundance in God's action through Christ, as evident in Paul's emphases on the "much more" (πολλῷ μᾶλλον) of God's activity in Christ or the superabundant grace (ὑπερεπερίσσευσεν ἡ χάρις) of divine love toward sinful humans.[77] By expelling the extravagance from divine love, the penal-substitutionary construal of Jesus' death effectively eliminates divine grace except in name only.

---

[75]*RPTSC*, 117 (2.3.6-8).

[76]See Conner's similar criticism at this point. "This theory was sometimes so stated as to make the impression that we owed our salvation to Christ but not to God. Christ purchased our salvation for us from God; it therefore was his gift to us, not God's. Christ was looked on as the impersonation of love, while God was the embodiment of justice; and Christ died to save us from God" (Conner, *Cross in the New Testament*, 144).

[77]Rom 5:10, 15, 17, 20.

Although other theoretical difficulties plague the penal-substitutionary theory, these ten aporias illustrate the extreme theological danger in the *RPTSC*'s standardization of this particular soteriology. The centrifugal forces of the theoretical difficulties in the penal-substitutionary construal of Jesus' death produce similar disintegrating dynamics for every doctrine implicitly or explicitly associated with and interpreted through this soteriology. For that reason, this theory miserably fails to release the vast resources in the meaning of Jesus' death for human experience and reality as a whole. Of all theories about the meaning of Jesus' death, perhaps this construal least adequately interprets that pivotal event for Christian experience.

Analogue. Episode Seven

On two of the most important occasions in the Hebrew people's salvific history with Yahweh, the people accused Moses and, by implication, Yahweh of delivering them from slavery in Egypt only to destroy them: on the first occasion, to be destroyed by Pharaoh's army in the wilderness; on the second occasion, to be destroyed by the Canaanite armies in the struggle for the promised land. Rather than courageously and faithfully facing the risks of their freedom as represented by the threats in the wilderness, the people construed the challenges to and the risks in the freedom given to them by Yahweh as evidence of sinister divine motivation and intention. The people desired to escape their freedom, to leave the wilderness, even if it meant returning to bondage in Egypt. Given their early experiences with Yahweh in the vast wilderness, not accidentally do the Hebrew scriptures often refer to salvation with the word יָשַׁע, which means to widen, to broaden, to make spacious, "to liberate," or even to remove constrictions.[78] In addition, the people rejected Moses, the person through whom Yahweh had chosen to disclose salvation to them, thereby again rejecting the liberation that Yahweh had provided for and had promised to them. Consequently, the people envisioned an opposite approach to their own salvation. As many

---

[78] *A Hebrew and English Lexicon of the Old Testament*, 1st ed., ed. Francis Brown, S. R. Driver, and Charles A. Briggs (Oxford: Oxford University Press, 1907; corr. repr. 1977) s.v. "[יָשַׁע]" (446-47). See also Georg Fohrer, "σῴζω and σωτηρία in the Old Testament," in *Theological Dictionary of the New Testament*, vol. 7, ed. Gerhard Friedrich, trans. and ed. Geoffrey W. Bromiley (Grand Rapids: Eerdmans, 1971) 970-80. As examples of this usage, see Num 10:9 and Exod 14:30.

episodes in the narratives about their sojourn in the wilderness attest, the people sought to secure their lives through their own abilities and efforts, through the smaller gods of their own imaginations and construction. The people's complaints implied that God actually oppressed and victimized them, that God in *reality* did not correlate to Moses's *discourse* about God. Thus, the people implied, and perhaps even endeavored to engender, conflict between Yahweh and Moses. Additionally, the people in their infidelity implicitly and extremely misrepresented the character of Yahweh in at least two ways: first, implying that Yahweh's interest in the people ultimately enriched a divine self-interest and did not actually express Yahweh's genuine concern for the people themselves; and, second, implying that Yahweh sacrificed nothing of the divine self for the people's liberation, but rather sacrificed the people for the sake of that selfish divine self-love.[79]

In similar ways, the PTSC's misrepresentation of the Christian doctrine of God in the *RPTSC* supports the committee's correspondingly distorted construals of both Christology and soteriology. By emphasizing its adherence to "orthodox" Christology, the *RPTSC* implicitly endorses the orthodox dogma of divine impassibility, thus also implicitly denying any suffering to God either prior to or during the life and death of Jesus. Also, despite this document's emphasis on divine forgiveness and salvation through Jesus Christ alone, the *RPTSC*'s unqualified definition of atonement as penal substitution implicitly misrepresents the character of God: as the divine victimizer of Christ; as a God who cannot suffer but will inflict suffering on others; as a God concerned only for divine glory and unconcerned for the genuine alterity of those who plead for liberation; as a God for whom the salvific activity ultimately expresses only a selfish divine self-love; as a God who establishes an immutable, legal, yet not genuinely personal, relationship with humans; and as a God who requires either punishment for sin and its consequences or payment to secure pardon, as a God for whom grace is not free by definition. Finally, with its emphasis on the penal-substitutionary theory of the atonement as the definitive or normative interpretation of the Christ's life and death, as the theory to which all Baptists in the SBC *must* assent in order to be designated "true Christians," the *RPTSC* implicitly adds, at least as a condition for good standing in the SBC and perhaps even as a

---

[79]Exod 14:5-15; 16:2-3; 17:1-7; 32:1-14; Num 11:1-23; 13:25-33; 14:1-45.

condition for salvation, some form of assent to its own theory of atonement. In short, with its mandatory and distorted Christology and soteriology, rather than emphasizing God's liberation through Christ, the *RPTSC* constricts life in Christ and imprisons Baptist Christians.

The authors of the *RPTSC* apparently have forgotten or intentionally have ignored the very meaning expressed by the name "Jesus," the Greek form of the Hebrew name "Joshua" or "Yeshua," a combination of the Hebrew name for God, יהוה, and the Hebrew verb for salvation mentioned previously, ישׁע: *Yahweh liberates, removes constrictions, brings into the open, makes spacious, or broadens.*[80] Baptists in the SBC continue repeatedly to express an awareness of this in their worship through the hymn, "There Is a Name I Love to Hear": "It [the name] tells me of a Saviour's love, Who died to set me free." As the English translation of the title of a book by Ernst Käsemann announces, "Jesus Means Freedom!"[81]

---

[80]Werner Foerster, "Ἰησοῦς," in *Theological Dictionary of the New Testament*, vol. 3, ed. Gerhard Kittel, trans. and ed. Geoffrey W. Bromiley (Grand Rapids: Eerdmans, 1965) 284-93.

[81]"There Is a Name I Love to Hear," lyrics by Frederick Whitfield (1855), in *The Broadman Hymnal* (Nashville: Broadman Press, 1940) no. 283, verse 1a; "There Is a Name I Love to Hear," lyrics by Frederick Whitfield (1855), in *Baptist Hymnal* (Nashville: Convention Press, 1975) no. 66, verse 1a; Ernst Käsemann, *Jesus Means Freedom*, 3rd ed., trans. Frank Clarke (Philadelphia: Fortress Press, 1972). In recent years, many genuine Baptists, now disaffected from the SBC, have reaffirmed this truth at the core of their own Baptist confessional commitments. See examples in the following studies: Alan Neely, ed., *Being Baptist Means Freedom* (Charlotte NC: Southern Baptist Alliance, 1988); Walter B. Shurden, *The Baptist Identity: Four Fragile Freedoms* (Macon GA: Smyth & Helwys Publishing, 1993).

Fractures
in the Model of the Church

But two men had remained in the camp; the name of one was Eldad and the name of the other Medad. And the Spirit rested upon them . . . and they prophesied in the camp. So a young man ran and told Moses and said, "Eldad and Medad are prophesying in the camp." Then Joshua the son of Nun, the attendant of Moses from his youth, answered and said, "Moses, my lord, restrain them." But Moses said to him, "Are you jealous for my sake? Would that all the Lord's people were prophets, that the Lord would put His Spirit upon them!" (Numbers 11:26-29 NASB)

. . . the ones who cause divisions, worldly-minded, devoid of the Spirit. (Jude 19 NASB)

Introduction

The Presidential Theological Study Committee formulated the *RPTSC*'s ecclesiological statements on the basis of several traditionally and distinctively Baptist perspectives. This committee, however, by its abuse of these distinctive emphases in the *RPTSC*'s model of the church, has also produced several fractures in the SBC's historic understanding of Christian community.

In the *RPTSC*'s formulations, the Presidential Theological Study Committee focused its ecclesiological efforts on three "distinctive principles of our Baptist heritage": (1) "the priesthood of all believers"; (2) "the autonomy of the local church"; and (3) "a free church in a free state." Rather than supplying full and healthy interpretations of these principles, however, with truncated formulations, this committee reductively altered the distinctive Baptist substance of these historic principles.[1]

---

[1] *RPTSC*, 117-18 (2.4.3-6). Clearly, Timothy George has designed the emphases and the structure of the *RPTSC*'s ecclesiological formulations on the basis of his own theological beliefs, concerns, and ideological construal of the SBC's history: see, for example, George, "Reformation Roots of the Baptist Tradition," 16-19; idem, "Renewal of Baptist Theology," 23-24.

To some extent, *only clues* within those ecclesiological formulations themselves suggest or imply the seriousness of these alterations. Once again, this situation exists primarily due to the rhetorical strategy inscribed into the *RPTSC*, a strategy in which the committee utilized traditional Baptist concepts and language, yet then only partially and sometimes intentionally to communicate very different meanings than historically conveyed in the SBC by that language. Nonetheless, as I have claimed and tried to demonstrate previously, the *RPTSC* consistently employs this camouflaging strategy. Consequently, as in preceding chapters, in this study of the *RPTSC*'s ecclesiology, I will attempt both to trace the explicit, as well as to expose the implicit, dangers in the *RPTSC*'s ecclesial model and to identify legitimate Baptist lines of resistance to those dangers in particular.

Although the *RPTSC*'s ecclesiological statements imply several other distortions as well, in the present chapter, I will limit my studies to the major aspects of the previously discussed problematic areas, as they arise from the *RPTSC*'s three major ecclesiological concerns. Because I have already partially examined the *RPTSC*'s three ecclesiological principles in the study of that document's rhetoric in Chapter Four, I will expand my studies of those three problematic areas beyond a concern with their connection to the *RPTSC*'s rhetorical strategy.

One major ideological shift underlies all of the *RPTSC*'s reductive alterations to these three distinctive Baptist emphases. In its model of the church, the *RPTSC* reverses the order of human spirituality, in terms of the relationship between the individual human and the human community, as historically and officially conceived by the SBC itself: a spiritual order, according to the SBC's confessional documents, in which the nature of Christian community arises from the human individual's direct or immediate access to and relationship with God.[2] Rather than understanding the individual Christian's relationship to God as the basis for the

---

[2]As examples, see the following documents: *PCU (1914)*, 74-77 (points 1-2, 4-5); "Fraternal Address of Southern Baptists," *Baptist Standard* 32 (26 February 1920): 20, 24; "The Soul's Competency in Religion under God: The Historic Baptist Principle for Today," in *Annual of the SBC* (1936): 108-15; *RIR (1938)*, 24; "A Pronouncement upon Religious Liberty," in *Annual of the SBC* (1939): 114-16 (hereafter cited as *PRL [1939]*); *SP (1946)*, 38; *BFM (1925)*, 72, 73, 74; *BFM (1963)*, 269, 270, 272-273, 275, 278, 279, 280; "Declaration of Human Rights," in *Annual of the SBC* (1978): 57-58 (hereafter cited as *DHR [1978]*).

formation, development, meaning, and operation of the Christian community, however, the *RPTSC* develops the relationship as the Christian community's hegemony over the individual Christian. This reversal represents the fundamental alteration of the distinctively Baptist substance in models of Christian community espoused both by Baptists in the SBC and by the SBC itself (at least, in most of the SBC's history). The Presidential Theological Study Committee has applied this basic change in Baptist ecclesiology through the reductive alterations of the three principles identified and reformulated in the *RPTSC*.

I. The Local Church's Hegemony over the Individual Christian

The *RPTSC* contains an assessment of the teaching about the priesthood common to all Christians, or the priesthood of all believers, as the first Baptist principle interpreted in its ecclesiological formulations. The *RPTSC* rightly commences its statement with this concept's emphasis on the individual human's "*direct access* to God through Jesus Christ," the aspect of the common priesthood that often tends popularly to control interpretations of this idea or teaching.[3] Nonetheless, as I have mentioned

---

[3]This dominant interpretation also reappears both in a relatively recent Church Study Course produced by the SBC on this topic (Dan Yeary, *Direct Access: The Doctrine of the Priesthood of Believers* [Nashville: Convention Press, 1987]) and in a study of this doctrine by Hobbs (Herschel H. Hobbs, *You Are Chosen: The Priesthood of All Believers* [San Francisco: Harper & Row, 1990]). Timothy George rightly distinguishes the more general anthropological concepts of "soul competency" and religious liberty from the concept of the priesthood shared by all Christians (George, "Priesthood of All Believers and the Quest for Theological Integrity," 284-87; idem, "Priesthood of All Believers," 85-87). In 1945 and 1946, the SBC officially noted this distinction. Regarding the concept of human competency before God, according to the SBC, "every man is endowed by the Creator with competence as a person to deal with God and with his fellowmen in all rightful relations." Furthermore, the SBC described religious liberty "as a basic right under God," by which it meant, "not only freedom of individual worship and fellowship without interference by the state," but "also specifically and insistently the right of propaganda through evangelism, education, and the development of Christian institutions." The SBC referred to the priesthood of all believers, by contrast, through its description of the Christian community as "a democratic body in which all the members are equally free and responsible participants" (*SP [1946]*, 38). Nonetheless, sometimes, in statements about various components of Baptist doctrine, the SBC has not sufficiently clarified the difference between these two concepts, sometimes identifying the human's "direct access" to God with the common Christian priesthood: "every true believer, by reason of his

in chapter 4, immediately the *RPTSC* qualifies its affirmation of this particular point. In one sense, the *RPTSC* properly qualifies any interpretation of this concept as exclusively an affirmation of "modern individualism," since, with the doctrine of the common priesthood, Protestant
Christians historically have emphasized the individual Christian's ministry
to others through various forms of communicating the gospel, as the
RPTSC itself accurately underscores: "it is a spiritual standing which
leads to ministry, service, and a coherent witness in the world for which
Christ died."[4] In another sense, however, before the *RPTSC* either
genuinely clarifies the extent of this freedom for the individual Christian
or accurately identifies the dialectical tension between the individual
Christian and the Christian community, this document embeds the
common priesthood within, *as if subservient to*, "a committed community
of fellow believers-priests [*sic*] who share a like precious faith." Timothy
George's perspective clearly has influenced this interpretation of the
common priesthood: for George, the common Christian priesthood "is
really a part of the doctrine of the church."[5]

---

union with Christ, is a priest unto God with free access to the divine presence" (*FASB
[1920]*, 11; also *PCU [1914]*, 74). Even W. Randall Lolley, formerly president of Southeastern Baptist Theological Seminary, interprets the doctrine of common priesthood
through the doctrine of direct access to God or the individual human's competency before
God (Lolley, "Individual Competency Basis for Belief in Priesthood of Believers," *Facts
and Trends* 25 [February 1981]: 4-5; similarly, cf. J. Terry Young, "Baptists and the
Priesthood of Believers," *Perspectives in Religious Studies* 20 [Summer 1993]: 142-44).
Nevertheless, by seeking to locate this doctrine exclusively within the doctrine of the
church, George too sharply distinguishes these concepts from one another.

[4]*RPTSC*, 117 (2.4.4); emphasis mine. See this awareness, for example, in some of the
careful historical studies of this concept: Cyril Eastwood, *The Royal Priesthood of the
Faithful: An Investigation of the Doctrine from Biblical Times to the Reformation*
(Minneapolis: Augsburg, 1963); idem, *The Priesthood of All Believers: An Examination
of the Doctrine from the Reformation to the Present Day* (Minneapolis: Augsburg, 1962);
Gerrish, *Old Protestantism and the New*, 90-105.

[5]*RPTSC*, 117 (2.4.4); George, "Priesthood of All Believers and the Quest for Theological Integrity," 285; idem, "Priesthood of All Believers," 86. A fundamentalist
caricature of moderate Baptist perspectives, constructed during the early years of the fundamentalist subjugation of the SBC, has finally motivated the promotion of this
interpretation of the common Christian priesthood in the SBC. In 1985, Paige Patterson,
one of the major architects of the fundamentalist agenda, clearly displayed this caricature
of diversity among Baptists in the SBC: "In this controversy, appeal to the doctrine of
'the priesthood of the believer' has become a popular tactic for justifying whatever belief
one might cherish" (Patterson, "Stalemate," *Theological Educator*, Special Issue, "The

The *RPTSC* contains two other examples of this tendency. First, without supplying sufficient elaboration on the meaning of the common Christian priesthood itself, and in connection with the Presidential Theological Study Committee's previous affirmations about confessions of faith, as I have noted in chapter 4, the *RPTSC* implies that, without the proper external or communal controls (or an ecclesially sanctioned confession of faith), the doctrine of the common Christian priesthood encourages "doctrinal minimalism" and "theological revision," "compromises a commitment to the gospel itself," or even becomes "a license for the masking of unbelief."[6] Second, this same tendency reappears toward the end of the *RPTSC*'s ecclesiological article, in its statement about the relationship between the Christian community and the state. There, as it affirmed religious liberty (stated summarily as, "God alone is Lord of the conscience"), the Presidential Theological Study Committee took the opportunity to stress the priority of the Christian community's *official* perspective over the individual Christian conscience: "the doctrine of religious liberty, far from implying doctrinal laxity or unconcern, guarantees *the ability of every congregation and general Baptist body to determine* (on the basis of the Word of God) *its own doctrinal and disciplinary parameters.*"[7]

Thus, as the first fracture in Baptist ecclesiology, although the *RPTSC*'s statements *apparently* remain faithful linguistically to the foundational and historic Baptist emphasis on the doctrine of the common priesthood, by subordinating the individual Christian to the Christian community, actually this document *intentionally minimizes* the historic emphasis on the centrality and value of the individual human or Christian as held by both Baptists in the SBC and the SBC itself. The *RPTSC*'s reductionistic alterations to the concept of the common priesthood generate, at least, two major problems.

Controversy in the Southern Baptist Convention," ed. Fisher Humphreys [1985]: 6).

[6]*RPTSC*, 113 (1.8).

[7]*RPTSC*, 118 (2.4.6); emphasis mine. Elsewhere, I have distinguished the two concepts, "soul competency" and "the common priesthood," from one another, as distinct though related dimensions in a conceptual genealogy of religious liberty (Pool, "Baptist Infidelity to the Principle of Religious Liberty," 15-17).

A. Equating Ecclesial Perspective with Christ's Perspective

Although the Presidential Theological Study Committee rightly began the *RPTSC*'s ecclesiological article by describing Christ as the source and leader of the church, nonetheless, a first problem emerges. On the basis of the committee's interpretation of the very difficult Pauline text, Ephesians 5:25, the *RPTSC* continues by boldly asserting that "the person who despises the church despises Christ."[8] While this statement expresses some truth, the context of its appearance suggests the operation of a very dangerous claim—without the *RPTSC*'s open and honest registration of that claim.

Again, in this particular context, the *RPTSC* construes the whole Christian community as the inhibitor of excesses promoted through abuse of the common priesthood by individual Christians, an inhibitor concretized in and as a "coherent witness."[9] In other places, the *RPTSC* construed this "coherent witness" in various ways: such as, "a positive biblical witness on basic Christian beliefs," or "a reaffirmation of major doctrinal concerns," or "the faith which was once delivered unto the saints," or "the fundamentals of the Christian faith," or "a confession of faith," or "our doctrinal confession." With these various designations, however, the *RPTSC* really and finally points to itself as that coherent witness.[10] Seemingly, according to the *RPTSC*, this coherent witness expresses the Christian community's only genuine, dependable, and objective voice, a large and uniform voice. For the *RPTSC*, that voice speaks loudly, clearly, truthfully, objectively, and rightfully above and against (drowning and, thereby, eliminating) any minor, marginal, subjective, or divergent vocalizations among the priests.

Although a number of serious issues attend such a perspective, one danger approaches as the most threatening of them all: the implicit identification of the Christian community's perspective with the Christ's own perspective. Once again, by identifying *doctrine about Christ* as *the living Christ*, the *RPTSC* deifies something creaturely, even if that creaturely reality takes shape as a confession of faith about the living God's gift of and loving interactions with the creation. I have previously identified the tendency of the *RPTSC* to deify the creature, of course, in earlier chap-

---

[8]*RPTSC*, 117 (2.4.1).
[9]*RPTSC*, 117 (2.4.4).
[10]*RPTSC*, 112, 113 (introduction; 1.1, 2, 5, 7).

ters. In the Presidential Theological Study Committee's efforts to establish an objective criterion for terminating conflict in the SBC, this committee has both removed the living Christ as the evaluator of every perspective and has emplaced the Christian community itself, as concretely re-presented in its one official voice or its confession of faith, as the criterion by which this community judges individual Christians and their differing perspectives.

Quite simply, those espousing such a position refuse to acknowledge the limitations of every creaturely perspective, even the perspective expressed as a communal voice. Limits in knowledge and understanding accompany every individual human and every human community. Furthermore, and more significantly still, all individual humans and all human communities sin. No creaturely reality, individual or social, non-Christian or Christian, has realized perfection in knowledge and virtue. God alone realizes such perfection. No matter how much knowledge it may possess, no matter how good, holy, or loving it may be, the Christian community always remains a creaturely reality and never becomes divine. For this reason alone, if one despises the church, for either valid or invalid reasons, one does not necessarily despise Christ.[11]

---

[11]Although the *RPTSC* does not mention the role of pastoral authority in this connection, given the *RPTSC*'s reversal of the relationship between the individual Christian and the Christian community, questions arise about the Presidential Theological Study Committee's presuppositions regarding the pastor's role in the articulation of a local church's doctrinal perspective and, hence, in the exercise of the Christian community's authority over the individual Christian conscience. The Presidential Theological Study Committee certainly conceived its own function toward Baptists in the SBC as a pastoral role: "this report addresses several issues of contemporary urgency *in a spirit of pastoral concern* . . . " (*RPTSC*, 113 [1.5]; emphasis mine). Nonetheless, the *RPTSC* does not mention or describe the nature of pastoral authority in the local church. I suspect, however, that the committee heartily endorses (especially in light of the *RPTSC*'s understanding of divine sovereignty) the concept of pastoral authority adopted by the SBC during its annual meeting in 1988, in which, on the basis of its claim that "the doctrine of the priesthood of the believer can be used to justify the undermining of pastoral authority in the local church," the SBC resolved "that the doctrine of the priesthood of the believer in no way contradicts the biblical understanding of the role, responsibility, and authority of the pastor which is seen in the command to the local church in Hebrews 13:17, 'Obey your leaders, and submit to them; for they keep watch over your souls, as those who will give an account' " ("Resolution No. 5—On the Priesthood of the Believer," in *Annual of the SBC* [1988]: 69). Furthermore, Richard Land strongly advocates this authoritarian model (although he uses the word "authoritative," instead, to describe it) of pastoral leadership: according to Land, not only is there "no

B. Eliminating the Prophetic Principle from Ecclesial Life

Second, and following from the previous problem, by introducing the *RPTSC*'s article on ecclesiology with the declaration that "the person who despises the church despises Christ," the Presidential Theological Study Committee has subtly inscribed its own warning above the gate into the SBC itself. *Do not criticize or critically evaluate the activities, theologies, policies, or leadership of the SBC itself, except under threat of reprisal, reprisal amounting to various forms and degrees of excommunication from, or termination of participation in, the community.* By subjugating the common priesthood to the ecclesial perspective with the previous warning, the *RPTSC* effectively eliminates the prophetic prin-

---

such thing as a great, God-honoring church which is pastor-led and not deacon and people supported," but "there is also no such thing as a great, God-honoring church which is deacon-led or congregation-led" (Land, "Pastoral Leadership: Authoritarian or Persuasive?" *Theological Educator* 37 [Spring 1988]: 80). Increasingly, at least among Baptist pastors, this concept of pastoral authority, as the criteriological qualifier of the priesthood shared by all Christians, dominates ecclesial life among Baptists in the SBC. For example, "if the church fails to honor the pastor as the spiritual leader of the church, it is showing evidence of rebellion against God's design for an orderly fellowship. . . . The human spirit rebels against submission, but God's order for the church is that the pastor provides the leadership and the laity provides the followership" (J. Gerald Harris, *Pardoned to be Priests* [Nashville: Broadman Press, 1988] 152, 156). Bill Leonard describes a " 'Clergification' of the Southern Baptist Convention," defined by him as "the increasing dominance of ordained professionals in the churches and denomination." Leonard accurately identifies one development leading to this problem as the confrontation of Baptists in the SBC "with one particular model for ministry which emphasizes the ultimate authority of the pastoral office": an "autocratic model for ministry," precisely the model defended by "Resolution No. 5" (Leonard, "Southern Baptists and the Laity," *Review and Expositor* 84 [Fall 1987]: 644, 645). Recently, other Baptist scholars have arrived at similar conclusions in their discussions of this issue: Grady C. Cothen, *What Happened to the Southern Baptist Convention? A Memoir of the Controversy* (Macon GA: Smyth & Helwys Publishing, 1993) 245-47; Arthur Emery Farnsley II, *Southern Baptist Politics: Authority and Power in the Restructuring of an American Denomination* (University Park: Pennsylvania State University Press, 1994) 75-89. No one has more forcefully identified this problem, however, than Carlyle Marney, when he describes the professional clergy among Baptists as "a kept harlotry" (Marney, *Priests to Each Other* [Valley Forge PA: Judson Press, 1974] 9). Across the course of the SBC's history, often Baptists have felt the need to caution themselves about misconstruals and abuses of pastoral authority: for example, Cephas C. Bateman, "Baptists Versus Authority of the Clergy," *Baptist Standard* 26 (23 July 1914): 6.

ciple from, and conserves the status quo (however oppressive, immoral, or sinful it might be or become) within, the Christian community.

Historically, however, confessions of faith officially authorized or adopted by the SBC have rejected (as authentic possibilities for both Baptists in the SBC and the SBC itself) all forms of Christian community that would establish and maintain the church or any ecclesiastical institution as the authority over individual Christians. The SBC as an institution, ironically, originally registered and has continued to maintain its disapproval and refusal of the local Christian community's hegemony over individual Christians, on the basis of the SBC's fundamental commitment to the priesthood of every Christian. Several examples from the SBC's confessional history illustrate these claims.

The SBC's "Pronouncement on Christian Union and Denominational Efficiency" (*PCU [1914]*), on the basis of its understanding of the common priesthood as the individual human's direct access and responsibility to God, declares that "we are bound to disapprove of all ecclesiastical systems which set up human authorities over the consciences of those whom Christ has made free." Similarly, because the SBC's *FASB (1920)* conceives "Christian religion" as "primarily the personal union of the individual with Christ by faith," it also describes "the direct relation of the soul to God in Christ" (or, in that document's perspective, the priesthood of all Christians) as "the guiding principle for Baptists." Hence, building upon that principle, the *FASB (1920)* understands the church as a community of "spiritual equals" in which the members are "under authority" to "no overlords or ecclesiastical superiors." According even to the SBC's "Pronouncement upon Religious Liberty" (*PRL [1939]*), again based upon the Baptist concept of the individual human's "direct access to God" or "grounded upon the competency of the human soul," the SBC declared "that the church of Christ, which in the Bible is called 'the body of Christ,' is not to be identified with any denomination or church that seeks to exercise ecclesiastical authority, but includes all the regenerated whoever and wherever they are, as these are led by the Holy Spirit." Furthermore, based on its understanding of the individual human's direct access to God, the SBC's "Statement of Principles" (*SP [1945, 1946]*) describes the church as both a voluntary community of Christians "responsible directly and only to Christ" and "a democratic body in which all the members are equally free and responsible participants." Finally, both *BFM* statements (1925, 1963) on this same foundation underscore freedom of Christian consciences from even the confessions of faith produced by the SBC: since "the sole authority for faith and practice among Baptists is the Scriptures of the Old and New Testaments," according to the *BFM (1925)*, "confessions are only guides in interpretation, having no authority over the conscience"; or, since "the sole authority for faith and practice among Baptists is Jesus Christ whose will is revealed in the Holy Scriptures," according to the *BFM (1963)*, "such statements have never been regarded as complete, infallible statements of faith, nor as official creeds carrying mandatory authority."[12]

Even though not always realized or followed practically, the SBC's consistent theoretical interpretation of the individual Christian's relation to the Christian community intentionally erects an impenetrable barrier against ecclesiastical control and oppression of individual Christians. Additionally, this historic emphasis on the high value of the Christian individual accentuates the strength in the priesthood of all Christians, rather than weakening it through its subjugation to the Christian community. With such a posture, the SBC has recognized historically the doctrine of the common priesthood as the legitimization for prophetically critical responses from individual participants in the Christian community toward abuses in, by, and through the Christian community itself. Thus, not only does the SBC's historic posture protect the individual Christian from every form of ecclesiastical control, but it also supplies the Christian community with a critical principle through which God's indwelling Spirit identifies abuse, distortion, or sin in the community itself.

When the *RPTSC* issues its veiled warning to Baptist Christians who might espouse different interpretations of various Christian doctrines, that document inhibits and effectively eliminates from the Christian community the prophetic principle within the common priesthood. By effectively divesting the Christian community of its prophetic principle, the *RPTSC* increases the probability of realizing two dangerous possibilities: on the one hand, the *RPTSC* promotes the concept of Christian community (or, as its authorized voice, its leadership) as impeccable, faultless, or infallible; on the other hand, and simultaneously, this document ignores and avoids the Holy Spirit's efforts within the community to convict the community itself of its own corporate sin, to heal its self-inflicted wounds, and to eliminate its abuses of itself and others.

---

[12]*PCU (1914)*, 74, 75; *FASB (1920)*, 8, 11, 13 (also "Fraternal Address of Southern Baptists," *Baptist Standard* 32 [26 February 1920]: 20, 24); *PRL (1939)*, 115; *SP (1946)*, 38; *BFM (1925)*, 71; *BFM (1963)*, 270.

II. Denomination as Church over the Local Church

As the *RPTSC* continues to minimize the common Christian priesthood in its apparent affirmation of the local church's autonomy, the first fracture produces a second one in the *RPTSC*'s ecclesiology—a fracture that actually begins to disintegrate the distinctive Baptist concept of Christian community, as historically affirmed by the SBC. The Presidential Theological Study Committee has designed its statement about the local church's autonomy principally both to legitimize all actions taken by the SBC and to reinforce a virtual unilateral loyalty from local Baptist churches to the SBC: for example, just as every local church "is free to order its own internal life without interference from any external group," according to the *RPTSC*, so too "this same freedom applies to all general Baptist bodies, such as associations and state and national conventions." The Presidential Theological Study Committee devoted more than half of its statement about the local church's autonomy to describing the local church's duty to give virtually unqualified support to the SBC. Also, as the negative side of the previous design, when the *RPTSC* claims to "decry all efforts to weaken our denomination and its cooperative ministries," once again, the *RPTSC* subtly warns all churches participating in the SBC against articulating criticism (whether justifiable or not) of the SBC, its activities, and its leadership.[13]

---

[13]*RPTSC*, 117 (2.4.5). Once again, Mohler's influence may have dominated the formulation of this statement. As chairperson of the Committee on Resolutions during the SBC's annual meeting in 1992, among a cluster of seven resolutions that he introduced to the SBC for adoption, Mohler recommended the adoption of two resolutions especially pertinent as preparatory components of and historical precedents for the ecclesiological section of the *RPTSC* presently under scrutiny. First, on Mohler's recommendation, the SBC adopted "Resolution No. 3—On Maintaining Trust with the Cooperative Program." The framer of this resolution designed it as a tool with which both to muzzle all criticism, whether legitimate or not, of the SBC by denominational entities or employees and to prevent participation by those same agents with groups which openly adopt critical postures toward the SBC. Referring to the boards, commissions, institutions, and the employees of these various entities, the SBC resolved "that we urge those entities and their personnel to maintain support of the Cooperative Program and avoid any conflict of interest, real or perceived, which would be occasioned by any participation with any organization, program, or meeting which would compromise support of the Cooperative Program." Second, also in this same connection and on Mohler's recommendation, the SBC adopted "Resolution No. 4—On the Autonomy of Baptist Churches and General Baptist Bodies." Although this second resolution explicitly affirms the autonomy of local

For Baptists in the SBC, this ecclesiological perspective contains two major and interdependent problematic features. First, the *RPTSC*'s perspective seems to indicate the committee's intention to shift Baptist perceptions of the SBC as a denomination: from the denomination as a general Baptist organization to the *denomination as The Southern Baptist Church*. Second, on the basis of that shift in Baptist perceptions of the SBC's nature, the *RPTSC* appears intent upon reversing the flow of authority between the local churches and the SBC: rather than affirming the SBC's submission to the authority of the local churches (by deriving its existence and resources from the gifts given by local congregations), the *RPTSC* seems to promote the *subservience of the local Baptist churches to the authority of the SBC*.

A. Toward Denomination as Church

The first major problem arises when the *RPTSC* defines the local church as "a gathered congregation of baptized believers who have entered into covenant with Christ and with one another to fulfil [*sic*], according to the Scriptures, their mutual obligations."[14] The *RPTSC*'s definition of a local church, however, fits almost every organized group of Christians, especially Christian denominations and, thus, even the SBC itself. More importantly at this stage, with such a definition of the local church, the Presidential Theological Study Committee both has revised the SBC's historic ecclesiology and, thereby, has dissolved the distinctively Baptist substance in its own ecclesiology.[15] Hence, by ignoring or eliminating essential components in historic Baptist definitions of the

---

churches, its framer designed it as a device to support perceived ecclesial disciplinary needs, with which principally to reverse the flow of accountability between the SBC and local Baptist churches: that is, doctrinally, morally, and administratively to require accountability from participating local Baptist churches to the SBC, primarily, rather than from the SBC to the local churches, although this resolution explicitly calls for mutual responsibility between the two parties. As the central component within its threefold resolution, the SBC resolved "that we confess our respective responsibility to maintain the integrity and scriptural discipline of every Baptist body in terms of faith, practice, membership, and programs, thus protecting the witness and purity of the church and denomination" (*Annual of the SBC* [1992]: 87-88).

[14]*RPTSC*, 117 (2.4.5).

[15]Robison B. James perceptively notes the absence of the distinctly Baptist substance from Mohler's entire fourteen-point theological program for the SBC (James, "Beyond Old Habits and on to a New Land," in *Beyond the Impasse?* ed. James and Dockery, 120).

local church, the *RPTSC* establishes the possibility of transforming the SBC itself, the denomination, into a national or an international denominational church.

1. *Ignoring Essential Components in the Definition of the Local Church.* By shifting an understanding of the SBC from a concept of denomination as a general Baptist organization to a concept of this denomination as The Southern Baptist Church, the *RPTSC* ignores, eliminates, or minimizes a variety of essential components in the SBC's historic definitions of the local church, components without which the SBC's historic and distinctive Baptist interpretation of Christian community disappears. This represents the *RPTSC*'s first step in the direction toward the denomination's (SBC's) hegemony over local Baptist churches. Consider the following examples.

(a) Although the *RPTSC* reaffirms its commitment to the church as "a gathered congregation of baptized believers" with "mutual obligations," this document conveniently omits the SBC's historic emphasis on the *equality shared by all members of local churches*, an equality arising necessarily from the SBC's historic emphasis on the equality of all humans before God. In contrast to the *RPTSC*'s omission, the SBC has consistently asserted its commitment to the equality of all members in the local church as a basic and non-negotiable principle of Baptist ecclesiology.[16]

(b) In addition, while the *RPTSC* reaffirms a commitment to the common Christian priesthood, it muffles the radical and risk-filled Christian freedom held within this doctrine, thereby minimizing the doctrine of the common priesthood. Similarly, although the *RPTSC* acknowledges the freedom of local Baptist churches and Baptist associations or conventions "to order" their own organizations "without

---

[16]*RPTSC*, 117 (2.4.5). The SBC has produced several significant and explicit affirmations of this Christian equality. As one example, in the *PCU (1914)*, the SBC describes ecclesial polity and ordinances (Baptism and the Lord's Supper) as "the formal expression of the spiritual life in Christ." On the basis of this conviction, according to the *PCU (1914)*, "the *equality of believers in the church*" follows as "the *necessary consequence of the equality of the status of men before God*" (*PCU [1914]*, 76-77 [emphasis mine]; similarly, cf. *FASB [1920]*, 8, 13; *SP [1946]*, 38; *BFM [1963]*, 275). Similarly, "it is necessary to resist all inequalities of basic rights and privileges in the church and in society, which arise out of racial prides and prejudices, economic greed, and class distinctions; everywhere proclaiming and practicing human brotherhood under the will and purpose of God" (*SP [1946]*, 39).

interference from any external group," the *RPTSC* does not reaffirm two interrelated and foundational ecclesiological components. First, the *RPTSC* ignores the SBC's historic affirmation of *the local church's autonomy as necessarily resulting from the radical freedom implicit in the priesthood of every Christian.* Consequently, second, the *RPTSC* avoids affirming *the radical freedom* from every external authority *in local ecclesial autonomy.* To the contrary, until the most recent years, the SBC has unflinchingly embraced the risk in the common Christian priesthood's freedom as the basis for the radical independence at the heart of the local church's autonomy.[17]

(c) Furthermore, despite the *RPTSC*'s affirmation of the local church's freedom "to order its own internal life without interference from any external group," this document totally neglects the SBC's historic

---

[17]*RPTSC*, 117 (2.4.5). "That each local church is, and in the nature of the case should be, self-governing and independent is a truth inseparable from the other truth that all men are directly responsible to God. The priesthood of all believers carries at its heart the necessity for self-government in church life" (*PCU [1914]*, 75). "This equality of believers in the church arises from the direct relation between each individual soul and the Lord Jesus Christ. He alone is the ruler of His people. It follows that each church is a self-governing body" (*FASB [1920]*, 8; similarly, cf. *BFM [1963]*, 275). Timothy George reverses this order, endowing the Christian community with authority over the individual Christian, due to his worry about the Christian community's "coherent witness": "What is at stake is the right of a *community* of believer-priests, whether local congregation, association, state or *national convention*, to define for itself, under the leadership of the Holy Spirit, the *acceptable doctrinal perimeters of its own fellowship*" (George, "Priesthood of All Believers and the Quest for Theological Integrity," 287; also idem, "Priesthood of All Believers," 88; emphasis mine; in the second version of this article, George himself italicizes the word "community"!). As an application of this reversal, Mohler dismissed Diana Garland, on 21 March 1995, from the deanship of the Carver School of Social Work at SBTS, as punishment for her questions and comments about Mohler's criteria for hiring new professors. Following Mohler's highhanded behavior, Marv Knox rightly criticized his actions as non-Baptistic, on the ground that he had violated the principle of the priesthood of all believers. According to Knox, since the trustees of SBTS fully supported Mohler's actions, and subsequently prohibited faculty from public disagreement with president Mohler, SBTS similarly has forsaken its Baptist identity: "Severed from the doctrine of the priesthood of the believer, an institution no longer remains Baptist" (Knox, "We Need a New Seminary 'for Such a Time as This,' " *Western Recorder* 169 [25 April 1995]: 5). More recently, the SBC's Executive Committee published an article in its official journal (quoting Timothy George, Mark DeVine, and Russ Bush) that both defends creeds in Baptist life and subordinates the common priesthood to the community's credal perspective (Dwayne Hastings, "Confessions of Faith: A Baptist Way of Life?" *SBC Life* 4 [October 1995]: 4).

understanding of *the political model on the basis of which the Christian community operates to order its own life: the democratic style and process necessitated, according to the SBC, by the previous dimensions of spirituality.* With this neglect, the *RPTSC* seems to prepare local churches as well as the SBC itself for officially sanctioned oligarchical, presbyterial, episcopal, monarchical, or autocratic models of polity and styles of pastoral leadership (or to legitimize such models and styles insofar as they have already appeared among Baptists in the SBC).[18]

(d) Finally, and perhaps the central factor influencing the previous omissions, although the *RPTSC* refers to Christ as the local church's source and guide, the *RPTSC* completely disregards the essential pneumatological dimension of ecclesiology. The *RPTSC neither refers to the Holy Spirit nor acknowledges the essential and presently neglected relationship between the Holy Spirit and the Christian community among Baptists in the SBC.* In its statement on the local church's autonomy, given the description of Christ as "Lawgiver" in the introduction to the *RPTSC*'s ecclesiological statement, with the nouns "covenant," "mutual obligations," and "doctrinal and disciplinary parameters," as well as with the infinitives "to order" and "to determine," and especially in light of the complete absence of references to the church's relation to the Holy Spirit, the *RPTSC* develops an imbalanced ecclesiology. The Presidential Theological Study Committee has constructed its ecclesiology predominantly on legal, objective, and deontological grounds, rather than growing

---

[18]*RPTSC*, 117 (2.4.5). In 1914, the SBC described democratic polity as a necessary (and, therefore, theological) corollary to the freedom of the individual Christian: "the freedom of the sons of God is a freedom which requires *democracy* for its adequate expression" (*PCU [1914]*, 75-76; emphasis mine). According to the SBC in 1938, "we believe that a church of Jesus Christ is *a pure democracy*, and cannot subject itself to any outside control, nor bend to a superior clergy. . . . We maintain, further, that Christ's ideal of a church, with its *pure democracy*, and the high value that it puts on the individual, is of priceless value, not only to preserve religious liberty but to promote civil liberty as well" (*RIR [1938]*, 24; emphasis mine). The SBC, in 1939, described "the organization of groups of obedient believers into churches of Christ, *democratic* in the processes and theocratic in the principles of their government," as one of the "principles that animate the activities of the Baptists, principles which they hold to be clearly taught in the New Testament" (*PRL [1939]*, 115; emphasis mine). Also, in both 1945 and 1946, the SBC described the church as "a *democratic* body in which all the members are equally free and responsible participants" (*SP [1946]*, 38; emphasis mine). Again in 1963, the SBC described the local church as "an autonomous body, operating through *democratic* processes under the Lordship of Jesus Christ" (*BFM [1963]*, 275; emphasis mine).

it from the more organic, personal, and pneumatological realities as the SBC has done historically in various ways.[19]

Thus, even the most concise definitions of the local church, as seen in various statements officially adopted by the SBC, include the previous essential components with which the SBC has distinguished the local church itself from all other Christian organizations (however closely related to the local churches those organizations may be). Nonetheless, in its own description of the local church, the *RPTSC* minimizes most of these components, when it does not omit these components altogether, and eliminates their essential positions within the ecclesiology historically advocated by the SBC. By subtly eliminating the previous components from the SBC's historic ecclesiology, the *RPTSC* dissolves the substance of the SBC's distinctive conception of Christian community and, thereby, enables the second step toward the SBC's hegemony over the local Baptist churches participating within it.

2. *Endowing the SBC with Ecclesial Status.* As the second step in the direction toward the denomination's dominance of the local churches, the *RPTSC* endows the SBC itself, the denomination, with an ecclesial status. I refer again to an example of this in the *RPTSC*'s rhetoric: its extensive use of such phrases as "Southern Baptists," "Southern Baptist belief," "Southern Baptist life," "the people of God called Southern Baptists," and related phrases, with more than either the geographical referentiality of the phrase "Baptists in the South" or the affiliational significance of the

---

[19]*RPTSC*, 117, 118 (2.4.1, 5, 6). The SBC, in 1920, referred to unity "under the guidance of *the Holy Spirit*" in its definition of the local church (*FASB [1920]*, 8; cf. *PCU [1914]*, 74-75; emphasis mine). In 1939, the SBC also described the church in a way that now cuts somewhat against the grain of the *RPTSC*: "We hold that the church of Christ, which in the Bible is called 'the body of Christ,' is not to be identified with any denomination or church that seeks to exercise ecclesiastical authority, but includes all the regenerated whoever and wherever they are, as these are led by *the Holy Spirit*" (*PRL [1939]*, 115; emphasis mine). In 1945 and 1946, the SBC also included a pneumato-logical reference in its statement about leadership in the local church: "its divinely called ministry is chosen by the church itself under the guidance of *the Holy Spirit*" (*SP [1946]*, 38; emphasis mine). Although the *BFM (1963)* does not refer to the Holy Spirit in its ecclesiological article, in its paragraph on the Holy Spirit within the article on the doctrine of God, the *BFM (1963)* does contain statements about the Holy Spirit's ecclesiological functions: "He cultivates Christian character, comforts believers, and bestows the spiritual gifts by which they serve God through His church. . . . He enlightens and empowers the believer and the church in worship, evangelism, and service" (*BFM [1963]*, 272).

phrase "Baptists in or of the SBC."[20] As particularly disclosive of this, one of the *RPTSC*'s numerous calls to Baptists in the SBC begins with the following phrase: "we call upon the Southern Baptist Convention, *its churches*, and *its institutions. . . .*" The sense with which one may legitimately refer to participating local Baptist churches as *the SBC's churches* differs vastly from the sense in which one may legitimately refer to the various institutions of the SBC as *the SBC's institutions*: the SBC owns its institutions, but not its participating local Baptist churches.[21] Only by dissolving the Baptist substance of the SBC's ecclesiology (as the previous step begins to do), however, could the *RPTSC* produce such a possibility for the SBC, the possibility of endowing the denomination itself with ecclesial status or, more specifically, the possibility of making it *The* Southern Baptist Church.

Clearly, as I have noted previously, one could easily identify in the SBC itself every component in the *RPTSC*'s definition of "a New Testament church" as "a gathered congregation of baptized believers who have entered into covenant with Christ and with one another to fulfil [*sic*], according to the Scriptures, their mutual obligations."[22] Under such a broad definition, certainly, even the SBC qualifies as a local church. Despite some camouflaging strategy to the contrary, the *RPTSC* indicates a general tendency to transform the SBC *from* a denomination understood as a Baptist assembly produced by and responsible to participating Baptist churches *into* a denomination understood as the larger expression of the local churches, as *The* Southern Baptist Church. In addition to the *RPTSC*'s definition of a local church, other examples support this claim as well.

The *RPTSC* implicitly equates all criticisms of and resistance to the fundamentalist agenda and credenda in the SBC (as supported, promoted, and represented by the *RPTSC*'s own content) as "efforts to weaken our denomination and its cooperative ministries."[23] Removing the SBC from the possibility of any criticism or resistance (whether justifiable or not) from Baptists and local Baptist churches in the SBC, however, effectively releases the SBC from its proper accountability both to the local Baptist

---

[20]For example, *RPTSC*, 112, 113, 114, 115, 116, 117, 118 (introduction; 1.3-5, 10; 2.2.1, 3, 5, 7, 13; 2.4.3; 2.5.2).
[21]*RPTSC*, 116 (2.2.13); emphasis mine.
[22]*RPTSC*, 117 (2.4.5).
[23]*RPTSC*, 117 (2.4.5).

churches which created and continue to support it and to the Baptist
Christians who comprise the SBC itself in any given year. Hence, such
distanciation of the SBC from any genuine accountability to the
participating local churches, its constituency, establishes the SBC as an
ecclesial entity with a status at least *equal to, if not actually superior to,*
the status of a local church.

Furthermore, the *RPTSC* clearly aims to guarantee for the SBC the
right to establish "its own doctrinal and disciplinary parameters."[24] Again,
although the SBC has produced doctrinal statements, historically the SBC
has qualified such statements in several essential ways: (a) the SBC's
doctrinal statements officially express only the consensus of those persons present during the annual meeting in which the SBC adopted them,
that is to say, the Convention for that year; (b) the SBC's doctrinal statements officially possess only a descriptive not a prescriptive status; (c)
the SBC's doctrinal statements do not hold any official legal or binding
authority over the SBC's entities or local Baptist churches participating
in the SBC, without the legal adoption of such doctrinal statements by
either the SBC's entities or its participating local churches.[25] As seen in

---

[24]*RPTSC*, 118 (2.4.6). This concern also appears quite early in the document: "None
of these principles, sacred to Baptists through the ages, is violated by voluntary, conscientious adherence to *an explicit doctrinal standard.* Holy living and sound doctrine are indispensable elements of true revival and genuine reconciliation among *any body of Christian believers*" (*RPTSC*, 114 [1.10]; emphasis mine). Clearly, George attributes key functions to covenants and creeds for discipline (as conflict resolution), especially because he
thinks that "discipline helped preserve the purity of the church's witness in the world,"
within the Christian community. George bemoans the disappearance of discipline's practice from Baptist communities. "As Baptists have evolved from small sectarian beginnings
into what one historian has called 'the catholic phase of their history,' both the covenantal
and disciplinary features of our church life have become marginal to our identity. The
loss of these historic distinctives has resulted in the crisis of Baptist spirituality which
pervades so much of our church life today" (George, "Renewal of Baptist Theology," 24;
cf. idem, "Reformation Roots of the Baptist Tradition," 17-18). This preoccupation obviously represents the resuscitation of an aggressively imposed scrupulosity that has sometimes appeared in the SBC's history. For example, B. A. Copass argued similarly. "If one
does not believe with the body of people to whom he belongs, he ought to get out. And
the others should insist that he do get out. Anything else is treason and nonsense. 'How
can two walk together except that they be agreed?' To withdraw fellowship from one who
differs in matters of faith is not an attempt to stifle freedom, but only getting rid of one
who does not belong to that body" (Copass, "Concerning Our Confession or Declaration
of Faith," *Baptist Standard* 26 [4 June 1914]: 2).
[25]*BFM (1925)*, 71; *BFM (1963)*, 269-70.

the *RPTSC*, the Presidential Theological Study Committee has obviously avoided in its own creed the SBC's historic qualifications to the doctrinal statements that it has produced. As I have noted in previous chapters, the *RPTSC* seeks to prescribe a very specific doctrinal perspective, endeavors to speak for all Baptists and local churches in the SBC, and desires to enforce this perspective on all dissenters from it, dissenting individuals and dissenting local churches. These prerogatives, understood only in a far more positive and much more restricted sense, however, properly belong only to the local Baptist church with respect to its own membership. Insofar as the *RPTSC* arrogates such prerogatives to the SBC, that document, at least implicitly and effectively if not theoretically, begins to transform the organization or denomination called the SBC into The Southern Baptist Church.

In its own historic self-descriptions, the SBC has consistently refused both to designate itself as a church or as The Southern Baptist Church and to present itself as such to other Christian groups and churches. In 1920, the SBC expressed this with simple clarity: "missionary and other religious associations and conventions are not ecclesiastical bodies," but "are simply voluntary bodies for coöperative purposes." In 1940, in reply to an invitation to become a member of the World Council of Churches (WCC), the SBC produced a similar, and even more pointed, statement as part of its rationale for declining the WCC's invitation: "our Convention has no ecclesiological authority" and "is *in no sense the Southern Baptist Church*."[26] In light of the SBC's historically consistent refusal of ecclesial status for itself, if Baptists in the SBC desire to preserve the SBC's authentic tradition, then they should flee from the *RPTSC* and everything similar to it.

B. Toward Subordination of Local Baptist Churches to *The* Southern Baptist Church

As the next interdependent problem of the second fracture in the *RPTSC*'s ecclesiology, and the goal of the *RPTSC*'s camouflaged efforts to endow the SBC with an ecclesial status, the *RPTSC* initiates a reversal in the flow of authority between the participating local Baptist churches and the SBC. I have previously identified several traces that suggest the operative presence of this goal in the *RPTSC*. The obvious applicability of the *RPTSC*'s definition of the local church to the SBC itself suggests

---

[26]*FASB (1920)*, 9; *RWCC (1940)*, 99, emphasis mine.

a dangerous possibility: that the *RPTSC* intends to extend denominational influence over local Baptist churches by construing the SBC as the larger ecclesial context for all participating local Baptist churches, or by reinterpreting the SBC both as the national reality expressed by the local Baptist church and to which all participating local Baptist churches must submit. In the Presidential Theological Study Committee's reconceptualization or revision of the relationship between the SBC and its participating local Baptist churches, local Baptist churches (as well as state conventions and local Baptist associations), at least conceptually, begin to become subordinate to the authority of the SBC as The Southern Baptist Church. In the *RPTSC*'s ecclesiology, the church resembles other Christian communities in which a centralized ecclesiastical organization controls all local churches (and other Christian organizations) as smaller expressions of the larger church.

The Presidential Theological Study Committee has carefully camouflaged this move, since most Baptists would immediately recognize and vehemently resist every *open* formulation of such non-Baptist ecclesiological and political revisions of the SBC. Furthermore, although understanding itself as a general Baptist body and even as a denomination, historically the SBC has not only consistently refused to describe itself as the church in any sense, as I have shown previously, but has also vehemently eschewed every pretense, as well as every actual exercise, of authority over its participating local Baptist churches, Baptist state conventions, and Baptist auxiliary organizations. In most of the SBC's history, authority has moved in the opposite direction: from the local churches to the convention, not vice versa.

Again, although quite obvious in the SBC's history, a variety of examples from some of the SBC's foundational documents support the previous claim. In the *FASB (1920)*, "articles of faith and practice" authorized in 1919 and published in 1920, the SBC clearly described the directional flow of authority between the local Baptist church and all other organizations: because Baptists "reject any and all forms of centralized church and ecclesiastical organization and government," the local Baptist church "conducts its own affairs in its own way and is *responsible to no other ecclesiastical body of any kind.*" In its confession of faith from 1925, the SBC stated this point similarly: *"such organizations have no authority over each other or over the churches."* In 1939, the SBC *refused to identify the church* or the body of Christ *"with any denomination or church that seeks to exercise ecclesiastical authority."* Again, in

1940, the SBC clarified its rationale for declining the WCC's invitation to membership in that organization: *"The thousands of churches* to which our Convention looks for support of its missionary, benevolent and educational program, *cherish their independence* and *would disapprove of any attempted exercise of ecclesiastical authority over them."* In 1945 and 1946, based on its definition of the local church both as "a voluntary fellowship of baptized believers" and as "responsible directly and only to Christ," the SBC applied its definition of the local church to the issues of Christian unity and cooperation in ministry: *"this cooperation should not issue in any ecclesiastical overlordship of the individually redeemed or their churches."* Even in the SBC's most recent confession of faith from 1963, the Convention has repeated its understanding of itself and similar organizations: *"Such organizations have no authority over one another or over the churches."*[27]

The SBC has consistently expressed the previous perspective and commitment in its "Constitution" for more than 150 years. For example, according to the SBC's original constitution in 1845, the SBC combined for missionary purposes "such portions of the Baptist denomination in the United States, as may desire *a general organization* for Christian benevolence, *which shall fully respect the independence and equal rights of the Churches"*; or more recently, "while independent and sovereign in its own sphere, the Convention *does not claim and will never attempt to exercise any authority over any other Baptist body,* whether church, auxiliary organizations, associations, or convention."[28] Given this powerful commitment (and promise), in its present drive to restructure the SBC, the current executive leadership cannot legitimately justify its own recent efforts, both subtle and blatant, to manipulate and to control the Woman's Missionary Union (WMU), an *auxiliary organization* of the SBC.[29] None-

[27]*FASB (1920),* 8, 14, 15; *BFM (1925),* 74; *PRL (1939),* 115; *RWCC (1940),* 99; *SP (1946),* 38, 39; *BFM (1963),* 279, emphasis mine.
[28]"Preamble and Constitution of the Southern Baptist Convention," in *Proceedings of the SBC* (1845): 3 (article II) (hereafter cited as *PCSBC [1845]*); "Constitution," in *Annual of the SBC* (1994): 4; emphasis mine.
[29]See "Covenant for a New Century, The Spirit and Structure of the Southern Baptist Convention: The Report of the Program and Structure Study Committee," in *Annual of the SBC* (1995): 45-46, 48, 64, 82, 86, 151-76 (hereafter cited as *CNC*). See the questions, discussions, and debates surrounding the conflict between the SBC's Executive Committee and the WMU: for example, Russell N. Dilday, "Arkansas WMU Director Questions SBC Restructuring," *Baptist Standard* 107 (12 April 1995): 13; Anna Turley,

theless, the SBC's encroachment on the WMU illustrates the operation
of the shift in the SBC's conception of its own authority, as suggestively
instantiated by the Presidential Theological Study Committee in the
RPTSC.

In another vein, one pertinent especially to the status of the *RPTSC*
itself, Mohler laments the SBC's lack of a doctrinal (and, hence, disciplinary) tool with which to regulate faith and practice *in participating
local Baptist churches*. According to Mohler, "Southern Baptists have *no*

"Look at WMU," *Western Recorder* 169 (2 May 1995): 4; "Restructure Committee Turns
Down WMU Request to Amend Proposal," *Baptist Messenger* 84 (18 May 1995): 9; Dee
Gilliland, "Does WMU Have a Place?" *Western Recorder* 169 (6 June 1995): 6; "FMB
Drops Lottie Moon Trademark Plan," *Western Recorder* 169 (13 June 1995): 2; "Rankin
asks Baptists to 'Pray For' WMU," *Western Recorder* 169 (5 September 1995): 2. As
another example, the SBC's Executive Committee has utilized its official publication, one
that purportedly speaks for the entire SBC, as the organ for criticism of the Baptist
General Convention of Texas (BGCT), regarding the BGCT's revision of its participation
in the SBC's Cooperative Program. Ironically, the SBC had to use funds given by Texas
Baptists, as well as funds given by other state conventions, to finance its criticism of
Texas Baptists in this publication by the SBC: "The Eyes of Baptists Are upon You,"
SBC Life 4 (October 1995): 14. Texas Baptists responded vehemently to this abuse of
power: Toby Druin, "BGCT Leaders Respond to SBC Publication," *Baptist Standard* 107
(18 October 1995): 3-4. This transgression by the SBC's Executive Committee represents
a dangerous departure from the SBC's historic understanding of the Convention's relationship to other general Baptist organizations. For example, as part of its annual report, the
SBC's Executive Committee, during the Convention's annual meeting in 1923,
recommended for adoption a fourfold definition of relationships between the SBC and
other general Baptist organizations or bodies. The SBC adopted this recommendation that
year. The present leaders on the SBC's Executive Committee would benefit by
remembering especially the second and fourth points in the SBC's definition of
relationships between general Baptist organizations and the SBC. "The *relation of the
Convention to all other Baptist general bodies is purely advisory*. It has *no authority over
the churches, over district associations, State Conventions, or other Baptist bodies of any
kind*, nor has any other Baptist general body any authority over the Convention. . . . In
all cases and degrees where the activities of the Convention are related to the activities
of other Baptist bodies, *the controlling principle is free and voluntary co-operation for
common ends*. Since *no Baptist body has authority over any other, there can be no
question of dictation on either side*. Among Baptists moral and spiritual rights and
obligations are mutual. Only confusion can result from a failure to recognize the
mutuality of these relations. *We co-operate, not by coercion, but by mutual consent.* Free
conference and frank discussion enable us to reach satisfactory conclusions for cooperative work. *We must never convert moral and spiritual into legal relations among
Baptist general bodies*" ("Defining the Work of the Convention," in "Report of Executive
Committee," in *Annual of the SBC* [1923]: 74).

effective Conventionwide doctrinal parameters for local churches, though all six SBC seminaries have statements of faith which must be signed by all permanent faculty. Much of the debate in the Southern Baptist conflict, and a considerable part of the traumatic controversy related to the seminaries, concerns the extent to which these statements of faith exercise a *regulative* function." Of course, as part of the remedy for his own diagnosis of the SBC's present illness, in one of his fourteen imperatives for "a renewed theological framework," Mohler prescribes such doctrinal parameters for the SBC and the churches participating in it: "*The Southern Baptist Convention, with the church and academy in partnership, must develop and articulate a set of dual doctrinal parameters.*"[30]

The previous examples illustrate the practical *drive* in the SBC's fundamentalist leadership *to depart from the SBC's biblical, historic, and official polity*. Baptists in the SBC need to remember that similar violations of polity and breaches of trust produced the original bifurcation of the Baptist denomination in the United States, generating the Southern Baptist Convention in 1845. The Baptists in the South who formed the SBC perceived the precipitating cause to be the exercise of "usurped authority" and "a manifest breach of trust," even to be "an usurpation of ecclesiastical power quite foreign to our polity" by Baptists of the North

---

[30]Mohler, "Call for Baptist Evangelicals and Evangelical Baptists," 234n.29, emphasis mine; idem, "Has Theology a Future in the Southern Baptist Convention?" 104. The SBC's Executive Committee repeated in its report for 1924, from the *DWC (1923)*, a portion of its previous annual report on these very issues. The committee wrote the following as the fourth point of this short document. "In all cases and degrees where the activities of the Convention are related to the activities of other Baptist bodies, the controlling principle is free and voluntary co-operation for common ends. Since no Baptist body has authority over any other, there can be no question of dictation on either side. *Among Baptists moral and spiritual rights and obligations are mutual.* Only confusion can result from a failure to recognize the mutuality of these relations. *We co-operate, not by coercion, but by mutual consent.* Free conference and frank discussion enable us to reach satisfactory conclusions for co-operative work. *We must never convert moral and spiritual into legal relations among Baptist general bodies*" ("Report of the Executive Committee," in *Annual of the SBC* [1924]: 25; emphasis mine).

Even Alvah Hovey, who advocated the use of creeds in religious denominations, held "that the adoption of one and the same creed is unnecessary to the welfare of the churches" and encouraged "every church to make or freely adopt its own articles of religious belief, holding them always subject to revision in the light of further truth drawn from the sacred record" (Alvah Hovey, "The Question of Creeds," *The Chronicle* 7 [April 1944]: 73).

against Baptists of the South, despite the key role of slavery in occasioning that crisis. Accordingly, the Baptists of the South understood the SBC's formation as the result of their own efforts to regain their equality in Christ with the Baptists of the North: "Thrust from the common platform of equal rights, between the Northern and Southern churches, we have but reconstructed that platform." The Baptists who formed the SBC adopted the same constitution of "the original union" and emphasized the basis of their action in that respect as "a Baptist aversion for all creeds but the Bible."[31] Given the present tendency toward violation, betrayal, distortion, and disintegration of the SBC's traditional polity, as evident in the *RPTSC*, can Baptists in the SBC expect anything less than a similar bifurcation of the SBC? Can the SBC's current leadership expect to control Baptists who remember the genuine polity at the foundation of the SBC? Can the SBC's leadership rightly condemn those faithful Baptists who depart from a distorted and recalcitrant SBC, as "thrust from the common platform of equal rights," in order to reconstruct that platform in a favorable, receptive, and healthy environment?

III. Denominational Church above the State

A third fracture appears in the *RPTSC*'s rendering of another ecclesiological principle on the basis of which the SBC has historically operated: the principle of ecclesial freedom in relationships with civil government. Under the heading "a free church in a free state," certainly a motto historically emblematic of the SBC's understanding of the church's relation to the state, the *RPTSC* affirms a concept of ecclesial liberty with two facets.[32] (a) On the one hand, and more negatively, as the first aspect of the church's relationship to the principle of religious liberty, the *RPTSC* denies the authority of civil government "to coerce religious commitments": stated more generally, Christian *freedom from* the state

---

[31]*SBCBUS (1845)*, 18, 19.

[32]*RPTSC*, 117 (2.4.6). This motto appears in several of the SBC's confessional statements. In 1914, the SBC described this motto as "an American axiom" (*PCU [1914]*, 76). In 1919 and 1920, the SBC used this motto to describe "the true ideal of the relations between church and state" (*FASB [1920]*, 13). In 1925 and 1963, the SBC referred to this motto as "the Christian ideal" (*BFM [1925]*, 74; *BFM [1963]*, 281). In 1939, the SBC affirmed its concept of the relation between church and state with this motto, varying it slightly and wisely, thus emphasizing the plurality of religious communities and the autonomy of local Baptist churches: "Free Churches within a Free State" (*PRL [1939]*, 115).

in all religious matters. (b) On the other hand, and more positively, the *RPTSC* describes the principle of religious liberty as the guarantor of "the ability of every congregation and general Baptist body to determine (on the basis of the Word of God) its [*sic*] own doctrinal and disciplinary parameters": again, stated more generally, Christian *freedom for* religious expression.[33]

In this ecclesiological reference to the principle of religious liberty, however, with only slightly altered language, the *RPTSC* merely *restates*, and *reverses* the order of, the same two facets of religious liberty that it previously had affirmed in its only other reference to this principle. In its "Part I," the *RPTSC* refers to the principle of religious liberty as the broader reality expressed through the production and use of confessional statements in the SBC. I repeat the two components of that earlier affirmation in the order in which they appear in the *RPTSC*'s first part. (a) On the one hand, and more positively, the *RPTSC* affirms for any Baptist group, including the SBC itself, "the inherent right to draw up for itself and to publish to the world a confession of faith whenever it wishes"—or, more generally, Christian *freedom for* religious expression. (b) On the other hand, and more negatively, the *RPTSC* rejects "state-imposed religious creeds and attendant civil sanctions"—or, generally, Christian *freedom from* civil government's involvement in religious matters.[34]

A. Truncated Affirmation of the Church's Separation from the State

Given the position of the *RPTSC*'s affirmation within its first part, however, there the *RPTSC* affirms the principle of religious liberty mainly to supply the theoretical framework with which to justify an affirmation of confessional statements in general and, hence, to legitimize the *RPTSC* itself as such in particular (even if implicitly). As the two components of that affirmation demonstrate, the goal of the *RPTSC*'s affirmation in its first part remains identical to the goal of the *RPTSC*'s latter rendering of religious liberty's ecclesiological significance: the aim to justify the production of common confessional or credal statements as tools for establishing disciplinary parameters for both local Baptist churches participating in the SBC and the SBC itself.

---

[33]*RPTSC*, 117-18 (2.4.6).
[34]*RPTSC*, 113 (1.7).

Nonetheless, *on the surface* of the formulations themselves, the *RPTSC appears* genuinely to re-affirm the principle of religious liberty in concert with the SBC's historical tendencies. To the contrary, however, the *RPTSC*'s statement concerning the relationship between the church and the principle of religious liberty contains one central and significant fault, an infidelity to the SBC's historic understanding of the *proper* relationship between religious communities and civil government. This fault radiates from the Presidential Theological Study Committee's selection of historic language with which to formulate its construal of the proper relationship between religious communities and civil government. Although the *RPTSC* employs the motto, "a free church in a free state," that document does not interpret this motto in harmony with the SBC's historic understanding of it.

According to the SBC's historic confessional statements, for Baptists in the SBC, this motto invokes the following interpretation of *the only proper relationship* between religious communities and the civil government: *the complete or absolute separation of religious communities or churches from civil government or the state.*[35] Elaborating its understanding of this concept with the aid of a fourfold typology in 1939, the SBC distinguished its own theory from three other inadequate and improper theories of the relationship between religious communities and civil government: (a) state above church; (b) church alongside state; and (c) church above state.[36]

Strangely, however, the *RPTSC* does not include the concise yet critical affirmation of the *complete* separation of church from state. Although the *RPTSC* unequivocally denies to the state or to "the temporal realm" any authority "to coerce religious commitments," or unambiguously does "reject state imposed religious creeds and attendant civil sanctions," the *RPTSC* does not explicitly address another equally important issue: *the control of civil government by religious communities. In its use of the SBC's historic motto, then, the RPTSC* explicitly affirms only a church free from the state, not a state free from the church.

During most of its history, when the SBC has affirmed its commitment to the complete separation of religious communities from civil

---

[35]*PCU (1914)*, 76; *FASB (1920)*, 12-13; *BFM (1925)*, 73-74; *RIR (1938)*, 24; *PRL (1939)*, 114-16; *SP (1946)*, 38; *BFM (1963)*, 281; "Resolution No. 2—Religious Liberty," in *Annual of the SBC* (1964): 78, 79, 80.

[36]*PRL (1939)*, 114.

government, the SBC has emphatically produced a double-edged principle with which to maintain this separation: (1) as the first edge of this principle, the SBC both affirmed its commitment to the freedom of religious communities from either positive or negative intervention by civil government and denied all religious functions (and identification with any particular religious community) to civil government itself; and (2) as the second edge of this principle, the SBC has both affirmed its commitment to the freedom of civil government from either positive or negative intervention by religious communities and denied all civil functions to religious communities themselves.[37] Nowhere in the *RPTSC* has the Presidential Theological Study Committee affirmed this second edge in the SBC's historic principle of the separation between church and state.

B. Toward a Calvinist Version of the Church's Relation to the State

The previous obvious and dangerous omission indicates, at the very least, the *RPTSC*'s reluctance to affirm the complete or absolute separation of religious communities from civil government. For the *RPTSC*, it appears that the principle of separation has only one edge, an edge used against civil government to protect religious communities, but lacking the complementary edge to protect civil government from religious communities. Also, the *RPTSC*'s *partial* affirmations of the separation between church and state, as well as the sense of anxiety communicated through its concerns about cultural and religious pluralism, suggest that the *RPTSC* actually favors and aims to realize, at least implicitly, the control of civil government by the values and aims of only one religious community: the community named the Southern Baptist Convention; or, at some time in the future when Baptists in the SBC have become "willing

---

[37]Although the SBC has affirmed various aspects of this double-edged principle in numerous statements through the years, in none of those statements, however, has it more clearly expressed this dual commitment than in two of the least remembered documents: (1) the *FASB (1920)*, the SBC's most comprehensive early confessional statement or articles of faith; and (2) its *SP (1945)* and *SP (1946)*. "As the state has no religious function, so also the church has no civil function" (*FASB [1920]*, 13). Again, regarding both church and state, "each must be left free to serve in its own divinely appointed sphere for the welfare of mankind; but neither undertaking to control the other or to be supported as such by the other" (*SP [1946]*, 38). Compare these statements to aspects of this principle contained in other confessional statements produced by the SBC: *BFM (1925)*, 74; *RIR (1938)*, 25; *PRL (1939)*, 115; *BFM (1963)*, 281.

to follow the mainline model" (as Mohler desires), The Southern Baptist Church.[38] Two significant factors tend to corroborate this suspicion.

1. *Recent Events in the SBC.* First, recent activities by leaders of the SBC, as well as decisions of the SBC influenced by those leaders, indicate the *erasure of commitment to the SBC's historic refusal* to ascribe civil functions to religious communities or, most specifically, to Christian communities. As one example, consider the following comparison.

Consistent with its history of affirming the absolute separation of religious communities from civil government, in 1964 the SBC adopted a resolution on religious liberty in which it issued the following appeal: "We appeal to the Congress of the United States to allow the First Amendment of the Constitution of the United States to stand as our guarantee of religious liberty, and we oppose the adoption of any further amendment to that Constitution respecting establishment of religion or free exercise thereof." In stark contrast to that instance of the SBC's historic stance on this principle, during its annual meeting in 1995, the SBC adopted a resolution in which, among other related claims, it issued two important calls: (1) a call upon the Congress of the United States to adopt a constitutional amendment related to prayer and religious expression in public schools; and (2) a call upon the SBC's Christian Life Commission to use its resources and personnel to influence the passage of such an amendment.[39]

As a second example, consider another comparison. The SBC has consistently resisted (whatever ambiguities such a posture may entail) the establishment of diplomatic relations between the government of the United States and Vatican City (as a collapse of the barrier that separates church and state from one another), even as recently as the SBC's annual meeting in 1993. Nonetheless, *in their own official capacities as leaders in the SBC,* in 1995, both Jim Henry, president of the SBC, and Richard Land, director of the Christian Life Commission, called on the Congress of the United States to initiate a study on the impact of gambling in this nation.[40] This recent activity discloses a double standard: apparently, the

---

[38]For example, *RPTSC*, 113, 114, 115, 116, 117, 118 (1.2; 2.1.5, 8; 2.2.4, 6-7, 9, 12-13; 2.3.2, 5-9; 2.4.4-6; 2.5.5); Mohler, "Call for Baptist Evangelicals and Evangelical Baptists," 235.

[39]"Resolution No. 2—Religious Liberty," in *Annual of the SBC* (1964): 80; "Resolution No. 5—On a Constitutional Amendment Regarding Prayer and Religious Expression," in *Annual of the SBC* (1995): 92-93.

[40]"Resolution No. 9—On Diplomatic Relations with the Vatican," in *Annual of the*

government's official relationships with the Roman Catholic Church collapse the wall between the church and state, but not similar relationships with the SBC!

In addition, as a third example, during its annual meeting in 1993, the SBC attempted to exert its influence to reproduce its own religious values (concerning human sexuality) at the political level in the United States. The resolution adopted by the SBC contains two revealing components: (1) a resolve to "urge" President Clinton "to affirm biblical morality in exercising his public office, recognizing that to do so is not inappropriate nor is it a violation of the separation of the institutions of church and state"; and (2) a resolve to "urge the more than 15 million Southern Baptists to use their influence with the President to urge him to stand for biblical morality and to reverse his stands on the issues aforementioned for the sake of our nation's survival."[41]

As a final example, although many others exist for comparison, Richard Land has recently defended efforts of right-wing and fundamentalist Christian groups to legislate various Christian values for all citizens in the United States of America.[42] Although Land uses much traditional rhetoric to defend the separation of religious communities from civil government, he disguises his deliberate efforts (and the similar efforts of those with whom the SBC's current leadership has allied itself) to collapse that barrier as exercises of religious freedom and political responsibility in this North American democracy.

2. *Calvin's Model of Christian Civilization.* A second factor increases the basis for suspicion of the *RPTSC*'s one-sided construal of the separation of religious communities from civil government: the political model employed by Calvin during the reformations of the sixteenth century. *In itself,* Calvin's model of the relation between church and state indicates nothing about the *RPTSC*'s explicit version of this relationship. Insofar as the *RPTSC* has consistently construed Christian doctrines

---

SBC (1993): 102-103; "SBC Leaders Call on Congress to Study Effects of Gambling," *Western Recorder* 169 (3 October 1995): 8.

[41]"Resolution No. 2—On President William Jefferson Clinton," in *Annual of the SBC* (1993): 95-96.

[42]" 'Radical . . . Right' Said Threat; Land Counters," *Baptist Standard* 107 (14 June 1995): 18; cf. the essays from similar perspectives in *Citizen Christians: The Rights and Responsibilities of Dual Citizenship,* ed. Richard D. Land and Louis A. Moore (Nashville: Broadman and Holman, 1994).

through a Reformed or Calvinistic framework, however, understanding Calvin's basic model illumines the *RPTSC*'s perspective and increases suspicion of the *RPTSC* at this point.

According to Calvin, God has placed humanity "under a twofold government": the first form of government "resides in the soul or inner man and pertains to eternal life"; the second form of government "pertains only to the establishment of civil justice and outward morality." Nonetheless, Calvin quite clearly gives "to civil government the duty of rightly establishing religion," among the state's many other functions. For Calvin, the state "also prevents idolatry, sacrilege against God's name, blasphemies against his truth, and other public offenses against religion from arising and spreading among the people." In effect, Calvin argues for the necessity of a "Christian state," a civil government without any toleration (much less freedom) for alternative or different religious or nonreligious ideas, values, or communities within its borders. Thus, although Calvin *theoretically* distinguishes the two realms from one another, Calvin *practically* collapses church and state into one another, effectively producing another form of Christian civilization or a Christian theocracy. Hence, the state, as the tool of divine justice, identifies, arrests, tries, convicts, and punishes any person deviating from the true Christian faith. According to Calvin, "the magistrate in administering punishments does nothing by himself, but carries out the very judgments of God."[43] On this ecclesiological basis, for example, the Genevan civil authorities, under Calvin's direction and with his zealous approval, arrested Miguel Servetus, a dissident Spanish Christian, tried and condemned him for heresy, then executed him by burning at a stake, on 27 October 1553.[44] In Calvin's perspective, although originating in God's election of individual humans to salvation from eternity for the divine glory, the community (that is, the Christian church-state) practically

---

[43]Calvin, *Institutes*, 2:1485, 1488, 1497, 1502 (4.20.1, 3, 10, 14).

[44]See the variety of documents written by Calvin, Servetus, the judges, and so forth, related to this event: for example, *The Reformation: A Narrative History Related by Contemporary Observers and Participants*, ed. Hans J. Hillerbrand (New York: Harper & Row, 1964; repr.: Grand Rapids: Baker Book House, 1978) 284-90; John Calvin, Geneva, to Phillip Melanchthon, 5 March 1555, in *John Calvin: Selections from His Writings*, ed. John Dillenberger, American Academy of Religion Aids for the Study of Religion, ed. Gerald J. Larson (Missoula MT: Scholars Press, 1975), 56. To be fair, Timothy George, referring to Calvin's treatment of Servetus, does offer a qualified criticism of "Calvin's coercive view of society" (George, *Theology of the Reformers*, 249).

assumes primacy over individual Christians; both the church and Christian civil government serve as "external means or aids by which God invites us into the society of Christ and holds us therein."[45]

More than likely, given the *RPTSC*'s dependence on other foundational Calvinistic concepts, the *RPTSC* at least presupposes several key components from this Calvinistic understanding of Christian community: such as, the community's primacy, despite both its origin in the divine election of individual humans and its service to the sanctification of elect humanity, over the individual; and the close identity of Christian church with Christian state. Hence, in light of the *RPTSC*'s omission of any reference to the historic Baptist commitment to the civil government's freedom from ecclesiastical control, in light of recent activities in the civil-political arena by the SBC and its leaders, in light of Calvinism's concept of the relation between church and state, the *RPTSC* appears to supply a veiled support for the move of a new SBC, as The Southern Baptist Church, toward some form of an Evangelical or Southern Baptist Church-State. Thus, although the *RPTSC* rejects the model of the *state above church* (in line with the SBC's historic position), implicitly the *RPTSC* has refused also to affirm the SBC's historic model of *absolute separation of church from state*. At the very least, the *RPTSC* has established the conditions for realizing the model of *church alongside state*, if not for realizing the model of *church above state*. In his famous address on religious liberty delivered in Washington, D. C., George W. Truett identified precisely this danger, retaining the doctrine of a state-church, as one major indication that "the Protestant Reformation of the Sixteenth century was sadly incomplete, . . . a case of arrested development."[46] Yet, the *RPTSC* seems to suggest, however partially or ambigu-

---

[45]Even the order of topics in Calvin's *Institutes* supports this claim: book one concerns knowledge of God as creator; book two addresses the way in which Christ discloses knowledge of God as redeemer; book three discusses the way in which humans receive Christ's grace and its benefits; and book four examines the external means for inclusion in God's community: see, especially, Calvin, *Institutes*, 2:1009-1521 (4.1-20); cf. Max Weber, *The Protestant Ethic and the Spirit of Capitalism*, trans. Talcott Parsons (New York: Charles Scribner's Sons, 1958) 98-128; Ernst Troeltsch, *The Social Teaching of the Christian Churches*, trans. Olive Wyon (New York: Macmillan Company, 1911; repr.: Chicago: University of Chicago Press, 1981) 2:581-625; William J. Bouwsma, *John Calvin: A Sixteenth-Century Portrait* (Oxford: Oxford University Press, 1988) 191-229.

[46]George W. Truett, *Baptists and Religious Liberty* (Nashville: Sunday School Board of the SBC, 1920) 23-24.

ously, some version of the Calvinistic model of the relation between civil government and the Christian community.

Analogue. Episode Eight

At Kibroth-hattaavah, when the formerly enslaved Hebrews began to loathe the manna from Yahweh and longed again for the rich foods in Egypt, Moses complained to Yahweh that he could not alone bear the burden of this people. In response to Moses, Yahweh commissioned seventy elders to share the burden of Moses. When Yahweh communicated the divine Spirit to the elders, they prophesied. Two others who had not met with Moses and the seventy elders, Eldad and Medad, also received Yahweh's Spirit and prophesied in the camp. Upon receiving a report of their unauthorized ministries, and indignant over this affront to the leadership of Moses, Joshua called upon Moses to restrain Eldad and Medad. To this misplaced loyalty, Moses replied with a surprising preference. Rather than scrupulously guarding his own role and authority, Moses preferred that Yahweh pour the divine Spirit on all the people, making prophets of them all. Moses, even as the mediator to the people of Yahweh's liberation, needed and wanted to share God's Spirit with all of the people. Yet, at least one of the people's leaders, Joshua, jealously sought to protect Moses's authority and to control the presence of God's Spirit among the people. Perhaps Joshua's jealous effort to protect the authority of Moses occurred because Joshua himself did not prophesy. In any case, Yahweh desired to distribute the divine Spirit to everyone in the community. The prophetic activity of Eldad and Medad functions as a sign of this divine intention.[47]

With the *RPTSC*'s article on the church, the Presidential Theological Study Committee has jealously guarded the Christian community's official perspective, a perspective formulated by no more than a small cadre of the SBC's fundamentalist leaders, virtually equating that perspective with Christ's own perspective. The *RPTSC* attempts to mask the committee's self-interest with three apparent affirmations of historic Baptist ecclesiological principles: the common priesthood, the local church's autonomy, and the church's freedom from the state. Nevertheless, due to its reversal of the relationship between individual Christians and the Christian community, as evident, for example, in the *RPTSC*'s

---

[47]Numbers 11:4-30.

devaluation of the common Christian priesthood, the Presidential Theological Study Committee has similarly misrepresented the nature of the Christian community itself, as historically understood by Baptists in the SBC, thereby similarly endeavoring to control the Spirit's work among Baptists in the SBC through the *RPTSC*'s definition of the Christian community. The *RPTSC*'s ecclesiological fractures, however, reveal far more about the psychological insecurities of the Presidential Theological Study Committee concerning their abilities adequately to address contemporary issues and trends, than about the SBC's historic ecclesiological principles themselves. Furthermore, the *RPTSC*'s ecclesiological formulas represent this committee's idealization of and nostalgia for, as Timothy George has described it elsewhere, some former "communitarian character of Baptist life,"[48] a communitarian character more accurately representing this committee's imaginative revision of the SBC's history than the SBC's actual history, a reality more desired than either biblical or historical (at least, among Baptists in the SBC itself).

[48]George, "Southern Baptist Theology," 25.

Epilogue

Living in Interesting Times, Brushing History against the Grain

In the preceding chapters, I have supported with ample evidence the guiding hypothesis of this book: *the RPTSC and its adoption by the SBC programmatically and officially establish the most severe threat among recent threats to distinctive Baptist Christian experience and community: credal Baptist Christianity or Baptist credalism.* I have also endeavored to demonstrate the validity of three related and elaborative hypotheses: (1) that the Presidential Theological Study Committee has camouflaged the *RPTSC*'s credalism; (2) that this credalism originates from and perpetuates a Calvinistic theological perspective; and (3) that the revision or reorganization of the SBC supplies a more effective political structure by which to enforce conformity to this new creed.

In light of even the slightest continued commitment by the SBC to its historic and foundational antipathy to creeds, this severe threat to the SBC is essentially self-defeating: the genuine Baptist vision, as interpreted and realized historically by the SBC, cannot dwell robustly and peacefully with credalism of any kind. In the confrontation between these two essentially incompatible interpretations of Christian life and experience, either the Baptist vision will reject credalism or else credalism will dim and finally extinguish the authentic Baptist vision.

By applying a criteriology of credalism to the *RPTSC*, I have exposed the Calvinistic credalism camouflaged in that document's formulations. Because the *RPTSC* and similar credal documents in the SBC represent anomalous phenomena within the Baptist vision as historically conceived and realized by the SBC, I have also resisted the *RPTSC*'s reductive approach to Baptist Christian experience in the SBC. Nevertheless, the *RPTSC*'s credalism no longer merely incubates in the SBC, but has begun to produce symptoms in its host, foreshadowing the imminent disintegration of the SBC's authentic Baptist substance. This theological and political virus, this credal religion with its Calvinistic genetic code, like the ebola virus, effectively perpetuates itself only by literally dissolving its Baptist host.[1] Unless the SBC quickly discovers, and immediately administers to itself, a vaccine against this deadly parasite, the SBC's Baptist substance will soon experience the final stages of this agonizing fate.

I. *Kairos,* Conscientization, and Documents of Brutality

In his assessment of the contemporary global situation, David Tracy quotes the invocation, "may you live in interesting times," primarily to recall its genre as "an ancient Chinese curse."[2] *Baptists of the SBC currently live in such interesting times.* This borrowed yet subdued façade on my own evaluation of the SBC's contemporary situation also understates the gravity of these critical moments in the SBC's life. Hence, unfortunately though temporarily, with this ironically muffled malediction, I have insulated the deafening cacophony of threat, tyranny, oppression, abuse, injustice, agony, and desperation in the *interesting times* of the SBC's present experience. These lamentable times in the SBC's life, perhaps more threatening than any previous moments in the SBC's history, nonetheless still offer opportunities for the SBC's positive transformation, however unlikely that bright possibility might be—as Grady Cothen once described the SBC's situation of controversy, " 'a moment of dangerous opportunity.' "[3] Although dark and dangerous, such a situation, according to Paul Tillich's keen distinction, differs from the ordinary, regular, and formal time that the Greek language designates with the word *chronos.* Rather, Tillich uses another Greek term from the Christian Scriptures, *kairos,* to characterize such a critical situation as "the right time" or "the moment rich in content and significance," the unique time or moment, previously unrealized and not repeatable, a time "laden with tensions, with possibilities and impossibilities," a time "qualitative and full of significance."[4]

---

[1]In order to develop a sense for the seriousness of the SBC's situation, see recent discussions of the Ebola virus as an enrichment of my metaphorical reference to this danger: e.g., Richard M. Preston, *The Hot Zone* (New York: Doubleday, Anchor Books, 1995).

[2]Tracy, *Dialogue with the Other,* 3.

[3]Linda Lawson, "Cothen Underscores Ideals," *Facts and Trends* 27 (Feb 1983): 5.

[4]See, as examples of this biblical concept, Mark 1:15; 13:33; Luke 8:13; 19:44; Romans 13:11-13; 1 Corinthians 7:29; 2 Corinthians 6:2; Titus 1:3; Revelation 1:3; 22:10; also, Paul Tillich, *The Protestant Era,* abridged ed., trans. James Luther Adams (Chicago: University of Chicago Press, 1957) 33.

I began my studies of the *RPTSC* with the intention of *restoring an awareness* of credalism's danger for Baptists, of counteracting the drowsiness among Baptists induced by fundamentalist or extreme right-wing sedatives. In this sense, then, these labors also invite all Baptists in the SBC to perceive and to acknowledge this particular kairotic moment in the SBC: more pointedly, these studies together constitute a plea both for such a consciousness or awareness and for actions to meet the demands of these interesting times in the SBC. The particular character of the SBC's present situation, however, requires a special type of awareness or consciousness among Baptists in the SBC: an awareness or consciousness appropriately designated as *conscientization* by some Latin Americans. According to Paulo Freire, a Brazilian educator, this concept, which he introduced with the Portuguese term *conscientização*, "refers to learning to perceive social, political, and economic contradictions, and to take action against the oppressive elements of reality."[5]

This type of awareness differs in several respects from a common understanding of consciousness as knowledge about something. First, rather than a passive reception of information from external sources, in conscientization, a group of people *actively develops its own awareness* or consciousness of a given situation; for Baptists in the SBC, my studies constitute an invitation to study the issue of credalism in the SBC for themselves. Second, through consciousness as conscientization, people do not depend unquestioningly on leaders alone; for Baptists in the SBC, such awareness will begin to appear only when the people begin to *teach themselves*, without absolute dependence on the SBC's official leadership. Third, to realize this consciousness, the people will accomplish this education on the basis of *a critical and creative use of their own values*; for Baptists in the SBC, this awareness will grow from those distinctive emphases repeatedly affirmed in the majority of the SBC's historic confessional statements and perspectives. Fourth, consciousness of a kairotic moment as conscientization occurs only as a *process*, a process left open.

---

[5]Tillich long ago issued a general "summons to a consciousness of history in the sense of the kairos" (Tillich, *Protestant Era*, 32). Paulo Freire, *Pedagogy of the Oppressed*, trans. Myra Bergman Ramos (New York: Continuum Publishing Company, 1989) 19n.1. Also see the following: Paulo Freire, *La educación como práctica de la libertad* (Montevideo: Tierra Nueva, 1969); Ernani Fiori, "Education and Conscientization," in *Conscientization for Liberation*, ed. Louis M. Colonnese (Washington DC: Division for Latin America-USCC, 1971) 123-44.

For Baptists in the SBC, achievement of the awareness to which these studies point will permanently affix both the mark of incompleteness and, thus, the mark of continuance to all consciousness of this particular *kairos* in the SBC. According to Gustavo Gutiérrez, a Peruvian Christian theologian, in consciousness as conscientization, the people themselves "make the transfer *from* a '*naive awareness*'—which does not deal with problems, gives too much value to the past, tends to accept mythical explanations, and tends toward debate—*to* a '*critical awareness*'—which delves into problems, is open to new ideas, replaces magical explanations with real causes, and tends to dialogue."[6]

Thus, the critical issues addressed by these studies, also coupled with my invitation to all Baptists in the SBC through them, even more emphatically qualify the current *kairos* for Baptists in the SBC as a *status confessionis*. The Latin word, *status*, originates from the Indo-European root-word *sta*, a root-word used to designate "a standing place," "something unmoving," something "firm" or "solid." The Latin noun *status*, then, refers both, concretely, to a standing position or posture and, more abstractly, to a condition, state, or situation. Similarly, the Latin noun, *confessionis*, produced by conjoining the Latin verb *fateri*, meaning "to acknowledge," and the Latin preposition *cum*, meaning "with" or "together," has developed from an Indo-European root-word, *bha*, which means "to speak." Contrastingly, from the same root-word, *bha*, originates also the English noun "infantry," foot soldiers who, similar to an *in-fant* or one not yet speaking, only follow orders or literally take the word of authorities and act without speaking.[7] Others always speak for and to the infantry. Soldiers in the infantry act as one unit; individuality diminishes. The word "infantry" has no singular form. The infantry follows orders or obeys commands and does not question the commander. By radical contrast, in a *status confessionis*, a people perceives its *hic et nunc*, the *here and now* of its time and place, as *an urgent occasion or kairos*, a *kairos* inviting it *to speak*, a *kairos* in and to which to speak *together or as many voices*, an urgent occasion in which to speak together *from a solid or decisive perspective*. According to Robert McAfee Brown, occasionally "the issues become so clear, and the stakes

---

[6]Gustavo Gutiérrez, *A Theology of Liberation*, rev. ed., trans. Caridad Inda and John Eagleson (Maryknoll NY: Orbis Books, 1988) 57; emphasis mine.

[7]See Joseph T. Shipley, *The Origins of English Words: A Discursive Dictionary of Indo-European Roots* (Baltimore: Johns Hopkins University Press, 1984) 25-26, 380-82.

so high, that the privilege of amiable disagreement must be superseded by clear-cut decisions, and the choice must move from 'both/and' to 'either/or.' " Brown describes just such a *kairos* as "a *status confessionis*, a 'confessional situation.' "[8] Baptists in the SBC find themselves in such a situation in relation to the credalism of both the *RPTSC* and similar documents in the SBC.

Generally, this *kairos* in the SBC holds two basic, though mutually exclusive, possibilities: *either* (1) the possibility for Baptists in the SBC to identify and intentionally to eradicate the credal virus replicating itself through the SBC's historic vitality, thus restoring the vigor of the SBC's genuine Baptist substance; *or* (2) the possibility for Baptists in the SBC to ignore and, thereby, to succumb to this theological and political viral dis-ease, thus acquiescing to the credal dissolution of the SBC's authentic Baptist substance. Obviously, my studies invite all Baptists in the SBC to realize the first possibility for both themselves and the SBC. Realization of that first possibility, or eradication of nascent credalism as well as tendencies toward that phenomenon, requires that Baptists in the SBC, as Walter Benjamin expresses it about history in general, "seize hold" of the memory of their tradition as that memory "flashes up at a moment of danger." As Benjamin continues, "in every era the attempt must be made anew to wrest tradition away from a conformism that is about to overpower it."[9] I have attempted to initiate the accomplishment of precisely this task and urgently invite all Baptists in the SBC to participate in this endeavor. Consequently, as a *status confessionis*, all Baptists in the SBC face a moment of decision during these interesting times.

Will Baptists in the SBC participate in this endeavor? Will Baptists in the SBC discern and resist credalism in the SBC? Development of the ability to acknowledge and to refuse the credalism camouflaged in the *RPTSC* depends essentially upon critical examination of both the *RPTSC* and the recent history that produced it, by brushing history against the grain, to borrow Benjamin's metaphor. For Benjamin, the critical task described by the previous metaphor operates on the basis of the following conviction: every "document of civilization" exists simultaneously as a

---

[8]Robert McAfee Brown, "Introduction: The Recovery of *Kairos*," in *Kairos: Three Prophetic Challenges to the Church*, ed. Robert McAfee Brown (Grand Rapids: Eerdmans, 1990) 7.

[9]Walter Benjamin, *Illuminations*, ed. Hannah Arendt, trans. Harry Zohn (New York: Harcourt, Brace, and World, 1968; New York: Schocken Books, 1969) 255.

"document of barbarism."[10] Hence, one must brush against the grain of history's civilized exterior, in order to discover and to resist the brutality of tyranny, distortion, manipulation, and oppression concealed beneath the surface.[11] Thus, the SBC's present *kairos* represents a confessional situation. My studies, however, invite the fulfillment of this *kairos* only in terms of the SBC's historic affirmation and practice of confessionalism, not in terms of the credalism historically refused by the SBC. To respond to this particular confessional situation or *status confessionis* by exposing and resisting credalism, consequently, expressly contradicts the status quo or the existing state of things in the SBC.

II. Environment for Credalism

With the phrase "status quo in the SBC," I do not refer merely to the presence either of a few isolated credal documents or of minor credal tendencies in actions and perspectives of a few leaders in the SBC. Rather, I identify the SBC's status quo as the entire environment that a cadre of fundamentalist leaders in the SBC has intentionally produced through and in which to conceive and to nurture credalism among Baptists in the SBC. Although in previous chapters I have identified various elements of the SBC's present status quo, my petition to Baptists in the SBC requires a brief characterization of the environment that has produced and continues to cultivate credalism.

A. Community as Monologue

Fundamentalist Baptist leaders engineered the prevailing status quo. According to official assessments from the majority of those leaders, one major issue necessitated their efforts to produce the environment that they continue scrupulously to protect and to extend: alleged widespread departures from conservative or orthodox Christian doctrines within the SBC (by its leaders and, especially, within its theological schools),

---

[10]Ibid., 256, 257.

[11]I have intentionally substituted the word "brutality" for the word "barbarism" in my extension of Benjamin's point, as an endeavor to remain consistent with his meaning without employing his term. In light of the term's derivation from the Greek word for an alien or a foreigner ("barbarian"), by substituting another term for the word "barbarism," I aim to avoid any negative evaluation of alterity in itself. The documents of civilization, in the very brutality they conceal, aim to subjugate and to reduce alterity: such documents do not affirm and seek to exclude or eliminate the barbarian (alien, foreigner) or the other and, in this sense, eschew a proper barbarity.

alleged doctrinal apostasy supposedly caused by false concepts of the nature of the Christian Bible itself. By opposing this alleged apostasy from a dependable Bible in the SBC with the ideographic theory of biblical inerrancy, and through a variety of other political tactics, that fundamentalist leadership incited and manipulated a shift in the SBC to the present status quo.

Within the SBC's current fundamentalist leadership, some leaders, such as David Dockery, naively continue to construe the source of the SBC's controversy as "primarily the result of a crisis of *biblical authority*," a crisis broadly construed also as both "a crisis of piety (living out a commitment to *biblical authority*) and a crisis of theology (articulating the meaning and significance of *biblical authority* for our generation in the midst of a changing and post-Christian culture)."[12] Among the originators of this fundamentalist conquest of the SBC, however, Paige Patterson explicitly identifies the controversy's source as the idiopathic drive for complete dominance of the SBC by a fundamentalist vision.

> In the early days of the controversy, conservatives pointed to the unassailable fact that there was no parity in the six seminary faculties. Some had no professing inerrantists on board, and none had more than a few. Moderates later discovered that conservatives did not desire "parity" but rather believed that every professor in Southern Baptist Convention seminaries should be an inerrantist. Some moderates felt that they had been deceived. However, *conservatives never asked for parity.* They simply noted that moderates, who claimed to be inclusive, in fact had been exclusive and doctrinaire.[13]

---

[12]Dockery, "Response," 223; emphasis mine. The SBC's Peace Committee (a group dominated by fundamentalist leaders), of course, officially inscribed this mythic assessment into the SBC's official records: "The primary source of the controversy in the Southern Baptist Convention is the Bible; more specifically, the ways in which the Bible is viewed" (*RPC [1987]*, 233).

[13]Paige Patterson, "Anatomy of a Reformation—The Southern Baptist Convention," 17 November 1994, TMs (photocopy), 15-16, Special Collections, Roberts Library, Southwestern Baptist Theological Seminary, Fort Worth TX; emphasis mine. Even James Henry, in his presidential address to the SBC in 1996, after acknowledging his own commitment to the theory of biblical inerrancy, indicated his suspicion of this possibility. "We are making strides in widening the participation level across a wider range of our Southern Baptist family, but there are a few who demonstrate a need to continually manipulate the procedures for denominational service and control beyond the call extended to Southern Baptists several years ago to return us to biblical authority. That call was a unifying factor for us, and that noble intention we salute. But to carry it beyond this, as a few seem determined to do, cast [*sic*] *suspicion on the original intent*" (Henry,

Despite the genuine significance of both the theological catalyst (the dispute about the nature of biblical authority) and human sin (the idiopathology of domination) in the production of the SBC's present status quo, and whether or not all of the aggressors consciously realized it, the real source of the controversy (the issue around which even these other factors revolve) concerns a struggle over the legitimate answer to one foundational question: *As theorized and realized historically by the SBC, for Baptists, what is the nature of Christian community and how does it operate?*[14] Historically, the SBC has operated with a concept of commu-

---

"The Southern Baptist Convention: Disintegration, Stagnation or Revitalization?" June 1996, TMs [photocopy], 8; Presidential Address, Southern Baptist Convention, New Orleans; emphasis mine). Patterson's previous comments, however, contradict his own earlier characterization of fundamentalist desires. "*Conservatives* do not seek 'control' of the Southern Baptist Convention, only the reducing of the bureaucratic structure and the return of the convention to the people. Conservatives do not insist that every decision and policy conform to their own thinking. They do not insist that everyone use the word 'inerrant' to describe his view of the Bible. They *do seek genuine parity* in the faculties and administrations of the schools and insist that employees of the convention never, under any circumstances, call into question any statement of the Bible or say anything that might be construed as disbelief in the veracity of the Scriptures" (Patterson, "Stalemate," *Theological Educator*, Special Issue, "The Controversy in the Southern Baptist Convention," ed. Fisher Humphreys [1985]: 10; emphasis mine).

Perhaps moderate Baptists thought fundamentalists wanted parity because Patterson, one of the principal leaders of the so-called "conservative resurgence," claimed this. Did the fundamentalists want parity or not? Patterson has made both claims. Given the logical principle of noncontradiction, did Patterson tell *the truth* in 1985 or in 1994? The two statements *do not correspond* to the same reality! Walter B. Shurden also perceived this blatant contradiction and camouflaged motive (Walter B. Shurden, "The Struggle for the Soul of the SBC: Reflections and Interpretations," in *The Struggle for the Soul of the SBC: Moderate Responses to the Fundamentalist Movement*, ed. Walter B. Shurden [Macon GA: Mercer University Press, 1993] 284-85).

[14]Ralph H. Elliott accurately perceives the mutual dependence between these three factors, in his recent autobiographical interpretation of the continuity between the SBC's fundamentalist controversy of the 1960s and the SBC's current plight: "The *authority* question has become so intertwined with *ecclesiology* and *power* that it is difficult to know which is the driving issue—the question of authority or the relish of the power struggle" (Elliott, *The "Genesis Controversy" and Continuity in Southern Baptist Chaos*, 39; emphasis mine). Walter Shurden, even more pointedly, expresses the intimate relationship between these issues. "To say that the Fundamentalist-Moderate Controversy focused on the nature and interpretation of the Bible is to fail to understand the heart of the conflict. . . . At bottom the Fundamentalist-Moderate war was a clash of worldviews" (Shurden, "Struggle for the Soul of the SBC: Reflections and Interpretations," 278).

nity in which participants acknowledge their equality with one another, arrive at common Christian vision and tasks through genuine prayer with God as well as in authentic dialogue with one another, and realize their common goals through shared power: in short, a concept of community in which the participants affirm and maintain all of the conditions for the possibility of cooperative Christian endeavors.

1. *Revising the SBC's Spirit: Eradication of Dialogue, Reduction of Alterity.* In striking contrast, fundamentalist leaders, through their manipulative and openly militant subjugation of the SBC, have systematically erased most (if not all) conditions of possibility for genuine cooperative Christian life in community from the SBC's historic practice of community, in order to establish the social dynamics of the SBC's present status quo on a theoretical basis very different from the SBC's historic perspectives. I have identified many of these erasures in previous chapters. The fundamentalist leaders of the SBC, however, have attacked with the greatest energy the most essential condition for community among Baptists in the SBC, the very spirit of the SBC itself: dialogue and the alterity that it represents.

Paulo Freire has accurately described the essential characteristics of dialogue, precisely those very characteristics rapidly disappearing from relationships among Baptists in the SBC. First, according to Freire, two dimensions constitute the essence of dialogue, or the word itself: *reflection* and *action*. Without the first dimension, reflection, dialogue becomes mere "activism"; without action, the second dimension, dialogue becomes "idle chatter" or mere "verbalism." The "true word" or dialogue both names the world and acts to transform it; genuine dialogue is praxis. Second, such action, the action of genuine dialogue or speaking the true word, belongs rightfully (or as a fundamental right) to every human, not merely to a few elite or privileged people. Dialogue does not occur when one person prescribes the true word for all, thus robbing others of their right to dialogue. As Freire expresses it, dialogue occurs neither as "the act of one person's 'depositing' ideas in another," nor as "a simple exchange of ideas to be 'consumed' by the discussants," nor as "a hostile, polemical argument" between persons committed only "to the imposition of their own truth" on others. Third, dialogue exists only on the foundation of *love* and as love, love both for the world and for humans. Fourth, genuine dialogue requires the dynamics of *humility*: commitment to the premise that the task of naming the world belongs to all people; openness to the contributions of others; refusal to construe oneself as a member of an elite group. Fifth, genuine dialogue "requires an intense *faith*" in the human's "power to make and remake, to create and to re-create," faith in the human's "vocation to be more fully human." Sixth, founded on love, humility, and faith, genuine dialogue produces *mutual trust*, a reality dependent upon the evidence provided by all parties in dialogue of their true intentions, of the consistency between their words and actions. Seventh, authentic dialogue requires *hope*: the realization of human "incompletion," coupled with the expectation through actions that such efforts may produce something new and necessary. Eighth, genuine dialogue occurs only when all participants "engage in *critical thinking*." Critical thinking includes several elements: discernment of "an indivisible solidarity" between the world and humans; perception of "reality as process, as transformation, rather than as a static entity"; constant immersion in action, "without fear of the risks involved"; and consistent engagement in the "humanization" of humans.[15]

Although many of the SBC's fundamentalist leaders continue explicitly to affirm the value and the need for dialogue, the fundamentalist conquerors of the SBC have systematically eradicated the previous requirements for genuine dialogue. On the surface, however, Mohler's perspective, for example, *seems* to indicate the inaccuracy of my previous claim in the thirteenth of his fourteen "imperatives for a renewed theological framework." According to Mohler, "Southern Baptists must engage in a genuine process of theological dialogue." Nevertheless, Mohler judges "prospects for genuine theological dialogue" to be "bleak," since "an institutionalized *two-party system* is now firmly fixed within the denomination." From his own pessimistic perspective, Mohler implicitly suggests the necessity for the institutionalization of a *one-party system*, in order to establish the possibility for genuine theological dialogue. With such a viewpoint, however, Mohler reveals his complete misunderstanding of dialogue itself. Genuine dialogue of any kind requires, at least, two parties. Yet, Mohler interprets the presence of two very different perspectives in the SBC as an obstacle to dialogue! For Mohler, genuine theological dialogue can occur only when both parties share the same perspective: in effect, when two parties become one or when both parties have arrived at agreement, then they can dialogue. According to Robison B. James, Mohler's approach to theological dialogue "could create the

---

[15]Freire, *Pedagogy of the Oppressed*, 75-81; emphasis mine.

impression that the results of the dialogue are being laid down before it starts." Mohler confirms the accuracy of James's criticism: "He is correct, at least in part, for I do not think that any genuine dialogue is possible, or could be profitable, if there is no established common ground."[16]

Representative of the fundamentalist leadership of the SBC, Mohler begs the question about the prospects for genuine theological dialogue, when he defines the doctrinal parameters (in several of his other, previous "imperatives") for the dialogue about the doctrinal parameters themselves.[17] Mohler's admission to begging the question reveals his discomfort with genuine alterity or otherness. As nonsensical as it may appear, for Mohler, only if two parties agree on the doctrinal parameters of the SBC (as defined by Mohler and the fundamentalist oligarchy) can the two parties (which really become one party) consider together the content by which to define the SBC's doctrinal parameters. If Mohler considers the *prospects* for genuine theological dialogue to be bleak in the situation that he describes as the SBC's two-party system, with his one-party system, he completely eliminates the *need* for any kind of dialogue at all. In effect, Mohler, first, refuses to converse with anyone whose perspective differs from his own: for example, in general, his writings tend to proceed by rhetorical argument and pronouncements, by tactics to defeat his opponents, rather than as genuine explorations of questions and dialogue. Second, by beginning with secured agreements to his own perspective from his partners in dialogue, Mohler eliminates questions and the need to answer them through dialogue. Mohler's pronouncements notwithstanding, however, genuine theological dialogue proceeds on the basis of common questions, not necessarily on the basis of shared conclusions. Furthermore, because dialogue requires the freedom of all participants, dialogue by its very nature entails risk, the risk that final and complete agreement will not occur through the processes of either conversation or argumentation.

One may find many similar examples in the writings and activities of other fundamentalist leaders in the SBC. This fear of the *other*, this elimination of dialogue, indicates the sort of community into which the deforming energies of this fundamentalist movement have shaped the

---

[16]Mohler, "Has Theology a Future in the Southern Baptist Convention?" 109, emphasis mine; James, "Beyond Old Habits and on to a New Land," 120; Mohler, "Response," 248.

[17]Mohler, "Has Theology a Future in the Southern Baptist Convention?" 99-109.

SBC. Anyone who refuses to ignore such abuses can detect the tendency of this fundamentalist movement, in virtually all of its actions and documents, both to eradicate all traces of diversity that might promote genuine dialogue and to eliminate every possibility for the reappearance of such diversity in the SBC. For example, rather than promoting dialogue and inviting all Baptists in the SBC to dialogue, Timothy George calls for decision: "Moderates must decide whether they can find a place to stand in the new order or else seek alternative alignments."[18] With respect to Baptists in the SBC who have different perspectives, this group dominates and does not cooperate. Some Baptists have accurately, if also ironically and homiletically, described this fundamental departure from the spirit of the SBC's historic operating procedures as a shift *from the Cooperative to the Coercive Program* in the SBC. One may also accurately describe this as the shift from community as dialogue to community as monologue.

2. *Revising the SBC's Structure: Toward Autocratic Forms of Polity.* During the SBC's first 150 years, the Convention's constitutional polity never legally or theologically permitted the SBC to operate legitimately as a hierarchical community with varying degrees of coercion and domination. From the origins of the destructive controversy in the SBC during the late 1970s, the fundamentalist conquest of the SBC has possessed political as well as theological characteristics. The fundamentalists realized, even at the beginning, that they could not ultimately control Baptist beliefs, unless they controlled the SBC's organizational and operational structures (with all of their economic and social implications and relationships).[19]

---

[18]George, "Conflict and Identity in the SBC," 195.

[19]Thus, most of those who opposed the fundamentalist aggression wrongly construed the efforts of the fundamentalists to be motivated solely by political concerns, despite fundamentalist protestations to the contrary. As Bill Leonard notes, however, by 1990, opponents of the SBC's fundamentalist leadership finally had acknowledged, and had begun to warn Baptists about, the fundamentalist goal to transform the SBC theologically as well as politically. "From the beginning of their takeover movement, the fundamentalists have insisted that the problems in the denomination were primarily, if not exclusively, theological. . . . In the early years of the debate, moderates insisted that the struggle was essentially political, the effort of a fundamentalist-oriented political faction to dominate convention life and distract the denomination from its unified goals of missions and evangelism. . . . Many moderates now warn that fundamentalists are changing not only the way the convention works but also the way Southern Baptists believe" (Leonard, *God's Last and Only Hope*, 66).

As late as 1987, however, the fundamentalist leaders of the SBC, through the SBC's Peace Committee (which they controlled), *both preferred* not to change the SBC's constitution and bylaws in order "to restrict the appointive powers" of the SBC's president *and recommended* "that the Cooperative Program be continued unchanged."[20] Nonetheless, the fundamentalist Baptist leaders, even in 1987, envisioned a structural change in the SBC that would favor their own very particular theological perspective over all other Baptist perspectives in the SBC. Only recently, however, have the fundamentalists who control the SBC finally accomplished a complete political (as well as theological) *de*formation of the SBC. As demonstrated in previous chapters of this book, since 1979 fundamentalist Baptist leaders have systematically manipulated both the political dynamics of the SBC and the Christian sentiments of Baptist messengers to the SBC's annual meetings, thereby successfully influencing the SBC to adopt a series of fundamentalist doctrinal and moral resolutions. With the culmination of those efforts in the *RPTSC*, the SBC's fundamentalist leadership has largely realized its theological transformation of the SBC. Because the victory of this theological revision would have remained hollow without the capacity to enforce practical conformity to its cognitive stipulations, however, the SBC's deformation required a political revision as well. The fundamentalist leadership did not stumble upon this insight. In an essay from 1992, Mohler openly expressed this fundamentalist perspective: "The only hope for the Southern Baptist Convention is a *renewed theological consensus* wedded to a *new model of convictional cooperation.*"[21]

Hence, by 1995, the SBC's Executive Committee, through its Program and Structure Study Committee, had unveiled and recommended its "Covenant for a New Century" (*CNC*), its blueprint for the revision of the SBC's organizational and operational spirit or character and structure.[22] The SBC adopted this recommendation in that year. The *CNC*, however, represents a degenerative contrast even to the report and recommendations of the Southern Baptist Convention Cooperative Program Study Committee, as adopted by the SBC during its annual meeting in June of 1983.[23] Mohler's presence on both the Presidential Theological

---

[20]*RPC (1987)*, 236, 241.

[21]Mohler, "Has Theology a Future in the Southern Baptist Convention?" 98.

[22]*CNC*, 45-46, 48, 64, 82, 86, 151-76.

[23]"Southern Baptist Convention Cooperative Program Study Committee Report and

Study Committee and the Program and Structure Study Committee was no mere coincidence. Mohler's participation on both committees should alert Baptists in the SBC to the tangible connection between the fundamentalist theological (*RPTSC*) and political (*CNC*) revisions of the SBC. Consistent with the authoritarian character of the *RPTSC*, the *CNC* intensifies the centralization and concentration of the SBC's operations and power, placing the SBC's governing mechanisms most firmly in the oligarchically autocratic grip of the SBC's Executive Committee.[24]

After fully activating the theological dimension in its fundamentalist project by producing the *RPTSC* and engineering its adoption by the

---

Recommendations," in *Annual of the SBC* (1983): 41-47. This committee's report occurred in the Executive Committee's report, and was adopted by the SBC as "Recommendation 5: Southern Baptist Convention Cooperative Program Study Committee Report and Recommendations," in *Annual of the SBC* (1983): 41-47. See especially the study committee's first recommendation to the SBC: "Recommendation 1—Principles of Cooperation," in *Annual of the SBC* (1983): 45.

[24]Since the SBC's adoption of the *CNC* in June 1995, numerous publications have appeared that illustrate the Executive Committee's intensification of its emphasis on the union of these theological and political aims. For instance, *SBC Life*, a tabloid published by the Executive Committee and completely slanted toward a fundamentalist ideology, has displayed this dual pattern in three recent issues: featuring parallel articles on both creeds or doctrinal orthodoxy and the SBC's political restructuration. See the following examples: Herb Hollinger, "Executive Committee Chairman Names Transition Group for PSSC Re-Organization," *SBC Life* 4 (October 1995): 2; Dwayne Hastings, "Confessions of Faith: A Baptist Way of Life?" *SBC Life* 4 (October 1995): 4; " 'Covenant for a New Century' Task Force Focuses on Transition," *SBC Life* 4 (November 1995): 13; Bill Haynes and Mark DeVine, "24 Theological Words Every Southern Baptist Should Know," *SBC Life* 4 (November 1995): 8-9; "Faculty Questionnaire: Midwestern Baptist Theological Seminary," insert in *SBC Life* 4 (November 1995); Jon Walker, "The Mythical Line between Indoctrination and Education," *SBC Life* 4 (December 1995): 3; Timothy George, "What Are You For?" *SBC Life* 4 (December 1995): 6; Morris H. Chapman, "SBC Requires Visionary Leadership through Transition," *SBC Life* 4 (December 1995): 7. McBeth also warns against restructuring the SBC, accurately identifying it as an increase, rather than a decrease, in bureaucracy. "Five SBC entities are abolished, but the proposed Great Commission Council erects a kind of 'Super Board' over the two mission boards. This creates yet another level of bureaucratic control. The proposals also enormously increase the power of the Executive Committee and concentrate it in fewer hands. This is a far cry from what was intended when the Executive Committee was created" (McBeth, "Cooperation and Crisis as Shapers of Southern Baptist Identity," 44). In this work, however, I have limited my studies to the *RPTSC* as the tangible evidence of the credalistic theological revision of the SBC. The *CNC*, nonetheless, certainly deserves a similar, if not more extensive, critical study.

SBC, the SBC's fundamentalist leadership materialized the political dimension of its project by formulating the *CNC* and also engineering its adoption by the SBC. Thus, when the SBC's Executive Committee has fully implemented the *CNC*, the political mechanisms will exist with which to enforce the theological perspectives affirmed and produced by the SBC's fundamentalist leadership, as summarized to date by the *RPTSC*. The aggressive right wing in the SBC apparently has engineered this dual project as a parallel to the Convention's work in 1925, when the SBC both adopted the *BFM (1925)* and approved the Cooperative Program. In addition, not accidentally did the unveiling of the *CNC* (following the adoption of the *RPTSC* in 1994) coincide with both the seventieth anniversary of the Cooperative Program and the 150th anniversary of the SBC itself. Even in 1992, Timothy George most certainly must also have perceived the symbolic significance of this parallel.[25] The SBC's current fundamentalist leadership, nevertheless, has refused to imitate the genuine Baptist character of the SBC's efforts in 1925.

B. Power as Domination

The fundamentalist revisions of the SBC's spirit and structure, therefore, both conceptually and operationally, have distorted power or authority in the SBC: from power used to *communicate power to and to share power with others*, to power as *the force with which to control*

---

[25]"In that same year [1925] the Convention would also approve the Cooperative Program, thus providing both a *confessional* and *organizational* basis for its consolidation and expansion" (George, "Conflict and Identity in the SBC," 196; emphasis mine). Andrew L. Pratt expresses this same suspicion about George. "One concern about George's program of theological renewal is its affinity to the political program of the current leadership of the Southern Baptist Convention. A doctrinal program that includes subordination of individual freedom to group orthodoxy, biblical authority understood as inerrancy, disparagement of biblical criticism, and warnings against both theological and denominational liberalism, provides a theological foundation for the political agenda of the current Southern Baptist Convention leadership. Another concern arising from this movement for theological renewal is its subtle melding of the Baptist and Reformed traditions" (Pratt, "A New Question in Baptist History: Seeking Theological Renewal in the 1990s," *Perspectives in Religious Studies* 20 [Fall 1993]: 265). Slayden Yarbrough has similarly evaluated the dual fundamentalist revision of the SBC: "The spirit of voluntarism, freedom, cooperation and trust as expressed in commitment to missions in 1845 can be contrasted with the current emphasis on theological and political parameters as a basis of unity" (Yarbrough, "The Southern Baptist Spirit, 1845–1995," *Baptist History and Heritage* 30 [July 1995]: 33).

others; from power as the *capacity to produce power for others*, to power as the *capacity to reduce the power of others*; from power as the *"communication of efficacy,"* to power as *coercion*; from *power with* others, to *power over* others; from power as *empowerment*, to power as *disempowerment*; from power as *cooperation*, to power as *repression*; thus, from power as *communion*, to power as *domination*.[26] This particular distortion has supplied perhaps the most essential condition for an environment in which to cultivate credalism in the SBC.

Nonetheless, these theological and political components depend upon one another. On the one hand, credal commitments with absolutist perspectives, require highly centralized and hierarchical structures of power to secure unalloyed conformity to those perspectives; without such political structures, such credal documents, however numerous or specific, remain impotent or ineffective. On the other hand, highly centralized and hierarchical structures of power require credal commitments as ideological legitimizations for the existence of such political realities; without such absolutist theological justifications, such political structures could not effectively withstand their relativization by the counterclaims of competing perspectives. Conjunctions between absolutist credal commitments and highly hierarchical structures of power, consequently, spawn various degrees of power as domination. In the 1920s, W. H. P. Faunce, then president of Brown University, accurately perceived and represented the relationship between such theological concepts and political structures: "Faith in God as dictator of the universe, as a being of arbitrary, irresponsible power, creates arbitrary, irresponsible, cruel men."[27] Specific credal documents, then, become devices for testing loyalties to political structures; political structures, by the same token, become means through which to guarantee adherence to specific credal perspectives.

---

[26]See Kyle Pasewark's excellent discussion of power as the communication of efficacy (Kyle A. Pasewark, *A Theology of Power: Being beyond Domination* [Minneapolis: Fortress Press, 1993] 196-235). In a description of dominating power as "antidialogical action," Freire identifies several characteristics of such action: (1) the desire and necessity to *conquer* or to impose objectives on the vanquished, a goal realized by depositing myths with which to preserve the new *status quo*; (2) the *division* of the vanquished majority, in order to maintain *control*; (3) *manipulation* of those who have entered the political process, anesthetizing them to prevent them from thinking; (4) *cultural invasion* of the vanquished, to curb their expression by supplanting their traditions with the conqueror's values and objectives (Freire, *Pedagogy of the Oppressed*, 133-61).

[27]W. H. P. Faunce, *Facing Life* (New York: Macmillan, 1929) 116.

Such a conjunction has occurred in the double fundamentalist revision of the SBC: theologically, as represented most comprehensively to date by the *RPTSC*; and politically, as represented most comprehensively to date by the *CNC*. This particular conjunction, between the *RPTSC* and the *CNC*, helps to explain the significant increase in the repression of different perspectives, as well as the oppression of various individual Baptists and groups of Baptists in the SBC's recent history. In spite of the serious abuses in the SBC's recent history, however, Baptists in the SBC have yet to experience among themselves the most frightening proportions of power as domination.

Some aspects of domination's most frightening proportions, however, have begun to disclose themselves even in the *RPTSC*. For example, the Presidential Theological Study Committee built its entire claim for the necessity of the *RPTSC* on the basis of a false set of assumptions about the SBC's history, especially about its recent history. The *RPTSC* represents the full blossom of a tendency that began to bud explicitly in 1979. *When an institution alters its memory in order to justify its self-contradictions, then power as domination maintains that institution.* The dissolution of the SBC's Historical Commission by instituting the *CNC* exemplifies this very claim. Thus, in the fundamentalist revision of the SBC's history, the fundamentalist leadership of the SBC has described the history of its conquest of the SBC as a popular revolution, a people's movement, a "conservative resurgence" arising from the Baptists in the pews of local Baptist churches.[28] Despite the emotional persuasiveness of such rhetoric for many Baptist people, the historical records themselves

---

[28]In 1987, Walter Shurden alerted Baptists about the fundamentalist revision of the SBC's history, specifically with respect to the SBC's historic unifying principle. "What has happened in recent years is that the fundamentalist movement among Southern Baptists has increasingly tried to rewrite our history by replacing that functional unity [for ministry, missions, and evangelism] with a theological unity. It is true that many denominations are united by theological uniformity. They have a creed to which people must subscribe in order to be a member of that church or denomination. Southern Baptists have always studiously avoided that. While we have confessed our faith together, we have confessed it with such flexibility that we can keep on working together without forcing each other in the same theological mold. But what fundamentalists have developed in recent years is the desire to see the Southern Baptist Convention unified around a theological pole rather than a ministry pole; a doctrinal pole rather than a functional pole" (Walter Shurden, "Southern Baptist Theology Today: An Interview with Walter Shurden," *Theological Educator* 36 [Fall 1987]: 31-32).

reveal something very different: the SBC's historical documents attest to
a movement initiated, controlled, and led almost completely, or with only
a few exceptions, by professional ministers, pastors, and preachers. To
put this another way, the so-called "conservative resurgence" actually
operated as a fundamentalist military *coup d'état*, not as a conservative
popular revolution. In a military *coup d'état*, a group of leaders gains
control of government by means of subterfuge and force, then misrepresents the means of its ascendancy to governorship as if, all along, it had
been a movement of the people themselves.[29]

As the previous example demonstrates, the fundamentalists who
control the SBC realize the intimate relationship between knowledge (in
this case, historical knowledge) and power. Those who *presently* control
the SBC certainly acknowledge the truth of Francis Bacon's assertion:
"for knowledge itself is power."[30] Rather than discovering a basis for
their power in the SBC's actual history, however, the fundamentalist
masters of the SBC have revised historical knowledge of the SBC, in
stark contrast to the attestations of Baptist historical documents themselves. Hence, those who have captured the SBC and now control its
institutions also govern the SBC on the basis of a reversal of Bacon's
insight: for the SBC's fundamentalist masters, *power is knowledge*. In
other words, if one controls the structures of power, one also can
determine, create, and shape the content of knowledge itself.

The previous discussion invites Baptists in the SBC to consider the
ultimate source of the drive to exercise power as domination: generally,
the emotion of fear; most specifically, a fear of diversity, a fear of the
other or alterity (heterophobia) based in an unnatural love of the same
(homophilia) or the self. The fundamentalist fear of the SBC's own
diversity and alterity also operates as agoraphobia or a fear of the

---

[29]"Dialogue with the people is radically necessary to every authentic revolution. This
is what makes it a revolution, as distinguished from a military *coup*. One does not expect
dialogue from a *coup*—only deceit (in order to achieve "legitimacy") or force (in order
to repress). Sooner or later, a true revolution must initiate a courageous dialogue with the
people. Its very legitimacy lies in that dialogue. It cannot fear the people, their expression,
their effective participation in power. It must be accountable to them, must speak frankly
to them of its achievements, its mistakes, its miscalculations, and its difficulties" (Freire,
Pedagogy of the Oppressed, 122).

[30]"Nam et ipsa scientia potestas est" (Francis Bacon, "Meditationes Sacrae," in *The
Works of Francis Bacon*, vol. 7, *Literary and Professional Works*, vol. 2, new ed. [Lon-
don: Longmans and Co., 1879] 241).

marketplace or the larger human public. The anxious antipathy toward both the alterity of broader human publics and the more narrow alterity within the SBC itself partially explains the SBC's practical maximization of self-examination (in terms of theological and political revisions) and minimization of ministry to others (in terms of missions and evangelism), despite the SBC's theoretical rhetoric about itself.

Has the exertion of power as domination by the fundamentalist leadership of the SBC actually affected Baptist experience and community in the SBC? As many teachers in Baptist colleges, universities, and seminaries already sadly acknowledge, Baptists in the SBC *presently* have begun to experience an ecclesial *millerandage*. With the term *millerandage*, the French describe the failure of young grapes to develop normally, due to poor weather during the flowering of the grapevines. The abnormal theological underdevelopment evident in present generations of Baptist students, especially students in the SBC's seminaries, resembles the *millerandage* in French vineyards. The environmental conditions produced in the SBC by its fundamentalist leadership, through the previous decades of controversy, have prevented the normal and healthy development, theological as well as emotional, of young Baptist Christians. This problem has begun to yield fewer, weaker, more confused, and less capable Baptist candidates for ministry. Current leadership in the SBC has mortgaged the future of cooperating Baptist churches against the intrigues surrounding the theological and political revisionism of the so-called "conservative resurgence." By supporting and encouraging the efforts of this militant movement, Baptist churches will soon reap a small and an even more unhealthy harvest of candidates for ministry. The fruit of this fundamentalist aggression has already begun to appear in many Baptist churches. The *RPTSC* represents another dangerous pollutant in the SBC's theological and political environment, a pollutant that will only increase the ecclesial *millerandage* on the branches of the vine who is Christ.

Will the action initiated by Ed Young, in appointing the Presidential Theological Study Committee in 1992, *make a difference* in the SBC? Baptists in the SBC who examine the *RPTSC*, as well as the spirit and structure of the SBC that now empowers it, surely must answer this affirmatively. Will Young's action, however, effect *a positive difference*, one consistent with the SBC's historic perspectives or genuine spirit and structure? Comparisons of the SBC's larger history with the last twenty years of its most recent history will lead many discerning Baptists in the SBC to answer this second question negatively![31]

III. On the Extremity of Liberty

In my resistance to the credalism in the *RPTSC*, as well as to the environment that has engendered and *currently* cultivates such phenomena, I do not resist all evaluations and criticisms of the SBC's historic confessional perspectives. As a consequence, neither do I resist change per se in the SBC. To the contrary, among the SBC's several confessional statements, the *BFM (1963)* most adequately identifies and reaffirms every Baptist's prerogative both to evaluate critically all confessional documents, including the *BFM (1963)* itself (as well as the *CSBI, CSBH, RPC [1987]*, and *RPTSC*), and to accept or reject such documents (or portions thereof) without reprisal within or from the SBC itself.

Nonetheless, on the basis of the previous principle, I do resist one change in particular that threatens the SBC: the elimination of this specific posture from the SBC's historic confessional perspectives, the erasure of a self-critical posture vis-à-vis documents like the *RPTSC*.[32]

---

[31]Illustrating his desire for change in the United States, Young reflected on his own experience: "My dad said to me many, many times down in the bucolic area of southern Mississippi where I was reared, 'Edwin, make a difference. Edwin, make a difference.' . . . He said, 'When you leave this world, leave it a little better than you found it.' Those were his exact words: 'Make a difference' " (H. Edwin Young, "Rebuild the Walls in America Today," in *Citizen Christians*, ed. Land and Moore, 24).

[32]One Calvinistic Baptist, Tom J. Nettles, describes three unhealthy attitudes toward confessions of faith. "The first . . . consists of a refusal to give legitimate conscientious affirmation to it in its proper sphere of influence. The second consists of imputing immutability to its phrases and words; the result of this is that it can become static and not dynamically related to vital theological concerns. The third consists of conceding the presence of extraordinary divine activity and guidance in the production of a confession so as to attribute to it the characteristics of inspiration." With his threefold assessment of confessional postures, of course, I concur. According to Nettles, however, "claims of providence in the production of the 1963 Baptist Faith and Message so as to render alteration impious, unfaithful, divisive, and pharisaical have appeared in our day. These represent lamentable lapses into an ironical creedalism and give to the confession a place that should be reserved for Scripture" (Nettles, "Creedalism, Confessionalism, and the Baptist Faith and Message," 152-53). Nettles attacks those who defend the *BFM (1963)*, however, only to support his criticism of those elements in the *BFM (1963)* that supply the conditions of possibility for resistance to full-fledged creedalism, not really in order for him to identify and to resist creedalism in the SBC. Within his Calvinistic communion, to the contrary, Nettles argues strongly both for the disciplinary use of creeds in the SBC and

Within its own first recommendation, even the SBC's fundamentalist-dominated Peace Committee implicitly supported this sort of resistance, emphasizing both the noncredal character of the *BFM (1963)* as a whole and the doctrinal formulations in that document as "parameters for cooperation" not as criteria for ecclesiastical discipline.[33] Hence, I resist the *RPTSC*'s revisions of the SBC's historic confessional perspectives, because those particular changes eliminate the critical posture from the SBC's historic perspectives, thereby eliminating the conditions of possibility for genuine Baptist polity and theologies.

A. Conservation and Revision

On the one hand, therefore, my position represents a conservative perspective among Baptists in the SBC.[34] Although one cannot fairly construe my own resistance to the *RPTSC* and similar documents as a reactionary response to the normal processes of institutional change, through my protest and resistance I do seek to conserve something essential: the conditions of possibility for authentic Baptist experience, ecclesial polity and activity, and theology as the foundations for the consensus required

---

(given the criteria of credalism derived from the *BFM [1963]*), therefore, for credalism itself (Nettles, "Missions and Creeds: Part I," 17-26; idem, "Missions and Creeds: Part II," *Founders Journal* 18 [Fall 1994]: 1-21). Earlier in his career, Nettles also promoted credalism through his naive efforts to revive the use of catechisms among Baptists in the SBC: see, e.g., Nettles, ed., *Baptist Catechisms* (Fort Worth TX: Tom Nettles, 1982).

[33]*RPC (1987)*, 240. Nonetheless, although Stephen Shoemaker moved to amend the *RPC*'s first recommendation to clarify the noncredal character of confessional statements with a third subpoint, the SBC unfortunately defeated his proposed amendment. The full text of Shoemaker's proposed amendment to the *RPC (1987)* follows: "We, (1) honoring the Baptist principle that our only creed is scripture, affirm the canon of Holy Scripture as our sole authority of faith and practice, and not make scripture of any interpretation of scripture, thereby adding to the Word of God, and that we, (2) honoring the Baptist principle of soul freedom and soul competence and of local church autonomy, affirm the competence and freedom of the individual person to interpret scripture for himself/herself and affirm the local church as the only governing interpreter of scripture for Baptist people in their congregational life" (*Annual of the SBC* [1987]: 57).

[34]Howard Wayne Smith, in his own response to a confessional statement in the Northern Baptist Convention, expressed this similarly: "In the light of the study it would also seem that the Baptist Conservative is he who asserts and defends the position that the distinctive message of the Baptists is their doctrine of the necessity of regeneration through faith only in a crucified, living Christ, obedience alone to Him, and the refusal to bear the bondage of human creeds by whomsoever formulated and declared" (Howard Wayne Smith, "Baptists and Creeds," *The Chronicle* 7 [April 1944]: 56).

to restore and maintain the SBC's genuine missionary and evangelistic purposes. My rejection of changes in certain elements of the *BFM (1963)*, therefore, discloses my desire to retain the conditions of possibility for genuine review and reinterpretation of Baptist doctrinal perspectives, even the conditions of possibility for the renewed refusal of ecclesiastical dogmas.

On the other hand, I do not object to many other changes. I do not resist every move of the SBC to transcend sectarianism, unless such moves really mean entering the new sectarianisms of contemporary North American evangelicalisms; instead, I support every Baptist effort to engage in dialogue with those who hold other perspectives, especially efforts to engage in dialogue with other Christian groups and denominations, whether Catholic or Pentecostal. Furthermore, I do not resist either the revision of existing confessions of faith or the writing of new confessional statements in the SBC, as long as the SBC produces such confessional statements in terms of the SBC's historic conception of confessions, refusing tendencies toward credalism. Additionally, I do not object to the reappropriation of the resources available in the broader Christian traditions, when such reappropriations proceed critically, identifying and refusing the distortions and problems also embedded in those traditions. I do not even resist a complete restructuring of the SBC, if such a political revision does not eradicate the very conditions of possibility for genuine Baptist polity and perspectives.

B. Toward Reclamation of Community as Genuine Dialogue

Given my plea for genuine dialogue as the essence of authentic community, how can I explain both my critical rejection of the *RPTSC* and my severe suspicions about the committee that produced the document? Obviously, such responses to credal phenomena do not promote polite conversation. The fundamentalist theological and political revisions of the SBC, however, have effectively eliminated most, if not all, conditions for *genuine* dialogue among Baptists with different perspectives in the SBC. In the SBC's present form, the SBC's dominating leadership only permits (at least without reprisal) voices to speak that articulate unqualified submission to and support of this new fundamentalist realm.

As Freire perceives, when a dominating group denies to other people "their primordial right to speak," then the oppressed people "must first reclaim this right and prevent the continuation of this dehumanizing aggression."[35] Timothy George, more than a decade ago, identified the mutual "confidence" of Baptists in one another as "the key to overcoming our present conflict with respect to our cooperative mission endeavor." George elaborated his claim: "Baptists must *believe in each other* even if they do not always agree with each other."[36] Precisely this mutual confidence or trust among Baptists in the SBC, however, has disappeared, and, with it, the living heart of dialogue itself. Only by *reclaiming and protecting the primordial right to speak* will the conditions for dialogue itself begin to reappear. On that basis alone can mutual trust again begin to blossom among Baptists in the SBC. When such trust finally blooms, then possibilities for the restoration of genuine dialogue will increase dramatically. With the studies of this book, I hope to reclaim the primordial right of all Baptists in the SBC both to speak and (despite diversity expressed through their discourse) to remain in the SBC. Thus, at this stage, I explain my responses both to the *RPTSC* and to the leaders in the SBC who produced it only as efforts toward reclamation of the right to dialogue as a historic perspective of the SBC. On the basis of the condition of equality in dialogue, as co-priests in Christ, Baptists organized the SBC. Only by reclaiming at least this condition, can Baptists in the SBC renew this convention's cooperative spirit. As a consequence of this aim, I offer the following petition to all Baptists in the SBC.

C. *Emergat Populus*

The Presidential Theological Study Committee has failed to fulfill one of its larger aims: "to move beyond the denominational conflict of recent years toward a new consensus rooted in theological substance and doctrinal fidelity."[37] If anything, this committee has accomplished exactly the opposite: intensifying and expanding the denominational conflict of the SBC's recent history, by imposing, through manipulative and deceptive means, a minority's distorted theological perspective as the doctrinal norm for the entire SBC. More than a century since he died, the piercing insight of John Leland (1776–1860), one of the greatest Baptist champions for religious liberty in North America, illuminates with startling honesty the seductively dangerous source of the SBC's current plight:

---

[35]Freire, *Pedagogy of the Oppressed*, 77.

[36]Timothy George, "The Southern Baptist Cooperative Program: Heritage and Challenge," *Baptist History and Heritage* 20 (April 1985): 12; emphasis mine.

[37]*RPTSC*, 113 (1.2).

That devil, who transforms himself into an angel of light, is often preaching
from these words: "*contend earnestly for the faith once delivered to the
saints.*" Whenever men are self-conceited enough to believe themselves
infallible in judgment, and take their own opinions for tests of orthodoxy,
they conclude they are doing God service, in vindicating his truth; while
they are only contending for their particular tenets. By this gross mistake,
the Christian world is filled with polemical divinity. I very much question,
whether there was ever more sophistry used among the old philosophers,
than there has been among divines.[38]

The *RPTSC* and related efforts in the SBC will only continue to
alienate that large majority of Baptists who remain committed to non-
Calvinistic and noncredal Baptist Christian perspectives. Nonetheless,
although God already has led many faithful Baptist Christians to leave
the SBC, God has also encouraged many other faithful Baptist Christians
to remain and, most importantly, to resist such reductive (and, therefore,
destructive) agenda and credenda among Baptists in the SBC. To achieve
peace does not always refer merely to the cessation or the prevention of
conflict. More often, the achievement of peace refers to the reestablish-
ment of the relations of genuine reciprocity and mutuality: struggles
toward a just social order or healthy structures of shared power. When
people had achieved these conditions in their communities, the ancient
Hebrews understood such an environment as *shalom* or peace. Baptists
have not yet reestablished those conditions within the SBC. Thus,
although open conflict during the SBC's annual meetings has largely
ceased, peace has not yet arrived.

1. *Facing an Oppressive Cessation of Conflict.* No matter how often
I survey either the causes of the SBC's lengthy and destructive conflict
or even the SBC's desperate straits, my heart still beats excitedly that this
very moment will give birth to liberty for *all* Baptists in the SBC.[39] Very
few Baptists remain united and, as yet, untouched by enslavement to the
SBC's young theological and political empire. No other group or insti-

---

[38]Leland, "Virginia Chronicle," 123; emphasis mine.

[39]In this section, I have freely adapted to the SBC's present situation components
from a speech written by Tacitus (ca. 55–120 CE), an ancient Roman historian, and
attributed by him to the Briton chieftain Calgacus. According to Tacitus, Calgacus
delivered his speech to a confederation of tribes in ancient Britain, as they faced a Roman
army led by Agricola, tribes the Romans had not yet fully reduced to servitude (Cornelius
Tacitus *De Vita Iulii Agricolae* 29-32).

tution inside or outside the SBC remains to support the few genuinely free Baptists. The very churches which participate in the SBC no longer remain free from menace, now that the legions of fundamentalist credalists threaten the SBC's genuine Baptist substance. Therefore, imitation of Christ, in a resistance motivated by the Spirit, with the Christian Scriptures in heart as well as in hand, the *strong* Baptist's confidence, also supplies the best safety even for the timid, lukewarm, apathetic, or compromising Baptist in the SBC. Former engagements, met by some Baptists with varying degrees of success against the so-called "Conservative Resurgence," left behind them hopes of help in the few remaining free Baptists. The most authentically conservative (yet not fundamentalist) of Baptists in all the SBC, dwellers in that inner Baptist shrine of liberty, have never felt the weighty chains of religious bondage, even preserving their very eyes from ecclesiastical tyranny's desecration and contamination of Christian freedom. On the extremity of liberty, those Baptists have lived unmolested to this day, defended by their remoteness and obscurity. Now, however, the uttermost recesses of the SBC's expanse lie exposed, ever magnifying the unknown.

Yet, no other allies exist to aid free Baptists: nothing stands either in front of them or behind them, except the more destructive fundamentalists, whose arrogance one cannot escape by obedience and self-restraint. These robbers of the SBC probe even the frontiers of Baptist freedom, now that the SBC's heart has succumbed to their all-devastating hands. Neither East nor West has glutted the fundamentalists. They covet, with the same lust, poverty as much as prosperity. As Timothy George himself could still observe without dissimulation in 1985, "the integrity of our worldwide missionary enterprise is undermined when the quest for personal power and denominational control takes center stage in our dealings with one another and in the oversight of our agencies and institutions."[40] The *plunder* of institutions, the *murder* of character and career, as well as the *rape* of holiness, piety, and fidelity, those who dominate the SBC falsely designate as polity and faith under two titles: (1) "Covenant for a New Century, the Spirit and Structure of the Southern Baptist Convention"; and (2) "Report of the Presidential Theological Study Committee." They create a desert and call it peace![41]

---

[40]George, "Southern Baptist Cooperative Program," 12-13.
[41]Israel's prophets often identified such contradictions among God's people. " 'For from the least to the greatest of them, every one is greedy for unjust gain; and from

The critical faith and confident doubt, exhibited by every Baptist in the exercise of the shared Christian priesthood, displease, frighten, and anger the SBC's fundamentalist masters. The very distance and seclusion from fundamentalist aggression in the SBC, in proportion as they secure genuine Baptists in their liberty, intensify fundamentalist suspicions about those lovers of Christian liberty. Only disunity and apathy among free Baptists, not the fidelity of fundamentalists to an allegedly divine cause or holy war, have permitted the fundamentalist conquest and revision of the SBC. The fundamentalist aggressors have possessed less of faith, hope, and love in the frenzied zeal of their aggression than they now possess of resentment, despair, and insecurity in the smug comfort of their domination.

Nonetheless, among those conquered by and serving among the fundamentalist aggressors, genuine yet captive Baptists remain. Through faithful and loving resistance to the fundamentalist revision of the SBC by Baptists who remain free, other Baptists among the aggressors themselves may glimpse their former liberty and begin to resist the oppressive realm as well.

The present situation for Baptists in the SBC differs in a variety of ways, but dramatically in one respect especially, from the situation of those Baptists who formed the SBC in 1845, the sad situation in which, nonetheless, they also finally rejoiced over the "*passing* calamity of division" among Baptists in the United States.[42] Despite various claims made both by those who now control the SBC and by those unfortunately driven from the SBC, however, the SBC's most recent calamitous divi-

---

prophet to priest, every one deals falsely. They have healed the wound of my people lightly, saying, "Peace, peace," when there is no peace' " (Jeremiah 6:13-14 RSV). " 'They have spoken falsehood and divined a lie; they say, "Says the Lord," when the Lord has not sent them, and yet they expect him to fulfil their word. Have you not seen a delusive vision, and uttered a lying divination, whenever you have said, "Says the Lord," although I have not spoken?' " (Ezekiel 13:6-7 RSV). "Their feet run to evil, and they make haste to shed innocent blood; their thoughts are thoughts of iniquity, desolation and destruction are in their highways. The way of peace they know not, and there is no justice in their paths; they have made their roads crooked, no one who goes in them knows peace" (Isaiah 59:7-8 RSV). Furthermore, both the commissioning of the Presidential Theological Study Committee and the *RPTSC* itself indicate the colossal failure of both the *RPC (1987)* and those who participated on the committee that produced the *RPC (1987)*, including H. Edwin Young himself.

[42]*SBCBUS (1845)*, 20; emphasis mine.

sion remains in process and has not yet completed itself. A time for rejoicing over the passing calamity has not yet arrived for Baptists in the present SBC. The calamity has not passed. However muted and concealed, the struggles continue: the struggle of fundamentalists to dominate, to restrict the freedom given to Baptists by God's own Spirit; and the struggle of free Baptists against such oppression, in the exercise of liberty to fulfill their callings from God. Baptists in the present SBC, by contrast to Baptists who formed the SBC in 1845, face an increasingly oppressive cessation of conflict.

Those who control the SBC, who have instituted the massive theological and political revisions of the SBC, have chiseled deeply, just inside and above the once-broad entrance to this organization, a new maxim for Baptists in the SBC: "We have constructed for our basis a new creed, acting in this matter against, in order to eliminate, the Baptist aversion for all creeds but the Bible." This epigram tersely announces the fundamentalist erasure of the SBC's genuine and historic Baptist perspective. The fundamentalist leaders who have engineered and activated the SBC's dual revision tightly clutch the name "Baptist," but, with their death grip, choke the life (the meaning as historically understood by the SBC) from that name. The SBC's fundamentalist lords retain the form of the name "Baptist," but not its content. Thus, one may describe most fittingly those who now dominate the SBC as *magni nominis umbrae*: shadows or unworthy descendants of a great name or an illustrious family.

As genuinely free Baptists in the SBC know, herein I only re-issue the alert sounded by many Baptists preceding me. In addition, I have not merely discovered in the *RPTSC* the sudden and unexpected appearance of this credal phenomenon among Baptists in the SBC, as if the credal phenomenon had lain dormant or inactive until this document's production, adoption, and employment. The fundamentalist leaders in the SBC labored several years, on a variety of components, to engineer the conditions necessary in the SBC for the formulation, adoption, publication, and application of such credal documents. *Nemo repente fuit turpissimus*: no one ever became dis-graceful suddenly or unexpectedly. As I have demonstrated in previous chapters, without question, in light of the SBC's history, this proverbial assessment accurately applies to those responsible for the *RPTSC*'s production.

As my references to the SBC's history in previous chapters have repeatedly indicated, the SBC has consistently resisted numerous abuses connected with the phenomenon of credalism. Most Baptists in the SBC deeply desire and urgently seek honesty and truth, not false assumptions about or misrepresentations of the SBC's history or its present situation. Most of these Baptists want ministers who serve and who build consensus, not commanders and dictators: ministers with honest purposes, not veiled and questionable intentions. Such Baptists thirst for communities that operate with democratic forms of congregational polity, not as aristocratic and oligarchic political hierarchies. Rather than manipulative forms of coercive tactics, genuinely free Baptists prefer both direct or open encounter over differences and dialogue toward accomplishment of common tasks. Historically, most Baptists in the SBC and the SBC itself have vehemently resisted the credalism produced by the previous abuses. Because the *RPTSC* represents the most dangerous manifestation of credalism in the SBC to date, genuinely free Baptists who remember the best of the SBC's historic perspectives will also resist this most recent threat to the SBC's Baptist substance.

2. *Petition to Baptists in the SBC.* In sixteenth-century Europe, Roman Catholics and mainstream Protestants (those following the teachings of Martin Luther and John Calvin, for example) often used the designation, "Anabaptist," to refer pejoratively to any Christian who practiced baptism as the immersion in water of persons only after their professions of faith in Christ.[43] The term, "Anabaptist," means "one who baptizes again." With this term, their opponents suggested that Anabaptists had submitted to a second baptism. The Catholics and mainline Protestants considered the baptism of infants as valid. Hence, according to the Christian status quo of sixteenth-century Europe, since the New Testament affirmed only one Lord, one faith, and *one baptism*, Anabaptists had departed from the true faith with their second baptisms. Thus, the ecclesiastical and political authorities commissioned special police

---

[43]During the sixteenth century, virtually any dissenter, whether Christian or not, might receive the label of "Anabaptist." I accept Hans Hillerbrand's threefold categorization of the radical reforming movements, or "Protestant radicalism," in the sixteenth century: Anabaptism (as represented by Felix Manz, Conrad Grebel, George Blaurock, Jacob Hutter, Michael Sattler, or Menno Simons); Spiritualism (as represented by Sebastian Franck, Nicolaus Storch, or Thomas Müntzer); and Antitrinitarianism (as represented by Miguel Servetus, Sebastian Castellio, Juan de Valdés, or Faustus Socinus) (Hillerbrand, *Reformation*, 214-21, 273-75). William R. Estep employs similar categories: Anabaptists, Inspirationists, and Rationalists (Estep, *The Anabaptist Story*, rev. ed. [Grand Rapids MI: Eerdmans, 1975] 15-16). With the term "Anabaptist," I refer specifically to the radicals in the first category.

units, known in German as *Täuferjäger* or hunters of Baptists, to apprehend the wayward and, therefore, dangerous Anabaptists. As punishment for their alleged apostasies or heresies, the authorities executed many Anabaptists. Numerous Anabaptists suffered execution by drowning. The city council of Zürich, on 7 March 1526, officially designated drowning as the punishment for those who participated in rebaptism: "Whoever hereafter baptizes someone will be apprehended by our Lords and, according to this present decree, be drowned without mercy." Subsequently, on 5 January 1527, the authorities of Zürich drowned the first victim of their persecution, Felix Manz.[44]

Sadistically and mockingly, the orthodox Catholics and Protestants, those who determined and controlled the structures of power in sixteenth-century Europe, executed the Anabaptists with the very symbol of their faith: drowning them by permanent submersion in the water of their own convictions. Similarly, the self-proclaimed orthodox (or fundamentalist and Calvinist) credalists in the SBC have submerged (and endeavored to drown) Baptists of the SBC in their own historic language and perspectives.

I began this section with a Latin title that, until now, I have neither translated nor explained: *emergat populus*. I translate this formulation as "may the people emerge," in order to address Baptists in the SBC with a petition, an invitation, a hope, or an anticipation. For this reason, I have expressed this petition or anticipation in the subjunctive mood rather than in the imperative mood, as an entreaty or a supplication rather than as a command or a mandate. Baptists in the SBC have proceeded together in their divine callings on the basis of individual convictions and voluntary decisions, cooperating by consent, not under coercion of any kind.[45] Hence, inasmuch as participating Baptists hope to preserve the SBC's genuine Baptist substance, they will similarly proceed together in the future. For too long and in too many ways during the SBC's recent history, the SBC's fundamentalist leadership has submerged the majority of Baptists or the people themselves, along with the SBC's genuine historic

---

[44]Hillerbrand, *Reformation*, 233, 234.

[45]The SBC has consistently refused to use coercion, vehemently insisting instead on the operation of consent, to produce cooperation: *PCSBC (1845)*, 659 (article 2); *SBCBUS (1845)*, 18-19; *PCU (1914)*, 75-76; *FASB (1920)*, 8-9, 14-15; *DWC (1923)*, 74; *BFM (1925)*, 74; *PRL (1939)*, 115; *RWCC (1940)*, 99; *SP (1946)*, 39; *BFM (1963)*, 275, 279; *BI (1963)*, 20-21, 30-31.

perspectives, beneath the waves of the chaotic fundamentalist miscon-strual of the SBC's Baptist substance, under the violent flood of the fun-damentalist agenda and credenda. At this moment of opportunity, a Bap-tist sentiment invites repetition. May the people emerge: *Emergat popu-lus*! May Baptists in the SBC emerge from the waters of domination that threaten to drown them with their own convictions, gasping for the breath of liberty that will deliver and sustain them.

Paige Patterson has described the Baptist state conventions of North Carolina, Kentucky, Virginia, and Texas as the SBC's "four weakest states," since those four conventions have not realized that "their future is with the Foreign Mission Board, the Home Mission Board and the seminaries over and above what is going on in each particular state."[46] Most assuredly, these states have resisted and continue to resist the coer-cive tactics of the SBC's leadership to initiate the deformation of the state conventions, identical to the processes of deformation presently operating in the SBC: deformations from congregational to oligarchical (or presbyterial or episcopal or papal) polity, from confessional spirituali-ty to credalism, from communities led by the Holy Spirit to organizations motivated by the drives, methods, attitudes, and profit-margin mentalities of international and corporate business.

In places, Baptists continue to emerge. If resistance to the oppressive fundamentalist forces constitutes weakness in the Baptist state conven-tions, I pray for such weakness to increase. Such weakness indicates the authentic Christian refusal to use or to submit to sinful forms of power.

> Because the foolishness of God is wiser than men, and the weakness of God is stronger than men [as the apostle Paul describes legitimate Christian power] God has chosen the foolish things of the world to shame the wise, and God has chosen the weak things of the world to shame the things which are strong, and the base things of the world and the despised, God has chosen, the things that are not, that He might nullify the things that are, that no man should boast before God. (1 Corinthians 1:25, 27-29 NASB)

Empowered by this divine Spirit, may Baptist people in the SBC emerge into Christ's bright, fresh, and broad liberty.

---

[46]Patterson, "Conversations with Evangelicals," 4; also see Mark Wingfield, "Patter-son Calls Kentucky One of SBC's 'Weak' States," *Western Recorder* 169 (15 August 1995): 6.

But you, beloved, building yourselves up on your most holy faith; praying in the Holy Spirit; keep yourselves in the love of God, waiting anxiously for the mercy of our Lord Jesus Christ to eternal life. (Jude 20-21 NASB)

1. May all Baptist Christians and churches in the SBC remember that the living God in Christ as attested by the Holy Spirit is the *ultimate* authority for Baptists: not ecclesiastical leaders of any kind, however coercive such leadership may be; not credal documents or statements, however full of either anathema or false humility they may be; not even the Bible itself, however sacred, certain, sufficient, and authoritative that book most assuredly is for Baptists in the SBC.

2. May all Baptist Christians in the SBC remember that all Christians have received from God a shared priesthood: exercising that priesthood *with* the professional ministers of their churches, *not under* them; and not trading their birthrights in Christ to any pastor or leader either from spiritual sloth or for mere intellectual and emotional security.

3. May all Baptist Christians and churches in the SBC realize that their decisions not to participate in the SBC's political processes and events, their decisions to avoid conflict, their minimizations of theological thinking and dialogue only allow the most unscrupulous leaders politically and theologically to dominate and, thus, to diminish the SBC which the churches continue to support.

4. May all Baptist Christians and churches in the SBC call the SBC's leaders, as well as the trustees, administrators, and employees of the SBC's institutions and agencies, to accountability for their actions: refusing blindly to trust words alone; considering deeds and their effects; and investigating the issues for themselves.

5. May all Baptist Christians and churches in the SBC withdraw their support both from the SBC as a whole and from all institutions of the SBC, when those entities have departed from the SBC's historic perspectives: especially when the SBC's leadership refuses to serve the Convention as the churches desire, and when the Convention's leadership has instituted, and persists in operating with, non-congregational polity.

6. May all Baptist Christians and churches in the SBC remember that their support, and theirs alone, has created and continues to sustain the SBC.

7. May all Baptist students in the SBC's seminaries and related institutions of higher education remember that, as Baptists in the SBC, by their gifts to and service in local Baptist churches, they also support the seminaries, universities, and colleges that they attend.

8. May all Baptist students in the SBC's seminaries and related institutions of higher education exercise their rights as well as their responsibilities to address constructively the elimination of the SBC's historic perspectives from the educational institutions in which they study, as well as the problems in the SBC that owns, or maintains direct or indirect relationships with, those educational institutions.

9. May all Baptist ministers and pastors in the SBC learn and teach the complete and genuine history of both the SBC and its leadership to the churches that they serve.

10. May all Baptist ministers and pastors in the SBC honestly inform their churches about the un-Christian events in the SBC that the faithful and sacrificial contributions of the churches and their members have actually financed and continue to sustain.

11. May all Baptist ministers and pastors in the SBC address courageously and honestly the fundamentalist leaders who have manipulated and deceived Baptists in the SBC.

12. May all Baptist ministers and pastors in the SBC resist the temptation to ignore the fundamentalist domination of the SBC, in order to fulfill personal ambitions for larger churches, for prizes of denominational employment, or for honors of denominational leadership.

13. May all Baptist employees of the SBC, its institutions, and its agencies remember that, as Baptists in the SBC, they also support the SBC and, therefore, possess both the privilege and the responsibility actively to identify and to resist wrongs in, or even erasures of the SBC's historic perspectives from, the agencies and institutions that they serve.

14. May all Baptist leaders of the SBC remember to whom they really owe their ultimate loyalties: God alone, not one another, not even the architects of the so-called "conservative resurgence."

15. May all Baptist leaders of the SBC trust in God alone, even when bullied with manipulative forms of piety into consenting to decisions or perspectives that their spiritual instincts refuse, remembering that God supplies the contexts and resources for genuine life and ministry.

16. May all Baptist leaders of the SBC refuse to compromise their sensitivity to the Holy Spirit's guidance, by accepting bribes of any

kind: whether those bribes appear as recommendations for positions in large churches, as appointments to boards of trustees in the SBC's institutions, or as employment opportunities in the SBC itself or in any institution of the SBC.

17. May all Baptist leaders of the SBC refuse to use employment opportunities either to bribe or to threaten other Baptists in the SBC in any way.

18. May all Baptist leaders of the SBC refuse to do evil, in order to accomplish any goal, however worthy such a goal may appear or may pretend to be.

19. May all Baptist leaders of the SBC refuse to consider and to promote themselves as members of an elite group or a spiritual aristocracy.

20. May all Baptist leaders of the SBC remember to serve and to cooperate in ministry, rather than to command or to coerce, either openly or manipulatively, those with whom they minister.

21. May all Baptist leaders of the SBC genuinely receive and learn from all priests in the body of Christ, refusing to identify the model of a North American corporate executive with the roles to which God has called them, and with which God has entrusted them, through election by the Baptists of the SBC.

Cataclysm. The Victory Worse than Defeat

I can only imagine, given the consistently aggressive and manipulative posture exhibited by fundamentalist leadership in the SBC's recent history, that the anticipations of my previous petition will probably go unheeded if not unavenged by that leadership. Nonetheless, the likelihood of vicious reprisals from such hands should never inhibit the pursuit of truth, justice, and beauty among genuine Baptists.[47]

---

[47]My predilection resembles the demeanor of both Martin Luther and Thomas Helwys toward the ecclesiastical and political leaders who opposed them. According to Luther, those leaders represented, as he designated it, "the kingdom of Babylon and the power of Nimrod, the mighty hunter." "And since I see that they have an abundance of leisure and writing paper, I shall furnish them with ample matter to write about. For I shall keep ahead of them, so that while they are triumphantly celebrating a glorious victory over one of my heresies (as it seems to them), I shall meanwhile be devising a new one. I too am desirous of seeing these illustrious leaders in battle decorated with many honors" (Martin Luther, "The Babylonian Captivity of the Church," trans. A. T. W. Steinhäuser, rev. Frederick C. Ahrens and Abdel Ross Wentz, in *Luther's Works* 36, *Word and Sacrament II*, ed. Abdel Ross Wentz [Philadelphia: Muhlenberg Press, 1959] 12, 17; also cf. idem,

The methods and doctrinal perspectives expressed through the *RPTSC*, as well as through the environment in which the SBC's fundamentalist leadership produced and promoted that document, have distorted the SBC's genuine perspectives and have manipulated Baptists in the SBC to affirm and to adopt those distortions. Thus, the leadership that dominates the SBC systematically dissolves the genuine Baptist substance of the SBC, by drowning Baptists in subtle distortions of their own historic language and perspectives. This fundamentalist violence to the SBC's historic perspectives has victimized the Baptist people themselves. The names of many faithful Baptists, those who resisted yet were vanquished and oppressed in various ways, now fill the *Taufbuch* or the baptismal register of those martyred in this fundamentalist oppression or

---

"The Pagan Servitude of the Church," in *Martin Luther: Selections from His Writings*, ed. John Dillenberger [Garden City NY: Doubleday, 1961] 250, 255). Thomas Helwys used Babylon as a metaphor as well, employing both Jeremiah 51:6 and Hosea 10:12 as the biblical bases for his work. "And shall we hold our peace because we are not eloquent? No, no, we have too long neglected our duties herein, and now through Gods grace we dare no longer do so: and therefore do we thus cry unto you the people of God, saying Babilon is fallen, she is fallen, Come out of hir, Come out of hir, for if you still partake with hir in hir sinnes, you shal certenly be partakers of hir plagues: and therefore also we say. Let him that is a thirst, Come: and let whosoever will, take of the water of life freely: and we call unto all valiant Archers that bend the bow, to come to the seige against this great Cité: and we pray all that are myndfull of the lord not to kepe silence, nor to give the lord rest, till he repaire, and untill he set up Ierusalem the praise of the world. And our continewall praiers unto the lord are, and shalbe that the lord will enlighten your understandings, and raise up all the affections of your soules and spirits, that you may apply your selves unto these thinges, so far as his word and spirit doth direct you, and that you may no longer be deceived and seduced by those false Prophetts who prophesie peace unto you when war and destruction is at the doore, which the lord give both you and them to see, that you may all flie unto the lord for your delivrance and salvation. Amen" (Helwys, "To the Reader," in *The Mistery of Iniquity*, facsimile repr. ed. H. Wheeler Robinson [London: Kingsgate Press, 1935; orig.: Holland, 1612]). Despite irregularities and differences from contemporary English, I have quoted the seventeenth-century language as it appears in the text itself. When Helwys published his book in England, it so angered King James I that, in 1612, the royal authorities imprisoned Helwys in Newgate Prison. According to most historians, Helwys had died by 1616: Michael R. Watts, *The Dissenters: From the Reformation to the French Revolution* (Oxford: Clarendon Press, 1978) 49; Robert G. Torbet, *A History of the Baptists*, rev. ed. (Valley Forge: Judson Press, 1963) 39. Henry W. Clark, however, placed the death of Helwys in 1626 (Clark, *History of English Nonconformity: From Wiclif to the Close of the Nineteenth Century*, vol. 1, *From Wiclif to the Restoration* [London: Chapman and Hall, 1911] 193).

drowning. Obviously, although the fundamentalists have not completed their work, among the many names contained therein, that *Taufbuch* lists at least the following victims of the fundamentalist theological and political revision of the SBC: Morris Ashcraft (SEBTS), Larry Baker (CLC), Isam Ballenger (FMB), Russell Dilday (SWBTS), Loyd Elder (BSSB), Randall Lolley (SEBTS), Molly Marshall (SBTS), Dan Martin (BP), G. Keith Parker (FMB), R. Keith Parks (FMB), Al Shackleford (BP), E. Frank Tupper (SBTS), Michael Willett (FMB), and many others.[48]

God most certainly grieves over this aggression and destruction, as Yahweh grieved over Israel's desire for Egyptian security, as Jesus even lamented over the Jewish people's infidelity to its divine calling. According to the Christian scriptures, just prior to his arrest, as Jesus entered Jerusalem on a donkey, during the people's messianic exultations and invocations of peace, Pharisees admonished Jesus to rebuke the people's excessive exaltation of him. The Gospel of Luke narrates Jesus' response to this encounter.

> And when He approached, He saw the city and wept over it, saying, "If you had known in this day, even you, the things which make for peace! But now they have been hidden from your eyes."

In the divine sorrow over Israel, as disclosed again through the grief of Jesus about Jerusalem, God lamented not only about Israel's infidelity, but also about the consequences of that false love toward God:

> "For the days shall come upon you when your enemies will throw up a bank before you, and surround you, and hem you in on every side, and will level you to the ground and your children within you, and they will not leave in you one stone upon another, because you did not recognize the time of your visitation." (Luke 19:41-44 NASB)[49]

Similarly, God sorrows over the fundamentalist aggression in and domination of the SBC. More sobering still, however, God grieves about the impending self-destruction of the SBC, if Baptists do not conscientiously and courageously resist the gradual dissolution of the SBC's genuine Baptist substance.

---

[48]See the lengthier catalogue of victims in one recent, privately published account of the fundamentalist conquest of the SBC: John F. Baugh, *The Battle for Baptist Integrity* (Austin TX: Battle for Baptist Integrity, Inc., 1996).

[49]Cf. Matthew 23:37-39; Luke 13:31-35; Ephesians 4:25-32.

The SBC's fundamentalist leadership has operated, and continues to operate, on the basis of an evolutionary principle: the survival of the fittest. Now that this new leadership has fully established coercive structures of power as the machinery by which the SBC operates, this environment of domination breeds new generations of similar leaders. The SBC's fundamentalist leaders have intentionally encouraged others to imitate them; yet, with that encouragement, they have unwittingly begun to produce the future leaders who will operate on the basis of the same evolutionary principle. With the departure of all diversity except fundamentalist perspectives, the newest dominators (in the increasing strength of their youth) will finally confront their aggressive forefathers (in the decreasing strength of their age). Hence, the SBC's *present* fundamentalist leadership has begun to engender a *future* fundamentalist leadership that will finally do to the fundamentalist patriarchs that which those original aggressors did to moderate Baptists in the SBC. Without significant help and healing, dysfunctional families perpetuate themselves in the next generation. For the SBC, this situation heralds the triumph of the rule of iron, not the blossoming of the Golden Rule.

Numerous Christian scriptures attest to the self-destruction of God's people. The apostle Paul's writings refer to this in a variety of ways. Paul reminded the Christians in Galatia that the harvest of a particular crop results from the planting of a certain kind of seed. More significantly, as Paul also announced to the Christians in Rome, God gives to the people who betray their relationships with God exactly that which they desire in their infidelity. According to the narratives of Israel's wandering in the wilderness, Yahweh even allowed an entire generation of the people to fulfill the desire of their fears: to die in the wilderness rather than to enter the struggle before them, thus never to taste the fruit of the promised land.[50]

Even as General Santa Anna besieged the Alamo, on 2 March 1836, the government of Texas, convening at Washington-on-the-Brazos, declared its independence from Mexico. Before receiving news about the Texan declaration of independence, William Barrett Travis, a co-commandant of the volunteers in the Alamo, on 3 March 1836 wrote to the colonies in Texas a lengthy and final appeal for aid. Carried by John Smith, Travis's final communiqué arrived at the Convention on Sunday, 6 March 1836, the day during which both the Alamo fell and bonfires

---

[50]Galatians 6:6-10; Romans 1:18-32; Numbers 13:25-33; 14:1-45.

consumed its dead defenders. In his letter, Travis boldly observed the following about both those with whom he served and those against whom they would stand together in the imminent final encounters.

> I will, however, do the best I can under the circumstances; and I feel confident that the determined valor, and desperate courage, heretofore evinced by my men, will not fail them in the last struggle: and although they may be sacrificed to the vengeance of a gothic enemy, *the victory will cost the enemy so dear, that it will be worse for him than a defeat.*[51]

Fierce combat during the following three days proved the truth of Travis's prophetic communiqué.

Without a doubt, the fundamentalists have vanquished their enemies in the SBC. Through their theological and political revisions of the SBC, however, the fundamentalists have effectively dissolved the SBC's genuine Baptist substance. The name "Baptist," as understood by the SBC for at least 130 years, really no longer belongs in the organizational name: "Southern *Baptist* Convention." The historic spiritual worth, value, significance, weight, or wealth—that is to say, the glory—of the name "Baptist" has almost completed its departure from the SBC. Even now, as credalism strengthens its grip through the theological and political revisions of the SBC, across the name "Southern Baptist Convention," a

---

[51]William Barrett Travis, commandancy of the Alamo, Bejar, to the president of the Convention, 3 March 1836, in "The General Convention at Washington, March 1-17, 1836," in *The Laws of Texas: 1822–1897*, vol. 1, pt. 2, ed. H. P. N. Gammel (Houston: 1838) 846 (26), emphasis mine; also in *Telegraph and Texas Register* (12 March 1836). Numerous collections include this letter: "Travis to Convention," in *The Papers of the Texas Revolution 1835–1836*, vol. 4, ed. John H. Jenkins (Austin: Presidial Press, 1973), 502-504 (2234); "William B. Travis to the President of the Convention," in *100 Days in Texas: The Alamo Letters*, ed. Wallace O. Chariton (Plano TX: Wordware Publishing, 1990) 304-305; "Travis' Last Appeal for Aid," in *Documents of Texas History*, 2nd ed., ed. Ernest Wallace, David M. Vigness, and George B. Ward (Austin TX: State House Press, 1994) 96-97. See Bill Leonard's interpretation of the response by Baptists in Texas to fundamentalist oppression in the SBC, as an analogue to the resolute independence of Texans during their revolutionary struggles (Leonard, "Lone Star Baptists," *The Christian Century* [20 April 1994]: 404-406). The Alamo itself also functioned symbolically for Moderate Baptists during the SBC's annual meeting in 1988, following the SBC's adoption of the reductive and deceptive "Resolution No. 5—On the Priesthood of the Believer" (*Annual of the SBC* [1988]: 68-69). According to Arthur Emery Farnsley II, "the moderates were shaken." As Farnsley reports it, "in a fit of rebellious anger, some of them marched to the Alamo singing 'We Shall Overcome' " (Farnsley, *Southern Baptist Politics*, 82).

new word has begun to appear, a judgment indelibly scorched into the coercive spirit of the new SBC: *Ichabod*.[52] Most certainly, the fundamentalist victory, as represented in the theological and political revisions of the SBC, has cost the victors more dearly than any sort of defeat they could have suffered, for it has cost the SBC its very soul: the SBC's glory has departed along with its genuine Baptist substance.

Only if Baptists in the SBC resist both the SBC's theological revision, as expressed through the *RPTSC*'s credalism, and its political revi-

---

[52]When the Philistines defeated Israel, captured the Ark of the Covenant, and killed the sons of Eli, on receiving the news, the old priest fell backward, broke his neck, and died. The pregnant wife of Phinehas, one of Eli's two slain sons, went into labor and gave birth to a son. Before she died as a result of the difficult delivery, Eli's daughter-in-law named her newborn son "Ichabod," a name that literally means "no glory." As she died, she explained her reasons for naming her son in this way. Israel's enemies had captured the Ark, and both her father-in-law and her husband had died: "and she said, 'The glory (*kabod*) has departed from Israel, for the ark of God was taken' " (1 Samuel 4:21-22 NASB). Clearly, in the Ark of the Covenant, the Hebrews perceived the divine glory and presence, just as the Ark's absence represented the departure of God's presence from their midst. This cycle of stories about the Ark's loss and return also contains fascinating and ironic references to Yahweh's glory. The basic meaning of the term "*kabod*," the Hebrew word meaning *glory*, contains the ideas of *weight, heaviness*, even *fat* or *wealth*, through which the term conveys the worth, importance, weightiness, honor, or significance of that which it describes or to which it refers. This word also connotes beauty, radiance, and light (Edmond Jacob, *Theology of the Old Testament*, trans. Arthur W. Heathcote and Philip J. Allcock [New York: Harper & Row, 1958] 79-82). After Eli died from his backward fall, the narrator explains that he broke his neck, because "he was old and heavy (*kabod*)" (1 Samuel 4:18 NASB). In this event, some ambiguity appears, however. As a righteous priest, the priest who had taught Samuel, Eli expressed something of the divine glory himself, inasmuch as age meant wisdom and weight meant honor and wealth among ancient Hebrews. Nonetheless, insofar as Eli's sons had abused their own priestly offices (1 Samuel 2:12-17, 22-25), a man from God had prophesied divine judgment against Eli's family, because Eli had tolerated the sins of his sons. Speaking with the voice of Yahweh, this prophet of God inquired as follows: "Why do you kick at My sacrifice and at My offering which I have commanded *in My* dwelling, and honor (*kabod*) your sons above Me, by making yourselves fat with the choicest of every offering of My people Israel?" (1 Samuel 2:29 NASB). Thus, perhaps in explaining Eli's broken neck by his age and heaviness, the narrator also seeks to emphasize the inertia in the senility, impotence, and indulgence of a priest who had compromised his calling. Later, the narrator adds that, while the Philistines kept the Ark, hemorrhoids afflicted them. The narrator explains this by saying that "the hand of Yahweh was heavy (*kabod*)" on them (1 Samuel 5:6, 11 NASB). Thus, the narrator discloses a paradox: the divine glory's presence burdens the unbeliever as much as its absence impoverishes and troubles the believer.

sion, as realized in the *CNC*, can the SBC regain its genuine Baptist substance. Without the resolute involvement of all Baptists in this task, however, a self-inflicted *cataclysm* approaches the SBC. In fact, perhaps the word "cataclysm" most fittingly designates the imminent destiny of the SBC for Baptists. Originating from the Greek noun, ὁ κατακλυσμὸς, constructed by combining two Greek terms, a preposition meaning "down" and a verb meaning "to wash," the word "cataclysm" designates a deluge, a flood, or an inundation. In the Septuagint or the Greek translation of the Hebrew scriptures, the translators used a form of ὁ κατα-κλυσμὸς to translate the Hebrew word for flood in the story of Noah's ark. The New Testament also uses nominal and verbal forms of this word in references to the narrative about Noah and the flood.[53] Given the attestation to God's grief over the world's sin prior to the flood in Genesis 6:5-6, one may poetically conceive the cataclysm on the world's sin as the loving tears of divine grief. Such a self-inflicted baptism, however, does not approach the SBC as blessing. The cataclysm unleashed by the theological and political revisions of the SBC approaches as destruction.

With these studies, I have endeavored to expose and to resist the deadly presence of credalism among Baptists in the SBC. I have argued, first, that the *RPTSC*, including the processes leading to its production and adoption, represents the most serious credal threat in the SBC's history. As a second essential dimension in my exposure of and resistance to the credalism promoted by this document, I have argued that this document, although credal, veils or camouflages its credalism with the SBC's historic confessional language. As a third essential dimension in this critical examination of the *RPTSC*, I have argued that this document's credal components arise primarily from a Calvinistic theological heritage and, although also veiled to some extent, promote a Calvinistic political agenda. In a fourth and final dimension of my study, I have argued that the restructuring of the SBC supplies the political structures of power with which to enforce credalism in the SBC. Analogically, I have referred to my exposure of and resistance to the credalism in the *RPTSC* as my decision against returning to Egyptian bondage. In this decision, I have tried to follow the apostle Paul's urgent advice to the Christians in Galatia: "It was for freedom that Christ set us free; therefore keep standing firm and do not be subject again to a yoke of slavery"

---

[53]Genesis 6:17 (LXX); Matthew 24:38-39; Luke 17:27; 2 Peter 2:5; 3:6.

(Galatians 5:1 NASB). I urgently invite all Baptists in the SBC to engage actively in this task as well. The cataclysm approaches.

> We are called to be God's prophets,
>   Spokesmen for the truth and right;
> Standing firm for godly justice,
>   Bringing evil into light.
> Let us seek the courage needed,
>   Our high calling to fulfill,
> That mankind may know the blessing
> Of the doing of God's will.[54]

Mox nox in rem.
Soon night, to the task!

---

[54]"We Are Called to Be God's People," lyrics by Thomas A. Jackson, tune ("Austrian Hymn") by Franz Joseph Haydn (1797), in *Baptist Hymnal* (Nashville: Convention Press, 1975) no. 405, verse 3; likewise *The Baptist Hymnal* (1991) no. 390. Although I prefer to use more gender-inclusive language than terms such as "spokesmen" and "mankind," I have chosen to quote the text of this hymn as it was written and is still used, not altering the text from which I have quoted. As the SBC declared in both 1945 and 1946, "the Christian movement is not isolated from the common concerns of mankind, but as a declarative, *prophetic movement* charged with a gospel for men in all relations, is a leavening and instructing agency in the midst of society for the good of the human race and the glory of God in the coming of His kingdom" (*SP [1946]*, 38-39; emphasis mine).

Appendixes

Appendix 1

"Resolution No. 3.
On the Presidential Theological Study Committee"

I have included the complete text of the SBC's "Resolution No. 3—On the Presidential Theological Study Committee," as printed in the SBC's annual proceedings (*Annual of the Southern Baptist Convention. One Hundred Thirty-Seventh Session. Orlando, Florida. June 14-16, 1994: 102*). I have indicated the page number from the SBC's *Annual* in brackets at the left margin of the page, at the beginning of the document.

[102] **145.** Tommy D. Lea (TX) moved the adoption of Resolution 3. Resolution 3 was adopted.

RESOLUTION NO. 3.
ON THE PRESIDENTIAL THEOLOGICAL STUDY COMMITTEE

WHEREAS, President H. Edwin Young appointed the Presidential Theological Study Committee, chaired by Timothy F. George and Roy L. Honeycutt, and including William E. Bell, J. Walter Carpenter, Jr., Mark T. Coppenger, Stephen D. C. Corts, Carl F. H. Henry, Herschel H. Hobbs, Richard D. Land, R. Albert Mohler, Jr., and William B. Tolar; and

WHEREAS, President Young commissioned the committee to examine those biblical truths that are most surely held among the people of God called Southern Baptists and, on this basis, to reaffirm our common commitment to Jesus Christ, the Holy Scriptures, and the evangelical heritage of the Christian church; and

WHEREAS, The report was announced in May 1993, and circulated among the messengers to the Southern Baptist Convention, meeting in Houston, Texas, June 15-17, 1993; and

WHEREAS, In light of the pressing need for a positive biblical witness on basic Christian beliefs, and in light of the questions raised in recent days concerning historic biblical and Baptist doctrine; and

WHEREAS, The report has been issued not as a new confession of faith, but rather as a reaffirmation of major doctrinal concerns set forth in the *Baptist Faith and Message* of 1963.

Therefore, Be it RESOLVED, That we, the messengers to the Southern Baptist Convention meeting in Orlando, Florida, June 14-16, 1994, commend the Report of the Presidential Theological Study Committee to the institutions and agencies of the Southern Baptist Convention as a guide to enable them to bear a faithful gospel witness to a culture in disarray, to be salt and light in a society that has lost its moral compass, and to serve as a resource for a new denominational consensus rooted in theological substance and doctrinal fidelity.

Be it finally RESOLVED, that we encourage the Executive Committee to print the full text of the Report of the Presidential Theological Study Committee in the *1994 Southern Baptist Convention Annual*, and we also encourage the Baptist Sunday School Board to publish and disseminate the report among Southern Baptists.

Appendix 2

"Report of the Presidential Theological Study Committee"

I have included here the complete text of the "Report of the Presidential Theological Study Committee" (*RPTSC*; from *Annual of the Southern Baptist Convention*. One Hundred Thirty-Seventh Session. Orlando, Florida. June 14-16, 1994: 112-18). In my citations of this document, I have referred to the version of this text as printed in the SBC's annual proceedings. For that reason, I have placed the page numbers of the text from the SBC's *Annual* in brackets at the beginning of each page (e.g., [113]). In my citations of the *RPTSC*, I have also referred to parts, articles, and paragraphs (e.g., [2.1.1]) in this document. Since I numbered the paragraphs in this document, I have included those numbers (or part designations) in brackets with each paragraph here.

[112]   **Report of the Presidential Theological Study Committee**

[Introduction] The Theological Study Committee was appointed by SBC President H. Edwin Young in 1992 and submitted its report in the spring of the following year. The purpose of this study group was to examine those biblical truths which are most surely held among the people of God called Southern Baptists and, on this basis, to reaffirm our common commitment to Jesus Christ, the Holy Scriptures, and the evangelical heritage of the Christian church. In light of the pressing need for a positive biblical witness on basic Christian beliefs, this report is published, not as a new confession of faith, but rather as a reaffirmation of major doctrinal concerns set forth in the *Baptist Faith and Message* of 1963.

Part I

[113] [1.1] In every generation, the people of God face the decision either to reaffirm "the faith which was once delivered unto the saints" (Jude 3) or to lapse into theological unbelief. Precisely such a challenge now confronts that people of God called Southern Baptists.

[1.2] As we approach the 150th anniversary of the founding of the Southern Baptist Convention, we are presented with unprecedented opportunities for missionary outreach and evangelistic witness at home and abroad. We must bear a faithful gospel witness to a culture in decline; we must be the salt and light in a society which has lost its moral compass. We must also pass on to the rising generation the fundamentals of the Christian faith and a vital sense of our Baptist heritage. To meet these goals, we seek to move beyond the denominational conflict of recent years toward a new consensus rooted in theological substance

and doctrinal fidelity. We pray that our effort will lead to healing and reconciliation throughout the Southern Baptist Convention and, God willing, to a
renewed commitment to our founding purpose of "eliciting, combining, and
directing the energies of the whole denomination in one sacred effort, for the
propagation of the gospel."

[1.3] Baptists are a people of firm conviction and free confession. Southern
Baptists have expressed and affirmed these convictions through *The Baptist Faith
and Message* confessional statements of 1925 and 1963.

[1.4] This committee affirms and honors *The Baptist Faith and Message*, as
overwhelmingly adopted by the 1963 Convention, embraced by millions of
faithful Southern Baptists and their churches, affirmed by successive convention
sessions and adopted by SBC agencies, as the normative expression of Southern
Baptist belief. Therefore, this committee declines to recommend any new
confession or revision of that statement.

[1.5] However, each generation of Southern Baptists faces unique and
pressing challenges to faithfulness which demand attention and test the integrity
of our conviction. This report addresses several issues of contemporary urgency
in a spirit of pastoral concern and a commitment to the unity of our Baptist
fellowship as well as the integrity of our doctrinal confession. These emphases
are intended to illuminate articles of *The Baptist Faith and Message*, consistent
with its intention and content, and are thus commended to the Convention, its
agencies, its churches, and the millions of Bible-believing, cooperating Southern
Baptists who freely join this Convention in its sacred work. We seek to clarify
our historic Baptist commitment to Holy Scripture, the doctrine of God, the
person and work of Jesus Christ, the nature and mission of the church, and
biblical teaching on last things. We reaffirm our commitment to these great
theological tenets since they are assailed, in various ways, by subtle compromise,
blatant concession, and malign negligence.

[1.6] We also affirm the historic Baptist conception of the nature and function of confessional statements in our religious and denominational life. Baptists
approve and circulate confessions of faith with the following understandings:

[1.7] • **As an expression of our religious liberty.** Any group of Baptists,
large or small, has the inherent right to draw up for itself and to publish to the
world a confession of faith whenever it wishes. As a corollary of this principle,
we reject state imposed religious creeds and attendant civil sanctions.

[1.8] • **As a statement of our religious convictions.** We affirm the priesthood of all believers and the autonomy of each local congregation. However,
doctrinal minimalism and theological revision, left unchecked, compromises [*sic*]
a commitment to the gospel itself. Being Baptist means faith as well as freedom.
Christian liberty should not become a license for the masking of unbelief.

[1.9] • **As a witness to our confidence in divine revelation.** The sole
authority for faith and practice among Baptists is the Bible, God's Holy Word.

It is the supreme standard by which [114] all creeds, conduct, and religious opinions should be tried. As in the past so in the future, Baptists should hold themselves free to revise their statements of faith in the light of an unchanging Holy Scripture.

[1.10] None of these principles, sacred to Baptists through the ages, is violated by voluntary, conscientious adherence to an explicit doctrinal standard. Holy living and sound doctrine are indispensable elements of true revival and genuine reconciliation among any body of Christian believers. Desiring this end with all our hearts, we commend the following report to the people of God called Southern Baptists.

Part II
Article One
Holy Scripture

[2.1.1] Southern Baptists have affirmed repeatedly and decisively an unswerving commitment to the divine inspiration and truthfulness of Holy Scripture, the Word of God revealed in written form. We believe that what the Bible says, God says. What the Bible says happened, really happened. Every miracle, every event, in every one of the 66 books of the Old and New Testaments is true and trustworthy. In 1900, James M. Frost, first president of the Baptist Sunday School Board, declared: "We accept the Scriptures as an all-sufficient and infallible rule of faith and practice, and insist upon the absolute inerrancy and sole authority of the Word of God. We recognize at this point no room for division, either of practice or belief, or even sentiment. More and more we must come to feel as the deepest and mightiest power of our conviction that a 'thus saith the Lord' is the end of all controversy."

[2.1.2] *The Baptist Faith and Message* affirms this high view of Scripture by declaring that the Bible "has God for it [*sic*] author, salvation for its end, and truth [*sic*] without any mixture of error, for its matter." The chairman of the committee who drafted this statement, Herschel Hobbs, explained this phrase by reference to II Timothy 3:16 which says, "all Scripture is given by inspiration of God." He explained: "The Greek New Testament reads 'all'—without the definite article and that means every single part of the whole is God-breathed. And a God of truth does not breathe error."

[2.1.3] Recent developments in Southern Baptist life have underscored the importance of a renewed commitment to biblical authority in every area of our denominational life.

[2.1.4] In 1986, the presidents of the six SBC seminaries issued the *Glorieta Statement* which affirmed the "infallible power and binding authority" of the Bible, declaring it to be "not errant in any area of reality." The miracles of the Old and New Testaments were described as "historical evidences of God's judgment, love, and redemption."

[2.1.5] In 1987, the SBC Peace Committee called upon Southern Baptist institutions to recruit faculty and staff who clearly reflect the dominant convictions and beliefs of Southern Baptists concerning the factual character and historicity of the Bible in such matters as (1) the direct creation of humankind including Adam and Eve as real persons; (2) the actual authorship of biblical writings as attributed by Scripture itself; (3) the supernatural character of the biblical miracles which occurred as factual events in space and time; (4) the historical accuracy of biblical narratives which occurred precisely as the text of Scripture indicates.

[2.1.6] In 1991, the Baptist Sunday School Board published the first volume of the *New American Commentary*, a projected 40-volume series of theological exposition on every book of the Bible. The commentary was intended to reflect a "commitment to the inerrancy of Scripture" and "the classic Christian tradition." The *Chicago Statement on Biblical Inerrancy* was adopted as a guideline more fully expressing for writers the intent of Article 1 of *The Baptist Faith and* [115] *Message.*

[2.1.7] In light of these historical commitments, we call upon all Southern Baptists:

- to foster a deep reverence and genuine love for the Word of God in personal, congregational, and denominational life;
- to use the Scriptures in personal evangelistic witnessing, since they are "able to make one wise unto salvation";
- to read the Bible faithfully and to study it systematically; and
- to encourage the translation and dissemination of the Bible throughout the world.

[2.1.8] We commend to all Baptist educational institutions and agencies the *Report of the Peace Committee* (1987), the *Chicago Statement on Biblical Inerrancy* (1978), and the *Chicago Statement on Biblical Hermeneutics* (1982) as biblically grounded and sound guides worthy of respect in setting forth a high view of Scripture. We encourage them to cultivate a biblical world view in all disciplines of learning and to pursue a reverent, believing approach to biblical scholarship that is both exegetically honest and theologically sound. There need be no contradiction between "firm faith and free research" as long as both are exercised under the Lordship of Jesus Christ and in full confidence of the truthfulness of His Word.

Article Two
The Doctrine of God

[2.2.1] The God revealed in Holy Scripture is the sovereign God who created the worlds and all therein, the God who called Israel out from the nations as a witness to His name, the God who spoke from a burning bush, and the God who decisively and definitively revealed Himself through His Son, Jesus Christ, through whom He brought redemption and reconciliation.

[2.2.2] Baptists, and all evangelical Christians, recognize the centrality of biblical theism. We honor and worship the one true God and our first act of worship is to acknowledge Him even as He has revealed Himself.

[2.2.3] This means that we affirm God's nature as revealed in Holy Scripture. He alone has the right to define Himself, and He has done so by revealing His power and His grace, seen in His absolute holiness and love.

[2.2.4] The biblical doctrine of God has been compromised in recent years as efforts to redefine God have rejected clear biblical teachings in the face of modern challenges. Southern Baptists cannot follow this course. As a fellowship of evangelical Christians we must recommit ourselves to the eternal truths concerning God, even as He has freely, graciously, and definitively revealed Himself. As Norvell Robertson, one of our earliest Southern Baptist theologians wrote: "The Word of God is truth. What He says of Himself is true [sic] . . . He alone knows Himself."

[2.2.5] Thus, we must submit ourselves to the knowledge God has imparted concerning Himself and His divine nature.

[2.2.6] First, Baptists affirm that God is limitless in power, knowledge, wisdom, love, and holiness. He suffers no limitations upon His power or His personality. He is not constrained by any external force or internal contradiction. We reject any effort to redefine God as a limited deity.

[2.2.7] Second, Baptists affirm that God, the Father of our Lord Jesus Christ, is none other than the God of Abraham, Isaac, and Jacob, of Sarah, and Rachel, and Ruth. God's self-revelation in Scripture is progressive, but fully consistent. He is the universal Creator and thus deserves universal recognition and worship as the one true God.

[2.2.8] Third, Baptists affirm that God is one, and that he has revealed Himself as a Trinity of three eternally co-existent persons, Father, Son, and Holy Spirit. We acknowledge the Trinity as [116] essential and central to our Christian confession, and we reject any attempt to minimize or compromise this aspect of God's self-disclosure.

[2.2.9] Fourth, Baptists affirm that God has revealed Himself as the Father of the redeemed. Jesus characteristically addressed God as His Father and instructed His disciples to do the same. We have no right to reject God's own name for Himself, nor to employ impersonal or feminine names in order to placate modern sensitivities. We honor the integrity of God's name and acknowledge His sole right to name Himself even as we affirm that no human words can exhaust the divine majesty. But God has accommodated Himself to us by naming Himself in human words.

[2.2.10] Fifth, Baptists affirm that God is the sovereign Creator of the universe, who called all things into being by the power of His Word, and who created the worlds out of nothing. His creative acts were free and unconstrained by any other creative force.

[2.2.11] Sixth, Baptists affirm that God is sovereign over history, nature, time, and space and that His loving and gracious providence sustains and orders the world.

[2.2.12] These statements, based upon Scripture and undergirded by historic Baptist confessions, force our attention to contemporary compromises which threaten the fidelity and integrity of our faith.

[2.2.13] We call upon the Southern Baptist Convention, its churches, and its institutions to beware lest revisionist views of God such as those popularly modelled in process and feminist theologies, as well as the esoteric doctrines of the New Age movement, compromise our faithful commitment to biblical truth.

Article Three
The Person and Work of Christ

[2.3.1] Jesus Christ is the center and circumference of the Christian faith. The God of heaven and earth has revealed Himself supremely and definitively in the Son, and the most fundamental truth of Christianity is that "God was in Christ, reconciling the world unto Himself" (II Cor. 5:19).

[2.3.2] Jesus Christ is the sole and sufficient Savior of the redeemed throughout the world and of all ages. He is the divine Word by which the worlds were created; He is also the unique and solitary Savior in whom alone there is redemption and forgiveness of sins. From beginning to end the Bible proclaims salvation through Jesus Christ and no other. The Church is commanded to teach and preach no other gospel.

[2.3.3] In His incarnation—an event in historical space and time—Jesus Christ was the perfect union of the human and the divine. He was truly God and truly man, born of a virgin and without sin, remaining sinless throughout His earthly incarnation. He was crucified, died, and was buried. On the third day, He rose from the dead, the first fruits of the redeemed. He ascended to the Father and now rules as King and Judge. He will consummate the age by His physical return to earth as Lord and King.

[2.3.4] Scripture bears faithful and truthful witness to Jesus Christ. The words and deeds of Christ set forth in the New Testament are an accurate record of what He said and did, even as the Old Testament prophetically revealed His identity and His purpose of redemption. The miracles of Jesus as revealed to us in Scripture were historical events which demonstrated Christ's identity and His power over sin, death, and Satan.

[2.3.5] All human beings, marked by original sin and their own individual sins, are utterly helpless before God and without excuse, deserving of eternal punishment and separation from God. Nevertheless, in Jesus Christ and His cross, God revealed both the extent of our lostness and the depth of His redemptive love. All human beings—in all places and of all ages—are lost but for [117] salvation through Jesus Christ. He is the only hope of salvation and the only Savior.

[2.3.6] Christ's redemption was wrought by His atonement which was both penal and substitutionary. Christ died in our place, bearing in His body the penalty for our sin and purchasing our redemption by His blood.

[2.3.7] The cross of Christ is thus the apex of God's plan of redemption, revealing God's absolute holiness and infinite love. The gospel of that cross is the only message which can and does save.

[2.3.8] The redeemed are justified before God by grace through faith in Jesus Christ, trusting in Him alone for their salvation and acknowledging Him as Savior and Lord.

[2.3.9] Therefore, Baptists must reject any effort to deny the true nature and identity of Jesus Christ or to minimize or to redefine His redemptive work. Baptists must reject any and all forms of universalism and bear faithful witness to salvation in Jesus Christ, and in Him alone. Furthermore, Baptists must join with all true Christians in affirming the substitutionary nature of Christ's atonement and reject calls—ancient and modern—for redefining Christ's reconciling work as merely subjective and illustrative.

Article Four
The Church

[2.4.1] We acknowledge Jesus Christ not only as personal Savior and Lord, but also as the Head, Foundation, Lawgiver, and Teacher of the church which is His building, body, and bride. The person who despises the church despises Christ, for "Christ . . . loved the church, and gave Himself for it" (Eph. 5:25).

[2.4.2] In the New Testament the word "church" sometimes refers to all of the redeemed of all ages but, more often, to a local assembly of baptized believers. Until Jesus comes again the local church is a "colony of heaven" (Phil. 3:20), a "sounding board" of the gospel (1 Thes. 1:8), and a fellowship through which God's people carry out the Great Commission of their Lord. The central purpose of the church is to honor and glorify God; the central task of the church is to bear witness to the gospel of Jesus Christ through evangelism and missions.

[2.4.3] In light of this mandate, we call upon all Southern Baptists to reaffirm our commitment to these distinctive principles of our Baptist heritage:

[2.4.4] •   **The priesthood of all believers.** Every Christian has direct access to God through Jesus Christ, our great High Priest, the sole mediator between God and human beings. However, the priesthood of all believers is exercised within a committed community of fellow believers-priests [sic] who share a like precious faith. The priesthood of all believers should not be reduced to modern individualism nor used as a cover for theological relativism. It is a

spiritual standing which leads to ministry, service, and a coherent witness in the
world for which Christ died.

[2.4.5] • **The autonomy of the local church.** A New Testament church
is a gathered congregation of baptized believers who have entered into covenant
with Christ and with one another to fulfil, according to the Scriptures, their
mutual obligations. Under the Lordship of Christ, such a body is free to order its
own internal life without interference from any external group. This same
freedom applies to all general Baptist bodies, such as associations and state and
national conventions. Historically, Baptist churches have freely cooperated in
matters of common interest without compromise of beliefs. We affirm the
wisdom of convictional cooperation in carrying out our witness to the world and
decry all efforts to weaken our denomination and its cooperative ministries.

[2.4.6] • **A free church in a free state.** Throughout our history, Baptists
have not wavered in our belief that God intends for a free church to function in
a free state. Since God alone is Lord [118] of the conscience, the temporal realm
has no authority to coerce religious commitments. However, the doctrine of
religious liberty, far from implying doctrinal laxity or unconcern, guarantees the
ability of every congregation and general Baptist body to determine (on the basis
of the Word of God) its [sic] own doctrinal and disciplinary parameters.

[2.4.7] We declare our fervent commitment to these distinctive convictions
of the Baptist tradition. We also call for a renewed emphasis on the faithful
proclamation of God's Word, believers' baptism by immersion, and the celebra-
tion of the Lord's Supper as central elements of corporate worship.

Article Five
Last Things

[2.5.1] With all true Christians everywhere, Baptists confess that "Christ has
died, Christ is risen, Christ will come again." The God who has acted in the past,
and is acting even now, will continue to act bringing to final consummation his
eternal purpose in Jesus Christ. Our faith rests in the confidence that the future
is in His hands.

[2.5.2] While detailed interpretations of the end times should not be made
a test of fellowship among Southern Baptists, we affirm with confidence the clear
teaching of Holy Scripture on these essential doctrinal truths:

[2.5.3] • **The return of Jesus Christ in glory.** Christians await with
certainty and expectancy the "blessed hope" of the outward, literal, visible, and
personal return of Jesus Christ to consummate history in victory and judgment.
As E. Y. Mullins put it, "He will come again in person, the same Jesus who
ascended from the Mount of Olives."

[2.5.4] • **The resurrection of the body.** In his glorious resurrection,
Jesus Christ broke the bonds of death, establishing his authority over it, and one
day He will assert that authority on our behalf and raise us. The righteous dead

will be raised unto life everlasting. The unrighteous dead will be cast into hell which is the second death (Rev. 20:14-15).

[2.5.5] • **Eternal punishment and eternal bliss.** Following the resurrection and judgment, the redeemed shall be forever with the Lord in heaven, a place of light and glory beyond description, and the lost shall be forever with the devil in hell, a place of utter darkness and inexpressible anguish. Nowhere does the Bible teach the annihilation of the soul or a temporary purgatory for those who die without hope in Christ.

[2.5.6] The second coming of Christ is the blessed, comforting, and purifying hope of the church. We call upon all Southern Baptists to claim this precious promise in every area of our life and witness, and thus "to live holy and godly lives as we look forward to the day of God and speed its coming" (II Peter 3:11).

Indexes

Index of Persons

Chapman, Morris H., viii, viiin.4, ix, 78, 79, 79n.1, 163n.20, 284n.24

Childs, Brevard S., 189n.33

Chrysostom, John, 173

Clark, Henry W., 304n.47

Clarke, Frank, 235n.81

Clement of Alexandria, 173

Clinton, President William Jefferson, 265, 265n.41

Cody, Z. T., 49n.15, 144n.4

Cole, G. A., 175n.7

Colonnese, Louis M., 273n.5

Conner, W. T., 198n.11, 217, 217n.40, 217n.41, 220, 220n.53, 221n.55, 222n.56, 222n.58, 223-24n.60, 226, 226n.63, 227n.64, 228-29n.68, 230-31n.71, 232n.76

Copass, B. A., 154-55n.3, 188n.31, 230n.69, 254n.24

Coppenger, Mark T., 1n.1, 3, 26n.24, 81, 83, 172, 173n.4, 181n.20, 197n.9, 204n.21, 311

Corts, Stephen D. C., 1n.1, 311

Cothen, Grady C., 4n.5, 244n.11, 272, 272n.3

Crockett, William, 133n.35

Cross, Frank Moore, 179n.16

Culpepper, R. Alan, 92n.34

Curtis, T. F., 61n.38

Cyril of Alexandria, 194n.5

Dansby, Karen, xix

Dargan, Edwin C., 48, 48-49n.14, 67n.3

Dehoney, Wayne, xin.5, 2-3n.3, 53, 53n.24, 155n.4

Delitsch, Friedrich, 179n.16

Denzinger, Henricus, 192n.2, 192n.3

Descartes, René, 174n.7

DeVine, Mark, 250n.17, 284n.24

Deweese, Charles, viiin.3, 6n.6, 35n.37, 128n.29

Dhorme, E. P., 179, 179n.16

Dilday, Russell H., vii, xiii, xiiin.7, xiv, 5n.5, 118, 119n.12, 305

Dilday, Russell, N., 257n.29

Dillenberger, John, 185n.27, 266n.44, 304n.47

Dinkins, David, xviii

Dobney, Henry Hamlet, 134n.35

Dockery, David S., xn.5, xin.5, 7n.7, 18n.17, 21n.19, 34n.35, 42n.5, 56n.30,

59n.35, 90n.29, 91n.32, 104n.58, 104n.59, 132n.33, 142n.2, 154n.3, 156, 156n.5, 156n.7, 161n.16, 248n.15, 277, 277n.12

Dorner, Isaak August, 185n.27

Draper, James T., Jr., 79, 79n.2, 145-46, 145n.7, 213n.34

Draughon, Walter D., III, 221n.55

Druin, Toby, 258n.29

Dudley, Bill, 81n.8

Dunn, James M., 29n.28

Eagleson, John, 274n.6

Eastwood, Cyril, 240n.4

Edmunds, Lidie H., 1n.**

Edwards, David L., 133n.35

Elder, Loyd, 305

Elliff, Tom, 162n.19

Elliott, Ralph H., xviii-xix, 161n.15, 278n.14

Ellyson, William, 49n.15,

Estep, William R., xviii, 7n.7, 51n.16, 88n.25, 163, 163n.20, 298n.43

Falkenberg, Steven D., 85n.18, 163n.21

Farnsley, Arthur Emery II, 244n.11, 307n.51

Faunce, W. H. P., 286, 286n.27

Ferguson, Robert U., Jr., xin.5, 7n.7,

Ferré, Frederick P., 166n.25

Fiddes, Paul S., 188n.31, 216n.39, 217n.41, 222n.57, 224n.60, 228n.65, 228n.67, 230n.70

Fiori, Ernani, 273n.5

Fletcher, Jesse C., 46n.9, 50n.16

Foerster, Werner, 235n.80

Fohrer, Georg, 233n.78

Franck, Sebastian, 298n.43

Franks, Robert S., 217n.42, 228n.65, 229n.69

Freeman, Harold, xviii

Freire, Paulo, 273, 273n.5, 279-80, 280n.15, 286n.26, 292-93, 293n.35

Fretheim, Terence E., 186n.28, 190, 190n.35

Frost, James Marion, 56n.30, 59, 59n.35, 86, 88n.26, 90, 97, 98-99, 98n.43, 98n.44, 99, 99n.45, 99n.46, 99n.48, 144n.4, 153, 154n.1, 315

Fudge, Edward, 133n.35

Fuller, R., 61n.38

Index of Topics

absolute certainty, 14, 19
absolute knowledge, 14
accommodation, divine, 173-76, 174n.6
affliction, divine, 201
agoraphobia, 288-89
Alamo, 306-307, 307n.51
alterity, 279-82, 288-89
ambiguity, xii, 63, 87, 123, 124, 136, 146, 168, 169, 264
Anabaptists, xiii, 208, 208n.28, 298, 298n.43, 299
analeptic intention, 27
Andover Newton Theological School, 84
annihilationism, 133-34, 133n.35, 321
anthropology (theological), 123-24, 193
Antitrinitarianism, 298n.43
aporetics of faith, 28-31
Ark of the Covenant, 308n.52
Arminianism, 144n.4, 148
arrogance of fundamentalists, 295
assailment of Baptist doctrine, 40-44
atonement, 82, 84n.16, 135, 144n.4, 175n.8, 191, 319
atonement, limited, 229-30n.69, 231, 231n.74
Augustinianism, 203, 204, 210
authority, 15-16, 49n.14, 58-59, 58-59n.35, 68, 70, 77-109, 142n.2, 147, 149, 167-68, 243n.11, 248, 250n.17, 254, 256, 258n.29, 259n.30, 277, 278n.14, 285n.25, 301, 314-15
autographs (of scripture), 153-61
autonomy of the local church, xvii, 70, 117, 126-28, 144, 237, 247, 249-50, 268, 291n.33, 314, 319

Babylon, 303-304n.47
baptism, 144, 205, 207, 249n.16, 298, 309, 320
baptismal register, 304
Baptist freedom fighters, xiii, xiv
Baptist identity, xiii, 47n.11, 56n.30, 132n.33, 141, 142n.2, 143, 145, 148
Baptist-hunter, xiv, 298-99
Baptists, General, 133-34n.35
Baptists, Particular, 133-34n.35
barbarity, proper, 276n.11

becoming human of God, 162, 187, 189, 193, 200, 201, 211, 212, 213, 214-15, 214n.37, 215, 224n.60
Beeson Divinity School, 147, 197n.9
BGCT, 258n.29
bondage, 22, 22n.21
BP, xxiv, 305
brutality, 276, 276n.11
BSSB, xxiv, 98-99, 101n.52, 107, 305, 316

Calvinism, 5, 47n.11, 100, 100-101n.51, 143, 143-44n.4, 144, 148, 156, 156n.5, 157, 158, 172, 172-73n.4, 183, 183n.24, 187, 193, 199, 202, 203, 204, 205, 206, 206n.26, 207, 209, 210, 212, 215, 218n.45, 225n.61, 231, 263-68, 299
Cambellism, 144n.4
cataclysm, 309
catechisms, Baptist, 291n.32
Chalcedon, Council of, 192, 194, 194n.7
challenge to reaffirm faithfulness to doctrine, 55-57
Chinese curse, 272
Christ, xii, 148, 158, 159, 161, 166-69, 242-43
Christian life, 149
Christology, 135, 147, 149, 182, 190, 192-201, 209-15, 318-19
Christus victor theory of atonement, 217, 221n.55
chronos, 272
clarity of the *BFM (1963)*, 52-55
CLC, xxiv, 264, 305
coercion, 15-16, 20-21, 21n.19, 60, 145, 258n.29, 259n.30, 262, 266n.44, 282, 298, 299, 299n.45, 300, 303, 308
Coercive Program, 282
Committee on Resolutions, 3n.3, 66n.3, 67n.3, 75, 80n.5, 80-83, 247n.13
communio, 9
community, xvii, 9, 17, 238-39, 250n.17, 278-85
competence before God, xvii, 122-24, 124n.22, 238-39, 239-40n.3, 245, 291n.33
conditional immortality, 133, 133n.35
Conditionalist Association, 134n.35

Index of Scriptures

Index of Documents

Against Returning to Egypt.
Exposing and Resisting Credalism in the Southern Baptist Convention.
by Jeff B. Pool.

Mercer University Press, Macon, Georgia 31210-3960.
ISBN 0-86554-553-7. Warehouse and catalog pick number: MUP/P162.
Text and interior designs, composition, and layout by Edmon L. Rowell, Jr.
Cover design and layout by Jim Burt.
Camera-ready pages composed on a Gateway 2000 via dos WordPerfect 5.1
    and WordPerfect for Windows 5.1/5.2 and printed on a LaserMaster 1000.
Text font: TimesNewRomanPS 11/13 plus ATECH Greek and Hebrew.
Display font: TimesNewRomanPS bf and bi.
Printed and bound by McNaughton & Gunn Inc., Saline, Michigan 48176:
    printed on web-fed 55# Writers Natural (360 ppi);
        perfectbound into 10-pt. cls stock with layflat lamination.
[March 1998]

021298elr

Against returning to Egypt :

320030101444968